FOURTEEN CENTURIES OF WAR
BETWEEN ISLAM AND THE WEST

SWORD

AND

SCIMITAR

RAYMOND IBRAHIM

with a Foreword by
VICTOR DAVIS HANSON

Da Capo Press

Da Capo Press
Hachette Book Group
1290 Avenue of the Americas, New York, NY 10104
www.dacapopress.com
@DaCapoPress; @DaCapoPR

Printed in the United States of America

First Edition: August 2018

Published by Da Capo Press, an imprint of Perseus Books, LLC, a subsidiary o
Hachette Book Group, Inc. The Da Capo Press name and logo is a trademark of the
Hachette Book Group.

The Hachette Speakers Bureau provides a wide range of authors for speaking events
To find out more, go to www.hachettespeakersbureau.com or call (866) 376-6591.

The publisher is not responsible for websites (or their content) that are not owned by
the publisher.

Library of Congress Cataloging-in-Publication Data has been applied for.

ISBNs: 978-0-306-82555-2 (hardcover), 978-0-306-82556-9 (ebook)

LSC-C

10 9 8 7 6 5 4 3 2 1

For Shechild, Minitaur, and Alfred.

t.
e

of

CONTENTS

FOREWORD

BY VICTOR DAVIS HANSON

RAYMOND IBRAHIM'S *SWORD AND SCIMITAR* IS A MUCH-NEEDED HIStory of landmark battles between Islam and the West. Ibrahim offers eight representative engagements across time and space from France to the Middle East, and over a millennium from 636 to 1683.

The study is first and foremost riveting military history. It offers blow-by-blow concise accounts of the eight battles, and interprets them in the context of the times—or rather, takes seriously what contemporary leaders claimed were their intentions and how they worked out their strategies. Such a first-hand approach requires extensive work in untranslated Arabic and occasional Greek sources, as well as a general background in comparative military history. For example, in his discussion of the pivotal battle of Yarmuk (near the current Syrian and Jordanian border), Ibrahim—who previously worked with various languages and manuscripts at the African and Middle Eastern division of the Library of Congress in Washington, D.C.—marshals together a diverse body of sources to offer a more accurate reconstruction of the battle that makes sense of how the numerically superior Byzantines suffered such an inexplicable and catastrophic loss.

Beyond its value as a meticulously researched chronicle of the major (and many minor) engagements between Islam and the West, the book advances larger cultural and religious arguments. Ibrahim's purpose is not to suggest inherent Western or Islamic cultural dynamism; indeed, he has selected four exemplary Western defeats (the fall of Constantinople, Hattin, Manzikert, and Yarmuk) balanced by four victories (second defense of

Constantinople, Las Navas de Tolosa, Tours, and Vienna). Instead, Ibrahim's evidence reveals certain recurring themes about the interaction between Islam and the West—an entity rarely any more defined as Christendom—that are presently either often ignored or underappreciated.

First, in most cases Islamic armies saw themselves as expansionary and messianic, eager to engage the West and annex its territory and convert its people. Inasmuch as Western armies were on the offensive, it was in the context of their belief that they were reclaiming areas of the Middle East, Northern Africa, Southern Europe, and Asia Minor that had been Roman or earlier belonged to the Hellenistic Greek world for over a half millennium before the birth of Islam. This may seem a self-evident point, but Ibrahim locates the tensions in the context of the times, in which Muslim forces at least saw themselves as absorbing formerly Westernized states and Western armies saw themselves as retrieving land that had been Roman or Greek for centuries.

Second, while there were localized and intramural political and tribal rivalries, Muslim armies went to war against the West more often as religious rather than as national or ethnic forces, and their warring against the Westerners was so seen as mostly a monolithic struggle against Christendom rather than particular European states. In turn, Western armies, while fragmented and marked by factions and political rivalries, still saw their common bond of Christianity as the only way to unite to fight off Islam.

Again, respective religious chauvinism seems another obvious observation, but quite often contemporary historians have tried to downplay any notion of a religious "clash of civilizations." In this context of religious tensions, Ibrahim often investigates diverse epochs and cultures rarely associated with the traditional theaters of conflict between Islam and Christendom, such as the lasting bitterness that followed in Russia from the so-called years of the Tartar yoke, and the Ottoman impediments to overland trade from Europe to the East that were catalysts for the Portuguese and Spanish voyagers to the New World, who initially had sought ways to squeeze Islam from both the West and new outposts in Asia.

Third, Ibrahim sees a continuity between past and present; that is, Muslim religious leaders and jihadists have characteristically seen Christianity as both antithetical to the Islamic world and inherently ripe for conquest or conversion. Westerners, in turn, have likewise over the centuries concluded that Islam was inconsistent with Christian values, and have seen tension and conflict rather than conciliation and peace as the more normal state of affairs. If current Islamists reflect age-old antipathies—compare the messaging of the Islamic State, their zealotry intentionally patterned after the dogma of their predecessors—so too Western reactions to them are far from sudden outbreaks of prejudice and xenophobia, but rather the self-defensive mechanisms of nearly 1,400 years.

Similarly, Ibrahim goes to some length to highlight little known methodologies of Muslim historiography—either due to linguistic difficulties or because criticism of them is considered politically incorrect. His critique is not that Muslim historiography is necessarily more or less reliable than Western sources of past conflict. Rather, Ibrahim argues that study of the craft of Muslim historians reminds us of how the Islamic world's account of religious tension with the West is remarkably consistent across time and different from the Western approach.

Fourth, often Muslims enjoyed as much, if not more protection living in Christian lands than did Christians in Islamic lands—and often without special taxes and levees predicated on their non-Christian status. In his descriptions of these battlefield collisions, Ibrahim demonstrates an asymmetry that is not just culturally relative, but instead reveals absolute different notions of forbearance. His point is not that Christians were saints and Muslims sinners, but that over the centuries, and with ample moral latitude given to the times, there was less of a Sermon on the Mount tolerance inherent in Islamic fundamentalism than in its Christian counterpart—and such antithetical customs were apparent before, during, and after battle with obvious ramifications for eventual outcomes.

Sword and Scimitar is first-rate military history and a product of solid scholarship and philological research. It characteristically offers candid appraisal of a rivalry that has now taken on quite different incarnations and played out on different fronts—from contemporary immigration to terrorism—but still in many ways remains an ancient existential struggle nonetheless.

Victor Davis Hanson
The Hoover Institution, Stanford University
May 1, 2018

What was, will be; what was done before, will be done again. There is nothing new under the sun.

—Ecclesiastes 1:9

PREFACE

THIS BOOK WAS ORIGINALLY CONCEIVED AS A MILITARY HISTORY between Islam and the West,* revolving around their eight most decisive battles and/or sieges (the first occurring in 636, the last in 1683†). As intrinsically interesting as this topic may be—my own master's thesis, written nearly twenty years ago under the chairmanship of noted military historian Victor Davis Hanson, was on the first and most decisive clash between Islam and the West, the Battle of Yarmuk—it soon became evident that there was a much larger but wholly forgotten backstory to this particular military history, the recollection of which can revolutionize the way the West understands its past, and thus its present, with Islam. As Bernard Lewis, one of the few modern historians to appreciate the totality of Muslim-Western history, explains, "We tend nowadays to forget that for approximately a thousand years, from the advent of Islam in the seventh century until the second siege of Vienna in 1683, Christian Europe was under constant threat from Islam, the double threat of conquest and conversion. Most of the new Muslim domains were wrested from Christendom. Syria, Palestine, Egypt, and North Africa were all Christian countries, no less, indeed rather more, than Spain and Sicily. All this left a deep sense of loss and a deep fear."[1]

Despite all this, the only conflicts highlighted today include the crusades, European colonialism, and any other Western venture that can be made to conform to the popular view that Europeans initiated hostilities

---

* Especial thanks go to my literary agent Peter Bernstein for representing, and to my acquiring editor Robert L. Pigeon for accepting the idea of this book.

† That Europeans and Muslims each won four is a happy coincidence of symmetry.

against non-Europeans. Even among less ideologically charged historians, the macrocosmic significance of the aforementioned millennium, when "Christian Europe was under constant threat from Islam," is unintelligible. They talk of "Arab," "Moorish," "Ottoman," or "Tatar"—rarely *Islamic*— invasions and conquests, even though the selfsame rationale—*jihad*— impelled those otherwise diverse peoples to assault the West.

None of this is helped by the fact that "most Muslims, unlike most Americans, have an intense historical awareness and see current events in a much deeper and broader perspective than we normally do."[2] Indeed, Muslim words addressed to and deeds performed in the West are often based on verbatim quotes and acts that Muslims have been saying and doing to Europe's ancestors for centuries. When Osama bin Laden opened his messages to the West with the words "Peace to whoever follows guidance," few knew that these irenic words were lifted directly from Islamic prophet Muhammad's "introductory" letters to non-Muslim kings; even fewer knew that Muhammad's follow-up sentence—which bin Laden wisely omitted— clarified what "following guidance" really means: "submit [to Islam] and have peace." When Yasser Arafat made a peace treaty with Israel in 1994 that was criticized by fellow Arabs and Muslims as offering too many concessions, the Palestinian leader justified his actions by saying, "I see this agreement as being no more than the agreement signed between our Prophet Muhammad and the Quraysh in Mecca"—that is, a truce that Muhammad abolished on a pretext once he was in a position of power and able to go on the offensive.[3] Whereas many of the world's Muslims make the connection and appreciate the continuity of the words and deeds of their politically active coreligionists, the West remains oblivious.

Which leads to the most timely aspect of this book. It definitively answers one of the most pressing questions of our time: Are militant Muslims—aka "terrorists," "radicals," "extremists"—being true to Islam, as they insist, or are they "hijacking" it for their own agendas, as we are told? This question has taken on renewed urgency with the rise of the Islamic State, which fashions itself after the caliphates of old and justifies every atrocity it commits—genocidal massacres, beheadings, crucifixions, mutilations, immolations, mass rapes, and enslavements—by citing Islamic doctrines.

A number of writers and analysts, myself included,[4] have sought to answer this question by showing that Islamic scriptures and their mainstream exegeses often do indeed support the Islamic State's and other jihadi organizations' actions. What few have done, however, is answer this question from a macro-historical perspective—that is, not by citing what most in the West instinctively dismiss as "abstract," "theoretical," and thus "open-to-interpretation" words of old scriptures, but by documenting what Muslims have actually *done* to and in the West for centuries. This is an admittedly more complex task that requires a familiarity with and distillation of a number of arcane texts written over the span of a millennium and in a variety of languages—not just key verses in the Koran and hadith. Yet within the context of its stated purview, this book does just that: it records a variety of Muslims across time and space behaving exactly like the Islamic State and for the same reasons.

Some words on methodology and various other caveats: what may seem a disproportionately large amount of space has been allotted to the first three chapters, which collectively center around three battles waged between 636 and 732. This was intentional: battles closer to our times are generally better documented, more detailed, and naturally seem more relevant due to their temporal proximity. Accordingly, they are already overrepresented in the modern literature, especially in contrast to their more distant and sparsely recorded counterparts. Yet, as shall be seen, there is no denying that Yarmuk (636) or the Second Siege of Constantinople (717) had far greater consequences than, say, the widely known and much celebrated Battle of Lepanto (1571).

Doing justice to nearly fourteen centuries of military history between Islam and the West without going over the allotted space was no easy task and required an unwavering fixation on matters of wars, their origins and consequences. As such, this book does not pretend to be a general history; that nonmilitant exchanges between the two civilizations existed, and that the totality of Islamic history is richer than and hardly limited to jihad, is acknowledged. Yet the fact remains: "For most of their common history, relations between the two communities were shaped by attack and counter-attack, jihad and crusade, conquest and reconquest."[5] Thus, while this book is not a *general* history of Western-Muslim relations, it is most certainly a history of the most *general* aspect of said relations—war—which is more than can be said for many academic books that masquerade as "general histories" of Islam and its interactions with other civilizations by placing peripherals and incidentals at center stage and sidelining the constants of war.

Tracing these constants, setting the record straight, and shedding light on contemporary questions would not have been possible without resorting to the original (but out of fashion or too cumbersome to wield) tool of the historian: primary sources, both Muslim and Western. Unlike many secondary histories—books heavy with their authors' subjective interpretations and light on objective substantiations—I have given the Muslims and Christians of the past, including those who fought and died, much space to tell their story. Their words—separated by centuries and continents—evince a remarkable continuity that is alone significant.*

A word of warning: premodern men—kings or chroniclers, Muslims or Christians—were by today's standards vociferously candid and spared no invective for what they deemed was the source of conflict—namely, the belief system of the other. Although their aspersions are usually seen as unnecessarily provocative hype and thus left out of polite histories, I have kept a fair amount in this book in the belief that they go a long way in explaining how each saw the other, and hence why they fought and died.

Concerning the oldest Muslim histories, which are our chief source for Islam's first two centuries, one Western school of thought holds them

---

* In an effort to eliminate confusions borne of inconsistencies, when quoting from (usually older) English translations of Arabic, Turkish, or Persian texts, I have taken the liberty of changing certain translations to transliterations. For example, if an English-language source of an Arabic text translates "Allah" to "God," I returned it to "Allah"; if it translates "jihad" to "Holy War," I returned it to "jihad"; if it translates "Allahu Akbar" to "God is Great[est]"—which is also a wrong translation in that the Arabic is a comparative, not superlative—I returned it to "Allahu Akbar." Koran translations are my own as checked against more mainstream translations (e.g., Pickthall, Dawood, Ali, and Shakir).

to be little more than foundational myths. Whatever the merits of this thesis, they have not dissuaded me from employing these earliest Arabic texts
(mostly limited to the Introduction and Chapter 1). After all, what Muslims
believe happened—and most Muslims treat the histories in question with
reverence—is more important than what *actually* happened (much of which
must remain conjectural anyway) and reveals how Muslims see their role
in history. Of course, by using these sources to highlight Muslim beliefs
does not mean that I also replicated their pious rationale, as many Western
historians are wont to do—much to the disservice of their audience. By
parroting hagiographical formulations—such as "Muhammad received a
revelation" to explain his subsequent behavior—such historians rarely offer
critical interpretations concerning motive.[†]

In conclusion, *Sword and Scimitar* documents how the West and Islam
have been mortal enemies since the latter's birth some fourteen centuries
ago. It does this in the context of narrating their military history, with a
focus on their most landmark encounters, some of which have had a profound impact on the shaping of the world. However, unlike most military
histories—which no matter how fascinating are ultimately academic—this
one offers timely correctives: it sets the much distorted historical record
between the two civilizations straight and, in so doing, demonstrates once
and for all that Muslim hostility for the West is not an aberration but a continuation of Islamic history.

Raymond Ibrahim
October 6, 2017

---

† Thus, according to John V. Tolan, "the Koran verifies his [Muhammad's] right to
more than four wives and specifies his right in particular to marry Zaynab, divorced
wife of his disciple and adopted son Zayd (33:37–38). This story, too, will be twisted
by the hostile pens of Christian polemicists, will be used to supplement their image
of Muhammad as lustful" (Tolan 2002, 29). Not only does Tolan fail to mention that
Zaynab and Zayd got divorced precisely because Muhammad desired the latter's wife,
but he appears irked that Christians "twisted" this story—that is, read between the lines
and understood Muhammad's "revelation" for what it was—instead of simply accepting
it as Allah's will, not to be questioned.

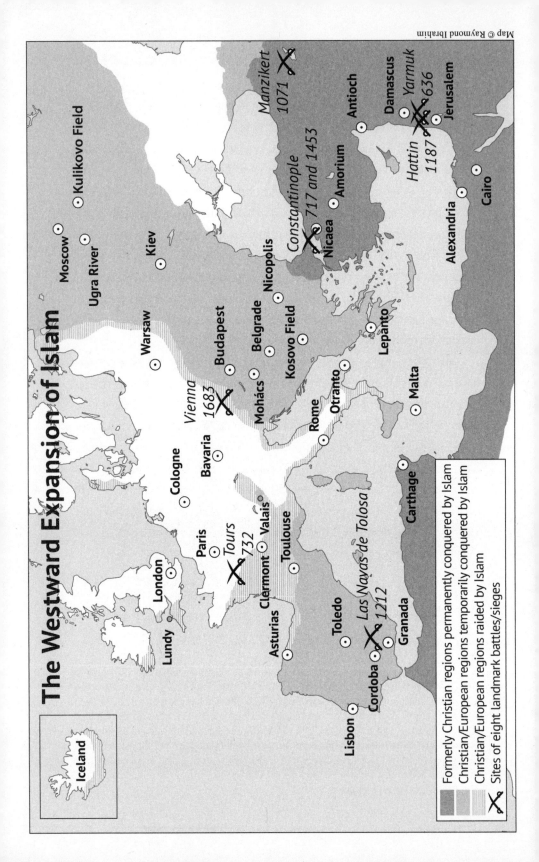

The Westward Expansion of Islam

Map © Raymond Ibrahim

Iceland

Lundy
London
Paris
Tours 732
Clermont
Valais
Toulouse
Asturias
Lisbon
Toledo
Cordoba
Granada
Las Navas de Tolosa 1212
Carthage
Cologne
Bavaria
Vienna 1683
Mohács
Budapest
Belgrade
Kosovo Field
Nicopolis
Rome
Otranto
Lepanto
Malta
Warsaw
Kiev
Ugra River
Moscow
Kulikovo Field
Constantinople 717 and 1453
Nicaea
Amorium
Antioch
Manzikert 1071
Damascus
Yarmuk 636
Hattin 1187
Jerusalem
Alexandria
Cairo

Formerly Christian regions permanently conquered by Islam

Christian/European regions temporarily conquered by Islam

Christian/European regions raided by Islam

Sites of eight landmark battles/sieges

JIHAD: THE ROOTS OF CONFLICT

I have been commanded to wage war against mankind until they testify that there is no god but Allah and that Muhammad is the Messenger of Allah. . . . If they do so, their blood and property are protected.

—Muhammad bin Abdullah, Prophet of Islam[1]

I have been made victorious with terror.

—Prophet of Islam[2]

If it were not a hardship for the Muslims, I would never idle behind from a raiding party going out to fight in the path of Allah. . . . I [would] love to raid in the path of Allah and be killed, to raid again and be killed, and to raid again and be killed.

—Prophet of Islam[3]

MUHAMMAD'S RISE TO POWER

B EFORE DELINEATING THE HISTORY OF WARFARE BETWEEN ISLAM and the West, its roots must first be comprehended. These begin and end with the Arabian founder and prophet of Islam, Muhammad bin Abdullah (570–632). In 610 he began telling his polytheistic tribesmen in Mecca that an angel (Gabriel) had called him to become Allah's messenger. The message was simple and revolved around the concept of submission—*Islam* in Arabic—to Allah's commandments (as delivered to and by Muhammad); whoever obeyed became a *Muslim* ("one who submits"). After twelve years of preaching Muhammad had only won over some one hundred converts,

1

mostly relatives. Although they originally let him preach unmolested, Mecca's tribal elites, the Quraysh, eventually wearied of his agitating against their gods and traditions and drove him out in 622. The prophet and his followers fled to, and the former eventually became master of, the oasis region of Yathrib, later dubbed Medina, the "Radiant." Now, with a considerable force of men under his control, Muhammad began to launch raids everywhere.

There was only one way to avoid the scimitar of Muhammad, captured in the following instructions he gave his followers: "Fight them [non-Muslims] until they testify that there is no god but Allah and Muhammad is his messenger; if they do so, then their blood [lives] and possessions are denied you."[4] His followers grew with every spoil-laden victory and were of two kinds: those vanquished by Muhammad, who chose Islam (submission) over slavery or death; and those impressed by Muhammad, who chose Islam (submission) in order to join his bandwagon and reap its rewards. All that both groups had to do was recite the *shahada,* Islam's first pillar and proclamation of faith: "There is no god but Allah and Muhammad is the messenger of Allah." Whether they sincerely believed the words or not was an academic distinction. In saying them, they made *submission* (Islam) to Muhammad's political authority and as such were good Muslims.

As Islamic histories will make clear in the coming pages, desire for what can be gained from or mere fear of Islam—both of which are seen as validating and thus exalting its power—were the primary impetus for conversion. That Muhammad had only won over some one hundred followers after a decade of peaceful preaching in Mecca—but nearly the whole of Arabia after a decade of successful raiding, "an average of no fewer than nine campaigns annually"[5]—speaks for itself. As Edward Gibbon observed, Muhammad "employ[ed] even the vices of mankind as the instruments of their salvation," and the "use of fraud and perfidy, of cruelty and injustice, were often subservient to the propagation of the faith."[6]

By 630, Muhammad's following had so grown that he could march ten thousand armed Muslims onto Mecca, whence he had been ignominiously driven out eight years earlier. An ultimatum was sent to the longtime naysayers and scoffers: "Embrace Islam and you shall be safe. You have been surrounded on all sides. You are confronted by a hard case that is beyond your power." When the Quraysh chieftain of Mecca—who, since Muhammad began preaching some two decades earlier, had only mocked and persecuted him as a false prophet—came to parley, Muhammad trumpeted, "Woe to you, Abu Sufyan; isn't it time that you recognize that I am Allah's apostle?" "As to that," replied the crestfallen pagan, "I still have some doubt." One of Muhammad's raiders instantly ordered him to "submit and testify that there is no god but Allah and that Muhammad is the apostle of Allah before you lose your head!"[7] Abu Sufyan, followed by the Meccans, proclaimed the *shahada* to resounding cries of "Allahu Akbar!"

Such is the bare-bones, hagiographic-free summary of Muhammad's rise from obscurity to power.

TRIBALISM DEIFIED

The appeal of Muhammad's message lay in its compatibility with the tribal mores of his society, three in particular: loyalty to one's tribe, enmity for other tribes, and raids on the latter to enrich and empower the former. For seventh-century Arabs—and later tribal peoples, chiefly Turks and Tatars, who also found natural appeal in Islam—the *tribe* was what *humanity* is to modern people: to be part of it was to be treated humanely; to be outside of it was to be treated inhumanely. This is no exaggeration: Muslim philosopher Ibn Khaldun (d. 1406) described the Arabs of his time (let alone those from Muhammad's more primitive era eight centuries earlier) as "the most savage human beings that exist. Compared with sedentary people they are on a level with wild, untamable animals and dumb beasts of prey. Such people are the Arabs."[8]

Muhammad upheld the dichotomy of tribalism, but by prioritizing fellow Muslims over blood relatives. Thus the *umma*—the Islamic "Super-Tribe" that transcends racial, national, and linguistic barriers—was born*;

---

* Although *umma* is often (and somewhat anachronistically) translated as "nation," it is etymologically related to "mother" (*umm*)—to one's closest kin—and thus better translated as "Super-Tribe."

and its natural enemy remained everyone outside it. The Islamic doctrine of *al-wala' wa al-bara'* ("loyalty and enmity"), which Muhammad preached and the Koran commands, captures all this.* The latter goes so far as to command all Muslims to "renounce" and "disown" their non-Muslim relatives—"even if they be their fathers, their sons, their brothers, or their nearest kindred"—and to feel only "enmity and hate" for them until they "believe in Allah alone" (Koran 58:22 and 60:4).† As one researcher summarizes, non-Muslims are described in the Koran as "vile animals and beasts, the worst of creatures and demons; perverted transgressors and partners of Satan to be fought until religion is Allah's alone. They are to be beheaded; terrorized, annihilated, crucified, punished, and expelled, and plotted against by deceit."[9]

Hence the jihad was born. As only two tribes existed—the Islamic *umma* in one tent and the dehumanized tribes of the world in another—Muslims were exhorted to attack and subjugate all these "infidels" in order to make their Super-Tribe supreme. This dichotomized worldview remains enshrined in Islamic law's, or sharia's, mandate that *Dar al-Islam* (the "Abode of Islam") must battle *Dar al-Kufr* (the "Abode of Infidelity") in perpetuity until the former subsumes the latter.‡ From here the argument

* Beginning with Muhammad's "Constitution of Medina," which asserted that "a believer shall not slay a believer for the sake of an unbeliever, nor shall he aid an unbeliever against a believer." Moreover, all Muslims were to become "friends one to the other to the exclusion of outsiders" (Ibn Ishaq 1997, 232). For Koran verses, see 4:89, 4:144, 5:51, 5:54, 9:23, and 60:1.

† According to Ibn al-Kathir's mainstream exegesis, Koran 58:22 refers to a number of Muhammad's close companions who, in keeping with their love for Allah, renounced and eventually slaughtered their own non-Muslim relatives: one slew his father, another his brother, a third—Abu Bakr, the first caliph—tried to slay his son, and Omar, the second caliph, slaughtered several relatives. (See Ibrahim, *Al Qaeda Reader*, which contains a nearly sixty-page treatise titled "Loyalty and Enmity"; al-Kathir's commentary appears on pp. 75–76.)

‡ The *Encyclopaedia of Islam* entry for "jihad" by Emile Tyan states that the "spread of Islam by arms is a religious duty upon Muslims in general. . . . Jihad [warfare to spread Islam] must continue to be done until the whole world is under the rule of Islam . . . Islam must completely be made over before the doctrine of jihad can be eliminated." There are, however, some caveats. Muslims may call off the jihad and make temporary truces with non-Muslims, but primarily only when Muslims are in

can be made that Muhammad's most enduring contribution to world history is that, in repackaging the tribal mores of seventh-century Arabia through a theological paradigm, he also *deified* tribalism, causing it to outlive its setting and spill into the modern era. Whereas most world civilizations have been able to slough off their historic tribalism and enter into modernity, to break with tribalism for Muslims is to break with Muhammad and his laws—to break with cardinal Islamic teachings.

JIHAD: THE WIN-WIN RAID

Numerous Koran verses and canonical (*sahih*) hadiths portray jihad as the noblest endeavor. "Lining up for battle in the path of Allah," Muhammad said, "is worthier than 60 years of worship."[8] Accordingly, whereas the rewards of the pre-Islamic tribal raid were limited to temporal spoils and came with the risk of death, the deified raid (jihad) offered rewards in the here *and* hereafter—meaning it was essentially risk-free—and thus led to a newborn fanaticism and sense of determination. As one Meccan scout reported after secretly surveying Muhammad's nascent Medinan army: "Yes, they are quite fewer than us. But death rides astride their camels. Their only refuge is the sword; dumb as the grave, their tongues they put forth with the serpent's deadly aim."[10]

Whoever survived the successful raid on the infidel was guaranteed all the usual spoils of war—plunder and slaves, including concubines[¶]; whoever died during this jihad was guaranteed similar but greater spoils in

---

a weakened state; once they are strong enough, existing truces may be annulled and the jihad resumed. Similarly, whenever Muslims are under infidel authority, they are permitted to feign friendship for and loyalty to their non-Muslim overlords—so long as the enmity is not extinguished from the heart (according to the Koran-based doctrine of *taqiyya,* more fully discussed in Chapter 6).

§ There is no dearth of references to the superlative quality of jihad, of which Muhammad also said, "I cannot find anything" as meritorious as jihad; he further likened jihad to "praying ceaselessly and fasting continuously" (Lindsay 2015, 70, 145).

¶ That the Koran has an entire sura (chapter 8) titled "Spoils" ("al-Anfal") is indicative of the importance of plunder during the jihad. Along with four wives, Muslim men are permitted to have as many infidel sex slaves as they can acquire (see Koran 4:3, 4:24, 33:50).

the afterlife. Either way, they won: "I guarantee him either admission to Paradise," said Muhammad, "or return to whence he set out with a reward or booty."[11] As for "the martyr"—the *shahid*—he "is special to Allah," said the prophet.* "He is forgiven from the first drop of blood [he sheds]. He sees his throne in paradise. . . . Fixed atop his head will be a crown of honor, a ruby that is greater than the world and all it contains. And he will copulate with seventy-two *Houris*."[12] The houris are supernatural, celestial women—"wide-eyed" and "big-bosomed," says the Koran—created by Allah for the express purpose of gratifying his favorites in perpetuity. That Islamic scriptures portray paradise in decidedly carnal terms—food, drink, gold, and "eternally young boys" who "circulate among" the believers also await the martyr—should not be surprising considering the aforementioned primitivism of Muhammad's society.[13]

Incidentally, Muhammad/Allah took a different approach to Muslims not inspired to fight on promises of temporal or eternal rewards: they "will be tortured like no other sinful human"[14] in hell, threatened Muhammad, with confirmation from Allah (e.g., Koran 8:15). At any rate, that the jihad's win-win nature motivated the early Muslims is widely attested and independently confirmed by past and present non-Muslim sources.† "It is almost as if they are driven by the very demons of Hell itself," a bewildered Byzantine official would proclaim of the soon-to-be invading Arabs. "They are in no wise tempted by comfort or safety. Instead, I dare say, they

---

* The salvific qualities of the sword in Islam resemble the salvific qualities of the cross in Christianity: whereas Saint Paul says that the sins "that condemned us" were "nailed to the cross" (Col. 2:14), Muhammad maintained that "the sword wipes away all sins" and "being killed in the path of Allah washes away impurity" (Cook 2005, 15; cf. Lindsay 2015, 183). The death-cultish aspects of jihad are especially evident in Muhammad's claim that "if it were not a hardship for the Muslims, I would never idle behind from a raiding party going out to fight in the path of Allah. . . . I [would] love to raid in the path of Allah and be killed, to raid again and be killed, and to raid again and be killed" (Lindsay 2015, 147).

† "As for religious enthusiasm and ardour for the holy war, it is certain that numerous Muslims were moved by this sentiment," writes historian Marius Canard. "There are numerous accounts describing combatants going to their deaths with joyful heart, seeing visions of the celestial *houri* who is calling to them and signaling to them" (Donner 2008, 66).

relish the ardor of battle and welcome the horrors of death."[15] According to a tenth-century Chinese source, "Every seventh day the king [of the Arabs] sits on high and speaks to those below, saying: 'Those who are killed by the enemy will be borne in heaven above; those who slay the enemy will receive happiness.' Therefore they are usually valiant fighters."[16]

Nor—and this is pivotal—were those who undertook jihad obligated to have sincere or pious intentions.‡ The cold, businesslike language of the Koran makes this clear. Whoever wages jihad makes a "fine loan to Allah," which the latter guarantees to pay back "many times over," always commensurate with their efforts (e.g., Koran 2:245, 4:95). Simply put, "Allah has *bought* from the believers their lives and worldly goods, and *in return* has promised them Paradise: they shall fight in the way of Allah and shall kill and be killed. . . . Rejoice then in the *bargain* you have struck, for that is the supreme triumph" (Koran 9:111, emphasis added).§

The instant forgiveness of sins granted to believers naturally became a license to sin for less believing Muslims. So long as they proclaim the *shahada* and pledge allegiance to Muhammad/Allah/*umma*, they can join and reap the rewards of jihad, no questions asked. Fighting in Islam's service—with the risk of dying—is all the proof of piety needed. Indeed, sometimes fighting has precedence over piety: many dispensations, including not upholding prayers and fasting, are granted those who participate in jihad. Ottoman sultans were actually forbidden from going on pilgrimage to Mecca—an otherwise individual obligation for Muslims—simply because doing so could jeopardize the annual jihad.[17] Similarly, according to

‡ This is even evident in the one hadith often cited to indicate that correct intentions are necessary: Muhammad was asked, "Men may fight out of a desire for booty, or for fame and glory. Who is it that fights in the path of Allah?" He responded, "Whoever fights so that the word of Allah may be highest is fighting in the path of Allah" (Bonner 2006, 51). Note that this explanation does not contradict fighting for selfish gain: simply fighting on the side of Islam makes one a de facto fighter for "the word of Allah," irrespective of intentions.

§ The Koran regularly employs mercantile language to describe the benefits of performing jihad—a "transaction that will save you from a painful punishment [hell]" (Koran 61:10). This has long been seen by non-Muslim cynics as reflective of the true author of the Koran, Muhammad the merchant.

the renowned Sunni jurisprudent Ibn Qudama (d. 1223), "One must fight under every leader, whether it be a respectable [meaning pious] man or a corrupt man."[18]

All this is important to keep in mind because many of the greatest jihadis* in the coming pages led otherwise un-Islamic lives (for instance by drinking alcohol or engaging in homosexuality). This fact has caused Western historians to disassociate these Muslims—and their often sadistic treatment of infidels—from Islam. Meanwhile Islamic historiography reveres them as good Muslims *precisely* because they waged successful jihads on the infidel. Others, like Khalid bin al-Walid, who mocked and warred on Muhammad only to proclaim the *shahada* once the latter took Mecca, were little more than mass-killing psychotics and rapists.

"THE WEST" (OR CHRISTENDOM)

Having gained a basic understanding of jihad, it is now necessary to examine Muhammad's dealings with and views on "the West." But as that term is fraught with problems and anachronisms—what other civilization is still named after a direction?—some clarifications are in order.

Like Islam, what is now referred to as the West was for centuries known and demarcated by the territorial extent of its religion (hence the older and more cohesive term, "Christendom"). It included the lands of the old Roman Empire—parts of Europe, all of North Africa, Egypt, Syria, and Asia Minor—which had become Christian centuries before Islam arrived and were part of the same overarching civilization.

In other words, the West is what remained of Christendom after Islam conquered some three-fourths of its original territory. As historian Franco Cardini puts it: "If we . . . ask ourselves how and when the modern notion of Europe and the European identity was born, we realize the extent to which Islam was a factor (albeit a negative one) in its creation. Repeated Muslim aggression against Europe . . . was a 'violent midwife' to Europe."[19] Resisting Islam defined Europe through the unity of Christianity. Similarly, after summarizing centuries of Islamic invasions, Bernard Lewis

---

* In Arabic, *mujahidin* (pl.) and *mujahid* (s.), literally one(s) who do(es) jihad.

writes, "Thus, at both its eastern and southwestern extremities, the limits and in a sense even the identity of Europe were established through first the advance, and then the retreat, of Islam."[20] Accordingly, Europe's self-identity never revolved around ethnicity or language—hence why such a small corner of the Eurasian landmass (Europe) still houses dozens of both, some widely divergent—but rather religion; it was the last and most redoubtable bastion of Christendom not to be conquered by Islam. Simply put, the West is actually the *westernmost* remnant of what was a much more extensive civilizational block that Islam permanently severed.

This is significant; inasmuch as the Middle East and North Africa are today culturally worlds apart from Europe, had Islam not interrupted the organic continuity and territorial integrity of Christendom, the classical Mediterranean would likely have remained part of the same civilization— what Plato, long before the advent of Christianity, called common "frogs around a pond."[21] Though accurate in other ways,† then, the term "the West" shortchanges its own history with and truncation by Islam. It further implies that all those "eastern" lands conquered by Islam were never part of "Western civilization," when in fact they were the original inheritors of its Greco-Roman and Christian heritage.

Indeed, because everything of importance—wealth, learning, civilization—was in the East, in 330, Roman emperor Constantine the Great built a new capital for the empire called New Rome, though later dubbed Constantinople in his honor, on land that is now part of modern-day Turkey. Although it quickly became the opulent center and capital of a burgeoning Christian empire; although it was Old Rome's direct successor and survived its fall by a thousand years; although everyone, friend and foe, called it "Roman"; and although it was Christendom's easternmost bulwark against Islam for centuries, since 1857 it and the empire it controlled have been known as Byzantium—another neologism that severs the continuity and integrity of the Roman Empire's (and thus West's) own history and heritage.‡

---

† First and foremost, in that the West no longer defines itself by the Christian religion.

‡ It was first used around 1556, but then in an exclusively poetic context; only in the nineteenth and twentieth centuries did it become synonymous with and eventually overshadowed the more accurate "Eastern Roman Empire."

(That said, and because of its brevity—"Byzantium" versus "Eastern Roman Empire"—both words are employed in the following history.)

Suffice to say, when Muhammad came onto the scene, the West consisted of the Christian world that existed along the old domains of Rome, and the symbolic representative of Christendom was the Roman emperor based in Constantinople. Therefore, to understand Muhammad's history with and law of war concerning the West is to understand his history with and law of war concerning Christianity.

THE PROPHET AND CHRISTIANITY

Although the Islamic prophet's relations with Christians and Jews (collectively referred to in the Koran as the "People of the Book") morphed over his career, his (meaning Allah's) final word was that both are infidel outsiders (e.g., Koran 5:51) and thus enemies. Muhammad's chief reason for denouncing Christianity revolved around Christ. While he agreed that Jesus was born of a virgin, performed miracles, and was essentially sinless, he rejected claims that Christ was crucified and resurrected. Muhammad/Allah especially denounced claims that Jesus was the Son of God—which is tantamount to the greatest crime in Islam, *shirk,* the idolatrous association of others with Allah, or polytheism.* Because it embodied all those doctrines he rejected, Muhammad "had such a repugnance to the form of the cross that he broke everything brought into the house with the figure upon it,"[22] and professed that one of Jesus's chief missions when he returns on Judgment Day will be to "break the cross" (a phrase that permeates the following history and into the present).[23]

Around the time Muhammad was becoming master of Mecca, he sent a letter† to Heraclius, the Christian emperor of the Eastern Roman Empire

---

* Also from the Koran: "Infidels are they who say Allah is one of three," a reference to the Christian Trinity (5:73); "Infidels are they who say Allah is the Christ, [Jesus] son of Mary" (5:17; see also 4:171).

† M. J. Akbar, a Muslim author, sums up the purported letter's significance for both Western and Muslim views of history: "A copy of [the letter] can be found in the Islamic section of the museum of Topkapi in Istanbul. This document is obviously an important element of the Muslim-Christian relationship in the Islamic perspective, and has been a consistent point of reference through the centuries. Ayatollah Khomeini

who had that same year just defeated the Persian Empire after decades of warring. The heart of the prophet's letter consisted of two Arabic words, *aslam taslam*—that is, "submit [to Islam] and have peace."[24] It was rejected. Muhammad responded in 629 by sending an expeditionary force of some three thousand Arabs chanting "victory or martyrdom!" into Christian territory.[25] The Romans, who for centuries considered their southern neighbors as leading a "beastly and blood-thirsty life,"[26] met and defeated them at Mu'ta (east of Jordan, near Karak).

Then, sometime in 630, even as Heraclius was ceremoniously restoring to Jerusalem what the Persians had earlier captured—the True Cross, a relic found centuries earlier under Constantine and believed to consist of fragments of Christ's cross—Muhammad declared eternal war on Christendom, as captured by Koran 9:29: "Fight those among the People of the Book [Christians and Jews] who do not believe in Allah nor the Last Day, nor forbid what Allah and His Messenger have forbidden, nor embrace the religion of truth, until they pay the *jizya* with willing submission and feel themselves subdued."[‡] In other words, Islam's three choices had come to Jews and Christians: either they converted, died fighting, or kept their religions by paying extortion money and accepting an inferior position as *dhimmis* in Muslim society.[§]

Then, claiming that the Christians were planning on invading Arabia to snuff out Islam, Muhammad "preemptively" led some thirty thousand

---

wrote a letter in a similar vein to Mikhail Gorbachev, fully conscious of the analogy. But too many writers in the West dismiss this letter as inauthentic, *unwilling to even consider the place it might have in Muslim thinking*" (2003, xxiii; emphasis added).

‡ Koran 9:29 and its brother verse, 9:5, are collectively known as the "Sword Verses," and according to mainstream Islamic jurisprudence have abrogated 124 verses that call for peace and tolerance.

§ This is evident in both the words *jizya* and *dhimmi*. The latter is rooted in the concept of "to find fault in" or "to affix blame to." Similarly, while *jizya* is often translated as "tribute," the root meaning of the word is to "repay," "recompense," or "compensate" for something. In other words, conquered non-Muslims were to purchase their lives, which were otherwise forfeit, with money. Some jurists spell this out, writing that "their [infidels'] lives and their possessions are only protected by reason of payment of jizya" (Ibrahim 2013, 22–24). For a comprehensive summary of the discriminatory and humiliating rules *dhimmis* were expected to adhere to, see "The Conditions of Omar" (Ibrahim 2013, 24–30).

Muslims to Tabuk, along the Roman-Arabian border. They stayed there for some three weeks; no Romans came, and the Muslims caravanned back to Medina.* Two years later, in 632, Muhammad was dead. In his lifetime, he had managed to rally the Arabs under the banner of Islam. On his death, some tribes sought to break away, including by remaining Muslim but not paying taxes (*zakat*) to Abu Bakr, Muhammad's father-in-law and successor, or caliph. Branding them all apostates, which in Islam often earns the death penalty, the caliph initiated the Ridda ("apostasy") Wars, which saw tens of thousands of Arabs beheaded, crucified, and/or burned alive. In 633 these wars—and in 634 the life of Abu Bakr—were over; Arabia's onetime factious tribes were once and for all united under the banner of Allah. It would fall to the second caliph, Omar bin al-Khattab (r. 634–644), to direct the full might of the once feuding Arabs—now one tribe, one umma, under Islam—against "the other."

"This same year," Theophanes the Confessor recorded a century and a half later, "there was an earthquake towards Palestine;† and a portent appeared in the heavens from the south, said to be a beam, pronouncing the attack of the Arabs. Thirty days it remained—from south to north. And it was sword-shaped."[27] Meanwhile, Emperor Heraclius began to be plagued by nightmares, wrote another chronicler, in which "he would be ravaged mercilessly by rats from the desert."[28]

---

* Though uneventful, the Tabuk campaign was important beyond its role in sealing the fate of all Christians and Jews via Koran 9:29. Many Arabs had beseeched their prophet to allow them to stay behind; as a result, Muhammad/Allah delivered a barrage of new verses that enticed with rewards, threatened with hellfire (e.g., Koran 9:81), and, most importantly, forever maligned those who would not commit to the jihad as *munafiqun,* "hypocrites."

† Arab sources (e.g., al-Tabari) also confirm an earthquake in Palestine during the initial Muslim invasions.

CHAPTER 1

ISLAM TAKES CHRISTENDOM BY STORM: THE BATTLE OF YARMUK, 636

And while the Church at that time was being troubled thus by emperors and impious priests, Amalek rose up in the desert, smiting us, the people of Christ, and there occurred the first terrible downfall of the Roman army, I mean the bloodshed at Ajnadayn and Yarmuk.

—Theophanes the Confessor[1]

It is neither hunger nor poverty that has driven us from our land [Arabia]. We, the Arabs, are drinkers of blood and we know there is no blood more tasty than that of the Greeks. That is why we have come, to spill and to drink your blood.

—Khalid bin al-Walid, the "Sword of Allah"[2]

WHEN THE ARABS INVADED ROMAN SYRIA IN 634, IT WAS MUCH larger than today and encompassed modern-day Israel, Jordan, and Palestinian territories. It was also profoundly Christian. Two of the original five apostolic sees—Antioch, where the followers of Jesus were first called "Christian," and Jerusalem, where Christianity was born—were in Syria. Due, however, to a dispute over the nature of Christ that began at the Council of Chalcedon (451) and which was racked with theological intricacies unintelligible to today's average Christian—some leading clergy on both sides now say the quarrel revolved around a semantic, not substantive point—the empire was divided.

Initial Arab incursions were seen as typical nomadic raids that would eventually meld back into the desert.* This did not happen. By 634 the Arabs en masse—some on horse or the dreaded camel,† others on foot—were deep into Roman Syria, slaughtering and pillaging. Once again, a wearied Heraclius, who had just experienced a decade of holy war against the Persians,‡ proceeded to muster his legions into Syria to squash these latest upstarts. Meanwhile, with every minor success the invaders experienced, thousands of more eager recruits swarmed into Syria from Arabia. Among them was Khalid bin al-Walid.

THE "SWORD OF ALLAH"

Khalid looms large in the Arab histories of the early Muslim conquests and is still seen today as the jihadi par excellence. A Meccan polytheist renowned for his military prowess, Khalid had for years dismissed Muhammad as a false prophet. But once the latter took Mecca, Khalid acclaimed Muhammad and entered the fold of Islam. The prophet gave him his "eagle," a black flag with white writing proclaiming the *shahada* (the Islamic State's flag is a facsimile). With it unfurled, Khalid became the scourge of infidels. He was among the three thousand jihadis sent to punish the Christians at Mu'ta in 629 after Heraclius rejected Muhammad's offer to "submit." The force of his swings were said to have shattered nine scimitars against his infidel enemies, prompting an impressed Muhammad to dub him the "Sword of Allah," an appellation that even early Christian chroniclers such as Theophanes (b. 758) knew.

---

* That the Arabs were previously never considered a threat is seen in that the *Strategikon,* an Eastern Roman military manual composed a few decades before the conquests, catalogues and recommends how to deal with all hostile and potentially threatening peoples to the empire—Persians, Avars, Turks, Huns, Franks, Lombards, Slavs, Antes—without mentioning the Arabs.

† Approximately one thousand years earlier and in the context of discussing Arabian camelback fighting, Herodotus wrote that horses "cannot endure the sight of the camel" (*The History,* book 7:87). While discussing a battle between the Arabs and Persians where the former used camels, al-Tabari agrees: "The Persian horses took fright and fled [from the camels]. . . . The Persians suffered from the camels more than the Muslims had suffered . . . from the elephants (al-Tabari 1992, 100).

‡ Who were simultaneously under attack and soon to be conquered by the Arabs.

Modern-day Muslims often have nothing but praise for Khalid's commitment to the jihad.§ But he had a darker side. During the Ridda Wars, Khalid accused Malik bin Nuwayra, a well-liked Arab chieftain, of apostasy from Islam. The Sword of Allah slaughtered him and, that same night, raped—Islamic chronicles call it "married"—his wife, Layla. Not content, he decapitated Malik, stood his head up between two stones, set it aflame, and cooked his evening meal in a cauldron above it. "And Khalid ate from it that night to terrify the apostate Arab tribes and others," writes Muslim historian Ibn al-Kathir. "It was said that Malik's hair created such a blaze as to thoroughly cook the meat."[3]

Several leading Arabs said Malik was a true Muslim and Khalid only accused him of apostasy to take his wife, whose beauty was renowned. Even Omar bin al-Khattab confided to then caliph Abu Bakr that "in the sword of Khalid there really is forbidden behavior," for he "transgressed against a Muslim man, killing him and then leaping upon his wife." Abu Bakr recalled Khalid back to Medina. Once there, the Sword of Allah, apparently trying to portray himself as a pious devotee of jihad—and thereby elicit sympathy or respect from his accusers—marched into the mosque wearing a battle-stained robe and "with his head wrapped in a turban of his in which arrows had become planted," explains a Muslim chronicler. Unimpressed, Omar marched "to him and pulled the arrows from his head and smashed them. Then he said, 'What hypocrisy, to kill a Muslim man and then leap upon his wife! By Allah, I would pelt you with stones.' Khalid b. al-Walid did not speak to him, and thought that Abu Bakr would only have the same opinion about him as Omar." To his delight, "Abu Bakr pardoned him and forgave him without punishment for whatever had happened in his recent campaign."[4]

When Omar continued pestering Abu Bakr—again warning that "in his sword there really is forbidden behavior"—the exasperated caliph put an end to the controversy: "Oh Omar, I will not sheathe a sword that Allah has drawn against the unbelievers!"[5] Expediency won the day. Better to unsheathe the Sword against the infidels than to sheathe it on account of some

---

§ See for example Pakistani army lieutenant-general A. I. Akram's *The Sword of Allah*, a glowing biography of Khalid.

moral shortcomings. Khalid was sent to do jihad in Christian Syria, where his popularity caused him to become "the commander of the Muslims in every battle."[6]

THE GREAT MUSTERING

By late summer 634, Emperor Heraclius had assembled and dispatched a large land force to repel the invaders. The Muslims responded by mustering at Ajnadayn (in modern day Israel). The opposing forces numbered between ten and twenty thousand fighters. "Against this army, the Moslems fought a violent battle, and Khalid bin al-Walid particularly distinguished himself," writes Muslim chronicler al-Baladhuri (d. 892). "At last, by Allah's help, the enemies of Allah were routed and shattered into pieces, a great many being slaughtered."[7] Several of the late prophet's closest companions fell on that day, while the bulk of the shattered Christian army managed to withdraw behind the walled cities of the north to fight another day.

Heraclius hoped the Arab invaders, after wreaking havoc and plundering, would eventually return to the desert whence they came, as usual. The invaders instead continued penetrating northward, leading to several more battles with and defeats of Roman forces. The battle of Marj al-Saffar, just south of Damascus, "was so violent that blood flowed along with water and turned the wheels of the mill."[8] By February 635, the walls of Damascus were breached by sword-waving Muslims crying triumphant Islamic slogans.[9] There, in the ancient city where Saul of Tarsus had become the Apostle Paul, another Christian bloodbath ensued.

Heraclius had no intention of forsaking Syria, which he had recently recovered from the Persians, to the even more despised Saracens. In late 635 the emperor "wrote to all who bear the Cross" and "awaited armies and regiments from the furthest reaches of the Roman Empire," writes Muslim chronicler al-Waqidi (747–823), author of the earliest and most detailed account of the Arab conquest of Syria.* Christian fighters from every

---

* Although I have opted to follow (and translate much of) al-Waqidi's outline and narrative—by far the most detailed and oldest Arab account of the Battle of Yarmuk—it should be noted that there are scattered references to Yarmuk in significantly older

corner—Armenians, Georgians, Greeks, Christian Arabs, supposedly even Slavs and Franks—marched to and assembled in Antioch "in the spirit of a Christian crusade."[10] Standing before them, the emperor harangued them to fight, to "protect yourselves, your religion, and your women."[11]

Often left out in modern histories is the profoundly religious nature of these early encounters. If the Arabs recited the Koran and chanted Islamic slogans, as all Muslim chroniclers report, the Roman camp was all but a Christian procession. After all, "Byzantium's role as the Christian Empire was central to its morale. Careful religious preparations preceded a battle"—including priests reciting prayers over fighters and parading relics and crosses before the troops—all of "which had a profound impact upon the men's mind."[12] Roman soldiers are regularly described as raising crucifixes aloft and shouting in defiance at the "Allahu Akbar"–yelling invaders. These were indeed holy wars, centuries before the crusades.

By late spring 636, Heraclius's multiethnic army, some thirty thousand strong, began their march south. On Khalid's advice, the Muslim forces, numbering approximately twenty-four thousand—with women, slaves, children, camels, and tents in tow—withdrew from their recently conquered territories and congregated by the banks of the Yarmuk River in Syria. They watched in amazement as the Roman throng—described by one Arab "as numerous as ants"[13]—slowly advanced. When the Christians finally made camp, it was reportedly seventeen miles long.

The supreme Muslim commander, Abu Ubaida, dispatched a hurried message to Caliph Omar complaining that "the dog of the Romans, Heraclius, has called upon us all who bear the cross, and they have come against us like a swarm of locusts."[14] Considering Muslim sources say that "to see Christendom fall was his [Omar's] delight," that "his meat was their humiliation," and "his very breathing was their destruction," reinforcements were forthcoming.[15]

Christian sources. Unfortunately, however, these give few details, noting only that it was an unmitigated disaster. Moreover, al-Waqidi is one of those early Arab chroniclers accused of overly embellishing. That said, because it is precisely his account that most Muslims follow, so too have I followed it—both to provide Western readers with an idea of what Muslims believe, and a detailed narrative.

Both Muslim and Christian positions were strategically sound. The Arabs, using their camels as obstacles along the perimeter of their camps, could if need be and per custom beat a hasty retreat into the deserts behind them. The Byzantines were only a day and a half's march away from recently recovered Damascus. Two ravines along the Wadi-Ruqqad and Yarmuk River dominated the landscape; each had vertical drops of one to two hundred feet in height—a deadly prospect for anyone fleeing in haste.

Heraclius appointed the Armenian Vahan, a hero of the Persian Wars, as supreme commander of his united forces. Although Abu Ubaida was supreme leader, Khalid, who commanded thousands of horsemen and camel-riders behind the infantry, continued to influence military decisions. In arms and armor, the Romans were better arrayed. Both infantry and cavalry relied primarily on swords (by now significantly longer than the ancient gladius), spears for thrusting, and javelins and arrows for hurling. Armor worn by the Arabs had been stripped from fallen Romans. For weapons they relied on the sword, spear, and bow.

Thus arrayed for battle, the Muslims and Christians faced each other for several weeks with little action aside from occasional skirmishing. The former bided their time and waited for reinforcements to arrive from Arabia, while Vahan, in keeping with the recommendations of the *Strategikon*—a military manual written by Emperor Maurice (d. 602) that recommended "endless patience, dissimulation and false negotiations, timing, cleverness, and seemingly endless maneuvering"[16]—sought to bribe, intimidate, and sow dissent among the Arabs. Because "vast numbers of the Arabs professed Christianity" at this time and "fought to the last for the Empire and the Cross,"[17] Vahan especially hoped his Arab horsemen of the Ghassan tribe, long the empire's auxiliaries on the Arabian frontier, would best know how to handle their southern kinsmen. He sent their "king" (or chief) Jabla to parley with the invaders on the belief that "steel can only be broken by steel."[18]

ISLAM, *JIZYA*, OR DEATH

Once in the Muslim camp, Jabla warned against the futility of fighting the combined forces of the Roman empire. He invited his southern kinsmen to keep all their plunder on condition that they withdraw back to Arabia. This would not do: "We have tasted blood and find none sweeter than the blood of Romans," Ubada bin al-Samat, one of the prophet's companions, informed him. As for the Christians' vast numbers, "Our fighters and heroes see death as gain and life as burdensome." Ubada then invited Jabla and his Christian tribe to embrace Islam as fellow Arabs, "for it will honor you in this world and the next." Jabla refused: "I will never break away from my religion." Ubada warned him that "there will never be peace between us unless you pay jizya or accept Islam." Jabla staunchly refused again. "By Allah!" exclaimed Ubada, "were treachery not so odious [Jabla had entered the Muslim camp under a flag of truce], I would have struck you down here with my scimitar!"[19]

If Vahan hoped that Jabla would be the Christian Arab steel to break the Muslim Arab steel, so too did the Muslims continue to harbor hopes of playing on Jabla's ethnic kinship. A more tactful delegation was sent to flatter the Ghassanian chief. They told him that as an Arab of noble lineage he would be greatly honored by the Muslims if only he converted to Islam. Jabla again turned the summons down: "I do not like that [Islam] or any other [religion], for I am attached to my own religion." He then spoke to them kindly, as kinfolk: "You are pleased with one thing [Islam], and we are pleased with another [Christianity]. You have your religion and we have our religion." The relentless emissaries then asked him merely to abstain from fighting alongside the Romans and base his decision on whether to convert on the battle's outcome. Again he refused, and again Muslim cajolery turned murderous: the delegation threatened to crush his skull and slaughter him. Equally infuriated, Jabla declared, "By Christ and the Cross, I will surely fight for Rome, even if against all my nearest kin!"[20]

Muslim sources highlight a similar exchange under a flag of truce between Khalid bin al-Walid and Supreme General Vahan. Meeting in the open field on horseback, the Armenian commander began by diplomatically blaming Arabia's harsh conditions and impoverished economy for giving the Arabs no choice but to raid Roman lands. Accordingly, the empire was pleased to provide them with food and coin on condition that they return home. "It was not hunger that brought us here," coolly responded

Khalid, "but we Arabs are in the habit of drinking blood, and we are told the blood of the Romans is the sweetest of its kind, so we came to shed your blood and drink it."[21]

Vahan's diplomatic mask instantly dropped and he launched into a ti- rade against the insolent Arab: "So, we thought you came seeking what your brethren always sought [plunder, extortion, or mercenary work] but alas we were wrong. You came killing men, enslaving women, plundering wealth, destroying buildings, and seeking to drive us from our own lands." Better people had tried to do the same but always ended up defeated, added Vahan in reference to the recent Persian Wars, before continuing:

As for you, there is no lower and more despicable people—wretched, impoverished Bedouins who know nothing but poetry.* Despite that, you commit injustices in your own nation and now ours. . . . What havoc you have created! You ride horses not your own and wear clothes not your own. You pleasure yourselves with the young white girls of Rome and enslave them. You eat food not your own, and fill your hands with gold, silver, and valuable goods [not your own]. Now we find you with all our possessions and the plunder you took from our coreligionists—and we leave it all to you, neither asking for its return nor rebuking you. All we ask is that you leave our lands. But if you refuse, we will annihilate you![22]

The Sword of Allah was not impressed: he began reciting the Koran and talking about one Muhammad. Vahan listened in quiet exasperation. Then, when Khalid began hinting at the possibility of "brotherly peace," the general eagerly inquired how this could be achieved. Khalid asked him to recite: "There is no god but Allah, and Muhammad is his slave and mes- senger, whom Jesus son of Mary prophesied." Responded Vahan, unenthu- siastically: "You have called me to abandon my religion and enter yours; this is impossible for me." "Then," concluded Khalid, "because you cling to your misguided religion, so too is it impossible for us to ever be brothers."[23]

_____

* A reference to the well-known Arab penchant for making verse.

Vahan continued trying to reason with him; he asked if simply saying the words (of the *shahada*) would suffice, or if actions were also required. Khalid replied, "You must also pray, pay zakat, perform hajj [pilgrimage] at the sacred house [in Mecca], wage jihad against those who refuse Allah . . . befriend those who befriend Allah [Muslims] and oppose those who oppose Allah [non-Muslims].† If you refuse, there can only be war between us. . . . And you will face men who love death as you love life." "Do what you like," resigned Vahan. "We will never forsake our religion nor pay you jizya."[24] Negotiations were over.

Things further came to a head—quite literally—when eight thousand Muslims marched before the Roman camp carrying the severed heads of four thousand Christian soldiers mounted atop their spears. These were the remains of five thousand reinforcements coming from Amman to join the main army at Yarmuk; the Muslims had ambushed and slaughtered them. Then, as resounding cries of "Allahu Akbar" filled the Muslim camp—and in keeping with Koran verses to "strike terror into the hearts of the infidels" by decapitating them (e.g., 8:12)—those Muslims standing behind the remaining one thousand Christian captives knocked them over and proceeded to hack their heads off before the eyes of their coreligionists, whom Arabic sources depict as looking on in "utter bewilderment."[25]

So it would be war. On the eve of battle, the Arabs "spoke of the fire of hell and the joys of paradise, and quoted the example set by the Holy Prophet in his battles," writes Pakistani general and military historian A. I. Akram. "The Muslims spent the night in prayer and recitation of the Quran, and reminded each other of the two blessings which awaited them: either victory and life or martyrdom and paradise."[26] No such titillation awaited the Christians; they were fighting for life, family, and faith. During his pre-battle speech, as clergymen marched with crosses and pronounced the death prayer on the kneeling men, Vahan explained that "these Arabs who stand before you seek to . . . enslave your children and women."[27]

---

† Essentially the Five Pillars of Islam, only in this case jihad against nonbelievers is a pillar instead of fasting. Also notable is Khalid's reference to the doctrine of "loyalty and enmity." Note, too, that none of the actions Khalid mentioned require proper intentions as discussed in the Introduction.

Another general warned the men to fight hard, otherwise "they shall conquer your lands and ravish your women." Such fears were not unwarranted. Even as the Romans were praying, Abu Sufyan—formerly one of Muhammad's greatest enemies who, like Khalid, happily converted rather than lose his head (see Introduction)—was prancing on his war steed and waving his spear around the assembled Muslims, exhorting them to "jihad in the way of Allah," so that they might "seize their [Christians'] lands and cities, and enslave their children and women."[28]

THE BATTLE OF YARMUK

The battle reportedly transpired over the course of six days. On the first day, sometime in late August 636, a large portion of the Byzantine army advanced and was met with a hail of arrows. Although man after man fell, the relentless phalanx continued to advance and struck the Muslim front hard. A bloody melee ensued. By sundown, both forces disengaged and returned to their respective camps. Casualties were not too high.

Having felt out his opponent's forces, over the next two days Vahan attacked the Arab center with just enough force to keep it bogged down while simultaneously hammering its wings; the Roman left flank, largely consisting of Slavs, especially pounded the Arab right (led by Amr bin al-As, another companion of Muhammad) hard. On both days the Christians broke through, pushing Allah's fighters back into their camps, where their womenfolk stood ready. Prior to battle, Abu Sufyan had told these female Arabs that, although "the prophet said women are lacking in brains and religion,"* they could still help by "striking them [Arab men] in the face with stones and tent poles" should they ever retreat to camp, "until they return [to battle] in shame."[29] Sure enough, whenever broken ranks of Muslim fighters fell back into camp, Arab women hurled stones at them, struck them—and

---

* A reference to a canonical hadith. After Muhammad told a group of Muslim women that "the majority of the dwellers of Hell-fire were you [women]," and they asked him why, he explained: "You curse frequently and are ungrateful to your husbands. I have not seen anyone more deficient in intelligence and religion than you" (*Sahih Bukhari* 1:6:301). Due to this and other remarks concerning female status, Muhammad's youngest wife, Aisha, once proclaimed: "You have made us equal to the dogs and the asses!" (*Sahih Muslim* 4:1039).

their horses and camels—with poles, and taunted them with verse: "May Allah curse those who run from the enemy! Do you wish to give us to the Christians? . . . If you do not kill, then you are not our men." Abu Sufyan's wife, Hind, reportedly even fought the advancing Romans while screaming, "Cut the extremities [meaning phalluses] of the uncircumcised ones!"[30] Said to be thoroughly humiliated by these indignities, the Muslims turned and drove back the advancing Romans to their original position. No gain was made, though many died on both sides.

Vahan initiated the fourth day of battle by again heavily pummeling the weakened Arab right. In a furious charge, Jabla's Christian Arab cavalry broke through the Muslim center and met Khalid's horse and camel, atop which were mounted the veterans of Islam's earliest caravan raids launched by Muhammad. Savage fighting killed many. The Christians eventually fell back as the Muslims advanced with triumphant cries of "Allahu Akbar." Although there were no women to chastise the retreating Christians, a multitude of archers unleashed volley after volley upon the rushing Arabs: "The arrows rained down on the Muslims. All one could hear was 'Ah! My eye!' In heavy confusion, they grabbed hold of their reins and retreated."[31] Some seven hundred Muslims lost an eye on that day (known in Islamic historiography as the "Day of Lost Eyes" or "Day of Wounding"). Seeking to exploit the Muslims' consternation, Vahan ordered his forces to pursue them. Arabs everywhere were slaughtered.

As the Muslims lay on the ground dying, they saw the houris—the celestial women promised those who die in the jihad—beckoning to them with open arms. Anecdotes permeate the Muslim chronicles. Thus, by the banks of the Yarmuk, one Muslim reported that he came upon a fallen comrade "smitten on the ground, and I watched as he lifted his fingers to the sky. I understood he was rejoicing, for he saw the houris." While waving his standard, another Arab chieftain told his men that a headlong charge against the "Christian dogs" is synonymous with a "rush to the embraces of the houris!"[32]

The fifth day passed uneventfully due to the previous days' exhaustion. Concerning the sixth and final day of battle, Muslim sources make much of the heavy infantry of the Christian right, referring to them as the "mightiest" of the Romans. These warriors reportedly tied themselves to-gether with chains as a show of determination and swore by "Christ and the Cross, and the Four Churches"* to fight to the last man.[33] Even Khalid expressed concern at their sight and show of determination. He ordered the Muslim center and left to engage and bog them down, while he led thou-sands of horsemen and camel-fighters round to the Roman left, which had become separated from its cavalry (possibly during an attempt at one of the complicated "mixed formation" maneuvers recommended by the *Strate-gikon*). To make matters worse, a dust storm—something Arabs were ac-customed to, their opponents less so—erupted around this time and caused mass chaos, as the Romans' large numbers proved counterproductive in these crowded and chaotic conditions. Now the fiercest and most desperate fighting of the war ensued; everywhere steel clashed, men yelled, horses screamed, camels bellowed, and sand blew in the confused mass. Unable to maneuver under these conditions, most of the Roman cavalry—carrying along a protesting Vahan—broke off and withdrew to the north.

Realizing that they were forsaken by the rest of the imperial army, the Christian infantry, including the "chained men," maintained formation and withdrew westward, the only place open to them. They were soon trapped between an Islamic hammer and anvil: a crescent of Arabs spreading from north to south continued closing in on them from the east, while a semicir-cle of the Wadi-Ruqqad's precipitous ravines lay before the Christians to the west. (Khalid had already captured the only bridge across the Wadi.)

As darkness descended on this volatile corner of the world, the final phase of war took place on the evening of August 20. The Arabs, whose night vision was honed by desert life, charged the trapped Romans, who, according to Muslim sources, fought valiantly. "Soon the terrain echoed with the terrifying din of Muslim shouts and battle cries. Shadows suddenly changed into blades that penetrated flesh. The wind brought the cries of comrades as the enemy stealthily penetrated the ranks among the infernal

---

* The Arabs may have mistook the Roman phalanx's tight formations for fetters. "Four churches" may be a reference to four of the five ancient churches, minus Rome, which were all Eastern and Orthodox: Alexandria, Antioch, Constantinople, and Jerusalem.

noise of cymbals, drums, and battle cries. It must have been even more terrifying because they had not expected the Muslims to attack by dark,"[34] which was one of Muhammad's strategies.†

Crowded and blinded as they were, the Christians could not properly maneuver and even lacked elbow room to utilize their weapons. Muslim cavalrymen continued pressing on the Roman infantry, using the hooves and knees of their steeds to knock down the wearied fighters. Pushed finally to the edge of the ravine, rank after rank of the remaining forces of the imperial army—including all of the "chained men"—fell down the steep precipices to their death. Several other soldiers, including officers, knelt, uttered a prayer, made the sign of the cross, and waited for the onrushing Muslims to strike them down.[35] No prisoners were taken on that day: "The Byzantine army, which Heraclius had spent a year of immense exertion to collect, had entirely ceased to exist.‡ There was no withdrawal, no rearguard action, no nucleus of survivors. There was nothing left."[36] As the moon filled the night sky and the victors stripped the slain, cries of "There is no god but Allah and Muhammad is his messenger" and "Allahu Akbar!" rang throughout the Yarmuk valley.

JIHAD IN JERUSALEM

When news of defeat reached him, Heraclius, in dismay, knew not what to do other than quit Antioch—which fell to the Arabs in the following year— and head for Constantinople. During his northwestern march through

---

† Muhammad so favored night raids for their surprise elements and the cover of dark they provided that, even though he was warned they would indiscriminately cause the death of women and children (whom he had earlier said should only be enslaved), he permitted them, since women and children were, to quote the prophet, "from among them," that is, infidels. See Ibrahim (2007, 161–171) for a complete discussion on the conditions and prerequisites that justify the waging of jihad even if those who should not be targeted—fellow Muslims, women, and children—get killed.

‡ Conflicting reports exist concerning the fate of Roman leadership. Vahan either fell fighting during his withdrawal, was tracked down and slaughtered by pursuing Muslims, or else ashamedly withdrew from the world and checked himself into a monastery. As for Jabla, one Muslim account says that after Yarmuk, the Christian Arab chief finally saw the light of Islam, converted, traveled to Medina to meet—but got into some scuffle with—Caliph Omar, recanted Islam, and fled back to the Christian north.

Anatolia, he ordered all Roman garrisons stripped and fortifications broken so that his pursuers would only find barren country. (Such was the beginning of the creation of that desolate no-man's-land that for centuries demarcated the frontier between Byzantium and its nemesis, Islam.[37])

Some weeks after Yarmuk, the triumphant Muslims—now rested, augmented with newly arrived recruits, and adorned with the arms of thousands of slain Christian soldiers—began their march to Jerusalem. After its patriarch, Sophronius, heard of the disaster at Yarmuk, he ordered the garrison to withdraw behind the Holy City's walls, and clandestinely sent the True Cross, which had only recently been recovered from the Persians, to Constantinople for safekeeping.[38] The patriarch's musings concerning these times are preserved in a sermon:

> Why are the troops of the Saracens attacking us? Why has there been so much destruction and plunder? Why are there incessant outpourings of human blood? Why are the birds of the sky devouring human bodies? Why have churches been pulled down? Why is the cross mocked? Why is Christ . . . blasphemed by pagan mouths? . . . The vengeful and God-hating Saracens, the abomination of desolation clearly foretold to us by the prophets, overrun the places which are not allowed to them, plunder cities, devastate fields, burn down villages, set on fire the holy churches, overturn the sacred monasteries, oppose the Byzantine armies arrayed against them, and in fighting raise up the trophies [of war] and add victory to victory.[39]

The majority of descriptions of the invaders written by contemporary Christians portray them along the same lines as Sophronius: not as men—even uncompromising men on a religious mission, as Muslim sources written later claim—but as godless savages come to destroy all that is sacred. Writing around the time of Yarmuk, Maximus the Confessor (b. 580) said the invaders were "a barbarous people of the desert . . . wild and untamed beasts, whose form alone is human, [come to] devour civilized government."[40] The intentional and widespread targeting of churches, crosses, and other Christian symbols/sacraments* prompted some to see the invaders as motivated by a diabolical animus. For Anastasius of Sinai (630–701), who was a child during the initial invasions and experienced nearly seventy years under Muslim rule, the "Saracens" were "perhaps even worse than the demons." After all, "the demons are frequently much afraid of the mysteries of Christ, I mean his holy body [the Eucharist], the cross . . . and many other things. But these demons of flesh trample all that under their feet, mock it, set fire to it, destroy it."[†] Interestingly, even the oldest Muslim sources confirm that Christians saw "these Arabs as demons."[41]

In November 636, the Muslims were besieging the walls of Jerusalem. After several months of being holed up and reduced to starvation, the desperate and plague-infested city capitulated in the spring of 637. The conquest of the Holy City was enough for Caliph Omar to pay it a personal visit from distant Medina. Once there, he noticed the Church of the Holy Sepulchre, a massive complex built in the 330s by Constantine over the site of Christ's crucifixion and burial. As the conquering caliph entered Christendom's most sacred site—clad "in filthy garments of camel-hair and showing a devilish pretense," to quote Theophanes—Sophronius, looking on, bitterly remarked, "Surely this is the abomination of desolation spoken of by Daniel the Prophet standing in the holy place."[42]

---

* As Sidney Griffith explains: "The cross and the icons publicly declared those very points of Christian faith which the Koran, in the Muslim view, explicitly denied: that Christ was the Son of God and that he died on the cross." Accordingly, "the Christian practice of venerating the cross and the icons of Christ and the saints often aroused the disdain of Muslims," so that there was an ongoing "campaign to erase the public symbols of Christianity [in formerly Christian lands such as Egypt and Syria], especially the previously ubiquitous sign of the cross. . . . There are archaeological evidences of the destruction and defacement of Christian images [and crosses] in the early Islamic period due to the conflict with Muslims they aroused" (2010, 14, 144–145).

† Anastasius was not speaking figuratively. He tells "of a certain John of Bostra who interrogated demonically possessed girls in Antioch. The demons told him (through the mouths of the girls) that the three things they feared the most were the cross, baptismal water, and the Eucharist; that, they continued, is why they preferred the religion of their 'companions,' the Saracens, who rejected all three" (Tolan 2002, 43, 44).

MARTYRDOM IN GAZA

Indeed, these were dramatic if not eschatological times. In the context of an earthquake that brought down an early mosque built atop the Temple Mount—and Muslims fervently breaking crosses from atop Jerusalem's churches[43] and even atop "the heads of Christians during processions and religious litanies"[44]—one of the more gripping but little known accounts to reach posterity concerns the conquest of nearby Gaza.[45] There, sixty Christian soldiers valiantly "fought day and night" and "continuously slew many of these Saracens" under the command of Amr bin al-As (who, after Yarmuk, began migrating to his next target, Egypt). The sixty fighters were eventually captured. Amr, apparently impressed by their mettle and eager to recruit them for the jihad, repeatedly "tried to force those [sixty] brought before him to desert their confession of Christ"* and submit to Islam. Every time they refused, they were sent to harsher, fouler dungeons.

Amr eventually sent them to a prison in Jerusalem, where Sophronius is said to have visited and exhorted them to remain steadfast. After ten months, Amr wrote to Abu Ubaida in Jerusalem and told him to "tell them [sixty prisoners] to deny their faith; and that if they agreed to deny Christ, to remove the irons from them and to send them on with great honour; and that if they refused to submit, to behead their chief, together with nine others, in front of them, so that, seeing this, the rest would, perhaps, be led by fear and deny their faith."

Abu Ubaida obliged, but the stubborn prisoners "did not submit to his commands, but all confessed together the faith of Our Lord Christ." Enraged, Muhammad's companion ordered their chief and nine others beheaded and the rest sent to a fouler dungeon. A month later, Amr ordered the remaining fifty prisoners returned to him. Unable to understand why they stubbornly refused to say the *shahada*—that is, utter some words—a frustrated Amr displayed their wives and children, before exclaiming:

> "How stiff-necked you are in your refusal to submit to us concerning our rites! If you submit to us, behold, you will have your wives and

---

* Meaning to stop claiming he is divine, the Son of God, part of a Trinity, died and was resurrected—all anathema to Islam and the Koran.

sons, and will be like us, and will be honoured just like one of us; but if you do not, you too will suffer what your fellow soldiers have suffered." Then the holy martyrs responded together to Ambrus [Amr], saying, "No one can separate us from the love of Christ, neither wives, nor sons, nor all the wealth of this world, but we are servants of Christ, the Son of the living God, and we are prepared to die for Him who died and rose for us." When the most cruel Ambrus heard this, he was filled with anger, his face changed, and he ordered the holy martyrs of Christ to be surrounded by a crowd of Saracens, and in this way he wickedly killed them ["by means of various tortures"] on account of their faith in Christ.[46]

This same Christian account asserts that Sophronius, who is known to have died a year after the conquest of Jerusalem, was actually beheaded for agreeing to convert some Muslims to Christianity.

Despite the popular claim that Islam bans forced conversion, the martyrdom of early Christians who refused to convert to Islam permeates both Muslim and Christian sources—it is still a very real phenomenon today—and was one of the chief reasons that premodern Christians saw only the spirit of Antichrist in Islam.[†]

THE MUSLIM CONQUEST OF EGYPT

In December 639, after rallying thousands of more Bedouins eager for plunder under the banner of Islam, Amr left Gaza for Egypt. As with Syria, when the Muslims reached the ancient land of the pharaohs, it had been profoundly Christian for centuries[‡]; it was home to some of Christendom's

---

[†] One of the earliest records on Islam, written soon after Muhammad's death, the "*Doctrina Iacobi nuper baptizati* [,] also implies that Muslims tried, on threat of death, to make Christians abjure Christianity and accept Islam" (Kaegi 1995, 109). As for the much touted Koran 2:256—"there is no compulsion in religion"—this seems more of an assertion, a statement of fact, than an imperative for Muslims to uphold. After all, it is true: no Muslim can *make* a non-Muslim convert. But that does not mean they cannot entice, cajole, and reward on the one hand, and enslave, extort, and slaughter on the other, those who refuse.

[‡] According to John Cassian, a Christian monk from modern-day Romania who visited Egypt about two and a half centuries before the Arab invasion, "the traveler from

earliest theological giants and church fathers, including Clement of Alexandria (b. 150), Origen the Great (b. 184), Anthony the Great, father of monasticism (b. 251), and Athanasius of Alexandria (b. 297), the chief articulator and defender of the Nicene Creed in 325, still professed by all major Christian denominations. The Catechetical School of Alexandria—"which generated the first systematic theology and the most extensive exegetic enquiry into Scripture"—was the oldest and "first great seat of Christian learning in the whole world."[47] Egyptian missionaries were reportedly even first to bring the Gospel to distant regions of Europe, including Switzerland, Britain, and especially Ireland.*

Once in Egypt, the Arab invaders besieged and captured many towns, "slaughter[ing] all before them—men, women, and children."[48] "Then a panic fell on all the cities of Egypt," writes an eyewitness of the invasions, and "all their inhabitants took to flight, and made their way to Alexandria."[49] In hot pursuit, Allah's fighters reached the walls of Alexandria in March 641. Mightily fortified—it had walls within walls—and with direct sea access for supplies and reinforcements, Alexandria was the most impregnable city the Muslims had yet encountered. To make matters worse, Heraclius, whose "mind, which had suffered some derangement [after Yarmuk], slowly recovered its balance in the seclusion of Chalcedon," was

---

Alexandria in the north to Luxor in the south would have in his ears along the whole journey, the sounds of prayers and hymns of the monks, scattered in the desert, from the monasteries and from the caves, from monks, hermits, and anchorites" (*Abba Anthony*, 6.)

* According to British historian and archaeologist Stanley Lane-Poole (d. 1931), "It is more than probable that to them [Egyptian Christians] we are indebted for the first preaching of the Gospel in England, where, till the coming of Augustine [who became the first archbishop of Canterbury in 597], the Egyptian monastic rule prevailed. But more important is the belief that Irish Christianity, the great civilizing agent of the early middle ages among the northern nations, was the child of the Egyptian church. Seven Egyptian monks were buried at Disert Uldith and . . . there is much in the ceremonies and architecture of Ireland in the earliest time that reminds one of still earlier Christian remains in Egypt. Everyone knows that the handicraft of the Irish monks in the ninth and tenth centuries far excelled anything that could be found elsewhere in Europe, and if the Byzantine-looking decoration of their splendid gold and silver work, and their unrivaled illuminations can be traced to the influence of Egyptian missionaries, we have more to thank the Copts for than had been imagined" (*British Quarterly*, 52).

"keenly alive to the importance of saving Egypt for the Empire."[50] He began assembling yet another army, one he planned on personally leading to Alexandria for a final, all-out effort to repulse the Muslims from the Christian empire's domains.

The siege lasted some six months. High in their walls, the Christians caused considerable damage with their projectiles to the Muslim besiegers, but Heraclius never came. This once valorous and charismatic hero, who had done much for the defense and glory of Christendom, was by all accounts now a broken man:

> The victor of the Persian heathen was vanquished by the unbelieving Saracens. . . . The man who was foremost in every fight where his personal courage was needed, and master of every movement on the battlefield—the man who six years ago would have met Khalid "the Sword of Allah" on equal terms in duel, and whose genius as a tactician would have baffled and crushed the raw valour of the Arab chieftains, never once led an army in the field against them. His hand and his brain alike were paralysed.[51]

Heraclius died on February 11, 641, aged sixty-six; he spent the last years of an otherwise long and distinguished reign watching his many achievements wither away to the Arabs. With no aid from Constantinople, Alexandria's gates could not hold; in September 641 they were opened to the usual triumphant cries of "Allahu Akbar."[52] A shady and treacherous Roman leader, known in Arabic sources as al-Muqawqas, facilitated the city's capitulation. This was likely Cyrus, a Byzantine clergyman who for a decade ruled over and persecuted the "schismatic" Egyptians for refusing to confirm the Council of Chalcedon. Whatever the terms of surrender were, a bloodbath followed the Muslim entry into Alexandria. They immediately "destroyed its walls and burnt many churches with fire," note the Coptic annals, including the ancient church founded by and containing the remains of Saint Mark, author of the eponymous Gospel, who also brought Christianity to Egypt around 50 AD.[53]

According to Muslim and Coptic historians, the Arab invaders also burned the Great Library of Alexandria. Amr sent a message to Caliph Omar inquiring what he should do with the tens of thousands of books and scrolls found within this massive building. Omar (in)famously responded: "If they agree with our Book [Koran], we do not need them; if they disagree, we do not want them. Burn them." The amount of ink-stained papyri—which if preserved would have rewritten history as we know it—were reportedly so great that, serving as fuel, it kept the many bathhouses of Alexandria, now enjoyed by its conquerors, continuously lit for six months, says Baghdad chronicler Abdul Latif.[54] Although most Western historians attribute the destruction of the great library to non-Muslims, the important point here is that Muslim histories and historians record it—meaning Muslims *believe* it happened—thus setting a precedent concerning how infidel books should be treated.

More than Syria, the loss of Egypt was "a source of great grief for the Romans."[55] Not only was it the beginning of the end of nearly one thousand years of Greek language and culture in Alexandria (following its founding by its Macedonian namesake in 332 BC), but as the seat of Hellenism, "even in the seventh century, [Alexandria was] the finest city in the world," and one of the wealthiest.[56] Heraclius's successors repeatedly tried to wrest the city from the Muslims: they briefly succeeded in 645, only to lose it again in 646; a large invasion fleet sent to Egypt in 654 also ended in failure.

Soon Egypt went from being a loss for, to being a base of operations against, eastern Christendom. In 649, Arab fleets from Alexandria invaded Constantia, the capital of Cyprus. "They found it entirely full of people. They established their rule over this town by a great massacre," writes Michael the Syrian. "They collected gold from the whole island, riches and slaves, and they shared out the booty." When they suddenly returned again, the already traumatized inhabitants were "seized with terror."[57] Sometime later, "the nation of the Saracens that had already spread through Alexandria and Egypt . . . came suddenly with many ships, invaded Sicily, entered Syracuse and made a great slaughter of the people—a few only escaping with difficulty who had fled to the strongest fortresses and the mountain ranges—and they carried off also great booty . . . and thus they returned to

Alexandria," writes Paul the Deacon (b. 720).[58] From this point on, Muslim powers "unleashed a wave of banditry and lawlessness which may well have been without precedent in the history of the Middle Sea"[59] (a theme to be examined more closely in Chapter 3).

What of the native Christian inhabitants of Egypt—the descendants of the pharaohs who converted to Christianity centuries before the Islamic invasion—known today as the Copts?* A brief look into their well-documented experiences under Islam sheds light on the experiences of all Christian populations that were conquered after Yarmuk. Although Muslim histories written two or more centuries after Egypt's conquest often portray Arab leaders as leaving the Copts alone on payment of *jizya,* "that they abhorred the religion of Islam is proved by every page of their history."[60] Entries such as the following by tenth century Coptic chronicler Severus are common: "The Arabs in the land of Egypt had ruined the country. . . . They burnt the fortresses and pillaged the provinces, and killed a multitude of the saintly monks who were in them and they violated a multitude of the virgin nuns and killed some of them with the sword."[61]

The oldest and most valuable chronicle was written around 650 by John of Nikiû, the bishop of the Nile Delta and an eyewitness of the invasions. According to him, "Whoever surrendered to the Muslims [alternatively referred to as "Ishmaelites"] was slaughtered, and no mercy was shown to the elderly, the women or the children . . . the Muslims [then] plundered the possessions of the fleeing Christians, deeming the servants of Christ as enemies of Allah."[62] His chronicle is so riddled with bloodshed that John often ends entries with, "But let us now say no more, for it is impossible to describe the horrors the Muslims committed."[63]

Soon began the caliphate's centuries-long "milking" of Egypt's wealth, beginning under Caliph Omar, who, in the words of the Spanish *Chronicle of 754,* "subjected Alexandria, that most ancient and prosperous metropolitan

---

* The word "Copt" is an English transliteration of an Arabic transliteration of the Greek word for "Egyptian," Αἰγύπτιος (pronounced ai-gypt-ios). The Arabs took the middle of three syllables, *gypt,* and pronounced it *qibt,* hence the English "Copt." That Egypt's most indigenous population was (and remains) Christian is therefore even evident in the name the Arabs applied to them, which denotes *Egyptian* and connotes *Christianity.*

city of Egypt, to the yoke of tribute."[64] According to eighth-century Muslim jurist Abu Yusuf, the second "rightly-guided" caliph* maintained that "Muslims eat them [Coptic Christians] as long as they live; if we perish, the children of our children eat their children."[65] Even Amr, whom Muslim histories portray as dealing moderately with the conquered populace—he left churches alone after the initial burning—receives a different rendering in the chronicles of the Coptic patriarchate and John of Nikiû: "He was a lover of money"; "he doubled the taxes on the peasants"; "he perpetrated innumerable acts of violence"; "he had no mercy on the Egyptians, and did not observe the covenant they had made with him, for he was of a barbaric race"; and "he threatened death to any Copt who concealed treasure."[66]

Yet it may be that Amr was not responsible. After Omar was assassinated in 644, Uthman, the third caliph, recalled Amr—that "willful, greedy, grasping man!" in the words of a contemporary Arab[67]—for not sending enough wealth from Egypt. Amr's replacement increased the caliphate's treasury double that of his predecessor prompting Uthman to boast how he had forced the "milk camels"—a reference to Egypt's indigenous Christian population—"to yield more milk."[68] Apocalyptic scenes permeate contemporary accounts concerning these times of wholesale extortion followed by starvation: "The dead were cast out into the streets and market-places, like fish which the water throws up on the land, because they found none to bury them; and some of the people devoured human flesh."[69]

In this manner, "Egypt had become enslaved to Satan," concludes John of Nikiû: "The yoke they [Arabs] laid on the Egyptians was heavier than the yoke which had been laid on Israel by Pharaoh. . . . When God's judgement lights upon these Muslims, may He do unto them as He did aforetime unto Pharaoh!"[70] No such judgment would come to pass. It would be the Copts' lot to lead lives synonymous with persecution. For it was they who bore the brunt of the great Roman persecutions under Emperor Diocletian in the early 300s; then they suffered under the Persians (619–629); then

---

* Because they were deemed ideal Muslim rulers, the first four caliphs are known in Islamic tradition by the Arabic appellation *Rashidun*, meaning "pious" or "rightly guided."

they suffered under the Roman Cyril (630–640); then they suffered under the Muslims—till the present.

Egypt is also instructive in showing how and why heavily Christian lands became Islamic. Early Muslim chronicles make clear that centuries of persecution and financial fleecing saw more and more Copts proclaim the *shahada,* making Egypt what it is today, a Muslim-majority nation. Thus, in his multivolume history of Egypt, Muslim historian Taqi al-Din al-Maqrizi (d. 1442) often concludes his many separate entries of Muslims burning churches, massacring and burning Christians alive, and enslaving their women and children, by saying, "Under these circumstances a great many Christians became Muslims."[71] Not all could persevere like the sixty martyred soldiers of Gaza.[†]

THE MUSLIM CONQUEST OF NORTH AFRICA

Like Egypt, seventh-century North Africa was one of the wealthiest regions of the Roman world; ancient ruins, relics of a bygone day, can still be seen in Libya, Algeria, and Morocco. Modern-day Tunisia rests atop the ruins of Rome's ancient rival, Carthage. Also like Egypt and Syria, when Islam invaded it, "North Africa was as firmly Christian as any other area of the empire. Cities and countryside were adorned with graceful churches."[72] It too had produced its share of great Christian theologians, chief among them

---

[†] This is to say nothing of the effects of the entrenched *dhimmi* system, which saw the increasingly impoverished native Egyptians slowly convert to Islam over the centuries. Consider the observations of Lord Alfred Butler, a nineteenth-century historian, concerning the institution of *jizya,* which he elsewhere refers to as a "vicious system of bribing the Christians into conversion": "although religious freedom was in theory secured for the Copts under the capitulation, it soon proved in fact to be shadowy and illusory. For a religious freedom which became identified with social bondage and with financial bondage could have neither substance nor vitality. As Islam spread, the social pressure upon the Copts became enormous. . . . The wonder, therefore, is not that so many Copts yielded to the current which bore them with sweeping force over to Islam, but that so great a multitude of Christians stood firmly against the stream, nor have all the storms of thirteen centuries moved their faith from the rock of its foundation." As for the popular claim that the Copts welcomed the Arabs as "liberators" against the Byzantines, Butler observes that "there is not a word to show that any section of the Egyptian nation viewed the advent of the Muslims with any other feeling than terror" (Butler 1992, iv–v, 236).

Saint Augustine of Hippo (in modern-day Algeria), the father of Western theology. The New Testament canon as we know it was confirmed by the Council of Carthage in 397.

The Muslim march west—the notion of "manifest destiny" is far older than the European colonization of America—continued with little respite after the conquest of Egypt. Outside the cultivated coastal cities dwelled the Berbers (from the Greek *barbaros,* or "barbarians"). A tribal, semicivilized people, they practiced a syncretic religion with pagan, Jewish, and Christian elements. The Muslims first warred on them as early as 642 in Barqa (modern Marj, Libya). A treaty was concluded on condition that the Berbers pay *jizya,* with the telling provision that "the people could sell their sons and daughters into slavery to raise the money."[73] Soon thereafter, Uqba bin Nafi, nephew of Amr bin al-As, set off to subjugate the rest of North Africa in the name of Islam. Around 666 and at the head of ten thousand men he "conquered the southern Tunisian cities . . . slaughtering all the Christians living there."[74] Muslim sources portray this hero of early Islam as waging countless raids, often ending with the complete ransacking and mass enslavement of cities.[75] Even "archaeological evidence from North Africa . . . points to the destruction of churches along the route the Islamic conquerors followed in the late seventh century."[76] But unlike their experiences with Christian populations, Uqba and other jihadis never knew when to stop slaughtering the Berbers—for the latter had no qualms about "converting" to Islam, that is, uttering some words about a certain Muhammad. As one medieval Muslim historian explains:

> He [Uqba] went to Ifriqiya [Africa] and besieged its cities, conquering them by force and putting the people to the sword. A number of Berbers converted to Islam at his hand and Islam spread among them until it reached the lands of Sudan [literally meaning the "black lands" in Arabic, i.e., sub-Saharan Africa]. Then Uqba gathered his companions and addressed them saying, "The people of this country are a worthless lot; if you lay into them with the sword they become Muslims but the moment your back is turned, they revert to their old habits and religion."[77]

The restless Uqba went on to raid the entire Mediterranean coast-line until he reached the Atlantic Ocean, whereupon he furiously rode his horse into the water while crying "Allahu Akbar"; slashing at the waves, he lamented: "If my course were not stopped by this sea, I would still ride on to the unknown kingdoms of the west, preaching the unity of Allah [*tawhid*], and putting to the sword the rebellious nations who worship any other god but him!"[78] This jihadi—who had earlier said, "I have sold myself to Allah most high" in conformity to Koran 9:111—finally died, or was "martyred," in battle in 683. In Islamic historiography, Uqba is to the conquest of North Africa what Khalid is to the conquest of Syria. And like the Sword of Allah, this venerated Muslim warrior also had a dark side: he was fond of enslaving for himself, and selling to others, innumerable Berber girls, "the likes of which no one in the world had ever seen."[79]

He was not alone. Hassan, another Muslim leader, made a career of abducting "young, female Berber slaves of unparalleled beauty, some of which were worth a thousand dinars."[80] Subsequent Muslim rulers of North Africa continued to attack and enslave the Berbers en masse, so that one modern historian rightly observes that "the Islamic jihad looks uncomfortably like a giant slave trade."[81] Arab chronicles record astronomical numbers of slaves, especially in the accounts of Musa bin Nusayr, a Yemenite chieftain who became the governor of Africa in 698, and who "was cruel and ruthless against any tribe that opposed the tenets of the Muslim faith, but generous and lenient to those who converted."[82] He waged "battles of extermination"—"genocides" in modern parlance—"killed myriads of them, and made a surprising number of prisoners."[83] According to historian Ahmad bin Muhammad al-Maqqari (c. 1578–1632), one of the most comprehensive sources on the Muslim conquest of North Africa:

> No sooner had Musa arrived in Africa proper, than hearing that some of the nations . . . had shaken off the yoke of Islam [as was their wont after perfunctorily saying the *shahada*], he sent against them his own son Abdullah, who soon returned with one hundred thousand captives. He sent Merwan, another of his sons, against the enemy in another quarter, and he also returned with one hundred thousand captives.[84]

In short, the number of Berbers enslaved "amounted to a number never before heard of in any of the countries subject to the rule of Islam" up to that time. As a result, "most of the African cities were depopulated, [and] the fields remained without cultivation." Even so, Musa "never ceased pushing his conquests until he arrived before Tangiers, the citadel of their [Berbers'] country and the mother of their cities, which he also besieged and took, obliging its inhabitants to embrace Islam."[85]

After a staunch resistance led by the Kahina—a charismatic Berber queen—was finally squashed by the Muslims, and she decapitated, the Africans, led by the Kahina's own sons, concluded that if they could not beat Islam, they had better join it. "When the nations inhabiting the dreary plains of Africa saw what had befallen the Berbers," al-Maqqari diplomatically explains, "they hastened to ask for peace and place themselves under the obedience of Musa, whom they solicited to enlist them in the ranks of his army." Musa agreed and left Arab teachers to instruct them in the finer points of jihad.[86]

So it was that the Berbers, who for decades had resisted the Muslims—occasionally (though nominally) converting whenever expedient—finally and fully submitted to Islam. In reward, the former slaves became the future slavers. Although many of them remained indifferent to the Arabian religion, it mattered not; they had formally accepted Muslim authority, and would soon be invading Europe and terrorizing the Mediterranean for over a millennium in the name of Allah. They who were formerly massacred and enslaved on an epic scale would be taught, upon conversion to the creed that had dehumanized them for decades, to dehumanize the other, the infidel, and thus become the ones to massacre, enslave, and plunder—always under the aegis of righteousness.

As for the last vestiges of Christian power, in 698, Carthage fell to Islam, bringing a close to centuries of Roman rule in North Africa. Musa "cruelly laid it to waste and leveled it [by fire] to the ground," writes Paul the Deacon.[87] Once the jewel of North Africa, Carthage was left desolate for two centuries, as Tunis became the new center of orbit. By 709, the whole of North Africa was under Muslim rule. All that was left to invade and plunder was Europe, where the last free Christians reigned. Their time to choose between conversion, *jizya,* or death was nigh.

THE MOST CONSEQUENTIAL BATTLE
"IN ALL WORLD HISTORY"

By now, the classical, Hellenistic world—the once Roman, then Christian empire—was a shell of its former self. Even archeology attests to this: "The arrival of Islam upon the stage of history was marked by a torrent of violence and destruction throughout the Mediterranean world. The great Roman and Byzantine cities, whose ruins still dot the landscapes of North Africa and the Middle East, were brought to a rapid end in the seventh century. Everywhere archeologists have found evidence of massive destruction; and this corresponds precisely with what we know of Islam as an ideology."[88]

It also corresponds precisely with what we know from the primary sources of history, as outlined in this chapter. To quote from a late seventh-century Christian manuscript that profoundly influenced later centuries of European thinking, aptly known as the *Apocalypse* and long believed to be prophetic: "All of the wood of the hillside will be extirpated, the beauty of the mountains will vanish, cities will become desolate, lands will become impassible because of the reduction of the human population and the earth will be polluted by blood and they [the Arabs] will gain hold of its fruit. For the tyrannically conquering barbarians are not men, but sons of the desert who will come to desolation, are ruined and will welcome hate."[89]

And yet the Islamic scimitar would not have been thousands of miles away from its Arabian homeland, poised to invade Europe through its easternmost and westernmost gateways (Chapters 2 and 3, respectively) had it been shattered at Yarmuk. This fact has prompted generations of historians, past and present, Christian and Muslim, to wonder: How and why did the Muslims win, especially considering that the Roman military was superior to them in virtually every way?

The earliest Christian and Muslim answers were at once similar and dissimilar. Both agreed that God was on the side of Muslims—but for radically different reasons. Christians agreed with Patriarch Sophronius: just as God had often punished the ancient Hebrews whenever they fell astray by raising ruthless pagan conquerors against them, so these new invaders were God's rod to chastise Christians for falling astray,* particularly, if the seventh-century *Apocalypse* is to be believed, for engaging in widespread acts of sexual immorality, including cross-dressing:

> Thus not because He loved them [Muslims] did the Lord God give them power to seize the land of the Christians, but because of the lawlessness of the Christians. The likes of it never had occurred nor may it occur in the entire generations of the earth. For why did men put on the clothes of adulterous women and prostitutes, adorn themselves as women and openly stand in the squares and markets of towns and change their natural practice for an unnatural one . . . ? Likewise, women did the same things as the men had done. Father, son and brother had intercourse with one woman who touched every kinsman. . . . For this reason God delivered them into the hands of the barbarians, that is, because of their sin and stench. The women will pollute themselves through the men who already are polluted and the sons of Ishmael will cast lots [for them].[90]

Speaking of Abraham's elder but outcast son whom the Arabs claimed as patriarch, biblical prophecies were also cited as proof of the Arabs' innate animus: Ishmael, it was foretold, "will be a wild donkey of a man; his hand will be against everyone and everyone's hand against him, and he will live in hostility toward all his brothers" (Gen. 16:12).

---

* After explaining how "the sword of the Saracens, beastly and barbarous, which truly is filled with every diabolic savagery" had prevented Christians from going on pilgrimage, Sophronius added, "If we constrain ourselves, as friendly and beloved of God, we would laugh at the fall of our Saracen adversaries and we would view their not distant death, and we would see their final destruction. For their blood-loving blade would enter their hearts, their bows will be shattered and their shafts will be fixed in them" (Donner 2008, 114–115).

While Muslims agreed that God—that is, Allah—empowered them against Christians because he was angry with the latter, his wrath was not due to any sin, but rather because they *were* Christians: because they believed in the Trinity, that is, because they committed the worst of all sins—*shirk,* polytheism—associating others with Allah. Additionally, then and now, for Muslims the conquests were, as one Muslim told a *dhimmi* monk in the seventh or eighth century, "the sign that Allah loves us and is pleased with our religion: He has given us authority over all religions and all peoples; they are slaves subject to us."[91]

Less hagiographically, some early Christian and Muslim sources attribute the initial Islamic conquests to the use of cunning and terrorism. The *Chronicle of 754* says that the "Saracens, influenced by their leader Muhammad, conquered and devastated Syria, Arabia, and Mesopotamia more by stealth than manliness, and not so much by open invasions as by persisting in stealthy raids. Thus with cleverness and deceit and not by manliness they attacked all of the adjacent cities of the empire."[92] (Another version of the *Chronicle* cites Arab "trickery . . . cunning and fraud rather than power."[93]) Similarly, in the context of discussing Muhammad's boast, "I have been made victorious with terror," Ibn Khaldun says, "Terror in the hearts of their enemies was why there were so many routs during the Muslim conquests."[94]

Finally, taking a middle view that fuses piety with ferocity, traditional Muslim historiography concerning why Muslims won holds that their win-win bargain with Allah—wherein the Muslim is rewarded with paradise either in the here or hereafter—enthused the Arabs' fighting spirit to no end. "The Muslim preachers did not cease to encourage the combatants [at Yarmuk]: Prepare yourselves for the encounter with the houris of the big black eyes," explains a later Persian scholar. "And to be sure, never has a day been seen when more heads fell than on the day of the Yarmuk."[95] Or to quote a companion of Muhammad speaking to a Byzantine official prior to the invasion of Egypt: "Do not deceive yourselves. We are not afraid of your numbers. Our greatest desire is to meet the Romans in battle. If we conquer them, it is well; if not, then we receive the good things of the world to come."[96]

The idea that Muslim fanaticism was responsible for the Arabs' victories was also adopted by European writers. As late as 1963, Lieutenant-General Sir John Bagot Glubb maintained that "it was religious enthusiasm which provided the impetus for the Arab conquests." He apparently knew what he spoke of: "I actually commanded, for thirty years, soldiers recruited from those very tribesmen who carried out the Great Arab conquests and who have remained unchanged for thirteen hundred years."[97]

In more recent times, when only material or economic explanations are taken as serious causal factors, the idea that Muslims were victorious due to a fanatical and martyrdom-driven zeal in battle has been dismissed by Western academics as a literary meme or device. In its place, a number of theories—some plausible, some strained, none enough to explain the victories at and after Yarmuk—appeared: Muslims won because the Romans and Persians were overly taxed from their own infighting; because of the Christological schism; because of infighting between the different ethnicities that made up the Roman army; and because of the desiccation of Arabia, which forced the Arabs to spread.[*]

Whatever reason the Muslims won, the fact remains: "Such a revolution had never been. No earlier attack had been so sudden, so violent or so permanently successful. Within a score of years from the first assault in 634 [Ajnadayn] the Christian Levant had gone: Syria, the cradle of the Faith, and Egypt with Alexandria, the mighty Christian See."[98] Just seventy-three years after Yarmuk, all ancient Christian lands between Greater Syria to the east and Mauretania (Morocco) to the west—approximately 3,700 miles—were forever conquered by Islam. Put differently, two-thirds (or 66 percent) of Christendom's original territory[†]—including three of the five most

---

[*] For a thorough examination of the various hypotheses, see *The Battle of Yarmuk: An Assessment of the Immediate Factors Behind the Islamic Conquests* (available at www. RaymondIbrahim.com).

[†] A general consensus around this two-thirds statistic has formed (e.g., Stark 2012, 199) and is confirmed by comparing maps of Christendom before and after the Islamic conquests. Eventually, and thanks (as shall be seen in forthcoming chapters) mostly to the Turks, "Muslim armies conquered three-quarters [or 75 percent] of the Christian world" (Madden 2004, 213).

important centers of Christianity—Jerusalem, Antioch, and Alexandria‡—
were permanently swallowed up by Islam and thoroughly Arabized. For
unlike the Germanic barbarians who invaded and conquered Europe in the
preceding centuries—only to assimilate into Christian culture, civilization,
and language (Latin and Greek)—the Arabs further imposed their creed
and language onto the conquered peoples so that, whereas the "Arabs" once
only thrived in the Arabian Peninsula, today the "Arab world" consists of
some twenty-two nations spread over the Middle East and North Africa.

This would not be the case, and the world would have developed in
a radically different way—there would likely be no more chapters to this
book—had the original floodgates on the banks of the Yarmuk not been inundated by Muslim invaders. Even without the power of hindsight afforded
to historians living more than a millennium after the fact, Anastasius of Sinai, who was a youth when Muslim forces overran his Egyptian homeland,
testified to the decisiveness of the battle by referring to it as "the first terrible and incurable fall of the Roman army. I am speaking of the bloodshed
at Yarmuk . . . , after which occurred the capture and burning of the cities
of Palestine, even Caesarea and Jerusalem. After the destruction of Egypt
there followed the enslavement and incurable devastation of the Mediterranean lands and islands. But those ruling and dominating the Roman Empire
did not understand these things."[99]

Put differently, because the Eastern Roman Empire failed to deal a
decisive blow to the invaders and send them back to Arabia, the unity of
the ancient Mediterranean was shattered and the course of world history
forever altered. Little wonder some historians hold that "the battle of the
Yarmuk had, without doubt, more important consequences than almost any
other in all world history."[100]

‡ With the caveat that Jerusalem fell back to Christian hands during the Crusades and
is today under Israeli authority.

CHAPTER 2

THE JIHAD REACHES AN EASTERN WALL OF STONE: THE SIEGE OF CONSTANTINOPLE, 717

Surely, Constantinople will be conquered [by my community]; how blessed the commander who will conquer it, and how blessed his army.

—Muhammad, Prophet of Islam[1]

He is deceiving. For do prophets come with swords and chariot? Verily, these events of today are works of confusion. . . . You will discover nothing true from the said prophet except human bloodshed.

—Jewish scribe, c. 634[2]

CONSTANTINOPLE:
THE BULL'S-EYE OF JIHAD

DESPITE THE CALIPHATE'S MANY TERRITORIAL CONQUESTS, THE UL-timate prize remained elusive. Constantinople—"New Rome," the Christian capital of the Eastern Roman Empire, or Byzantium—still stood in defiance after all the others had fallen to the scimitar of Islam. Con-quering its "slaves of the cross" and their "Roman dog" of an emperor became an obsession. "To them [Muslims] it was a vexation that the Cross maintained its dominion, in competition with Allah," writes scholar Julius Wellhausen; "in their conception, the war against the Byzantine emperor was preferable to all others, and they incessantly devoted themselves to this war."[3]

This fixation traced back to Muhammad. In the context of his Tabuk campaign against the Romans, the prophet had inaugurated unending war on Christians as captured in Koran 9:29 (see Introduction). His desire to see Constantinople fall to Islam was such that Muhammad promised—prophesized—great honors, rewards, and the forgiveness of all sins to any Muslim involved in its capture.[4]

Muawiya bin Abu Sufyan (b. 602)—a general at Yarmuk whose jihadi pedigree was impeccable—sought that honor.* Since becoming governor of Syria three years after that fateful battle, he had regularly eyed the road to Constantinople. In 650 he sent his men as far north as Euchaita (an Armenian Christian town); they sacked it and held the entire population captive. Michael the Syrian describes what happened next:

> When Mu'awiya arrived he ordered all the inhabitants to be put to the sword; he placed guards so that no one escaped. After gathering up all the wealth of the town, they set to torturing the leaders to make them show them things [treasures] that had been hidden. The Taiyaye [Arabs] led everyone into slavery—men and women, boys and girls—and they committed much debauchery in that unfortunate town: they wickedly committed immoralities inside churches. They returned to their country rejoicing.[5]

Soon thereafter, Muawiya sent another squadron that "embarked on devastation and pillage" in the Armenian regions around Lake Van and into Georgia. Once again, "they took captive the population, set fire to the villages and returned to their country joyfully."[6]†

---

* Both Muawiya's parents also fought at Yarmuk: his father, Abu Sufyan, had exhorted his fellow fighters to wage "jihad in the way of Allah" and "take their [Christians'] lands and cities, and enslave their children and women," while his mother, the formidable Hind, cried to her fellow womenfolk to "cut the extremities [phalluses] of the uncircumcised ones!"

† Even before he became caliph, as governor of Syria (639–661) Muawiya sent an Arab expedition to the island of Kos, off the coast of Asia Minor: they "laid waste and

In 661 Muawiya became caliph and founder of the Umayyad dynasty. As supreme leader of the Muslim *umma,* he moved the caliphate's capital from Medina to Damascus—closer to the promised prize, Constantinople—and continued directing raids deep into Roman territory. At age seventy-two, Muawiya launched a series of mass expeditions, the largest yet, in a final, all-out effort to take New Rome. Though the ensuing battles and sieges were long and brutal—they began in 674 and ended in 678 and are now collectively referred to as the First Siege of Constantinople—few details are extant.

Theophanes simply writes that "the deniers of Christ equipped a great fleet," consisting of some one hundred thousand fighters.[7] "On being informed of so great an expedition of God's enemies against Constantinople," Emperor Constantine IV, a great grandson of Heraclius, "built large biremes bearing cauldrons of fire and dromones equipped with siphons" to meet them. This is the first mentioned use of "Greek fire," or as the Byzantines themselves called it, "sea fire," an inflammable composition that continued to burn even while floating atop water—history's first flame thrower, apparently invented by a Syrian refugee who had fled the Arab advance.

After the massive Muslim fleet arrived "in the region of Thrace" adjacent to Constantinople, "everyday there was a military engagement from morning until evening . . . with thrust and counter-thrust. The enemy kept this up from the month of April until September. Then, turning back, they went to Kyzikos [on the westernmost tip of Asia Minor, facing Constantinople], which they captured, and wintered there. And in the spring they set out and, in similar fashion, made war on sea against the Christians." After some five years of this, and after they had "lost a multitude of warriors and had a great many wounded, they turned back with much sorrow."[8]

---

pillaged all its riches, slaughtered the population and led the remnant into captivity, and destroyed its citadel." Next they "moved into Crete and pillaged it" before they "devastated" Rhodes in 654. Then they "plundered all the lands of Asia, Bithynia, Pamphylia. There was a serious plague in the lands of Mesopotamia. The Taiyaye pillaged anew and laid waste [to lands] as far afield as Pontus and Galatia" in central and northwest Asia Minor, respectively (Ye'or 2010, 275–276).

Concerning this first notable Christian victory over the hitherto unstoppable warriors of Allah, eminent Byzantine scholar George Ostrogorsky writes: "The Arab attack which Constantinople experienced then was the fiercest which had ever been launched by the infidels against a Christian stronghold, and the Byzantine capital was the last dam left to withstand the rising Muslim tide. The fact that it held saved not only the Byzantine Empire, but the whole of European civilization."[9]

"WHITE WOMEN": THE FORGOTTEN LURE OF JIHAD

Two years later, in 680, Muawiya died at age seventy-eight, and with him the dream of becoming the one to conquer Constantinople—the one he had heard the prophet prophesize of when still a youth. But honors and riches were not the only things that had motivated him. Muslim chronicles say his pivotal role in Islam's first schism, the First Fitna—which saw Muawiya ascend to the caliphate on a pyramid of dead Muslim bodies—had, as he aged, instilled in him a brooding fear of the hellfire awaiting him; hence the first Umayyad caliph's obsession with conquering Constantinople, which might appease Allah into overlooking the crimes of his youth.[*]

Be that as it may, beneath the prophecy and piety lay more carnal motives for eyeing the great city. New Rome was by far the wealthiest city in all *Dar al-Kufr,* or the Abode of Infidelity. Unbelievable splendors and fabulous treasures were said to be hidden behind its high walls. Nor were beautiful, inanimate objects the only things waiting for the taking; beautiful, *animate* objects—potential slaves, especially women—were also waiting to be seized.

Because it will reoccur throughout and motivate the course of this history, here it is necessary to examine the origins of a rather sordid Muslim motif that developed around this time. As one Western academic of Muslim origin (rather euphemistically) explains:

---

[*] "Muawiya aimed to see the downfall of the Christian Byzantine Empire because reportedly whoever was involved in the capture of the capital city of Constantinople would have all his sins forgiven" (P. Davis 1999, 99).

The Byzantines as a people were considered fine examples of physical beauty, and youthful slaves and slave-girls of Byzantine origins were highly valued. . . . The Arabs' appreciation of the Byzantine female has a long history indeed. For the Islamic period, the earliest literary evidence we have is a hadith (saying of the Prophet). Muhammad is said to have addressed a newly converted Arab: "Would you like the girls of Banu al-Asfar [the yellow (haired?) or pale people]?"[10]

Muhammad's question was meant to entice the man to join the Tabuk campaign against the Romans and reap its rewards—in this case, the sexual enslavement of attractive women. In other words, as "white-complexioned blondes, with straight hair and blue eyes," to quote another academic, Byzantine women were not so much "appreciated" or "highly valued" as they were lusted after.[11]

But any sense of compliment ended there. As contemptible and corrupt infidels—or simply to support the fantasy that they were eager to be sexually enslaved—Muslims habitually portrayed Europe's Christian women, beginning with those they first encountered in neighboring Byzantium, as sexually promiscuous by nature. Thus, for Abu Uthman al-Jahiz (b. 776), a prolific court scholar, the females of Constantinople were the "most shameless women in the whole world"; "they find sex more enjoyable" and "are prone to adultery." Abd al-Jabbar (b. 935), another prominent scholar, claimed that "adultery is commonplace in the cities and markets of Byzantium"—so much so that even "the nuns from the convents went out to the fortresses to offer themselves to monks."[12]

For all these reasons and more, European Christian women, typified by neighboring Eastern Roman women, became Islam's "beautiful femme fatale who makes men lose their self-control," as Nadia Maria el-Cheikh, author of *Byzantium Viewed by the Arabs,* explains:

Our [Arab/Muslim] sources show not Byzantine women but writers' images of these women, who served as symbols of the eternal female—constantly a potential threat, particularly due to blatant exaggerations of their sexual promiscuity. In our texts, Byzantine women are strongly associated with sexual immorality . . . .While the one quality that our [Muslim] sources never deny is the beauty of Byzantine women, the image that they create in describing these women is anything but beautiful. Their depictions are, occasionally, excessive, virtually caricatures, overwhelmingly negative.[13]

Such fevered fantasies—which "are clearly far from Byzantine reality"—existed only in the minds of Muslim men and "must be recognized for what they are: attempts to denigrate and defame a rival culture. . . . In fact, in Byzantium, women were expected to be retiring, shy, modest, and devoted to their families and religious observances. . . . The behavior of most women in Byzantium was a far cry from the depictions that appear in Arabic sources."[14]

Even so, if the jihad could not breach the walls of Constantinople and dominate these lusty hussies of imagination, it would find an alternate route. Thus began the caliphate's centuries-long slave trade arrangement with pagan Scandinavian pirates who shared in Islam's hostility for Christians. Starting in the mid-600s and for nearly three centuries thereafter, "Viking raids were elicited by the Muslim demand for white-skinned European slaves."[15] Indeed, it is "impossible to disconnect Islam from the Viking slave-trade," argues M. A. Khan, a former Muslim from India, "because the supply was absolutely meant for meeting [the] Islamic world's unceasing demand for the prized white slaves" and for "white sex-slaves."[16] Emmet Scott goes so far as to argue that "it was the caliphate's demand for European slaves that called forth the Viking phenomenon in the first place."[17]

CHRISTIAN VIEWS ON ISLAM MATURE

Because it is a common but false notion that negative Western views of Islam first began during the crusades—when imperial popes and greedy knights sought to demonize Muslims and their prophet to justify their "colonial" aspirations in the East—here another segue is necessary to establish context for the upcoming centuries of wars. If Muslims saw Constantinople as the last bastion where Christian "dogs" still dared defy Allah—and thus as the kingdom most deserving of being conquered and plundered of its wealth and women—how did Christians see Islam? As seen in Chapter 1, the invading Arabs were initially viewed as godless raiders devoted only to destruction and rapine, with a sometime hatred for Christian symbols. This is unsurprising considering that they were all pagans only a few years before; even during the initial invasions, many if not most Arabs and Bedouins had joined the Muslim caravan solely for the prospects of booty.

Yet even among the earliest Christian notices are scattered references to a prophet and a creed. Thus, writing around 650, John of Nikiû said that "Muslims"—the Copt is apparently one of the first non-Muslims to document that word—were not just "enemies of God" but adherents of "the detestable doctrine of the beast, that is, Mohammed."[18] The oldest parchment that alludes to a warlike prophet was written in 634, a mere two years after Muhammad's death. It has a man asking a learned Jewish scribe what he knows about "the prophet who has appeared among the Saracens." The elderly man, "with much groaning," responded: "He is deceiving. For do prophets come with swords and chariot? Verily, these events of today are works of confusion. . . . You will discover nothing true from the said prophet except human bloodshed."[19] Others confirmed that "there was no truth to be found in the so-called prophet, only the shedding of men's blood. He says also that he has the keys of paradise, which is incredible."[20]

Muhammad is first mentioned by name in a Syriac fragment, also written around 634; only scattered phrases are intelligible: "many villages [in Homs] were ravaged by the killing [of the followers] of Muhammad and many people were slain and [taken] prisoner from Galilee to Beth," and "some ten thousand" other Christians were slaughtered in "the vicinity of Damascus." Writing around 640, Thomas the Presbyter says that "there was a battle [probably Ajnadayn] between the Romans and the Arabs of Muhammad in Palestine twelve miles east of Gaza. The Romans fled. . . . Some 4,000 poor villagers of Palestine were killed there. . . . The Arabs ravaged the whole region"; they even "climbed the mountain of Mardin and killed many monks there in the monasteries of Qedar and Bnata."

A Coptic homily, also written around the 640s, is apparently the earliest account to associate the invaders with (an albeit hypocritical) piety. It counsels Christians to fast, but not "like the Saracens who are oppressors, who give themselves up to prostitution, massacre and lead into captivity the sons of men, saying, 'we both fast and pray.'"[21]

But it is only toward the end of the seventh and beginning of the eighth centuries that learned Christians became acquainted with and scrutinized the theological claims of Islam. The image of Muslims went from bad to worse. The Koran, that "most pitiful and most inept little book of the Arab Muhammad," was believed to be "full of blasphemies against the Most High, with all its ugly and vulgar filth," particularly its claim that heaven amounted to a "sexual brothel," to quote the eighth century's Nicetas Byzantinos, who had and closely studied a copy of it. Allah was denounced as an impostor deity, namely Satan: "I anathematize the God of Muhammad," read one Byzantine canonical rite.[22]

But it was Muhammad himself—the fount of Islam—who especially scandalized Christians: "The character and the history of the Prophet were such as genuinely shocked them; they were outraged that he should be accepted as a venerated figure," writes Norman Daniel, an expert on Christian views of Islam throughout the centuries.[23] Then and now, nothing so damned Muhammad in Christian eyes as much as his own biography, written and venerated by Muslims.* For instance, after proclaiming that Allah had permitted Muslims four wives and unlimited concubines (Koran 4:3), Muhammad later declared that Allah had delivered a new revelation (Koran 33:50–52) offering him, the prophet alone, a dispensation to sleep with and marry as many women as he wanted—prompting his child-bride Aisha to quip, "I feel that your Lord hastens in fulfilling your wishes and desires."†

---

* An interesting anecdote concerning a twelfth-century debate between a Christian monk and a Muslim cleric is well representative of this ongoing phenomenon. As the former continued reciting the misdeeds of Muhammad, the Muslim accused him of "blasphemy" against "our Prophet Muhammad" whom "you mock with insolence!" to which the monk replied: "Upon my life, we do not bring anything from ourselves but from your Book and your Koran." (See Hakkoum 1989.)

† The full (and canonical) hadith: "Narrated Aisha: I used to look down upon those

Based, then, on Muslim sources, early Christian writers of Semitic origins—foremost among them Saint John of Damascus (b. 676)—articulated a number of arguments against Muhammad that remain at the heart of all Christian polemics against Islam today.* The only miracle Muhammad performed, they argued, was to invade, slaughter, and enslave those who refused to submit to him—a "miracle that even common robbers and highway bandits can perform." The prophet put whatever words best served him in God's mouth, thus "simulating revelation in order to justify his own sexual indulgence";[24] he made his religion appealing and justified his own behavior by easing the sexual and moral codes of the Arabs and fusing the notion of obedience to God with war to aggrandize oneself with booty and slaves.†

Perhaps most importantly, Muhammad's denial of and war on all things distinctly Christian—the Trinity, the resurrection, and "the cross, which they abominate"—proved that he was Satan's agent. Thus, "the false prophet," "the hypocrite," "the liar," "the adulterer," "the forerunner of Antichrist," and "the Beast" became mainstream epithets for Muhammad among Christians for over a thousand years, beginning in the late seventh

---

ladies who had given themselves to Allah's Apostle and I used to say, 'Can a lady give herself (to a man)?' But when Allah revealed: 'You (O Muhammad) can postpone (the turn of) whom you will of them (your wives), and you may receive any of them whom you will; and there is no blame on you if you invite one whose turn you have set aside (temporarily).' (33:51) I said (to the Prophet), 'I feel that your Lord hastens in fulfilling your wishes and desires'" (*Sahih Bukhari* 6:60:311).

* Many modern academics portray this fact—that the polemics first made against Islam continued to be made with little variation centuries later—as proof that medieval Christians mindlessly copied and mimicked the early arguments against Islam without much reflection. On the contrary, because these early polemics were so comprehensive and well thought out, they continue to be cited to this day by even former Muslims as cause for them to apostatize.

† This latter point is key: it is not that Christians were "above" Muhammad's worldly incentives, but rather that they knew and feared the temptation. "Christians were recommended, for example, to practice marital continence, where the reverse was encouraged by Islam." As such, "it is not possible to exaggerate the horror that the clergy felt for a doctrine which . . . either permitted or encouraged things that men in any case would not give up," such as violence and sex, which at least Christianity sought to tame (Daniel 1962, 266).

century.[25] Indeed, for people who find any criticism of Islam "Islamophobic," the sheer amount and vitriolic content of more than a millennium of Western writings on Muhammad may beggar belief.[‡]

Nor did the theological claims behind the jihad escape scrutiny (and subsequent ridicule). In his entry for the years 629–630, Theophanes the Confessor wrote:

> He [Muhammad] taught his subjects that he who kills an enemy or is killed by an enemy goes to Paradise [Koran 9:111]; and he said that this paradise was one of carnal eating and drinking and intercourse with women, and had a river of wine, honey and milk, and that the women were not like the ones down here, but different ones, and that the intercourse was long-lasting and the pleasure continuous; and other things full of profligacy and stupidity.[26]

Similarly, in a correspondence with a Muslim associate, Bishop Theodore Abu Qurra (b. 750), an Arab Christian, gibed: "Since you say that all

---

‡ Even charitable historians such as Oxford's Norman Daniel—who rather gentlemanly leaves the most disturbing accusations against Muhammad in their original Latin in his survey of early Christian attitudes to Islam—makes this clear: "The two most important aspects of Muhammad's life, Christians believed, were his sexual license and his use of force to establish his religion"; for Christians "fraud was the sum of Muhammad's life. . . . Muhammad was the great blasphemer, because he made religion justify sin and weakness." Due to all this, "there can be no doubt of the extent of Christian hatred and suspicion of Muslims" (Daniel 1962, 274, 107, 265). Regrettably, however, modern academics and writers have twisted these facts around by claiming that negative Christian views of Muhammad began only after and as a pretext for the crusades—even though these "Islamophobic" views trace back to and remained consistent after the seventh century. Thus, for best-selling author of religious history Karen Armstrong, it is only "since the Crusades, [that] people in the west have seen the prophet Muhammad as a sinister figure. . . . The scholar monks of Europe stigmatised Muhammad as a cruel warlord who established the false religion of Islam by the sword. They also, with ill-concealed envy, berated him as a lecher and sexual pervert at a time when the popes were attempting to impose celibacy on the reluctant clergy" ("Balancing the Prophet," *Financial Times,* April 27, 2007). Similarly, Georgetown University's John Esposito bizarrely claims that "five centuries of peaceful coexistence [between Islam and Christendom] elapsed before political events and an imperial-papal power play led to [a] centuries-long series of so-called holy wars that pitted Christendom against Islam and left an enduring legacy of misunderstanding and distrust" (Andrea 2015, 1).

those who die in the holy war [jihad] against the infidels go to heaven, you must thank the Romans for killing so many of your brethren."[27]

A BUILDUP OF FANATICISM

None of this would do, and it came at a bad time. Growing Christian knowledge—and thus mockery—of Islamic teachings coincided with the caliphate's humiliation after the First Siege of Constantinople. Worse, Byzantium had followed up on its victory by recovering some of its lost territory, and—adding insult to injury—even exacting tribute from the Umayyads. All of this prompted an even more fanatical, specifically anti-Christian, response.* Although it began under Caliph Abd al-Malik (r. 685–705), it was during the reign of his son, Caliph Al-Walid (r. 705–715)—that "great hater of Christians," to quote a chronicler—that the jihad resumed and the spirit of "Anti-Christ" intensified.[28]

In the first year of his reign, Al-Walid ordered the Muslims to penetrate deep into Armenia, "where they captured all the magnates and leaders of the people, brought them together, and burned them alive."[29] In the following year, he had the venerated basilica dedicated to John the Baptist in Damascus, which the Arabs had initially vouchsafed to the Christians, demolished, and built the Great Mosque of Damascus (aka the Umayyad Mosque) atop it. And so it went. "Though lacking in divine favor," the *Chronicle of 754* grudgingly admits, "he crushed the forces of almost all neighboring people, made Romania [Anatolia] especially weak with constant raiding, [and] nearly brought all the islands to their destruction."[30]

Any challenge to Islam was not tolerated during this renewed burst of fanaticism. Thus "Walid ordered that Peter, the most holy Metropolitan of

---

* Which even had symbolic aspects: From the start, gold coins minted by the Roman empire had the image of the cross on one side. These continued to be circulated in the caliphate after the Arab conquests, until Malik ordered that one or two arms of the cross be effaced so the image no longer resembled a cross; in its place were carved Islamic slogans, especially the *shahada*. Moreover, high above—and thus looking down on—the Church of the Sepulchre, Christendom's holiest site, al-Malik constructed the Dome of the Rock, a mosque with several inscriptions carved on it openly denouncing Christian truths, particularly the Trinity. Such disavowal did not stop the early caliphs from closely copying Byzantine architecture, including for the buildings of Mecca, even the Ka'ba.

Damascus, should have his tongue cut off because he was publicly reproving the impiety of the Arabs," writes Theophanes. Peter was then exiled to and beheaded in Arabia, "where he died a martyr on behalf of Christ after reciting the holy liturgy."[31] Another anecdote especially highlights Al-Walid's animus for the cross and its followers: After ordering Shamala, a still-Christian Arab, to "stop disgracing" Arabs by "worshipping the Cross," Shamala refused. Outraged, Al-Walid had him tortured; afterward he asked him again to convert to Islam or else prepare to "eat his own flesh." The Christian Arab again refused, and the order was carried out: Muslim henchmen "cut off a slice from Shamala's thigh and roasted it in the fire, and they thrust it into his mouth."[32]

The caliph also meant to be the one to avenge Islam on Constantinople and began vast preparations for another all-out siege. In 715, word reached Emperor Anastasios II that Muslims were felling entire forests in Lebanon, "Land of the Cedar," and constructing tens of thousands of war ships for an upcoming expedition.[33] Roman vessels were issued to intercept and engage the Arabs on the island of Rhodes. On the heels of this battle, a Byzantine court ambassador returning from Damascus reported that the "Saracens were preparing an armament by sea and land, such as would transcend the experience of the past, or the belief of the present."[34] As many as 200,000 Muslim fighters were coming to Constantinople: 120,000 by land, 80,000 by sea.

Apprehensive of the onslaught about to be unleashed, Anastasios began to refortify the walls of Constantinople, furnish them with catapults and other siege weapons, and gather adequate provisions and food stores—a daunting task for a city that then had as many as half a million people. Citizens unable to stockpile enough food to last three years were evacuated. In a last-ditch effort, Constantinople sought to spare itself by offering the caliph a large tribute in gold. It would not do; nothing less than total capitulation to Islam would suffice this time.

Alas for Al-Walid, his dream of conquering Constantinople never materialized: in 715—the same year he condemned Peter to death—the caliph died at age forty-seven. But his brother and successor, Suleiman, another son of Abd al-Malik, shared the same ambitions and continued preparations with increased vigor, thanks to another prophecy;* and he continued oppressing Christians. When visiting Medina once, he gifted his local favorites with four hundred Greek slaves; they "could think of nothing better to do with them than slaughter them," as a Muslim poet scoffed in verse.[35] Those whom his forces conquered were either forced to convert to Islam or financially bled dry. Suleiman wrote to the governor of Egypt and commanded him "to milk the camel [reference to indigenous Coptic Christians] until it gives no more milk, and until it milks blood."[36] His tax collector, Osama bin Zayd, "used particularly barbarous means to extract money from the Christians. With hot iron bars he impressed a symbol on the body of each taxpayer. If a monk or Christian layman was discovered without the sign, Osama first amputated the victim's arms and then beheaded him. Many Christians converted to Islam in order to avoid punishment as well as to be freed of tribute."[37]

Once all was complete, Suleiman summoned his younger brother, Maslama, and commanded him to lead Islam's combined forces to Constantinople and "stay there until you conquer it or I recall you."[38] The young emir embraced the honor: soon "I [will] enter this city knowing that it is the capital of Christianity and its glory; my only purpose in entering it is to uphold Islam and humiliate unbelief."[39] In late 715, Maslama, at the head of 120,000 jihadis, crossed into the Eastern Roman Empire's territory and, with "both sword and fire, he put an end to Asia Minor," wrote a near contemporary chronicler.[40] Then he wintered his men.

THE ADVENTURES OF KONON AND MASLAMA

During this downtime, Maslama crossed paths with a Byzantine general named Konon (b. 685); he spoke fluent Greek and Arabic and was intimately acquainted with and had spent his entire life fighting Muslims,

---

* "When Solomon became Caliph, he was informed by many learned men that the name of the Caliph who should take Constantinople should be the name of a prophet; and there was none among the Ommiad [Umayyad] kings whose name was the name of a prophet except him. And he was eagerly desirous of doing it and made preparations for this purpose; never doubting that it was he who should perform this" (Jeffery 1944, 20–21).

beginning in the north Syrian town of his birth, Mar'ash.[†] First conquered by Khalid bin al-Walid in 637, Mar'ash had been fortified with Muslim fighters and used as a base to launch raids on Byzantium for decades, until it was recaptured by the Christians shortly after the failed First Siege, at which time Konon was born. Almost instantly Islamic raids began anew, until 694, when emir Muhammad bin Marwan utterly annihilated the frontier town and, in the words of Konon, who was then nine years old, "decapitated a number of Christians."[41]

Born and bred on fighting Muslims, this Konon's renown as "an expert in the art of war" soon reached Constantinople.[42] He quickly rose to the highest echelons of the military and was said to be a favorite of Emperor Anastasios. However, in November 715, Anastasios was deposed, retired to a monastery, and Konon was stationed—some might say exiled—at a battalion in Isauria, close to where Maslama was wintering in Anatolia. After playing something of a cat-and-mouse game with the mammoth Muslim army, Konon met and parleyed with Maslama. Citing his background as a "fellow Arab" and his grievances against the court of Constantinople, Konon indicated a willingness to betray the Byzantines, and a bargain was soon struck: Maslama would allow Konon to reach Constantinople and militarily support him in a bid to become emperor; in return the Byzantine general would open the city's gates to him. Maslama instantly dispatched emissaries to inform the people of Constantinople that the only way the Muslim army would "leave you, your country, your religion, and your churches in peace" is if they accepted his new vassal as "king."[43]

Constantinople was having its own internal problems and was heavily divided. On arriving, Konon forced Emperor Theodosius—who two years earlier had usurped Anastasios—to abdicate. Leaderless, the people swiftly concluded that the redoubtable thirty-two-year-old general was the ablest man to defend them against the coming storm and hailed him emperor. In

---

† Konon's experiences are similar to those of all non-Muslims who shared a frontier with Islam, "where anxiety always reigned and emptiness spread; properties there were abandoned, cultivated fields were left to lie fallow, the populations took refuge in the walled cities," to quote French medieval historian C. E. Dufourcq (Bostom 2005, 419).

late March 717, inside Hagia Sophia—or "Holy Wisdom," one of Christendom's oldest and greatest cathedrals—Konon was crowned Emperor Leo III, the name history remembers him by.

By now Maslama and his army had crossed the Hellespont at Abydos and were in Thrace. After sacking and pillaging several more towns, the Muslims finally reached and surrounded the walls of Constantinople in the summer of 717. Having heard that Leo had indeed become emperor, Maslama eagerly sent messengers to inquire when the Syrian would drop the city's gates, to which Leo replied, "Never." Shocked, the emissaries asked if Leo really meant to renege on his more powerful ally. "I am of the opinion that in breaking faith with him lies the exaltation of Christianity, and the defense of that is the best of rewards," responded the new emperor.[44] Furthermore, unless Maslama left forthwith without attacking any more Christians, "he will meet with real war, very different from that in which he has been engaged." Suleiman, the head of the Muslim mission, was devastated: "If the emir Maslama does not learn of this except through me, by Allah, he will kill me!" cried the emissary. "Your death is of less consequence to me than the loss of my kingdom," coolly replied the new guardian of Christendom, and left the negotiation table. Sure enough, when Maslama heard of this "great calamity," his "wrath was extreme," notes the Muslim chronicle, and, as the hapless messenger had predicted, he was crucified.[45]

While Greek sources confirm that the emperor "tricked" Maslama, who was "waiting on Leo's promises,"[46] Muslim sources are unsparing of the emir[*]: al-Tabari simply concludes that Leo so deceived Maslama as if the latter "was a plaything of a woman."[47] In Maslama's defense, the notion that, as fellow "Arabs," nominal Christian Semites could easily be made to side with Muslim Arabs against Rome was logically consistent (as evident in the high hopes and failed attempts of the Muslims to convert the Christian Arab chief, Jabla, at Yarmuk). Moreover, based on his lifelong

---

* One Muslim historian has Leo boast, "If Maslama had been a woman, and I had then chosen to seduce her, I would have done it, and he would never have refused me anything that I desired of him" (Brooks 1899, 23).

experiences with Muslims, Leo likely knew that they welcomed such sub-terfuges and played it to great effect.

THE SIEGE OF CONSTANTINOPLE

On August 15, 717, Maslama began bombarding the city. Battering rams, catapults, and other siege engines of war—that had been hauled over hundreds of miles by thousands of mules and camels—were activated against the stone walls of Constantinople with great violence, though to little effect. First built by Constantine the Great as defensive bulwarks surrounding his New Rome, successive emperors had continued to refortify as well as build higher and thicker walls, so that by the time Islam arrived the city was ensconced behind layers of cyclopean walls. Because these barricades had withstood countless sieges over the centuries—including the First Siege of recent memory (674–678)—Leo knew that as long as sea communications remained open, the city should stand. Maslama responded by blockading it. He ordered trenches dug around his camp to prevent any surprise sallies from Constantinople, let his men ravage the entire countryside, and waited for 1,800 vessels containing an additional 80,000 fighting men to approach through the Bosporus and engulf the city.

The Muslim warships arrived two weeks later, on September 1, heavy-laden with equipment and cumbersome (the Arabs then still had little naval experience, certainly in comparison to the Greeks). Suddenly Leo ordered the ponderous chain that normally guarded the harbor cast aside. Then, "while they [Muslim fleets] hesitated whether they should seize the opportunity . . . the ministers of destruction were at hand."[48] Leo sent forth the "fire-bearing ships" against the Islamic fleet, which was quickly set "on fire," writes Theophanes, "so that some of them were cast up burning by the sea walls, others sank to the bottom with their crews, and others were swept down flaming."[49]

Matters went from bad to worse when Maslama received word that the caliph, his brother Suleiman, had died of "indigestion" (by reportedly devouring two baskets of eggs and figs, followed by marrow and sugar for dessert). The new caliph, Omar II—Suleiman's more pious cousin, known

for his "scrupulous observance of the law [sharia]"[50]—seemed more interested in consolidating Islam's borders than extending them, and was initially inattentive to the Muslim army's needs. It did not matter; when he
was caliph, Suleiman had told his younger brother, "Stay there [Constanti-
nople] until you conquer it or I recall you." Neither had happened; now the
latter option was no longer possible. Maslama stayed, and winter set in.

Not new to besieging Constantinople, the Muslim force was not taken
unawares. The invading army was well provisioned from the start and had
augmented its stores with the plunder of numerous towns during its drive
to the city. Several caravans had also brought wheat to sow and harvest—a
wise move, as by now the Thracian countryside had been so thoroughly
ravaged that it could not be foraged. The original plan was to wait it out in
this fashion while Constantinople starved. But the Muslim navy's failure
to blockade the city rendered the plan ineffective: the Christians were still
ferrying in provisions; time was on their, not the Muslims', side.

Then, "one of the cruelest winters that anyone could remember" arrived, and, "for one hundred days, snow covered the earth."[51] All Maslama
could do was assure his emaciated, half-frozen men that "soon! Soon supplies will be here!"[52] But they did not come; worse, warlike nomadic tribesmen known as Bulgars—whence the nation of Bulgaria—accustomed to
the terrain and climate began to harry any Muslim detachment that left the
starving camp in search of food.

By spring, Muslim reinforcements and provisions finally arrived by
land and sea. But the damage was done; frost and famine had taken their
toll on the Muslims encamped outside the walls of Constantinople. "Since
the Arabs were extremely hungry," writes Theophanes, "they ate all their
dead animals: horses, asses, and camels. Some even say they put dead men
and their own dung in pans, kneaded this, and ate it. A plague-like disease
descended on them, and destroyed a countless throng."[53]

Even so, knowing that such a massive force—which had taken years
to assemble and had severely taxed the caliphate's resources—was already
at the walls of Islam's archrival was too much of a temptation for Omar to
order a withdrawal. The new caliph also knew that nothing could bolster
his credentials as the conquest of that one infidel kingdom that remained

a thorn in Islam's side. Thus, while the Muslim land force recuperated, a new navy, composed of eight hundred ships, was outfitted in the ports of Alexandria and Libya. The fleet arrived under the cover of night and managed to blockade the Bosporus. Having learned the lesson of Greek fire, the prudent ships kept their distance.

Just as the beginning of the end seemed to have arrived for Constantinople, sudden delivery—and from the least expected source—came: the crews manning the caliphate's new navy were not Arab Muslims but Egyptian Christians. Because the caliphate's fighting men had been spread thin, with many dying during the current siege, the caliph had no choice but to rely on infidel conscripts (whether as fighters or more likely rowers is unclear). Much to Omar's chagrin, the Egyptian sailors "of these two fleets took counsel among themselves, and, after seizing at night the skiffs of the transports, sought refuge in the City and acclaimed the emperor; as they did so, the sea," writes Theophanes, "appeared to be covered with timber."[54]

Not only did the Muslim war galleys lose a significant amount of manpower, but the Copts provided Leo with useful information concerning Muslim formations and plans. With this new intelligence, Leo lifted the boom and unleashed the fire ships. Considering the loss of manpower and general chaos that ensued after the Egyptian desertion, the confrontation—or rather conflagration, for the waves were again aflame—was more a rout than a battle.

Seeking to seal his victory, Leo had the retreating Muslim fleets pursued by sea. The neighboring Bulgar tribes—who, though having no great love for the Christian empire, had even less for the new invaders—were persuaded by Leo's "gifts and promises" to attack and massacre as many as twenty-two thousand of the battle-weary and starved Muslims.[55] To make matters worse, a "report was dexterously scattered that the Franks, the unknown nations of the Latin world, were arming by sea and land in defense of the Christian cause, and their formidable aid was expected."[56] (Come the Franks eventually would, but not for another 380 years; in fact, the Muslims would come to the Franks first, in the following chapter.)

By now, Caliph Omar II realized all was lost. Maslama, who could only have welcomed the summons, was recalled. On August 15, 718—exactly one year since it began*—the siege of Constantinople was lifted. But the Muslims' troubles were far from over. Nature—or from a Byzantine perspective, God—was not through with them: a terrible storm swallowed up many ships in the Sea of Marmara; and the ashes from a volcanic eruption on the island of Santorini set others aflame. Of the 2,560 ships retreating back to Damascus and Alexandria, only ten reportedly survived—and of these, half were captured by the Romans, leaving only five to reach and tell the tale to the caliph. In all, of the original 200,000 Muslims who set out to conquer the Christian capital, plus the additional spring reinforcements, only some 30,000 eventually made it back by land.†

Constantinople's unexpected salvation—particularly in the context of nemesis-like sea-storms and volcanoes that pursued and swallowed up the fleeing infidels—led to the popular belief that divine providence had intervened on behalf of Christendom, saving it from "the insatiable and utterly perverse Arabs," in the words of contemporaries.[57]

By way of collective punishment—which is still meted out to infidel minorities in the Muslim world‡—a vindictive Omar, failing to subdue the infidel dogs across the way, was quick to project his wrath on the infidels under his authority. In the words of the chronicler Bar Hebraeus: "And because of the disgrace which came upon the Arabs through their withdrawal from Constantinople, great hatred against the Christians sprang in the heart of Omar and he afflicted them severely."[58] Theophanes gives specifics:

> In the same year [when the siege was lifted], after a violent earthquake had occurred in Syria, Omar banned the use of wine in cities and set about forcing the Christians to become converted; those that converted he exempted from tax [*jizya*], while those that refused to do so he killed and so produced many martyrs. . . . He composed a letter

---

* Though some historians date the start of the siege to July, not August, 15.

† The figures are those of Theophanes, though Arabic sources also cite astronomical numbers, including 150,000 Muslim deaths during the campaign.

‡ In places like Egypt and Pakistan, entire Christian villages and their churches have in recent months and years been attacked and/or torched to the ground by Muslim mobs in "retribution" for the offensive behavior—real or perceived—of individual Christians (see Ibrahim 2013, 172–179).

concerning religion addressed to the emperor Leo in the belief that he would persuade him to convert.[59]

INTERFAITH DIALOGUE (EIGHTH-CENTURY STYLE)

Such letters issued by newly made caliphs calling on infidel kings to renounce their beliefs and submit to Islam are common and follow the pattern of Muhammad's missives to Heraclius and others. Leo responded with his own letter, "the first known Byzantine text which refutes Islam, and it shows knowledge of the subject much wider than that of other contemporary polemicists."[60] In it, Leo, "who was as zealous in his Christian faith as Omar was in his, refuted Islam on the basis of the Christian Gospel as well as on the basis of the Koran."[61] Standard Christian shock at the "incredulity" of the Arabs for believing that Muhammad, whose "tremendous imposture" should be self-evident, was a prophet was only one of the frank emperor's many criticisms:

> Nor do I wish to pass over in silence the abominable authorization given you [Muslims] by your legislator [Muhammad] to have with your wives a commerce that he has compared, I am ashamed to say, to the tilling of fields [e.g., Koran 2:223]. As a consequence of this license, a goodly number of you have contracted the habit of multiplying their commerce [sex] with women, as if it were a question of tilling fields. Nor can I forget the chastity of your Prophet and the manner full of artifice whereby he succeeded in seducing the woman Zeda.§ Of all these abominations the worst is that of accusing God of being the originator of all these filthy acts, which fact has doubtless been the cause of the introduction among your compatriots of this disgusting law [treating women as "tilling fields"]. Is there indeed a

---

§ Zaynab, wife of Zayd ibn Haritha. When the latter learned of Muhammad's attraction to his spouse, he divorced her for the prophet's sake. Allah followed up by delivering a new "revelation" encouraging Muhammad to marry Zaynab despite the otherwise dubious circumstances. The affair, which is documented in the Koran and other early Islamic sources, was arguably the most scandalous thing to reach Christian ears, as seen here in Leo's reference.

worse blasphemy than that of alleging that God is the cause of all this evil?[62]

As for paradise, Leo wrote: "We [Christians] do not expect to find there springs of wine, honey or milk. We do not expect to enjoy there commerce with women who remain forever virgin," for "we put no faith in such silly tales engendered by extreme ignorance and by paganism." But "for you who are given up to carnal vices, and who have never been known to limit the same, you who prefer your pleasures to any good, it is precisely for that reason that you consider the celestial realm of no account if it is not peopled with women" for sex, a reference to the houris.[63]

Something of a premodern defender of human rights, Leo further informed Omar that he "ought to be ashamed of the fact that at so modern a time as ours, when God has delivered the human race by breaking the bonds of the law, you announce yourself as a defender of circumcision." Worse, whereas circumcision had a symbolic place in God's "ancient law" for men, "among you, not only males but also the females, at no matter what age, are exposed to this shameful practice."[64]

Finally, the differences between Christ's peace and Muhammad's jihad were for the emperor those between light and darkness*: "You call 'the Way of God'† these devastating raids which bring death and captivity to all peoples. Behold your religion and its recompense [death and destruction]. Behold your glory ye who pretend to live an angelic life."[65]

Despite his comprehensive response, Leo expected his words to fall on deaf ears. For what "could one expect from you, when I see you, even now, excited by a species of fanaticism worthy of a pagan, exercising such cruelties towards the faithful of God [Christians], with the purpose of converting them to apostasy, and putting to death all those who resist your designs, so that daily is accomplished the prediction of our Savior: 'The time will

* This dichotomy was echoed throughout the centuries. Thus, for English philosopher Robert Holkot (d. 1349), "it is not possible to teach the life of Christ unless by destroying and condemning the law of Machomet" (Wheatcroft 2005, 182).

† A reference to the Arabic phrase *fi sabil Allah*, which appears frequently in the Koran, is variously translated as "in the way/cause/path of Allah," and is all but synonymous with and certainly connotative of jihad.

come when everyone who puts you to death will believe he is serving God' [John 16:2]. For you are far from thinking that in killing all those who resist you, you are putting yourself to an eternal death."[66]

According to one tenth-century Christian account, when Omar read Leo's response, "the Caliph was very confused." But eventually the "letter produced on him a very happy effect. From this moment he commenced to treat the Christians with much kindness. He ameliorated their state, and showed himself very favorable towards them, so that on all hands were heard expressions of thankfulness to him."[67] That he was assassinated some two years after his exchange with Leo lends some credence to this claim. The official Muslim story is that Omar initiated a series of altruistic reforms that significantly lessened the burdens and taxations of his subjects, so that the Umayyad aristocracy, seeing their income diminish, had him assassinated in 720. Naturally, if these reforms were associated with a more lenient or favorable attitude to Christians, his murderers would have had even more reason to kill the apostate caliph. Of further interest to reflect on is that according to Arab chronicles, in the moments before he died, Omar "forgave" and even helped his assassin, a lowly slave who had poisoned him, escape—a remarkably "Christian" thing for the imperial head of what had hitherto been a ruthless war machine devoted to enslaving and plundering all and sundry.[68]

THE WALL STANDS

Whatever the case may be, the damage was done, the lesson learned. It would be some seven centuries before any Islamic power would again attempt to breach the stone walls of Islam's archenemy. "Expeditions went out as before, but no more attempts were made against Constantinople, which is to say that no strategic attempts were made to eliminate or defeat the adversary. The yearly raids, by sea and by land, became the main characteristic of the warfare." Nevertheless, "the conquest of Constantinople was [to remain] a transcendent, religious goal for the Muslims, especially after their failure in 717–718 to accomplish it."[69]

Indeed, the enormity of this defeat had a direct impact on the codification of jihad. "We must remember that the Islamic law of war itself came into existence during this period, largely in response" to the failed and humiliating siege.[70] Convinced that the caliphate was not doing its duty against the Byzantines, austere, radicalized Muslim *ulema* traveled to and spent their lives along the Christian-Muslim frontier of Anatolia, which eventually stabilized along the Taurus mountain range. The Muslim-held side became known as the *ribat*, or frontier with infidels, and they *murabitun*, those dedicated to doing jihad along the dangerous frontiers.[71] There, they collated, authenticated, and studied Muhammad's teachings on jihad—and then lived them out during constant raids on the Romans. These prototypical "lone wolf" jihadis made clear in both their writings and actions that individual Muslims could not wait for or depend on an imam to proclaim a jihad on infidels—an idea still very much alive today. Muhammad had said, "Every community has its monasticism (*rahbaniya*), and the monasticism of my community is jihad in the path of Allah;" as such, these warrior monks preceeded the crusading military orders by centuries.[72]

Even the oldest extant Arabic manual on jihad, *Kitab al-Jihad* ("Book of Jihad"), was compiled by one of these frontier warriors, namely, Abdallah bin Mubarak. Born a decade after the failed siege of 717, he committed his life to studying and waging jihad on the Anatolian border until his death in 797. He and other zealous fighters became the stuff of legend and inspired generations of aspiring jihadis, till the present. Thus, Ali bin Bakr, who "went to live along the Arab-Byzantine frontier in the eighth century," was once "wounded in battle, so that his entrails came spilling out onto his saddle. He stuffed them back, used his turban as a bandage to bind them in place, and then proceeded to kill thirteen of the enemy" to cries of "Allahu Akbar."[73] As for Abdallah bin Mubarak himself, he too "served as a model of zeal in volunteering. His piety and asceticism gave him enormous strength"—"he would bellow like a bull or cow being slaughtered" during battle—and "his fellows continued to be drawn to his power after his death."[74] His *Book of Jihad* remains a classic among militant Muslims around the world.

Of course, it was not all austerity and bellowing; the usual lures were there. "In describing the eventual conquest of Constantinople, the apocalyptic sources" which the frontier jihadis pored over told "of gold, jewels, and virgins," and predicted that the conquerors "will ravish 70,000 [Christian maidens] as long as they wish in the Royal Palace."[75]

The Second Siege of Constantinople was a long time coming, had the full backing of the caliphate, and was laden with prophetic predictions. That the Eastern Orthodox Christian kingdom was able to repulse the hitherto unstoppable forces of Islam is one of Western history's most decisive moments. As seen in the previous chapter, the last time a large expanse of land was left open to the scimitar of Islam (following Roman defeat at Yarmuk), thousands of square miles were permanently conquered. Had Constantinople—the bulwark of Europe's eastern flank—fallen, large parts or even the whole of Europe could have become the northwestern appendage of the caliphate as early as the eighth century (thereby significantly shortening the rest of this book). The earliest chroniclers knew this and referred to August 15, the day the siege was lifted, as an "ecumenical date"— that is, a day for all of Christendom to rejoice.[76]

Nor should the architect of this victory be forgotten: "By his successful resistance Leo saved not only the Byzantine Empire and the eastern Christian world, but also all of western civilization," says historian A. A. Vasiliev.[77] Yet, true to the vicissitudes and ironies of *Byzantine* history— that word has not come to mean "convoluted" for nothing—by the time Leo died, "in the Orthodox histories he was represented as little better than a Saracen," primarily for his role in the iconoclasm debate.* While other defenders of Christendom would be memorialized, it would be Leo's lot to be all but anathematized—an unfortunate fact contributing to the historical obfuscation of this otherwise pivotal encounter.

---

* Leo went on to ban the veneration of icons, which had been and continues to be customary in traditional Christianity. Although he had some support, the pro-icon faction eventually triumphed, and from there the emperor was remembered with disrepute.

CHAPTER 3

THE JIHAD REACHES A
WESTERN WALL OF ICE:
THE BATTLE OF TOURS, 732

Penetrating northward into Europe, the Muslims did "not pass a place without reducing it, and getting possession of its wealth, for Allah Almighty had struck with terror the hearts of the infidels."

—al-Maqqari, Muslim historian[1]

[Then] the men of the north stood as motionless as a wall, they were like a belt of ice frozen together, and not to be dissolved, as they slew the Arab with the sword."[2]

—Latin chronicle c. 754

THE MUSLIM CONQUEST OF SPAIN

LAST WE LEFT MUSA BIN NUSAYR IT WAS THE YEAR 709 AND the Umayyad Muslim governor had subjugated the whole of North Africa. Then, "looking round him," he "saw no more enemies to attack, no more nations to subdue," writes al-Maqqari, a Muslim historian. So Musa "wrote to his freedman Tarik [Tarek, a Berber chieftain], who was governor of Tangiers, and ordered him to get himself and troops ready to make an incursion into the opposite land of Andalus"[3]—that is, Spain.*

---

* Al-Andalus (and its derivatives, e.g., Andalusia) is believed to be etymologically based on an Arabic corruption of the word "Vandal," apparently the earliest Germanic barbarian group to invade and be known to the inhabitants of North Africa.

As with most of the territory Islam conquered in the previous chapters, when Muslims invaded Spain, it too had been Christian for centuries[†] (with a notable Jewish minority). In the early fifth century, the western-based Goths, or Visigoths[‡]—one of many pagan tribes to have overrun the Western Roman Empire—settled in Spain. Though they had originally embraced a heretical form of Christianity (Arianism), by 589 they had converted to and were assimilated in to mainstream Christianity (which in the West meant Catholicism).

Musa's initial reconnaissance missions to Spain returned with reports of great splendors and beauty—both animate and inanimate—further whetting Muslim ambitions.[§] During one of the subsequent raids in 710, the Muslims "made several inroads into the mainland, which produced a rich spoil and several captives, who were so handsome that Musa and his companions had never seen the like of them."[4]

The feeling was not mutual. It appears that the westernmost people of Europe saw Islam's newest converts, the Berbers, much the same way as the easternmost people of Europe saw Islam's original converts, the Arabs: unfavorably. According to al-Maqqari's chronicle,

> Whenever some of the scattered tribes of Berbers inhabiting along
> the northern coast of Africa happened to approach the sea shore, the

---

[†] The presence of Christianity in Spain stretches back to the time of the Apostles (Rom. 15:28).

[‡] The prefixes *Visi*goth and *Ostro*goth are simply different ways of saying *west*ern and *east*ern Goths, respectively.

[§] Islam's initial crossing from North Africa into Spain was, according to Muslim history, facilitated by a disgruntled nobleman—of Greek, Gothic, or North African origin is unclear—known as Julian. He had sent his beautiful daughter to be tutored at King Roderick's court in Spain—only for Roderick to sexually seduce her. Now, wanting revenge, Julian went to and offered Tarek his many boats to ferry the Muslims to Spain. What makes this story suspect is that, in order to win Tarek's trust, Julian supposedly offered him his two other daughters as hostages: trusting one's daughters to a barbarian chieftain heavily involved in the slave trade seems a contradictory way for a father to avenge himself on another man who proved untrustworthy with his daughter.

fears and consternation of the Greeks* would increase, they would fly
in all directions for fear of the threatened invasion, and their dread of
the Berbers waxed so greatly that it was instilled into their nature, and
became in after times a prominent feature in their character. On the
other side, the Berbers having been made acquainted with this ill-will
and hatred of the people of Andalus towards them, hated and envied
them the more, this being in a certain measure the reason why even
a long time afterwards a Berber could scarcely be found who did not
most cordially hate an Andalusian [people of Spanish/Christian de-
scent], and vice versa.[5]

Once on Spanish soil, the Islamized Berbers' "cordial hate" manifested
itself. Thus, during another early raid, a Berber chieftain "set fire to their
houses and fields, and burnt also a church very much venerated amongst
them. He then put to the sword such of its inhabitants as he met, and, making a few prisoners, returned safe to Africa."[6]

Successful raids further bolstered dreams of wholesale conquest. By the
end of April 711, Tarek was ready. At the head of "an army of seven thousand men, chiefly Berbers and slaves, very few only being genuine Arabs,"[7]
he made his fateful voyage to Spain through the Pillars of Hercules, and
landed on what is now, in honor of the invader, called Gibraltar ("Tarek's
Hill" in Arabic). To make clear that retreat was not an option, Tarek ordered
all their boats burned on touching European soil: "We have not come here
to return. Either we conquer and establish ourselves here or we will perish."[8]

The invaders proceeded to ravage the land, with an eye at placing terror into the hearts of the infidels. One anecdote, documented in the oldest
Muslim chronicle of Spain's conquest, Ibn 'Abd al-Hakam's (b. 803), is especially telling:

When the Moslems settled in the island, they found no other inhabitants there than vinedressers. They made them prisoners. After

* The term "Greek" is used here either generically to mean "white/Christian" or in
reference to Greek/Byzantine-held islands off the Spanish mainland.

that they took one of the vinedressers, slaughtered him, cut him into pieces, and boiled him, while the rest of his companions looked on. They also boiled meat in other cauldrons. When the meat was cooked, they threw away the flesh of the man which they had boiled; no one knowing that it was thrown away: and they ate the meat which they had boiled, while the rest of the vinedressers were spectators. These did not doubt but that the Moslems ate the flesh of their companion.[†]

Once released, the horrified Christians fled and "informed the people of Andalus that the Moslems feed on human flesh," creating panic across the countryside.[9]

A message was quickly dispatched to King Roderick in Toledo, the capital of Visigothic Spain: "This, our land has been invaded by people whose name, country, and origin are unknown to me. I cannot even tell thee whence they came—whether they fell from the skies, or sprang from the earth!"[10] At the head of thousands of armed nobles, Roderick went to meet the Muslim army, which by now had been augmented by an additional five thousand reserves from Africa for a total of twelve thousand fighters congregated near a body of water in southern Spain, believed to be the Guadalete River.

Tarek, seeing the Christian army approaching, rallied his men around him and exhorted them: "Whither can you fly—the enemy is in your front, the sea at your back. By Allah! There is no salvation for you but in your courage and perseverance."[11] Once again, however, carnal incentives lurked beneath the pious talk. Tarek even managed to fuse the seizure of those two most enticing rewards—untold riches and beautiful women—as well as invoke the stereotype of eager-to-be-ravished European women, in one succinct sentence: "You must have heard numerous accounts of this island, you must know how the Grecian maidens, as beautiful as houris [sexual, celestial women], their necks glittering with innumerable pearls and jewels, their

---

[†] There has always been speculation that the Africans actually did feast on their captives' flesh, and the Muslim historian, somewhat embarrassed, embellished the story by portraying the Muslims as only pretending to eat.

bodies clothed with tunics of costly silks sprinkled with gold, are awaiting your arrival, reclining on soft couches in the sumptuous palaces of crowned lords and princes." Covering all bases, Tarek also invoked Allah's win-win bargain: If, after "rush[ing] on like so many brave men to the fight" any Muslim happened to die in battle, "know that the recompenses of Allah await you" in paradise.[12]

As the two forces clashed, Tarek espied Roderick and cried out, "This is the King of the Christians!" whereupon a mad rush was made for the Visigoth.[13] Records of what actually happened thereafter are sketchy and contradictory, but it is clear that there were divisions among the Spanish nobles, and that one or more factions abandoned Roderick in the midst of battle. At any rate, the Muslims scored a decisive victory against the Western Goths. "Allah killed Roderick and those with him," says al-Hakam, "and opened* the way for the Muslims; and never was there in the West a more bloody battle than this—for the Muslims did not withdraw their scimitars from them for three days."[14] The king either fell in battle or was killed soon thereafter, and the remainder of his forces retreated to their own districts. Others were not as lucky: "So great was the number of the Goths who perished in the battle, that for a long time after the victory the bones of the slain were to be seen covering the field of action."[15] Thus ended "nearly three hundred and fifty years of the Goth's rule in Spain," concludes the *Chronicle of 754.*[16] Roderick's sword-bearer, Pelagius, better known as Pelayo, retreated to the north of the Peninsula, into the rugged mountains of Asturia, whence a new and long chapter—literally, Chapter 6—of Muslim-Christian fighting would soon begin.

Meanwhile, "Allah filled with terror and alarm the hearts of the *mushrikin* ["polytheists," or Christians], and their consternation was greatly increased when they saw Tarek penetrate far into their country," writes al-Maqqari.[17] The Muslim chieftain again met—and again beat—some of

---

* In Arabic and other Muslim languages, the historic Islamic conquests are never referred to as "conquests" but rather as *futuh*—"openings" for the light of Islam to enter. In this context, every land ever invaded and/or seized by Muslims was done "altruistically" to bring Islam to wayward infidels, who are seen as the unjust aggressors, getting only what they deserved—death or slavery—for resisting Islam.

Roderick's remnants at Ecija, at which point all concerted resistance collapsed. As more carcasses drew more vultures, so "when the people on the
other side of the straits [in Africa] heard of this success of Tarek, and of
the plentiful spoils he had acquired, they flocked to him from all quarters,
and crossed the sea on every vessel or bark they could lay hold of. Tarek's
army being so considerably reinforced, the Christians were obliged to shut
themselves up in their castles and fortresses, and, quitting the flat country,
betake themselves to their mountains."

And so it went; Tarek continued to penetrate northward into Spain, "not
passing a place without reducing it, and getting possession of its wealth, for
Allah Almighty had struck with terror the hearts of the infidels."† Like their
eastern coreligionists from the previous century, the earliest Christians of
Iberia saw the Muslim invaders as godless cutthroats motivated solely by
plunder and rapine, not permanent conquest—certainly not in the name of
any new religion;‡ "they were under a belief that his [Tarek's] object in the
attack was only to gain spoil and then return to his country."[18]

None of this should suggest, as some modern Western historians do,
that Spain willingly capitulated to the Muslims, seeing that their rule was
no harsher and possibly more lenient than the Visigoths'. Muslim chroniclers often write of how "the Christians defended themselves with the utmost vigour and resolution, and great was the havoc which they made in
the ranks of the faithful." Thus in Cordoba, a number of leading Visigoths
and their people holed themselves up in a church. Although "the besieged

---

† Whether because it corresponds with the Koran's calls to "strike terror into the
hearts of the infidels" (e.g., 3:151, 8:12) or whether because it was deemed strategic,
Muslim chroniclers often point out that their historic coreligionists terrorized those
who resisted Allah and his prophet. Thus, according to al-Maqqari, Tarek continued
to have bodies of fallen Christians butchered and cooked in front of their captive comrades. Afterward he "allowed some of the captives to escape, that they might report to
their countrymen what they had seen. And thus *the stratagem produced the desired
effect,* since the report of the fugitives contributed in no small degree to *increase the
panic of the infidels*" (emphasis added; Maqqari 1964, 276).

‡ The one notable exception is the *Chronicle of 741,* which states that "the Saracens
worship Muhammad" and "affirm him to be an apostle of God and a prophet" (Wolf
1990, 39).

had no hopes of deliverance, they were so obstinate that when safety was offered to them upon condition either of embracing Islam, or paying *jizya,* they refused to surrender, and the church being set on fire they all perished in the flames." The ruins of this church became a place of "great veneration" for later generations of Spaniards, adds the Muslim chronicler, because "of the courage and endurance displayed in the cause of their religion by the people who died in it."[19]

Over in Africa, Musa "grew jealous and spiteful" upon hearing of Tarek's ongoing exploits; "and, fearing lest, by prosecuting the conquest, Tarek should take all the spoil and glory for himself, and leave none for him, sent Tarek a severe reprimand . . . together with an injunction not to move from where he was until he should join him."[20] Though he admired their prowess, Musa remained mistrustful of Tarek and his nation: "The Berbers are the people who most resemble the Arabs in activity, strength, courage, endurance, love of war, and hospitality," he once said, but "they are the most treacherous of men. They have no faith, and they keep no word."[21] Once face to face, the Arab governor berated his Berber subordinate for essentially upstaging him; he publicly flogged and even contemplated executing him. When Musa finally asked, "Why did you disobey me?" Tarek wisely responded, "To serve Islam."[22] The two were reconciled, though Musa now held the reins of jihad, as countless more Africans swarmed into the southwestern tip of Europe. And so "the Saracens set up their savage kingdom in Spain, specifically in Cordoba," lamented an anonymous eighth-century chronicler, whence they continued penetrating deeper into the Peninsula until even "Toledo, victor over all peoples, succumbed, vanquished by the victories of the Ishmaelites."[23]

As with the Arab conquests of Syria and Egypt in the previous century, some early Muslim and Christian sources attribute Muslim victory to trickery and terror. According to al-Hakam, "When the Muslims conquered Spain, they looted it and committed many frauds";[24] the *Chronicle of 754* elaborates: "While he [Musa] terrorized everyone in this way, some of the cities that remained sued for peace under duress and, after persuading and mocking them with a certain craftiness, the Saracens granted their requests without delay.* When the citizens subsequently rejected what they had accepted out of fear and terror, they tried to flee to the mountains where they risked hunger and various forms of death."[25]

AMBITIOUS JIHADIS AND ENVIOUS CALIPHS

At any rate, Musa and his men continued hacking their way to the northernmost regions of Spain, "destroying on their way all the churches, and breaking all the bells," notes the Muslim historian.[26] By 715, he stood at the foot of the Pyrenees mountains, the gateway between the Iberian Peninsula and Europe proper. Just as he had eyed Spain once North Africa had been totally subjugated in 709, now that the former had also been overrun, the ambitious Muslim warlord and "the greater number" of Muslims "eagerly desired to penetrate into the lands of the Franks"—that is, north of the Pyrenees, into Gaul.[27]

But there was more to it. According to Muslim historiography, "It is confidently believed that, elated with success, Musa conceived the project of returning to the East by way of Constantinople; for which purpose he intended to march from Andalus [Spain] at the head of his brave troops, until, by making his way through the countless Christian nations that inhabit the great continent [of Europe], he should arrive at the court of the eastern caliphs" in Damascus.[28] In other words, in 715, at the height of Muslim preparations to besiege Constantinople (last chapter), Musa apparently hoped to reach and perhaps even sack the great city first—and he would do it by taking everything between it and Spain.

His ambitions did not go unnoticed. The same envy he bore against Tarek was borne against him. In 715, Musa was recalled to Damascus. He and his Berber subordinate made the long journey across North Africa, bringing with them thousands of camels laden with immense treasures and thirty thousand captives as a flesh-tribute to the Umayyads. Unfortunately for Musa, he arrived right when Caliph Al-Walid, who apparently favored

---

* Both Alfonso X's and Archbishop Rodrigo's histories indicate that Christian leaders often capitulated to the invaders under ostensibly lenient terms, which the Arabs reneged on once they were in absolute control.

him, died. The new caliph, Suleiman, apparently envious of the Muslim conqueror's successes in Spain, confiscated all of Musa's booty and had him "paraded with a rope around his neck" and thrown into prison.[29]

Later that same year, Abdul Aziz, Musa's son whom he had left to govern Spain, was assassinated by fellow Muslims on the accusation that he had apostatized from Islam. Although he was notorious for taking the Visigothic "daughters of kings and princes, whom he treated as concubines and then rashly repudiated,"[30] he eventually married King Roderick's widow. Jealous Muslim chieftains accused her of influencing the emir to the point of converting him to Christianity. Thus, one day, while Abdul was in the monastery of Santa Rufina—then transformed into a mosque—assassins rushed in and slaughtered him. They sent his head to Damascus; after parading it in public, Caliph Suleiman hurled it at the disgraced and now broken Musa. He died soon thereafter in 716 or 717, possibly in prison. Such was the end of the man who had only recently harbored hopes of conquering all of Christendom in the name of Islam.

Nothing is known of the fate of Tarek, but it is believed that the Berber too, having incurred not just the envy but contempt of Suleiman, died in complete obscurity, possibly reduced to begging in the Middle East.

The conquerors of Spain were not the first to be treated thus; many of Islam's earliest heroes ended ignominiously—not at the hands of their infidel enemies but of resentful caliphs. This includes the great Khalid bin al-Walid: after sacking Mar'ash in 637 and returning in triumph with splendorous spoils—Mar'ash would later avenge itself by giving birth to Emperor Leo III—Khalid became so popular that then Caliph Omar dismissed him from military service. Thus at the peak of his career, the Sword of Allah was retired to Emesa (Homs), where he died four years later in obscurity. At his funeral, the embarrassed caliph explained how he had "not dismissed him because of suspicion, but the people venerated him excessively and I was afraid that they would put their trust in him."[31] Omar added that he would even have appointed the Sword as his successor had he not died prematurely. Similarly, Amr bin al-As—another hero of Yarmuk and conqueror of Egypt—was ignominiously yanked twice from his governorship of Egypt due to the whims of caliphs, under unclear circumstances.

JIHAD IN THE HEART OF EUROPE

But Allah is no respecter of persons, and individuals are irrelevant when it comes to the jihad, which continued unabated into Gaul, then known as Francia, the Kingdom of the Franks. Originally a Germanic tribe that had migrated to Roman Gaul in the fifth century, the warlike Franks had been the dominant force of Europe since 500. For them, "being a Frank meant being a warrior. War, bravery in battle, and success on the battlefield were essential elements of kingship. . . . Reading the most important chroniclers of the time, one cannot escape the sensation that the supremacy of the ruler was based upon how many opponents he had slain in face-to-face combat."[32] But unlike other barbarians—Ostrogoths and Longobards for instance—the Franks had assimilated into Latin Christendom well over two centuries earlier and were on their way to becoming "champions of the faith."

In 719, the Muslim governor of Spain, al-Samh bin Malik al-Khawlani reached and "made Narbonne his own and harassed the people of the Franks with frequent battles," says the *Chronicle of 754*:

> Assembling his forces . . . [al-Samh next] came to attack Toulouse and surrounded it with a siege, trying to overcome it with slings and other types of machines. Informed of this turn of events, the Franks gathered together under the command of Eudes [duke of Aquitaine, also known as Odo the Great], their commander. There, at Toulouse, while the battle lines of both armies were engaging with one another in serious fighting, the Franks killed as-Samh, the leader of the Saracen forces, along with that portion of the army gathered with him, and pursued the remaining part as it slipped away in flight.[33]

Coming on the heels of the Muslim defeat along the walls of Constantinople in 718, Toulouse was yet another massive blow to Umayyad prestige; the Muslims of Spain would lament this disastrous defeat in verse for centuries to come. Meanwhile, the pope in Rome celebrated the victory and hailed Eudes as Christendom's champion.

Emboldened, the duke of Aquitaine declared independence from the Frankish empire, which since 717 was ruled by the battle-hardened Charles

Martel, "a man who had proved himself a warrior from his youth and an expert in things military,"[34] and who was just then preoccupied with fighting pagan Saxons, Teutons, and Swabians along his realm's northern and eastern borders. To prevent further Muslim attacks and further declare independence from Charles, Eudes formed an alliance with one Uthman, a neighboring Berber chieftain situated just north of the Pyrenees. "To satisfy his desires," Eudes gave Uthman his daughter in matrimony, and it is possible that the Berber was first baptized.[35] What is certain is that Uthman was disaffected by reports of ongoing Arab oppression of fellow Berbers in Spain and Africa (though Muslim, Arabs still continued to look down on and mistreat the Berbers).* He cooled on the jihad against infidels—were his people not Muslim and still being treated as infidels?—and like Eudes entered the alliance with an eye to breaking free from his overlords in Cordoba.

This would not do. In 731, Abdul Rahman al-Ghafiqi—a "warlike man" and survivor of Toulouse who bore a special grudge against Francia— became the new governor of Spain.[36] He learned that Uthman had not only ceased raiding but had allied himself to the infidels. Denouncing him as a renegade, Abdul "angrily prepared an expedition for battle and fiercely pursued" Uthman deep into the mountains, where, knowing what was in store for him if captured, the apostate leapt over the precipice to his death.[37] The Berber's Christian wife, Eudes's daughter Lampagie, "a girl of remarkable beauty," was seized and—along with the trophy-head of her former spouse—sent to adorn the harems of the caliph in Damascus.[38] Next, Abdul Rahman, "seeing the land filled with the multitude of his army, cut through the rocky mountains of the Basques so that, crossing the plains, he might invade the lands of the Franks." Eudes sent urgent word to, and implored the aid of, the man he had recently tried to break away from, Charles; the Frankish chief—aka the mayor of the palace—counseled patience: "If you

---

* As one example, around 719, the then Arab ruler of Spain "penalized the Moors who had long been dwelling in Spain on account of the treasure they had hidden [meaning plunder they had kept for themselves]. He kept them in sackcloth and ashes," continues the Christian chronicler, "infested with worms and lice, bound in jail and weighed down with chains, and he tortured them during interrogation" (Wolf 1990, 136).

follow my advice, you will not interrupt their march, nor precipitate your attack. They are like a torrent, which it is dangerous to stem in its career. The thirst of riches, and the consciousness of success, redouble their valor, and valor is of more avail than arms or numbers. Be patient till they have loaded themselves with the encumbrance of wealth.[†] The possession of wealth will divide their councils and assure your victory."[39]

Unable to stand by and watch his lands ravaged, Eudes tried to make a stand at Bordeaux, but was defeated and the city pillaged; he tried to make another stand at the Garonne River, and was again defeated—"so utterly that God alone knew the number of slain and wounded."[40] With something of tail between legs, Eudes fled to Paris and Charles. Now, with no one to stop the invaders, a new chapter of woe unfolded in Francia, as summarized by an anonymous, apparently Arab, chronicler:

> The men of Abdul Rahman were puffed up in spirit by their repeated successes, and they were full of trust in the valour and the practice in war of their Emir. So the Moslems smote their enemies, and passed the River Garonne, and laid waste the country, and took captives without number. And that army went through all places like a desolating storm. Prosperity made those warriors insatiable. . . . For everything gave way to their scimitars, which were the robbers of lives. All the nations of the Franks trembled at that terrible army, and they betook them to their king Caldus [Charles], and told him of the havoc made by the Moslem horsemen, and how they rode at their will through all the land of Narbonne, Toulouse, and Bordeaux.[41]

---

† Interestingly, this is the same advice offered in an Eastern Roman military treatise attributed to Emperor Nikephoros Phokas (featured in the next chapter) and written primarily with Muslims in mind: "Instead of confronting the enemy as they are on their way to invade Romania [Anatolia], it is in many respects more advantageous and convenient to get them as they are returning from our country to their own. They will then be worn out and much the worse for wear after having spent such a long time in the Roman lands. They are likely to be burdened with a lot of baggage, captives, and animals" (Dennis 2008, 157–159).

The destruction was profound: "The memory of these devastations, for Abdul Rahman did not spare the country or the people, was long preserved by tradition," writes Edward Gibbon; the "richest spoil was found in the churches and monasteries, which they stripped of their ornaments and delivered to the flames." "Alas, what a misfortune!" responded the Franks. "What an indignity! We have long heard of the name and conquests of the Arabs; we were apprehensive of their attack from the East [should they have gotten over the walls of Constantinople during the siege of 717–718]: they have now conquered Spain, and invade our country on the side of the West."[42]

By the early 730s Muslims controlled all the major cities of the Frankish Mediterranean coastline, between the Pyrenees and the Rhône; and they ruled with an iron fist. "As a warning to others, [they] burned a bishop alive" in neighboring Cerdanya in 730.[43] Not content, Abdul and his hordes continued to penetrate deeper north into Francia, ravishing the countryside and despoiling "every church and monastery in their path."[44] Their immediate target was Tours, where they heard the Basilica of Saint Martin—one of Western Christendom's holiest sites—contained untold treasures. "To spread as much terror and accumulate as much loot as possible, Abdul Rahman divided his army, probably some 80,000 strong, into several columns and sent them pillaging."[45]* Town after town fell, and the caliph in Damascus rubbed his hands with glee as he received, "among other things, male and female slaves, and seven hundred of the best girls, besides eunuchs, horses, medicine, gold, silver, and vases," says al-Hakam.[46]

As the Muslims wreaked havoc throughout Francia, Charles, having secured his northern and eastern borders, began rallying his liegemen in Paris. He set off with as many as thirty thousand battle-hardened Franks to intercept the invading army. Meanwhile, Abdul "destroyed palaces, burned churches, and imagined he could pillage the basilica of St. Martin of Tours" during his drive north, laments a Christian chronicler. "It is then that he

---

* The chroniclers give astronomical numbers concerning the Muslims, some putting them at more than 300,000. Suffice to say, the Franks were greatly outnumbered, and there seems to be a consensus on the figures of 80,000 Muslims against 30,000 Franks, reached by Paul Davies and others.

found himself face to face with the lord of Austrasia, Charles, a mighty warrior from his youth, and trained in all the occasions of arms."[47]

THE BATTLE OF TOURS

So it was that in the year 732—precisely one hundred years after the death of Islam's prophet Muhammad, a century which had seen the conquest of thousands of miles of formerly Christian lands—the scimitar of Islam found itself in the heart of Europe, facing that continent's chief military power, the Franks. The invading hordes consisted mainly of Berbers who "fought from horseback, depending on bravery and religious fervor to make up for their lack of armor or archery. Instead, the Moors fought with scimitars and lances. Their standard method of fighting was to engage in mass cavalry charges, depending on numbers and courage to overwhelm any enemy; it was a tactic that had carried them thousands of miles and defeated dozens of opponents. Their weakness was that all they could do was attack; they had no training or even concept of defense."[48]

Except for mounted nobles like Charles, the Franks, influenced by the Romans they had conquered, were now primarily an infantry force. Relying on deep phalanx formations and heavy armor—the typical infantryman bore seventy pounds of iron—the Franks were as immovable as the Muslims were mobile. Along with their shields, which the Franks received upon entry into adulthood, their arms consisted of swords, daggers, spears, and two kinds of axes, one for wielding and the other for hurling—the notorious *francisca,* which became so conflated with the Franks that either they were named after it or it after them.[†]

---

† The symbolic significance of receiving their shields on reaching manhood—and that "war, bravery in battle, and success on the battlefield were essential elements of [Frankish] kingship"—is reminiscent of the Spartans of old (whose lives revolved around warfare, and whose mothers told them whenever they set off to "come back with your shield or on it." A story concerning Clovis (d. 511), the first king to unite the Franks, further indicates the high esteem Franks had for their arms: "You keep neither your spear nor sword nor axe in serviceable order," Clovis once reproached a man during a war assembly. He then snatched and hurled the man's axe to the ground in disgust. When the disgraced warrior bent to pick it up, Clovis pulled out his own axe and smote the man dead. Although it was repayment for a previous insult, that it was

Having arrived somewhere between Poitiers and Tours, the latter being the Muslim target, the Franks took advantage of the familiar and densely wooded terrain. They secured the high ground, which not only served to provide shelter and mask their inferior numbers, but could also impede the much anticipated Muslim cavalry charge. Once the invaders arrived, the two contending armies faced each other for six or seven days, neither wanting to make the first move. No fool, Abdul knew that behind the miles of dense woods, the best Francia could muster had assembled in large numbers. Worse, and as Charles had predicted, the Muslims' gain was now their bane: having plundered numerous towns and churches on their northern drive, they were overwhelmed with booty. Nor did any one contingent or tribe trust leaving their share to the protection of another. Abdul used this downtime to begin transporting the booty south for safekeeping. Charles awaited more of his men to arrive from the furthest outposts of his domains. Then, on October 10—the European climate was getting too cold for the Africans and Arabs, and their supplies and foraging areas had dwindled—Abdul commenced battle. To the loud cries of "Allahu Akbar!," charge after charge they came.[49] An anonymous medieval Arab chronicler describes the battle in rather epic terms:

> Near the river Owar [Loire], the two great hosts of the two languages [Arabic and Latin] and the two creeds [Islam and Christianity] were set in array against each other. The hearts of Abd al-Rahman, his captains and his men were filled with wrath and pride,* and they were the first to begin to fight. The Muslim horsemen dashed fierce and frequent forward against the battalions of the Franks, who resisted manfully, and many fell dead on either side, until the going down of the sun.[50]

------

done in the context of honoring one's weapons went a long way to exonerate Clovis (Santosuosso 2004, 55).

* That the Muslims were filled with "wrath and pride" against the infidel Franks comes out often in Arabic histories. When asked about the Franks some years earlier, Musa had haughtily replied: "They are a folk right numerous, and full of might: brave and impetuous in the attack, but cowardly and craven in the event of defeat. Never has a company from my army been beaten" (W. Davis and West 1913, 362).

Entirely consisting of wild headlong charges, the Muslim attack proved ineffective, for "the men of the north stood as motionless as a wall, they were like a belt of ice frozen together, and not to be dissolved, as they slew the Arab with the sword. The Austrasians [eastern Franks], vast of limb, and iron of hand, hewed on bravely in the thick of the fight," continues another chronicler.[51] The Franks refused to break ranks and allow successive horsemen to gallop through the gaps, which nomadic cavalry tactics relied on. Instead, they tightened their ranks and, "drawn up in a band around their chief [Charles], the people of the Austrasians carried all before them. Their tireless hands drove their swords down to the breasts [of the foe]."[52]

Military historian Victor Davis Hanson offers a more practical take: "When the sources speak of 'a wall,' 'a mass of ice,' and 'immovable lines' of infantrymen, we should imagine a literal human rampart, nearly invulnerable, with locked shields in front of armored bodies, weapons extended to catch the underbellies of any Islamic horsemen foolish enough to hit the Franks at a gallop." As expected, the battle was a wondrous mess: "Muslims would ride up in large bodies, slash at the clumsier Franks, shoot arrows, and then ride away as the enemy line advanced." In response, "each Frankish soldier, with shield upraised, would lodge his spear into either the horsemen's legs or the face and flanks of his mount, then slash and stab with his sword to cut the rider down, all the while smashing his shield—the heavy iron boss in the center was a formidable weapon in itself—against exposed flesh. Gradually advancing en masse, the Franks would then continue to trample and stab fallen riders at their feet—careful to keep close contact with each other at all times."[53]

At one point, Allah's warriors surrounded and trapped Charles, but "he fought as fiercely as the hungry wolf falls upon the stag. By the grace of Our Lord, he wrought a great slaughter upon the enemies of Christian faith," Denis the chronicler extolled. "Then was he first called 'Martel,' for as a hammer of iron, of steel, and of every other metal, even so he dashed and smote in the battle all his enemies."[54]

As night descended on the field of carnage, the two bloodied armies disengaged and withdrew to their camps. At the crack of dawn, the Franks prepared to resume battle, only to discover that the Muslims had all fled under the cover of darkness. Their master, Abdul, had been killed in fighting the day before, and the Berbers—freed of his whip and having tasted Frankish mettle—apparently preferred life and some plunder over martyrdom. They all fled back south—still looting, burning, and enslaving all and sundry as they went. Aware that his strength lay in his "wall of ice," Charles did not give chase.

The aftermath "was, as all cavalry battles, a gory mess, strewn with thousands of wounded or dying horses, abandoned plunder, and dead and wounded Arabs. Few of the wounded were taken prisoner—given their previous record of murder and pillage."[55] The oldest sources give astronomical numbers of slain Muslims—hundreds of thousands—with only a small fraction of slain Franks. Whatever the true numbers, significantly less numbers of Franks than Muslims fell in that battle. Even Arab chronicles refer to the engagement as the "Pavement of Martyrs," suggesting that the earth was littered with Muslim corpses.

"The joyful tidings were soon diffused over the Catholic world,"[56] and the surviving chronicles of the day—including that of the aforesaid and anonymous Arab—portray this victory in epic if not apocalyptic terms. Even in distant England, fiery comets appeared for two weeks prior, "striking terror into all who saw them," wrote the Venerable Bede; "seeming to portend awful calamity to east and west alike," these falling stars "indicated that mankind was menaced by evils. . . . At this time, a swarm of Saracens ravaged Gaul with horrible slaughter; but after a brief interval in that country they paid the penalty for their wickedness," concluded the "Father of English History," who died just three years after the battle at Tours.[57]

CHARLES: FROM THE "HAMMER" TO THE "GREAT"

Although a decisive victory, the Muslim menace did not disappear overnight. Pockets of raiders still swarmed north of the Pyrenees and along the Mediterranean coast. "Almost every year of the reign of Charles until his death in 741 was spent in warring to unite Gaul or to rid Europe of Islam."[58] Two years after Tours, Uqba bin al-Hajjaj, the new governor of

Spain, invaded Francia "to avenge the defeat at Poitiers and to spread Islam." His large land force remained in Gaul for nearly four years, during
which time he carried raids as far as Lyons, Burgundy, and Piedmont,
and forced some two thousand Christians to convert to Islam on pain of
death.[59] The Hammer returned to the rescue: "Charles overthrew the tyrants who claimed rule over all of Francia and so completely defeated the
Saracens, who were attempting to occupy Gaul, in two great battles, one
in Aquitaine at the city of Poitiers [or Tours, 732] and the second near
Narbonne near the River Berre [in 737], that he forced them to return
to Spain," writes Einhard the chronicler (b. 770).[60] Thanks to Charles's
follow-up victories, including another significant one in 739, the Muslims
became a spent force and were eventually driven back beyond the Pyrenees into Muslim-occupied Spain.

But if the Pyrenees became a dam against the rising tide of Islam, the
jihad soon overflowed into the Mediterranean basin, and the entire coastline of Europe and its islands were awash with nonstop raids. Due to these
Islamic attacks, which were exacerbated by coterminous invasions from
surrounding pagan peoples—Vikings, Saxons, and Magyars, all of whom
left unbelievable destruction in their wake, the pope in Rome eagerly sought
to unite Western Europe, which had been devoid of an emperor since 476.
Another Frankish chief, another Charles—in fact, the grandson and namesake of Charles Martel—came to the rescue. On Christmas Day in the year
800 inside the Basilica of St. Peter in Rome, Pope Leo III crowned Charles
the Great, better known as Charlemagne (742–814), as the first Holy Roman Emperor. The shouts of acclamation that thundered in St. Peter's "pronounced the union, so long in preparation, so mighty in its consequences,
of the Roman and Teuton, of the memories of the civilization of the South
with the fresh energies of the North," wrote James Bryce (d. 1922), a British
jurist and historian. "From that moment modern history begins."[61] And yet,
it all came in response to more than a century of nonstop jihad. As eminent historian Henri Pirenne correctly put it, "Without Islam the Frankish
Empire would probably never have existed and Charlemagne, without Mahomet, would be inconceivable."[62]

Posterity would celebrate Charlemagne for many things—from unifying the West to his love for scholastic learning—but it is his dealings with Islam that are germane here. As the defender of Christendom, he became the quintessential Christian warrior, a proto-crusader. Not content with keeping Muslims out of his domains, his exploits—and those of his descendants, including his son and successor Louis the Pious, who marched into Muslim Spain and established a buffer state in Catalonia—were celebrated in heroic epics and poems (the *chansons de geste*) and inspired generations of future crusaders.

Charlemagne was but a child when the Umayyad caliphate (661–750) finally fell. Along with making it unpopular, the "failure [of Constantinople's siege, 717–718] brought a grave moment for Umayyad power," explains Bernard Lewis. "The financial strain of equipping and maintaining the expedition caused an aggravation of the fiscal and financial oppression which had already aroused such dangerous opposition. The destruction of the fleet and army of Syria at the sea walls of Constantinople deprived the regime of the chief material basis of its power."[63] For a war machine whose legitimacy was coterminous with its ability to conquer and expand,* successive failures—including at Tours less than two decades later, and the final expulsion of Islam from Francia—could not have helped. Thus, in 750, when Charles was eight, a new Muslim dynasty, the Abbasids, usurped and purged all the Umayyads in a bloodbath—minus one emir who fled to and reestablished the Umayyad house in Spain.

It is in this context that Charlemagne maintained cordial relations with the Abbasid caliph Harun al-Rashid: they shared the same enemies—the Umayyad remnant in Muslim Spain. Moreover, Charlemagne actively cultivated the friendship of Muslim rulers in order to help *dhimmi* Christian populations, as explained by Einhard, who personally knew Charles:

---

* Khalid Yahya Blankinship, American historian and convert to Islam, confirms that the Umayyad "caliphate constituted the jihad state par excellence. Its main reason for existence aside from maintaining God's [Allah's] law, was to protect Islam and to expand the territory under its control, and its reputation was strongly bound to its military success" (1994, 232).

He was very enthusiastic in supporting the poor, and in that spontaneous generosity which the Greeks call alms, so much so that he made a point of not only giving in his own country and his own kingdom, but even overseas when he discovered that there were Christians living in poverty in Syria, Egypt and Africa; and at Jerusalem, Alexandria and Carthage he had compassion on their wants, and used to send money. The reason that he zealously strove to make friends with the [Muslim] kings beyond seas was that he might get some help and relief to the poor Christians living under their rule.[64]

Charlemagne himself made a pilgrimage to Jerusalem, where he purchased a hostel to welcome Christian pilgrims—most of whom were "devout men and women from Egypt and other lands by then under Muslim rule"[65]—and built a church and library for their use.

IF NOT BY LAND, THEN BY SEA

Needless to say, the golden age of Charlemagne could not outlast the jihad, the former of a temporal, the latter a timeless nature. In 846 Muslim fleets landed on the coast of Ostia, near Rome. Unable to breach the walls of the Eternal City, they sacked and despoiled the surrounding countryside, including, to the shock of Western Christendom, the venerated basilicas of St. Peter—where Charlemagne was crowned—and St. Paul, which were built by Constantine in the fourth century. The invaders vandalized the two holy shrines, desecrated the tombs of Christendom's two most revered apostles, and stripped them of their treasures, including a large golden cross, a silver table earlier donated by Charlemagne, and numerous rich liturgical vessels and jeweled reliquaries.

This sacrilege prompted Pope Leo IV (d. 855) to erect strong walls and fortifications along the right bank of the Tiber to protect the basilicas and other churches from further Muslim raids.[66] Anticipating the crusades by over two centuries—and for the same reasons—he also decreed that any Christian who died fighting Muslim marauders would earn heaven, so bad was the devastation.[67] Not ones to be deterred, "in 849 the Muslims attempted a new landing at Ostia; then, every year from around 857 on, they threatened the Roman seaboard," explains French medieval historian C. E. Dufourcq:

> In order to get rid of them, Pope John VIII [who also offered remission of sins for Christians who died fighting the invaders] decided in 878 to promise them an annual payment [or *jizya*] of several thousand gold pieces; but this tribute of the Holy See to Islam seems to have been paid for only two years; and from time to time until the beginning of the tenth century, the Muslims reappeared at the mouth of the Tiber or along the coast nearby.[68]

For this was the first great age of Muslim piracy. Having gone as far as they could on land, Muslims from Spain and all throughout the North African coast spent their energy invading the Mediterranean islands. Though some had already been raided in previous centuries, the Balearic Islands, Corsica, Crete, Cyprus, Malta, Sardinia, and Sicily were utterly devastated and occupied during the ninth.* Mass slaughter and/or slavery, the imposition of *jizya,* and the destruction of churches all but depopulated these tiny Christian islands. As one example, during the invasion of Crete in 826, Muslims forced Christians to convert to Islam, and that island's capital, Candia, was turned into one of the busiest slave markets.[69]

---

* The following entry from Ibn al-Athir's history dealing with southern Italy and Sicily is indicative of the quantity and quality of these raids: "Another raid [in 835] directed at Etna and the neighboring strongholds resulted in the burning of harvests, the slaughter of many men and pillage. Another raid was again organized in the same direction by Abu al-Aghlab in 221 [according to the Muslim calendar, which in this case corresponded to Christmas Day, 835]; the booty brought back was so extensive that slaves were sold for almost nothing. . . . In the same year, a fleet was sent against the [neighboring Christian] islands; after having taken rich booty and conquered several towns and fortresses there, they returned safe and sound. In 234 [August 5, 848], the inhabitants of Ragusa made peace with the Muslims in exchange for surrendering the town and what it contained. The conquerors destroyed it after having taken away everything that could be transported. In 235 [July 25, 849], a troop of Muslims marched against Castrogiovanni and returned safe and sound, after having subjected that town to pillage, murder and fire." (Ye'or 2010, 289–290).

Religious hostility always accompanied the raid; for "it was to the amusement of the Saracens to profane, as well as to pillage, the monasteries and churches. At the siege of Salerno a Musulman [Muslim] chief spread his couch on the communion table, and on that altar sacrificed each night the virginity of a Christian nun."[70] Such wanton depravity was par for the course: "The raids are a constant element [of the jihad], always considered praiseworthy and even necessary. This is a feature of pre-modern Islamic states that we cannot ignore. In addition to conquest, we have depredation; in addition to political projects and state-building, we have destruction and waste."[71]

Unsurprisingly, by the tenth century, the once highly trafficked Mediterranean—that for centuries had been the world's greatest economic highway uniting East and West, first in the classical civilization of Rome, and then in Christendom—became a "Muslim Lake," the hunting ground for pirates and slavers.[†] Thus the "Muslims controlled the Mediterranean on all sides," writes Ibn Khaldun. "Their strength and their power were considerable. Nowhere on this sea could the Christian nations do anything to resist the Muslim fleets. They crisscrossed these seas incessantly as conquerors and obtained successes there marked by conquests and acquisition of booty."[72]

Because much of the existing wealth had already been plundered in the previous centuries, these raids on coastal Europe thrived on capturing

---

[†] Several historians have been adamant about this point: "From now on, the 'Middle Sea' (or Mare Nostrum ['Our Sea'], as the Romans called it) would no longer be a highway, but a frontier, and a frontier of the most dangerous kind. War and piracy became the norm—in some areas for the best part of a thousand years. And this is something that has been almost completely overlooked by historians, especially those of northern European extraction. For the latter in particular, the Mediterranean is viewed through the prism of classical history. So bewitched have educated Europeans been by the civilization of Greece and Rome, that they have treated the more recent part of Mediterranean history—over a thousand years of it—as if it never existed" (Scott 2014, 162–163). Similarly, "the consequences of Muslim piracy were important factors in the crisis [Europe's decline between the ninth and tenth centuries], indeed sometimes decisive, producing social and economic as well as psychological and cultural distress: there was a drastic decline in navigation in general, a reduction in the number of Christian ports and coastal towns, widespread impoverishment, a contraction in the monetary economy and, finally, general fear and anxiety" (Cardini 2001, 18).

and selling "white slaves [who] were a particularly desirable commodity."[73] Indeed, the "House of Islam in the tenth century had little use for any of the produce and natural resources of Europe, except one; the bodies of the Europeans themselves. Young women and boys were preferred, but during the tenth century Europeans of almost any age or class, and in almost any part of the continent, could find themselves in chains and on a ship bound for North Africa or the Middle East."[74] Muslims even managed to settle in and for decades launch raids from Valais, Switzerland.

Similarly, Vikings, "motivated by Arab gold," continued raiding northern Europe in search of potential slaves.[75] The results of these incessant raids are well known even if the cause is forgotten: increasingly impoverished and illiterate Europeans withdrew from the coastlands and fled to the fortresses and castles of the highlands, where they pledged their vassalage to whichever lord or knight could protect them. Europe's "Dark Age" had begun.[*]

THE JUDGMENT OF HISTORY

Of all the battles surveyed in this book, Tours has, beginning with the contemporary chronicles up until the modern era, been one of if not the most celebrated in the West. For although the Mediterranean was lost, and although raids on the coastline became a permanent feature, Islam was confined to the Iberian Peninsula, leaving Western Europe to develop organically. Thus, well into the twentieth century many Western historians, such as Godefroid Kurth (d. 1916), still saw Tours as "one of the great events in the history of the world, as upon its issue depended whether Christian Civilization should continue or Islam prevail throughout Europe."[76] In reality, the Frankish victory stands in relation to and complements the arguably more decisive Eastern Roman victory fourteen years earlier. For starters, the siege of Constantinople was lifted in 718—auspiciously the same year

---

[*] Thus, "the classic tradition was shattered," writes historian Henri Pirenne, "because Islam had destroyed the ancient unity of the Mediterranean" (1939, 28). After the conquest of Egypt, the importation of papyrus into Europe terminated almost overnight, causing literacy rates to drop back to their levels in pre-Roman times.

Charles Martel became ruler of Francia—and he and Leo III were contemporaries. More significantly, whereas the Hammer smashed a large, pestilent force, the Lion overcame all that the caliphate could hurl in a committed, yearlong siege dedicated to conquering Islam's archenemy, Constantinople. Hence, if the Muslims fled Tours after just one day of heavy fighting, those before the walls of Constantinople persevered for one year against all odds—including frost, Bulgar raids, and the starvation-induced eating of corpses and feces. Most importantly, had Leo not resisted, had Muslims overrun Europe from the east, Charles may well have found himself fighting Islam on two fronts, leading to a probably different outcome.

None of this should take away from the relative importance of Tours. Whatever else was happening in the east, Charles's victory heralded the end of Islam's advance into Western Europe. Nor should its inspirational significance for posterity be overlooked. Even so, contemporary academics have dramatically downgraded the importance of Tours. After announcing that "the old drums-and-bugles approach will no longer do," the authors of *The Reader's Companion to Military History* say that "economics" and "changing attitudes . . . have altered our views of what once seemed to matter most. . . . The confrontation between Muslims and Christians at Poitiers-Tours in 732, once considered a watershed event, has been downgraded to a raid in force."[77] They argue that Muslims invaded France to plunder, not conquer it; and although European chroniclers stress the macro significance of Tours, modern naysayers argue that most of their Arab counterparts barely mentioned it, suggesting the battle was unimportant in Muslim eyes.

These points are unconvincing. For starters, they dismiss the stated goal of Spain's first Muslim ruler, Musa bin Nusayr: penetrating and conquering all of Europe, from the Pyrenees in the west to Constantinople in the east, and thus concluding the circuit of jihad that began a century earlier. Nor was such a task unthinkable. If Muslims had conquered all the southern domains of Rome—Syria, Egypt, North Africa, and into Spain—why not return by way of conquering all the northern domains of Rome, that is, the whole of continental Europe, culminating with the great prize,

Constantinople itself? That Abdul's vast hordes "came out of Spain with all their wives, and their children . . . in such great multitudes that no man could reckon or estimate them" further suggests plans of colonization.[78]

Moreover, as mentioned in the Introduction, all who fought under the banner of jihad—from many of Muhammad's first Arab recruits, to the Bedouins who were always eager to join the jihadi caravan, to the Berber masses that first entered Europe—were always motivated by the promise of plunder. Such motives never clashed with Islam, the deity of which incites his followers to war on the promise of booty, both animate and inanimate—so much so that an entire sura, or chapter of the Koran, "al-Anfal," is named after and dedicated to the spoils of war. In short, the acquisition of booty and territorial conquests always went hand-in-hand and were the natural culmination of jihad. As French medievalist C. E. Dufourcq explains:

> In principle, the Arabs never attempted to annex lands when they launched an initial attack against a new objective; they would always begin with a reconnaissance mission—a raid or a landing by night. That way they carried off some booty, sounded out a region, determined whether or not they had an interest in returning there to establish their dominion, and then reckoned the effective military force needed for that eventual enterprise of conquest, according to the degree of resistance that they had met.[79]

This is precisely how the initial Arab incursions into Roman Syria were conducted. Spain too: Tarek's invasion in 711 was little more than a raid for booty and slaves; as al-Maqqari noted, the Christians "were under a belief that his object in the attack was only to gain spoil and then return to his country."[80] Yet because these spoil-driven raids were not stopped and only served to whet appetites, more and more Africans swarmed into Spain so that by 718 it became the westernmost appendage of the Umayyad caliphate. Had Abdul Rahman's men not been stopped by force of arms at Tours—had they instead killed Charles and continued to overrun Francia— they would have stayed.

As for Muslim historians being conspicuously silent, this is somewhat true.* The earliest and most comprehensive Arabic histories devoted to chronicling the Islamic conquests—al-Baladhuri's, al-Tabari's, and al-Waqidi's—do not even mention Tours. The few Muslim sources that do are very curt. All that ninth-century chronicler al-Hakam has to relay is that "Abdul Rahman was a righteous man, and he raided the Franks, the furthest enemies from al-Andalus. He plundered much booty and triumphed over them. . . . [Later] he went out again to raid them and was martyred along with most of his companions."[81]

Such terseness ultimately reminds one of an observation Edward Gibbon made concerning the dearth of Byzantine sources concerning the early Muslim conquests: "The Greeks, so loquacious in controversy, have not been anxious to celebrate the triumphs of their enemies."[82] The same can be said of Muslims.

---

* Yet Creasy and Speed write, "The enduring importance of the battle of Tours in the eyes of Moslems is attested not only by the expressions of 'the deadly battle' and 'the disgraceful overthrow,' which their writers constantly employ when referring to it, but also by the fact that no further serious attempts at conquest beyond the Pyrenees were made by the Saracens" (1900, 168).

CHAPTER 4

ISLAM'S NEW CHAMPIONS: THE BATTLE OF MANZIKERT, 1071

> [A Muslim youth said:] "Apostle of Allah, I have traveled far and wide . . . but of all the places I have seen, I never saw a place like the land of the Rum [Byzantine Anatolia, modern-day Turkey]. Its towns are close to each other, its rivers are full of water, its springs are gushing . . . and its people are extremely friendly—except that they are all infidels." And he described it at such great length that the blessed mind of the Apostle became very fond of Rum indeed. [So Allah declared:] "My blessed apostle has taken a liking to Rum, so I on my part must grant that province to his *umma*. May they pull down its monasteries and set up mosques and madrasas in their places."
>
> —the *Battalnama*, early Turkish epic[1]

AMORIUM: THE LAST STRAW

WITH THE FALL OF THE UMAYYAD CALIPHATE (IN 750), THE SU-premacy of the Arab began to wane. Not only was the new Abbasid caliphate (750–1258) moved to Baghdad and run by a Persian bureaucracy, but its soldiery increasingly consisted of non-Arab slaves. Credited with perfecting the institution of military slavery, Caliph Mu'tasim (r. 833–842) managed to put it to great use. In 838, after a decades-long stalemate, the caliph—at the head of eighty thousand slaves—burst into Amorium, one of the Eastern Roman Empire's largest and most important cities. They burned and razed it to the ground and slaughtered countless; everywhere there were "bodies heaped up in piles," writes Michael the Syrian. The invaders locked those who sought sanctuary inside their churches and set the buildings aflame; trapped Christians could be heard crying "*kyrie eleison*"—"Lord have mercy!"—while being roasted alive. Hysterical "women covered their children, like chickens, so as not to be separated from them, either by sword or slavery."[2]

About half of the city's seventy thousand people were slaughtered, the rest hauled off in chains.[3] There was such a surplus of human booty that when the caliph came across four thousand male prisoners he ordered them executed on the spot. Because there "were so many women's convents and monasteries" in this populous Christian city, "over a thousand virgins were led into captivity, not counting those that had been slaughtered. They were given to the Moorish and Turkish slaves, so as to assuage their lust," laments the chronicler.[4] (One wonders if Mu'tasim had enticed his slaves beforehand by regaling them with stories of how Byzantine women, including nuns, were especially good at and eager to have intercourse, as Abbasid luminaries had claimed.*) Among the many slaves the caliph carted off were forty-two notables, mostly from the military and clerical classes. During their lengthy captivity in Iraq they were repeatedly ordered to accept Islam but refused; in 845, after seven years of torture and temptation failed to make them renounce Christ for Muhammad, they were beheaded and their bodies dumped into the Euphrates River. (The Eastern Orthodox Church still commemorates their martyrdom on March 6.)

By all accounts, the sack of Amorium had a traumatic effect on the Eastern Roman Empire, beginning with its emperor, Theophilus (r. 829–842); for Amorium was his hometown, and the caliph had specifically chosen it for that reason—to make the sting hurt all the more. And indeed, when the young emperor heard of the atrocities committed at and the utter ruin of Amorium, he suddenly fell ill. Theophilus remained in poor health and died three years later at age twenty-eight, reportedly from sorrow. Yet for others, Amorium provoked more rage than grief. A "never again"

---

* See pp. 48–49.

attitude against the caliphate was in the air, and the Christian empire was soon on a warpath of vengeance.

Thus, in the late 850s and for the first time since the disaster at Yarmuk over two centuries earlier, General Bardas (d. 866) marched a large army across the Euphrates, far into Muslim territory, and launched raids on the coast of Egypt, slaughtering several emirs. Next, East Roman Emperor Basil I (r. 867–886) cleared the Adriatic of Muslim pirates in a joint effort with Holy Roman Emperor Louis II. He liberated Cyprus and marched against—and annihilated—an Arab army in Mesopotamia. Before pressing his advantage, Basil was distracted by the growing might of the Bulgars (the pagan people who were persuaded by Emperor Leo III's "gifts and promises" to help lift the Second Siege of Constantinople in 718); their empire reached its zenith between 893 and 927. Basil and his successors spent some seventy years in a tug of war with the Bulgars. But "although the government in Constantinople needed to deal with them, [once again] the judicious use of bribery, diplomacy, or the threat of force kept that front sufficiently quiet that the government could focus most of its attention on the Moslems."[5]

"THE BEARER OF VICTORY"

Finally, with the ascendancy of Nikephoros II Phokas (912–969)—first a general and twenty years later emperor—a concerted proto-crusade against Islam was launched. Likened to "the legendary Hercules in courage and strength," it was his severe piety and monkish austerity that was most remarked upon by friend and foe alike. While still a general, "Nikephoros himself claimed that he wished to maintain his customary moderate lifestyle unaltered, avoiding cohabitation with a wife, and refraining from eating meat," writes Leo the Deacon (b. 950). But the monks, whom he held "in exceedingly great honor," urged him to marry the wife of deceased Emperor Romanos, "who was distinguished in beauty."[6] Matthew of Edessa (d. 1144), an Armenian chronicler writing at a time when Armenia had little love for Constantinople, concurs: "He was a kind, saintly, and pious man, filled with every virtue and uprightness, victorious and brave in all battles, compassionate to all the Christian faithful, a visitor to widows and captives, and a protector of orphans and old people."[7]

That said, whenever he was on the warpath, Nikephoros—his name means "Bearer of Victory"—brought "frightful and heavy slaughter upon the Muslims."[8] Like Emperor Leo III before him, his people had hailed from a region along the Anatolian frontier (Cappadocia) that had been ravaged by constant Muslim raiding;[*] he bore a grudge against and knew Islam well.[†] The following is a typical account of his exploits from Leo the Deacon's chronicle:

> Nikephoros devastated the surrounding [Muslim-held] regions [in Anatolia between 961–963] like a thunderbolt, ravaging the fields and enslaving whole towns with thousands of inhabitants. When he had destroyed everything in his path with fire and sword, he attacked the fortresses, most of which he captured at the first assault. As for those that had strong defenses because of their walls and the multitude of inhabitants, he brought up his siege machines against them, and waged a relentless war, urging his men to fight fiercely. Each one readily obeyed his commands. For it was not only with words that he encouraged and persuaded them to be of good courage but also by his deeds, since he always used to fight in an extraordinary fashion

---

* Back in 715, Cappadocia was still "remarkable for the density of its population," the "abundance of its vineyards," and "magnificent trees of every kind," wrote a chronicler. But "it was laid waste" when Maslama passed through it in 716 on his way to besiege Constantinople. After his failure, he returned along the same route and again "pillaged and devastated all that region which he transformed into an arid desert" (Bostom 2005, 596).

† Unlike previous Christian rulers who believed that "the Arabs were animated solely by the expectation of booty and a barbarous love of war," and who "failed to take into account the influence which could be exerted on combatants by the promise of heavenly reward," historian Marius Cannard notes that "only Nikephoros Phokas understood, trying in vain to persuade the Byzantine church to adopt a doctrine similar to the Muslim doctrine of martyrdom" (Donner 2008, 67). The Orthodox patriarch refused to sanction the emperor's belief that Christians who fought and died against Muslims were absolved, though the idea would eventually find fertile ground in Catholic Europe and culminate in the Crusades a century hence.

in the van of the army, ready to meet any danger that came his way, and to ward it off valiantly. Thus in a very short time he captured and destroyed more than sixty Agarene [Muslim] fortresses, carried off an enormous amount of booty, and crowned himself with a victory more glorious than that of any other man.[9]

In 961, after 135 years under Islamic occupation, Nikephoros liberated Crete; in 965, he took Tarsus and Cyprus.* He fought fire with fire and sought to terrorize Muslims as they had terrorized Christians—including by hurling their decapitated heads back over their fortifications.[10] He scorned all Muslim attempts at negotiations and spurned offers of submission and tribute. "Against the forces of Islam, it was war to the death" for Nikephoros.[11] In 968 he set out for Syria itself, conquering Homs and Tripoli; in 969 Aleppo and Antioch were back under Christian control after more than three hundred years of Islamic occupation. "His conquest, almost to the suburb of the Holy City and of Damascus, took Byzantine rule further into Arab territory than at any time since the Moslem banners first streamed out of Arabia three centuries before."[12]

To Muslims, Nikephoros was known as the "Pale Death." Arabic sources tell of a "monstrosity of a man" who was "unyielding with the Muslims."[13] Ibn al-Athir says "Muslims feared him greatly" and not infrequently fled the field of battle on the rumor that he was on the march.[14] At one point, he even captured "the sword of the most accursed and impious Muhammad,"[15] to quote Leo the Deacon, "which he had taken as plunder."† Nikephoros made no secret of his contempt for Islam and ordered his men to gather and burn any copies of the Koran they found.‡ After reconquering Tarsus, he ordered his herald to proclaim that those Muslims "who desire

---

* Cyprus had fallen back to the Muslims seven years after Basil I had liberated it.

† "It may be assumed that the sword of Muhammad mentioned here was the famous sword the Prophet wielded on the battlefield of Badr (624). It was called Dhu'l-fakar (the Cleaver of Vertebrae)" (Leo the Deacon 2005, 126n).

‡ He was not alone in this. Before him, in 866, Pope Nicholas sent a letter to the Bulgarians ordering them to burn any books captured from the Muslims because they were harmful and blasphemous (Kedar 2014, 32; Fletcher 2004, 67).

security of property, of their lives, and the lives of their children," and "who desire just laws and fair treatment," to accept Christian rule. "But those who want fornication, tyrannical laws and practices, extortion, [and the] confiscation of property," must "go to the land of Islam." In a letter to the caliph, the emperor "threatens to march against Baghdad, Egypt, and Jerusalem," writes a modern historian. "He insults the Muslims, in the person of their prophet, and says that his next campaign will be against Mecca to establish the throne of Christ."[16]

The Eastern Roman Empire's victories against Islam reached such heights that a military treatise on fighting Muslims, long believed to have been written by Nikephoros himself (though more likely written jointly with or by his brother, General Leo Phokas), opens with an apologia:

> [The treatise might not offer] much application in the eastern regions at the present time. For Christ, our true God, has greatly cut back the power and strength of the offspring of Ishmael and has repelled their onslaughts. Nonetheless, in order that time, which leads us to forget what we once knew, might not completely blot out this useful knowledge, we think we ought to commit it to writing. If in the future, then, some situation should arise in which Christians need this knowledge, it will be readily available.[17]

Yet in the midst of these triumphant times, Byzantine court intrigues and conspiracies were never far away. Along with his incessant warring, which fiscally strained the empire and led to unpopular taxations, Nikephoros's severe piety was always a double-edged sword: if it endeared him to the Christian peasant or relieved *dhimmi*, it provoked the disdain of the profligate denizens of court. Several aristocrats made no secret of their dislike for the "swarthy" emperor.[18] As John the Deacon explains:

> [Nikephoros] was strict and unbending in his prayers and all-night standing vigils to God, and kept his mind undistracted during the singing of hymns, never letting it wander off to worldly thoughts.

Most people considered it a weakness in the man that he wanted everyone to preserve virtue uncompromised, and not to debase the scrupulousness of justice. Therefore he was relentless in the pursuit of these, and seemed implacable and harsh to wrongdoers, and annoying to those who wanted to lead an unprincipled life.[19]

But it was his young wife—"You conquered all but a woman" is inscribed on his mausoleum—that was his undoing. Finding little tenderness in her warrior-monk husband, Empress Theophano fell for his nephew, the charismatic and athletic general John Tzimiskes (who could supposedly vault himself over three horses before landing in the saddle of the fourth). Fair-skinned, blond-haired, with "manly and bright" blue eyes, but of a somewhat diminished stature, he appeared the antithesis of the emperor.[20] John had fallen out of favor with his uncle of late and was banished, but the empress implored her husband to recall him, and the forgiving man did. Before long the two lovers hatched a plot.

On the cold and snowy night of December 10, 969, well past midnight, John and a number of accomplices were drawn up into the palace in baskets let down from a window. With swords upraised, they crept into Nikephoros's chamber only to find his bed empty. The austere emperor was, per custom, sleeping on the floor. He was rudely awoken by a sword slash to his face and a barrage of kicks. Startled and "covered all over with blood and stained with red," all Nikephoros could do was implore Heaven for aid. "John, sitting on the imperial bed, ordered [them] to drag the emperor over to him. When he was dragged over, prostrate and collapsing on the floor (for he was not even able to rise to his knees, since his gigantic strength had been sapped by the blow of the sword)," John proceeded to berate him, claiming that his ungrateful uncle had banished him out of jealousy.[21] Leo the Deacon has the rest:

The emperor, who was already growing faint and did not have anyone to defend him, kept calling on the Mother of God for assistance. But John grabbed hold of his beard and pulled it mercilessly, while his fellow conspirators cruelly and inhumanly smashed his jaws with their sword handles so as to shake loose his teeth and knock them out of the jawbone. When they had their fill of tormenting him, John kicked him in the chest, raised up his sword, and drove it right through the middle of his brain, ordering the others to strike the man, too.[22]

The slain emperor's head was hacked off and his mutilated body hurled out the window into the snow below. Such was the ignominious end of this scourge of Islam, the Pale Death of Saracens, at age fifty-seven. The court quickly forgot him but others did not: the church beatified him, the frontier poets sang his exploits, and the monks of Mount Athos still venerate him as their founder.

The empress was hurried off to a convent for her role in the assassination. As for her coconspirator, deemed the ablest man to lead—and perhaps as reward for getting rid of the puritanical Nikephoros—the pragmatic court hailed John Tzimiskes emperor. Whatever else may be said of him, John took up his uncle's crusade with vigor. Although he was often occupied fighting the Bulgars and their allies, "victoriously and full of rage [John] made war against the Muslims and filled the whole land with slaughter and blood." One Muslim region after another—Mosul, Beirut, Damascus, Tiberius, Nazareth, Acre, Tripoli—fell to him, and the whole of northern Syria was devastated. He announced that "all Phoenicia, Palestine, and Syria have been freed from the bondage of the Muslims," and began preparations to march onto Jerusalem itself.[23] But Nemesis saw to it that the man who assassinated his uncle in cold blood—a deed, it was said, that ever after haunted him—would suffer a similar fate: an aristocratic landowner with a grudge poisoned and killed John in 976. Even so,

[t]he campaigns of Nicephorus Phocas and John Tzimiskes once again made the Byzantine empire a great power in the east. Significantly, they were also consciously holy wars, the first since Heraclius's war with the Persians. In previous wars with the Muslims the Byzantines had all too often been on the defensive, with the retaining of Christian

territory their aim, not its expansion. However, both Nicephorus and John declared their wars to be for the glory of Christendom, aimed at rescuing the holy places and destroying Islam.[24]

And there was more glory yet to come. After John came Basil II,[*] whose victories against Islam were such as to contribute to the vindictive Fatimid caliph of Egypt's order to destroy all churches in his territory.[25] "Never in the seven centuries since its founding by Constantine had the Eastern Roman Empire reached such a pinnacle of power as it attained in 1025, at the end of the reign of Basil II, the grim man of steel known to history as the Bulgar Slayer."[26]

This would not last. Due to a century of successes at the hands of the aforementioned emperors—from Basil I to Basil II—a false sense of security prevailed. Vigilance was abandoned; rule "passed into the hands of a series of dotards, sensualists and courtesans—female rule once again predominated." The twenty-nine-year reign of Empress Zoe, "a middle-aged harlot," saw her marry and divorce—often by blinding or murdering— several men.[27] Concern for the frontier and the struggle against Islam was dropped; the empire's resources were squandered on the fancies of the civil bureaucracy, which came to rule in all but name.

FROM SLAVES TO SELJUKS

All this came at a bad time, for important changes were taking place in the lands of Islam. Since Caliph Mu'tasim had used slave soldiers to great effect at Amorium, the fateful decision to rely exclusively on them was taken. Because he had especially preferred Turkic slaves—of whom he said,

---

* This Basil quickly "learned from the revolts of the aristocrats to despise them and to trust no one. Putting behind him the pleasures to which he was devoted in his youth, he made himself into a man of pure muscle and iron determination. He . . . became a loner, taking advice and counsel from none and apparently never marrying. Austere, rough and dour, rejecting the luxuries, ceremonies, spectacles and panoply of court life, contemptuous of the rhetoric that Constantinopolitans so much admired, Basil spurned the capital and took his troops into the field to stay with them years on end, campaigning in winter as well as summer" (Friendly 1981, 56).

"No people in the world [are] braver, more numerous, or more steadfast"—countless were imported into the caliphate.[28] At first the Turks "marched with the Arabs as subjects and not as masters," but by the tenth century the slaves had become the masters; the Abbasid caliph remained as a mere figurehead to bestow Islamic legitimacy on them.[29]

As with other nomadic peoples before them, early Turkic tribesmen found natural appeal in and converted to "the universal, primitive Islam at war with its infidel neighbors."[30] The perspicacious Muslim philosopher Ibn Khaldun appreciated the parallels. After portraying Arabs as "wild, untamable (animals) and dumb beasts of prey," he wrote, "In the West, the nomadic Berbers . . . are their counterparts, and in the East, the Kurds, the Turkomans, and the Turks."[31] In short, "if taking lives and ravaging the lands of the infidel were the means by which the ends of expanding Islam were served, then the new [Turkic] converts' traditional pleasures were now happily endowed with a pious rationale."[32]

That the jihad—meaning plunder-driven raids against the "other"—is the primary aspect of Islam to jibe with the early Turks is evident in their oldest epic, *The Book of Dede Korkut* (based on oral traditions). In it, the newly converted Turkic peoples engage in pagan practices either frowned on or banned by Islam: they eat horse meat and drink wine and other fermented drinks; they bestow names on their sons only after they behead an enemy in battle; and their women are, in comparison to Muslim women, relatively free and independent. Only in the context of raids on the "infidel"—which becomes synonymous for "tribal outsider" or "enemy"—is Islam evident in their lives. "I shall raid the bloody infidels' land, I shall cut off heads and spill blood, I shall make the infidel vomit blood, I shall bring back slaves and slave-girls. I shall show my cleverness," is a typical pre-battle boast.[33] "They destroyed the infidels' church, they killed its priests and made a mosque in its place. They had the call to prayer proclaimed, they had the invocation [or *shahada*] recited in the name of Allah Almighty. The best of the hunting-birds, the purest of stuffs, the loveliest of girls . . . they selected," is a typical account of these new converts' pious exploits.[34] Otherwise, Islam is absent from their lives. As the translator of *Dede Korkut* remarks, "The enemy throughout is equated with 'the infidel,' and when the heroes are in trouble they invoke the Prophet Muhammad, and perform the rites of Muslim prayer. But there is no mention of their doing so when they are not in trouble."[35]

Although the Persian and Arab establishment was originally unimpressed by Turkish piety,[*] they praised the new converts because they "fight in the way of Allah, waging jihad against the infidels," which always went a long way to exonerate otherwise un-Islamic behavior.[36] By 1037 the Seljuk tribe rose to the top, its leaders becoming the true power-wielders—literally, the *sultans* of the Abbasid caliphate. Because they "became Moslems at a time and place where ardour for holy war against infidel [Christian] and dissident [Fatimid Shias in Cairo] was flaming, the Seljuks seized the torch with the zeal of the convert."[37] Just when the spirit of jihad was beginning to wane and lose significance under the less warlike and Persianized Abbasid caliphate, "under Turkish influence, Islam regained the zeal of the early Arab conquests and reopened holy war against its Christian foes[†] on a significant scale."[38]

ARMENIA RAVAGED

The nearby Christian kingdom of Armenia was first to receive the brunt of Turkic Islam. In 1019 "the first appearance of the bloodthirsty beasts . . . the savage nation of infidels called Turks entered Armenia . . . and mercilessly slaughtered the Christian faithful with the sword," writes Matthew of

---

* Of the Turks, one Arab wrote, "Their faults in general are that they are blunt-witted, ignorant, boastful, turbulent, discontented and without a sense of justice. Without any excuse, they will create trouble and utter foul language. . . . Their merit is that they are brave, free from pretense, open in enmity and zealous in any task allotted to them" (Friendly 1981, 51).

† This point—that the "spirit of militant Islam suited the Turkish fighting spirit perfectly; [that] the desire for plunder was legitimized by pious service to Allah" (Crowley 2014, 24)—comes out often. Bernard Lewis goes so far as to say that, due to Islam's "simple intensity" and "because their conversion to Islam at once involved them in Holy War . . . the converted Turks sank their national identity in Islam as the Arabs and Persians had never done. . . . Turkish Islam was dedicated from the start to the defense or advancement of the faith and power of Islam, and never lost this militant quality" (2003, 88, 95).

Edessa, a chief source for this period.[39] The Armenians fought hard and might have continued to defend themselves, but in 1045—and partially due to the old Christological controversy against the "schismatic" Armenians—Byzantine Emperor Constantine IX, a profligate husband of Zoe, annexed and disarmed portions of their kingdom, carting much of its wealth back to Constantinople. In this manner, "the sterile, effeminate and ignoble nation the Greeks," to quote the aggrieved Armenian chronicler, "delivered up [Armenia] to the Turks."[40]

Four years later, in 1049, the founder of the Seljuk Empire himself, Sultan Tughril Bey (r. 1037–1063), reached the unwalled city of Arzden, west of Lake Van, and "put the whole town to the sword, causing severe slaughter, as many as one hundred and fifty thousand persons." After thoroughly plundering the city—which reportedly contained eight hundred churches—he ordered it set ablaze and turned into a desert. Arzden was "filled with bodies" and none "could count the number of those who perished in the flames." The invaders "burned priests whom they seized in the churches and massacred those whom they found outside. They put great chunks of pork in the hands of the undead to insult us"—Muslims deem the pig unclean—"and made them objects of mockery to all who saw them." Eight hundred oxen and forty camels were required to cart out the vast plunder, mostly taken from churches. "How to relate here, with a voice stifled by tears, the death of nobles and clergy whose bodies, left without graves, became the prey of carrion beasts, the exodus of women of high birth led with their children into Persian slavery and condemned to an eternal servitude![‡] That was the beginning of the misfortunes of Armenia," laments Matthew. "So, lend an ear to this melancholy recital."[41]

And so it went. During the siege of Sebastia (modern-day Sivas) in 1060, six hundred churches were destroyed and "many [more] maidens, brides, and distinguished ladies were led into captivity to Persia." Another

---

‡ Other contemporaries confirm the devastation visited upon Arzden. "Like famished dogs," writes Atistakes, "bands of infidels hurled themselves on our city, surrounded it and pushed inside, massacring the men and mowing everything down like reapers in the fields, making the city a desert. Without mercy, they incinerated those who had hidden themselves in houses and churches" (Friendly 1981, 134).

raid on Armenian territory saw "many and innumerable people who were burned [to death]."[42] The atrocities are too many for Matthew to recount, and like earlier quoted chroniclers from different nations and centuries he frequently ends in resignation: "Who is able to relate the happenings and ruinous events which befell the Armenians, for everything was covered with blood. . . . Because of the great number of corpses, the land stank, and all of Persia was filled with innumerable captives; thus this whole nation of beasts became drunk with blood. All human beings of Christian faith were in tears and in sorrowful affliction, because God our creator had turned away His benevolent face from us." Armenia was reliving its first Islamic nightmare: "Calamity and destruction have fallen upon us like a whirlwind, and the tempestuous winds of the evil Ishmaelites of old [Arabs] have haunted us,* giving us neither respite nor rest," bemoaned the monk.[43]

Nor was there much doubt concerning what fueled the Turks' animus: "This nation of infidels comes against us because of our Christian faith and they are intent on destroying the ordinances of the worshippers of the cross and on exterminating the Christian faithful," one David, head of an Armenian region, explained to his countrymen. Therefore, "it is fitting and right for all the faithful to go forth with their swords and to die for the Christian faith."[44] Many were of the same mind; the sources tell of monks and priests, fathers, wives, and children, all shabbily armed but zealous to protect their way of life, coming out to face the invaders—to little avail.

Anecdotes of faith-driven courage also permeate the chronicles. During the first Muslim siege of Manzikert in 1054, when a massive catapult pummeled and caused its walls to quake, a Catholic Frank holed up

---

* The Arabs, not the Turks, were the first Muslims to invade and terrorize Armenia: "in the reign of Abdallah [Abbasid Caliph al-Mansur, r. 754–775] and on the orders of Yazid, Armenia was struck by extremely onerous taxation," notes one Christian chronicle. "The infernal avarice of the implacable enemy was not satisfied with devouring the flesh of the Christians, the flower of the country, nor with drinking their blood as we drink water; Armenia in its entirety suffered horribly from the absolute lack of money. Every individual, even by giving all he had, his clothes, his food stuffs and prime necessities, did not succeed in paying his ransom and redeeming his person from torture. Gibbets, presses and gallows had been set up everywhere; nothing but fearful and continual torture was seen everywhere" (Ibrahim 2007, 200–201).

in with the Orthodox Armenians volunteered to sacrifice himself: "I will go forth and burn down that catapult, and today my blood shall be shed for all the Christians, for I have neither wife nor children to weep over me." (Clearly many lay Christians transcended the arcane and abstract schisms of the church councils.) The Frank succeeded and returned to gratitude and honors. Adding insult to injury, the defenders catapulted a pig into the Muslim camp while shouting, "O sultan [Tughril], take that pig for your wife, and we will give you Manzikert as a dowry!" "Filled with anger, Tughril had all Christian prisoners in his camp ritually decapitated."[45]

During this whole time, Constantinople showed little interest in what was happening along its eastern borders. The indifferent and "squanderous" lifestyle of Empress Zoe (r. 1028–1050) "was the beginning of the utter decline in our national affairs and the cause of our subsequent humiliation," lamented historian and court insider Michael Psellus (b. 1018).[46] Her successors were little better. "Neither Constantine [IX] nor his advisers gave any evidence that they appreciated at the time the danger of the Seljuk raids, mounting in frequency, extent and success during his reign."[47] The best they did is make treaties with Sultan Tughril; and when roaming bands of Turks broke the treaty by invading and terrorizing Christian territory, and Constantinople objected, the sly sultan feigned innocence by saying he was unable to control these premodern "lone wolves," even as they continued raiding deeper and deeper into western Anatolia.

Military recruits from the sturdy Anatolian peasants that Byzantium had for centuries relied on drastically fell during this time; "indifferent foreigners were enlisted, arms, artillery and warlike stores neglected, and castles and fortresses allowed to fall in ruin."[48] In short, "the legacy of the civilian bureaucrats and of the emperors who were their nominees and puppets—profligate spenders on their own ostentations and miserly providers for their armies—was a defenseless Asia Minor. Turks raided at will, ever further to the west."[49]

In 1063, Sultan Tughril, aged seventy, died peacefully and was eventually succeeded by his thirty-six-year-old nephew, Muhammad bin Dawud Chaghri—known to posterity as Alp Arslan, a Turkish honorific meaning

"Heroic Lion."* Muslim sources portray this Muhammad as fanatically pious but just. Nizam al-Mulk, his vizier and a formidable man himself, said of the young sultan: "He was exceedingly imperious and awe-inspiring and, because he was so earnest and fanatical in his beliefs and disapproved of the Shafi'i rite [one of the four orthodox schools of Sunni Islamic jurisprudence†], I lived in constant fear of him."[50] As usual, extreme Muslim piety manifested itself before Christian eyes as extreme hostility. For Matthew of Edessa, Sultan Muhammad was "like a beast crazed by its bloodthirsty nature," a "drinker of blood," a "venomous serpent," a "ferocious beast."[51] For Michael Attaleiates (b. 1022), a contemporary Greek chronicler, the sultan was simply the "Antichrist."[52]

Between 1064 and 1065, Sultan Muhammad, "going forth full of rage and with a formidable army," invaded Christian Georgia and laid siege to Ani, the fortified capital of Armenia, then a great and populous city. The thunderous bombardment of Muhammad's siege engines caused the entire city to quake, and Matthew describes countless terror-stricken families huddled together and weeping. Once inside, the Muslims—reportedly armed with two knives in each hand and an extra in their mouths—"began to mercilessly slaughter the inhabitants of the entire city . . . and piling up their bodies one on top of the other. . . . Beautiful and respectable ladies of high birth were led into captivity into Persia. Innumerable and countless boys with bright faces and pretty girls were carried off together with their mothers."[53]

But the most savage treatment was always reserved for those visibly proclaiming their Christianity: clergy and monks "were burned to death,

---

* Contemporary descriptions portray him as "very awe-inspiring, dominating," a "great-formed one, elegant of stature. He had long, thin whiskers, which he used to knot up when shooting arrows. And they say his arrow never went astray. . . . From the top button of his hat to the end of his moustaches it was two yards" (Hillenbrand 2007, 217).

† Sultan Muhammad was so dedicated to the Hanafi *madhhab* (or Islamic school of jurisprudence) that he always kept a *qadi* (sharia jurist) by his side, including in battles. Whatever disagreement he had with the Shafi'i rite, it did not concern jihad or related topics, as all four Sunni schools are in agreement that non-Muslims are de facto enemies that must be warred on in the name of Islam (see Introduction).

while others were flayed alive from head to toe." Every monastery and church—before this, Ani was known as "the City of 1001 Churches"—was pillaged, desecrated, and set aflame.‡ A zealous jihadi—or "nefarious infidel" to Christian eyes—climbed atop the city's main cathedral "and pulled down the very heavy cross which was on the dome, throwing it to the ground," before entering and defiling the church. Made of pure silver and the "size of a man"—and now symbolic of Islam's might over Christianity—the broken crucifix was sent as a trophy to adorn a mosque in modern-day Azerbaijan.[54]

Not only do several Christian sources document the sack of Armenia's capital—one contemporary succinctly notes that Muhammad "rendered Ani a desert by massacres and fire"[55]—but so do Muslim sources, often in apocalyptic terms: "I wanted to enter the city and see it with my own eyes," one Arab explained. "I tried to find a street without having to walk over the corpses. But that was impossible."[56]

And so it went. In 1067, the Muslims devastated the area surrounding Edessa. Their commander "went back to Persia laden with many captives and countless booty. He presented the sultan with as many as two thousand attractive young slaves, both boys and girls."[57] These must have been the crème de la crème of seventy thousand Christians sold into slavery around the same time in Aleppo, according to contemporary Muslim records.[58]

PRELUDE TO WAR

In 1068, Eudocia, another unscrupulous Byzantine empress, married Romanus Diogenes (b. 1030), an aristocrat from an ancient and distinguished military family with large landholdings. She was apparently infatuated with him; for according to Attaleiates, one of Romanus's generals who campaigned with him for years, "The man not only surpassed others in his good qualities but he was also pleasant to look at in all respects."[59] He was, however, "very harsh and violent in his judgments," writes Michael the

---

‡ Considering that Ani had some 100,000 residents, that it had 1,001 churches, as Matthew of Edessa and others say, is not farfetched, as that comes out to one church for every 100 residents, in an era when everyone attended church.

Syrian, and once had the nose of a soldier hacked off for stealing the donkey of a Muslim after the emperor had given his peace.[60] Still, compared to the effete, corrupt, and dissolute Byzantine rulers of the last half century or so, it must have been refreshing that "one thing alone satisfied him: that he marched against his foes."[61] Indeed, Romanus's courage bordered on hubris or naivety, for he would often go unarmed and without escort to parley with barbarous enemies, complained his generals.*

The new emperor was committed to reversing the jihadi tide that had recently engulfed Armenia and was edging westward across the Anatolian plain. In 1069 he amassed a large army consisting of Greeks, Franks, Bulgarians, Turcomen, Normans, Georgians, Armenians, and Christian Arabs.[62] Although they made for great numbers, decades of disregard had taken its toll on the military: "Here one could see an appalling sight," reflected the contemporary chronicler John Skylitzes (b. 1040). The men were "deprived of their full armour," lacked "swords and other weapons of war," and were "short of war horses and other equipment[†] because no emperor had campaigned in this area for a long time. . . . All that caused great despondency in the hearts of those who saw them, when they reflected on the state to which the Roman armies had come and from which they had fallen."[63]

Undaunted, Romanus "marched forth and went against the country of the Muslims," writes Matthew. He met them in central Anatolia, near Phrygia, and drove them back, capturing all their plunder and freeing all

---

* "I who was present [during an enemy surrender] did not approve of the simplicity of the emperor who mingled without body armour among murderous men who pass their lives in recklessness and madness," wrote Michael Attaleiates (Hillenbrand 2007, 230). Psellus confirms that Romanus "exposed himself to danger without a thought of the consequences" [1966, 355]).

† In other words, they were treated the exact opposite of how the militarily successful Nikephoros Phokas and/or his brother Leo recommended troops should be treated: "They certainly ought to receive their salaries and money for provisions regularly, as well as gifts and bonuses, more than are customary or stipulated. Not lacking anything, therefore, they will be able to use these to obtain the best horses and the rest of their equipment. With a joyous spirit and a willing and exultant heart they will choose to brave dangers on behalf of our holy emperors and all the Christian people. . . . [For] these are the defenders and, after God, the saviors of Christians who, so to speak, die each day on behalf of the holy emperors" (Dennis, 215–217).

their slaves. Next, and to avenge the recent selling of seventy thousand Christians, he launched a "violent assault" on northeast Aleppo. The terrified Muslims, "improvised crosses in their hands, went in the direction of the gates to the emperor," and fell at his feet imploring him to spare them. He "took pity on the town and accepted its submission."[64]

Romanus's successful drive continued into 1070: he expelled the Muslims out of Cappadocia, and at Khilat near Lake Van met and defeated the forces of Sultan Muhammad; the heroic lion barely managed to flee. Just then Romanus was recalled to deal with a Norman uprising in the west. Muhammad took full advantage of the Christian army's withdrawal and, returning with fire and sword, conquered what his predecessor and uncle could not: the important city of Manzikert just north of Lake Van. "When the Greek emperor [Romanus] Diogenes heard the news of this recent calamity brought, roaring like a lion[‡] he commanded all his numerous forces be collected; so edicts were issued and heralds sent forth throughout all the lands of the West."[65]

At the head of a mammoth but largely mercenary army—"as numerous as the sands of the sea" and consisting of some seventy thousand men—Romanus was back in Anatolia in early 1071 and making his way to Manzikert.[66] Muslims interpreted this massive march as Christendom's attempt to exterminate Islam once and for all. "They swore oaths that they would drive out the caliph, appoint the catholicos in his place, destroy mosques and build churches," one Muslim chronicler projected. Romanus was coming "out intending to conquer the world and destroy the religion [Islam] and to overcome sultans and to give help to devils," another fumed. The emperor "had resolved to destroy the lands of Islam," yet another succinctly jotted.[67]

On the faulty belief that Sultan Muhammad and his men were away south fighting Shia Fatimid incursions and unable to arrive in time—certainly not with a comparable host—the emperor decided to split his

---

[‡] The emperor's impetuous nature comes out in contemporary accounts; thus, "in a bout of anger and as he was of courageous temperament, the Byzantine emperor decided on war. . . . Full of boastfulness and anger, he crossed the sea as if it was terra firma" (Hillenbrand 2007, 238).

force in half, sending the Normans and other mercenaries, under Roussel de Bailleul, a Norman knight and mercenary, to Khilat, while he went to and easily recaptured Manzikert. Made confident by this victory, he divided his forces yet again, sending reinforcements to Bailleul and a foraging party of some twelve thousand to Georgia. Such was "his ignorance of military science," berated Psellus, a court intriguer and no friend of Romanus, that "he scattered his forces. . . . So instead of opposing his adversaries with the full force of his army, less than half were actually involved."[68]

For Muhammad and his swift cavalry, augmented by other Islamic forces and totaling some forty thousand horsemen, were galloping to Khilat.[69] According to Muslim sources, once there, they swiftly smashed the Christians, cut off the nose of their "Russian leader" (the Norman Bailleul?), and captured their "greatest cross," which Muhammad sent as a trophy to the caliph in Baghdad.[70] Byzantine sources offer a different and more plausible account, suggesting that Bailleul let Khilat fall with nary a struggle; that he instantly withdrew all his men—approximately half of the Roman force—not to Manzikert, where his emperor awaited them, but northwest to safety. This reading is bolstered by the fact that, even before Romanus set off on his crusade, the court intriguers—including his wife the empress, whom he grew contemptuous of for trying to control him*— were scheming against him.[71] Moreover, many of the mercenaries, men like Bailleul himself, disliked the emperor for favoring and trying to rebuild the native-born Anatolian troops that had been left to falter in recent decades.

At any rate, after capturing Khilat, Muhammad, with exact knowledge of Romanus's whereabouts, quickly galloped his forces northeast to Manzikert. Meanwhile, the emperor, totally unaware of the close proximity of his enemy, began marching to Khilat to ascertain why Bailleul had failed to arrive. The Roman vanguard suddenly found itself engulfed by Turkic arrows; many were slain while others quickly fell back onto the main army and told the tale: the sultan was here, and with a large host.

---

* "The more she tried to dominate him, to treat him, who was really her master, like a lion in a cage, the more he fretted at her restraining influence and glared at the hand that kept him in check," writes Psellus, who knew them both. "To begin with, he growled inwardly, but as time passed his disgust became obvious to everyone" (1966, 350).

Once the two forces had set camp, Muhammad sent a delegation to parley with Romanus on "the pretext of peace"† though in reality "stalling for time," explains Michael Attaleiates. This only "roused the emperor to war." Romanus spurned the emissaries, forced them to prostrate themselves before him, and commanded them to tell their sultan that "there will be no treaty . . . and no going home except after I have done in the lands of Islam the like of what has been done in the lands of Byzantium."[72] Besides, for Romanus to return to Constantinople after amassing (and boasting of) such a large military with only a truce to show for it would not do. It was now or never.

Having "dismissed the ambassador with the greatest contempt," Romanus incited his men to war with "words of extraordinary violence," says Attaleiates.[73] More temperately, the army chaplain reminded all that this was no ordinary enemy they were fighting, but a committed one that earnestly believed he was doing God's work by destroying Christianity. As proof he quoted Christ: "The hour is coming when whoever kills you will think he is offering his service to God," that is, Allah (John 16:2).[74]

All this time, Turkic horsemen harried the Roman army with their traditional hit-and-run tactics, always careful to avoid melee combat. For the Turkish way of war—like that of other tribal peoples from the Asian steppes, including the Huns before and the Mongols after them—was almost exclusively based on ambush tactics that required swift horses and even swifter arrows.‡ As the Byzantine army made final preparations, mounted Turks would suddenly appear in furious charges, loose volleys of arrows, and then retreat—only to reappear again in a different place. "The Turks pass their lives in trickery and deepest design, accomplishing everything through contrivance and unabashed fabrication," the vexed general Attaleiates jotted, as he saw his men fall one by one to arrows.[75]

---

† One Muslim source confirms that the peace mission was a ruse "to discover their [military] condition" (Hillenbrand 2007, 75).

‡ "Basically, the success of the Turks lay in the unity of man, horse, and weapon—the bow and arrow," says Turkish historian Mehmet Koymen. "No other people in history made use of those three elements as harmoniously as did the Turks" (Friendly 1981, 120).

THE BATTLE OF MANZIKERT
(OR "THAT DREADFUL DAY")

On the morning when battle seemed imminent, mass was celebrated and a great crucifix paraded before the troops, as they knelt in prayer. The emperor was described from the Muslim camp as sitting "on a throne of gold; above him was a golden cross studded with priceless jewels and in front of him was a great throng of monks and priests reciting the Gospel" and "carrying crucifixes in their hands."[76]

The religious element was no less prominent in the Muslim camp where preparations for this grand jihad were being made.* Everywhere prostrated on the ground the Turks "prayed to Allah Most High that he would make his religion triumph, that he would reinforce their hearts with patience, that he would enfeeble their enemy and that he would cast fear into their hearts." The sultan reminded them of Islam's win-win scenario: "If we are given victory over them, [well and good]. If not, we will go as martyrs to the Garden." A reminder—or threat—was also issued to those not sufficiently inspired by these promises: Allah's wrath, in the guise of "fire and ignominy," would take whoever dared retreat before the infidels (Koran 8:15–16). "We are with you!" cried the men in unison when he finished his harangue.[77]

Muhammad reportedly waited until Friday—when Muslims everywhere would be congregated in mosques and beseeching Allah for victory— to initiate battle. The Abbasid caliph in Baghdad is said to have produced a sermon laden with jihadi-martyrdom rhetoric to be read in mosques throughout the lands.† When Friday at last dawned, Sultan Muhammad

---

* This is well attested to in the earliest Muslim accounts. Koran verses (e.g., 61:10–11) portraying jihad as the greatest service to Allah, are regularly juxtaposed with the words and deeds of the sultan, who is portrayed as the *ghazi* par excellence. While some modern academics claim that the jihadi sentiment permeating this and other battles are hagiographical accretions, one expert on Manzikert warns, "It would be unwise . . . to assume the Muslim accounts are exclusively retrospective and simply reflect a pious recasting of history by later generations of Muslim historians" (Hillenbrand 2007, 113). Moreover, if not more importantly, it is, once again, what Muslims *believe* happened—not the often unknowable what *really* happened—that determines how they see their place in history.

† It read in part: "O Allah! Raise the banner of Islam and its helper. . . . Help those

Islam's New Champions   115

appeared in a pure white tunic (indicating his sacrificial status as a martyr); he dismounted, fell face first to the earth, and made supplication: "O
Allah! I have placed my trust in you and have come closer to you through
this jihad . . . help me to fight jihad against the enemies, give me from your
presence a sustaining power, and make that which is difficult easy for me."‡
On rising, the "mountains trembled" as wave after wave of "Allahu Akbar!"
was cried out of countless throats.[78]

Muhammad then issued his final orders to his eunuch general, Taranges: "Win or be beheaded."[79] Taranges, writes another contemporary
chronicler, "divided his army into several groups, set traps and organized
ambushes, and ordered his men to surround the Byzantines and to riddle
them with arrows."[80] Finally, as "martial music resounded from both sides
and the dust of the battlefield billowed up like clouds in the sky," the two
armies met on Friday, August 26, 1071.[81]

The battle ensued in the usual way: Turkic horseman, in a crescent formation that hid their fewer numbers, sped forward and unleashed volleys of
arrows, before swiftly retreating. Throngs of Roman men and horses fell;
some even broke rank and fled. One "important detachment, whose men
were not from amongst those who shared in the worship of God [that is,
pagan Turkic mercenaries], betrayed the emperor and crossed over to the
enemy side."[82]

Undaunted, Romanus, commanding from front-center, maintained the
line and marched his forces forward. Because the Anatolian terrain is filled
with gorges, passes, and mountain ranges, his men continued to fall "to the
traps and ambuscades" of the Muslims and "suffered great losses." Still
undeterred and "determined to risk all," the impetuous emperor continued

---

fighters in your paths who have expended themselves in obedience to you, and who
have given their utmost in their making of a covenant with you. . . . Strengthen his [Sul-
tan Muhammad's] hand to glorify your religion . . . for he has abandoned tranquility for
the noble path of pleasing you; and by expending his wealth and his life he has pursued
the paths of your commands which he has obeyed and pursued. For you speak and your
word is truth: 'O you who believe! Shall I show you a commerce that will save you
from a painful doom? You should believe in Allah and his messenger, and should strive
for the cause of Allah with your wealth and your lives' (Koran 61:10)" (Hillenbrand
2007, 53–54).

‡ Allusions and references to Koran 48:13–18.

"advancing slowly, expecting to encounter the Turkish host, engage them in close combat, and thus bring matters to a head"—Byzantium's traditional strategy for defeating nomadic horsemen.[83] But because the Turks had unlimited terrain to fall back on, Romanus's men never managed to corner and finish them off. The battle remained a running fight: as the heavily armored infantry slowly advanced, Muslim horsemen charged and shot arrows at them and then retreated. When the day was nearly spent, Romanus ordered an about-face back to camp, the only place to feed his men and water their horses. Once he turned his back, the Turks launched an all-out assault, "hurling themselves fiercely upon the Byzantines with terrifying cries."[84]

It was then that treachery struck: General Andronicus, who commanded the rear of the army—now its head, as it marched back to camp—said the emperor's reversed standards meant that he had fallen, and proceeded to march his men, many of whom were hired by and loyal to Constantinople's conspirators, back to camp. Other units, believing a retreat had in fact been sounded, broke ranks and fled from the main army. And the ancient Christological schism that initially broke out in 451 continued to haunt the empire: large contingents of Armenians, "whom they [Byzantines] wanted to force into adopting their heresy," wrote Michael the Syrian, "were the first to take flight and to turn their backs in the battle."[85]

Havoc ensued. "All were shouting incoherently and riding about in disorder; nobody could say what was going on. . . . It was like an earthquake with howling, sweat, a swift rush of fear, clouds of dust, and not least Turks riding all around us," Attaleiates later remembered:

> Then each entrusted his salvation to flight with as much impetus, haste or strength as he had. Thereupon the enemy pursued, killing some, taking others captive, trampling yet others. The affair was very painful, surpassing any lament or dirge. For what could be more piteous than for the entire imperial army to be driven away in flight and defeat by savage and relentless barbarians and the emperor, helpless, to be surrounded by barbarian weapons.[86]

Indeed, the Islamic horsemen—now augmented by hitherto hidden contingents—swiftly exploited the broken ranks, especially to the right and rear, and surrounded the center, where stood Romanus and his Varangian Guard (the empire's elite unit of Nordic warriors who were always attached to the emperor they served). A berserk-style melee erupted, as "free-roaming stallions and armed defenders fought to the death and swarmed round vengeance," to quote a Muslim chronicler waxing poetically: "Vanguards met vanguards and cutting swords were struck by cutting swords. Arrow points sang and spears danced. Spears became twisted, horsemen orbited, the cups [of death] circulated and heads flew." Even Sultan Muhammad—who found "the taste of thrusting [of lances] and the striking of blows delightful"—was espied swinging "about him explosively to right and left, bringing down the foe now with the sword, now with arrows and javelins."[87]

As for Romanus, he was always more at home surrounded by enemies than by the denizens of court, who had anyway proven to be just as hostile:

> [Once he saw that he was] abandoned and completely cut off from help, [he] unsheathed his sword and charged at his enemies, killing many of them and putting others to flight. But he was surrounded by a crowd of adversaries and was wounded in the hand. They recognized him and he was completely encircled; an arrow wounded his horse, which slipped and fell, dragging its rider down with it. Thus the emperor of the Romans was captured and led in chains to the sultan.[88]

Worse, the once proud and imperious Romanus became the first Roman emperor in over a thousand years to experience the ignominy of being taken prisoner from the field of battle.

Still, he had made a valiant last stand* and was only captured "when he became weary towards the evening," says Attaleiates, at which point the rest of the imperial army dissolved, some in flight, most in death. "Those

---

* The valor of the emperor at Manzikert is attested to in several contemporary accounts:

who escaped were but a tiny fraction," notes Psellus. "Of the majority, some were taken captive, the rest massacred."[89] The entire Varangian Guard was slaughtered. One Muslim chronicle confirms that the Christians "were killed to such an extent that a valley there where the two sides had met was filled [with their corpses]."[90]

Sultan Muhammad declared victory and, as the stars shined above the bloodied fields of Manzikert, renewed cries of "Allahu Akbar!" resounded, as the victors scoured the earth and despoiled the dead.[*] The sultan hurriedly dispatched "the cross and what had been taken from the Byzantines" to Baghdad, and "the caliph and the Muslims rejoiced. Baghdad was decorated in an unprecedented fashion and domes were erected. It was a great victory the like of which Islam had not seen before," writes a later Damascene historian. Henceforth, the Heroic Lion would also be known as Abu al-Fath (Father of Conquest, or Liberation, based on perspective[†]) and "the Guardian of Sharia."[91]

THE INGLORIOUS AFTERMATH

Once he accepted that the battered and chained man led before him with a rope around his neck was indeed the Roman emperor—for neither Romanus nor Muhammad ever expected to meet each other under such circumstances—the sultan leapt from his throne like a mad man, commanded

---

Romanus "launched himself into the thick of the battle. He knocked down several very valiant Persian fighters and caused disarray in their ranks," says a contemporary Armenian account. Once surrounded, he "defended himself vigorously for a long time," says Attaleiates; for, "as he was a soldier experienced in war and conversant with many dangers he warded off his assailants and killed many, but he was finally wounded in the hand by a sword and, since his horse had been shot down with arrows, he stood fighting on foot" (Hillenbrand 2007, 240, 234–235). Even the normally critical Psellus begrudgingly writes, "According to my several informants he actually killed many of them and put others to flight" (1966, 356).

* Afterward, "they sent most of the wicked infidels to the abode of perdition. . . . So much valuable plunder, such as money, goods, captives, animals and attendants, fell into the hands of the Muslims that the scribe of the sky would be in a state of confusion from writing it all down," notes one Muslim chronicler (Hillenbrand 2007, 92).

† On why the word al-fath ("the opener") is translated as "the conqueror," see footnote on p. 72.

Romanus to kiss the ground, and stepped on his neck. He repeatedly berated the emperor, including for spurning his emissaries and offers of peace.
The unrepentant Romanus deigned only to offer the curtest responses to
his captor's fiery upbraiding. He merely had done what was "possible for a
man, and which kings are bound to do, [and] I have fallen short in nothing.
But God has fulfilled his will. And now, do what you wish and abandon
recriminations."[92]

Putting the laconic Roman to the test, the sultan asked the emperor
what he would do if their positions were reversed. Romanus's frank
answer—"the worst!"—impressed him: "Ah! By Allah, he has spoken the
truth!" exclaimed the Turk. "If he had spoken otherwise, he would be lying.
This is an intelligent, tough man. It is not permissible that he should be
killed."[93] In the end, Muhammad released Romanus on several conditions,
including an exorbitant Byzantine tribute (portrayed as *jizya* in the Muslim
sources)—half a million gold coins followed by 360,000 annually[94]—and
the return of several cities, including Antioch and Edessa.[95] He sent Romanus back to Constantinople with a Muslim escort; they carried a banner
above the head of the disgraced emperor that read, "There is no god but
Allah and Muhammad is his messenger."[96]

Although much has been made by Western historians concerning Muhammad's apparent magnanimity, it completely accorded with sharia, which
recommends that Muslim leaders dispense with captives in whichever one
of three ways—execution, slavery, or freedom (often by ransoming)—best
serves Islam's interests. Considering that the sultan's Fatimid rivals were
launching devastating raids on his domains and that the execution of their
emperor might provoke a renewed Roman offensive, whereas clemency to
Romanus might ease hostilities, Muhammad wisely concluded on release
for ransom. Even Romanus himself had shrewdly told the sultan that "killing me will not be of any use to you."[97]

A final, ironic aspect concerning Romanus's captivity is worth relaying: early Christian chroniclers, who often depict Sultan Muhammad as
a bloodthirsty Antichrist figure, concede that he behaved magnanimously
with Romanus; Muslim historians, who often depict Muhammad in glowing

terms, portray him as behaving meanly and pettily with Romanus. In this, one wonders if Christian and Muslim authors projected their own ideals concerning how victors should treat the vanquished. "You are too trivial in my view for me to kill you," the sultan is said to have declared before his Turks in Muslim sources. "Take him to the person who pays most." When no one reportedly wanted to purchase the "Dog of the Romans," Muhammad scoffed that that was "because the dog is better than he is!" "He struck him three or four blows with his hand and [when Romanus collapsed] he kicked him a similar number of times"; he "put him in chains and fettered his hand to his neck"; he pulled his hair and put his face to the ground, while informing him, "your troops [are] food for the Muslims."[98] And so on. Whatever really took place in that tent, it is this rendition of contemptuous supremacy, documented in Islam's chronicles, that Muslims acknowledge.

At any rate, Constantinople's anti-Romanus faction never expected to see the emperor alive again—and worse, coming back to reclaim his throne. The least the sultan could have done is rid them of the fellow. Confusion and anxiety reigned in the palace, and "Eudocia found herself in an embarrassing position," writes Psellus. "She was unable to decide what to do next . . . pulling her veil over her head she ran off to a secret crypt below ground."[99] His enemies mocked the disgraced emperor and accused him of not just losing to but being the sultan's puppet. Something of a civil war between those loyal to Romanus and those loyal to his opposition broke out. In the end, holed up in a tower, the spent man eventually capitulated: "There he stood, a strange, melancholy spectacle, all his hopes gone," writes the chronicler. He agreed to retire to a monastery, was instantly "forced to don the black robe of a monk," and had his hair quickly sheared off, "not caring who did it."[100]

But even this would not do; his usurpers feared a comeback from the ambitious man and sent "cruel and harsh men," writes John Skylitzes to ambush Romanus. They "gouged out his eyes pitilessly and inhumanely. Carried forth on a cheap beast of burden like a decaying corpse, his eyes gouged out and his face and head swollen and full of worms and stench, he lived on a few days in pain and smelling foully before his death" in the summer of 1072.[101] According to another account, after he was blinded, Romanus spent his final days, "hit[ting] his head against a wall until he died."[102]

Such was the end of the emperor who meant to turn the tide on the resurgent jihad. While no Nikephoros Phokas in his generalship against and triumphs over Islam, Romanus shared his ignominious fate. Constantinople's perennial conspirators destroyed yet another man who had fought for God and empire; and in both cases Muslim posterity told of Allah's vengeance on the Dogs of Rome who most defied him. Romanus's ashes were sent to and buried in a monastery he had recently built, and his wife, the empress who had made and unmade him, was exiled to a convent.

Reportedly shocked at Romanus's treatment—and denied the great tribute and concessions promised him—Sultan Muhammad pledged: "I shall consume with the sword all those people who venerate the cross, and all the lands of the Christians shall be enslaved."[103] (One wonders how this vow presaged anything new or different from what Muhammad, his forbears, and followers had already been doing in word and deed in "the lands of Christians.") He did not live to fulfill his promise, as treachery cuts both ways.

Soon after his glorious victory, the sultan sped east to quell a rebellion. He met stiff resistance at a fortress commanded by one Yusuf al-Harani, a fellow but recalcitrant Sunni Muslim. The sultan "gained its submission only by deceit, promising Yusuf safety and the retention of his holdings."[104] The rebellious Muslim accepted—not because he was deceived, but because he was preparing his own deception. That night, Yusuf held a great feast with his family and friends. "Then during the night he savagely slew his wife and three children with his own hands, so that they might not fall into the hands of the sultan and be his slaves."[105] On the following day, he went before the sultan—with the same daggers he had used on his children concealed—and pretended to do obeisance. As Yusuf had expected, Muhammad reneged on his clemency and instantly ordered that the former rebel "be tied hands and feet to four stakes, to be executed by a firing squad of archers." Yusuf instantly "fell upon the sultan and plunged the two knives into his body."[106] Muhammad's guards cut the assassin down but the damage was done: Muhammad bin Dawud Chaghri—Alp Arslan, Heroic Lion and Defender of Sharia—died from his wounds days later.

THE TURKS' YARMUK

The sultan would be honored by Muslims in general, Turks in particular, for centuries to come. For the "victory of the Seljuq sultan at Manzikert was not just a military triumph over the Byzantine emperor. His capture symbolized the subjugation of Christianity by Islam. Manzikert was perceived to be the first step in an epic story in which Turkish-led dynasties would defeat the Christians and proclaim the triumph of Islam."[107] Accordingly, when the nine hundredth anniversary of Manzikert was held on August 26, 1971, it "was heralded by widespread jubilation in Turkey" and correctly portrayed as "the beginnings of Turkification and Islamification of Anatolia."[108] Prime Minister Recep Tayyip Erdoğan and other top-ranking officials continue participating in Manzikert celebrations, and the battlefield is treated as sacred. A statue of Sultan Muhammad on rearing stallion stands near where the battle is believed to have been fought; the inscription says the sultan only had 15,000 men, the enemy 210,000.

In short, Manzikert was for the Turks what Yarmuk was for the Arabs. In both battles—and according to the Muslim narrative—outnumbered Muslims won because, seeing their readiness to be martyred for his cause, Allah had enabled them to triumph over the infidels. Even Michael Attaleiates, who was at the battle, noted that the Turks "attributed everything to God, as they had accomplished a greater monument of victory than they could have under their own strength."[109] But there are other, less hagiographical similarities: as at Yarmuk, the Roman army at Manzikert consisted of various nations, with tensions and disunity between them; and whereas Roman defeat at Yarmuk was followed by the conquests of Syria and Egypt, Roman defeat at Manzikert was followed by the conquest of hitherto stalwart Anatolia, or Asia Minor.

For, before his assassination, the Heroic Lion commanded the Turks: "Henceforth all of you be like lion cubs and eagle young, racing through the countryside day and night, slaying the Christians and not sparing any mercy on the Roman nation."[110] This they did; and "the emirs spread like locusts, over the face of the land,"[111] invading every corner of Anatolia, sacking some of ancient Christianity's most important cities, including Ephesus, home of Saint John the Evangelist; Nicaea, where Christendom's creed was formulated in 325; and Antioch, the original see of Saint Peter. "All that was left were devastated fields, trees cut down, mutilated corpses and towns driven mad by fear or in flames." Hundreds of thousands of Anatolian Christians were reportedly massacred or enslaved.[112] Still racked by civil strife, the rapidly shrinking Byzantine empire offered one last battle in 1076 at Myriokephalon, and again failed. By the early 1090s, the Turks had taken the last Christian bastion, Nicomedia, only 2,500 feet away from Constantinople, across the narrowest point of the Bosporus strait.

The Eastern Roman Empire lost much after Manzikert. It lost the richest and most fertile part of its empire, whence its hardiest soldiers and not a few warrior-emperors (including Leo III and Nikephoros II) historically came from; it lost its prestige and reputation as the world's greatest power for seven centuries—not just in the eyes of Muslims who had still been reeling under the shadow of defeat from the empire's tenth-century comeback, but Western eyes as well. As Steven Runciman put it, "The Battle of Manzikert was the most decisive disaster in Byzantine history. The Byzantines themselves had no illusions about it. Again and again their historians refer to that 'dreadful day.'"

It was in fact the beginning of "the longest death-rattle in history"[113]— one that would culminate three chapters hence.

CHAPTER 5

CHRISTENDOM STRIKES BACK:
THE BATTLE OF HATTIN, 1187

They will slaughter the priests at home, defiling the holy places
[churches], and they will lie with their wives in the revered and holy
places where the mystical and bloodless sacrifice is performed. The
holy vestments, they will place these on their horses, they will spread
them on their beds and they will tie their cattle in the coffins of the
saints. They will be corrupted murderers, like a fire testing the race of
the Christians.

> —The *Apocalypse* (a seventh-century document long deemed
> prophetic)[1]

Who is to revenge all this, who is to repair this damage, if you do not
do it? . . . Rise up and remember the manly deeds of your ancestors, the
prowess and greatness of Charlemagne, of his son Louis, and of your
other kings, who destroyed pagan [and Muslim] kingdoms and planted
the holy church in their territories.

> —Pope Urban II[2]

NEWS OF GREAT PERSECUTION

RUMOR OF THE GREAT TRIBULATION EXPERIENCED BY THE CHRIS-
tians of the East reached those of the West in the years following
Manzikert. It was a terrible and unvarying tale, brought forth by many.*

---

* Indeed, there is no dearth of contemporary writings documenting the atrocities Eastern Christians suffered. Whether an anonymous Georgian chronicler tells of how "holy
churches served as stables for their horses," the "priests were immolated during the

"Far and wide they [Muslim Turks] ravaged cities and castles together with their settlements," wrote a Frankish eyewitness. "Churches were razed down to the ground. Of the clergymen and monks whom they captured, some were slaughtered while others were with unspeakable wickedness given up, priests and all, to their dire dominion and nuns—alas for the sorrow of it!—were subjected to their lusts."[3] Alexios I Komnenos (r. 1081–1118), Constantinople's first able emperor in decades, elaborated in a letter to Count Robert of Flanders:

> The holy places are desecrated and destroyed in countless ways. . . . Noble matrons and their daughters, robbed of everything, are violated one after another, like animals. Some [of their attackers] shamelessly place virgins in front of their own mothers and force them to sing wicked and obscene songs until they have finished having their ways with them . . . men of every age and description, boys, youths, old men, nobles, peasants and what is worse still and yet more distressing, clerics and monks and woe of unprecedented woes, even bishops are defiled with the sin of sodomy and it is now trumpeted abroad that one bishop has succumbed to this abominable sin.[4]

Atrocities were not limited to Asia Minor or its indigenous Christians: "As the Turks were ruling the lands of Syria and Palestine, they inflicted injuries on Christians who went to pray in Jerusalem, beat them, pillaged them, [and] levied the poll tax [jizya]," writes Michael the Syrian;[†]

Holy Communion itself," the "virgins defiled, the youths circumcised, and the infants taken away," or whether the princess at Constantinople tells of how "cities were obliterated, lands were plundered, and the whole of Rhomaioi [Anatolia] was stained with Christian blood"—it was the same scandalous tale of woe (Bostom 2005, 609).

† Before becoming a charismatic preacher of the First Crusade, even Peter the Hermit (b. 1050) suffered accordingly during an earlier pilgrimage to Jerusalem. When he finally reached the Holy Sepulchre "he saw many forbidden and wicked things occurring there. . . . [So] he sought out the patriarch of the holy church of Jerusalem and asked why gentiles and evil men were able to pollute holy places and steal away offerings from the faithful, using the church as if a stable, beating up Christians, despoiling

moreover, "every time they saw a caravan of Christians, particularly of those from Rome and the lands of Italy, they made every effort to cause their death in diverse ways."[5] Such was the fate of one German pilgrimage to Jerusalem in 1064. According to one of the pilgrims:

> Accompanying this journey was a noble abbess of graceful body and of a religious outlook. Setting aside the cares of the sisters committed to her and against the advice of the wise, she undertook this great and dangerous pilgrimage. The pagans captured her, and in the sight of all, these shameless men raped her until she breathed her last, to the dishonor of all Christians. Christ's enemies performed such abuses and others like them on the Christians.[6]

It is often suggested that it was only during these times, when the Turks were running amok, that Christians living around the Holy Land were persecuted. This is incorrect. Similar bouts of persecution regularly erupted under other Muslim peoples and dynasties from the very start. Thus, in the early eighth century under the Umayyads, some Arabs—described as "untamed and beastly, illogical in mind and maniacs in their desires"[7]— captured, tortured, and executed seventy Christian pilgrims in Jerusalem for refusing to convert to Islam (minus seven who complied under torture). Shortly after that, another sixty pilgrims were crucified in Jerusalem. In the late eighth century, under the Abbasids, Muslims destroyed two churches and a monastery near Bethlehem and slaughtered its monks. In 796, Muslims burned another twenty monks to death. In 809, and again in 813, multiple monasteries, convents, and churches were attacked in and around Jerusalem; Christians of both sexes were gang raped and massacred. In

---

pilgrims through unjust fees, and inflicting on them many sufferings." The frustrated patriarch threw up his hands in exasperation: "Why do you reprimand me and disturb me in the midst of my fatherly cares? I have but the strength and power of a tiny ant when compared to those proud men. We have to redeem our lives here by regular tribute payments [*jizya*] or else face death-dealing punishment" (Rubenstein 2015, 69). A similar exchange continues to this day whenever Western observers chastise Mideast Christian minorities for not "standing up for themselves."

929, on Palm Sunday,* another wave of atrocities broke out; churches were destroyed and Christians slaughtered. In 936, "the Muslims in Jerusalem made a rising and burnt down the Church of the Resurrection [the Holy Sepulchre] which they plundered, and destroyed all they could of it," records one Muslim chronicler.[8] As Rodney Stark puts it, "Almost generation after generation, Christian writers recorded acts of persecution and harassment, to the point of slaughter and destruction, suffered at the hands of Muslim [Arab, Persian, and Turkish] rulers."[9]

That said, the persecution and carnage had reached apocalyptic levels by the 1090s.

THE CALL FROM CLERMONT

It was in this context that, on November 27, 1095, Pope Urban II (r. 1088–1099) made his famous appeal to the knights of Christendom. According to Robert the Monk, who may have been present at the Council of Clermont in France, Urban held nothing back:

> They [Muslim Turks] have completely destroyed some of God's churches and they have converted others to the uses of their own cult [mosques]. They ruin the altars with filth and defilement. They circumcise Christians and smear the blood from the circumcision over the altars or throw it into the baptismal fonts. They are pleased to kill others by cutting open their bellies, extracting the end of their intestines, and tying it to a stake. Then, with flogging, they drive their victims around the stake until, when their viscera have spilled out, they fall dead on the ground. They tie others, again, to stakes and shoot arrows at them; they seize others, stretch out their necks, and

---

* As something of a modern-day parallel, on Palm Sunday, April 9, 2017, Islamic terrorists bombed two Coptic Christian churches in Egypt, leaving forty-five worshippers dead and dozens injured. In fact, Muslim terror attacks on churches during Christian holidays—especially Christmas Eve, Easter, and New Year's Eve, which in Eastern Orthodox nations are celebrated in church—are regular occurrences and in recent years have left hundreds dead in Muslim nations from Pakistan to Nigeria. (See, "Why Easter Brings Out the Worst in Islam," at www.RaymondIbrahim.com, for more.)

try to see whether they can cut off their heads with a single blow of a naked sword. And what shall I say about the shocking rape of women? . . . Who is to revenge all this, who is to repair this damage, if you do not do it? . . . Rise up and remember the manly deeds of your ancestors, the prowess and greatness of Charlemagne, of his son Louis, and of your other kings, who destroyed pagan [and Muslim] kingdoms and planted the holy church in their territories.[10]

When Urban concluded by calling on Western Christians to undertake an armed pilgrimage to Jerusalem—both to help fellow Christians and to liberate the Sepulchre of Christ—all in assembly, lay and laity alike, shouted a resounding, "God wills it!"

This was a long time coming. Just as the Turks were hardly the first Muslims to attack Christendom, so was Urban hardly the first Christian leader to try to rally Christendom against Islam in the spirit of a holy war. More than two centuries earlier and due to constant Muslim raids on churches in Rome and elsewhere, popes Leo IV (d. 855), Nicolas I (d. 867), and John VIII (d. 872) also offered Christians who died fighting Muslims remission of sins. In his *Taktika,* Byzantine emperor Leo VI (d. 912) "speaks with some respect of the doctrine of the [Islamic] holy war and of its military value, and even suggests that Christians might be well advised to adopting something of the kind."[11] Decades later Emperor Nikephoros Phokas tried "in vain to persuade the Byzantine church to adopt a doctrine similar to the Muslim doctrine of martyrdom," to no avail.[12]

Similarly, after Egyptian Fatimid caliph Hakim bi-Amr Allah (r. 996–1021) ordered the destruction of some thirty thousand churches in Egypt and Greater Syria[13]—including Jerusalem's Church of the Holy Sepulchre, which was torn to its foundations and Christ's tomb vandalized in 1009—Pope Sergius IV (d. 1012) issued an encyclical mourning its "destruction," which "plunged the entire church and the city of Rome into deep grief and distress." Accordingly, "with the Lord's help we intend to kill all these enemies and restore the Redeemer's Holy Sepulchre." Christians from everywhere were called to come to the fight and fear nothing, "for God has promised that whoever loses the present life for the sake of Christ will gain another life which he will never lose. For this is not a battle for an earthly kingdom, but for the eternal Lord."[14]

Even Pope Urban's immediate predecessor, Pope Gregory VII (d. 1085), had issued an encyclical three years after Manzikert, "to all who are willing to defend the Christian faith." In it, he descried "a race of pagans"—elsewhere he refers to them as "Saracens"—who, "with pitiable cruelty has already almost up to the walls of Constantinople laid waste and with tyrannical violence has seized everything; it has slaughtered like cattle many thousands of Christians."[15] Grieving was not enough: "The example of our Redeemer and the duty of brotherly love demand that we set our hearts on delivering our siblings. Just as He offered His life for us, so we should offer our lives for our siblings."[16]

In short, when he spoke at Clermont in 1095, Pope Urban was drawing on a long legacy. After the Fatimid Shia caliph had annihilated the original Church of the Holy Sepulchre in 1009, a smaller structure had been rebuilt around Christendom's holiest site in 1048; now this too was under attack, Urban explained, by those "enslaved by demons."[17] Christians had to act now or never.

For whatever reason—chroniclers cited the work of the Holy Spirit—Urban accomplished what his predecessors could not. His emissaries traveled far and wide and the message at Clermont snowballed to every corner of Western Christendom. The Saracens were once again persecuting the faithful, once again defiling the Lord's tomb. As many as one hundred thousand people from all walks of life—not just knights, but peasants and priests, women and children—hastened to "take the cross"* and prepare for an armed pilgrimage to Jerusalem.[18] Fulcher of Chartres, a priest and chronicler who traveled with the earliest crusaders, wondered at what he saw: "Little by little and day by day the army grew. . . . You could see a countless number from many lands and of many languages. . . . Whoever heard of such a mixture of languages in one army?" Along with the

---

* Crosses were generally sewn on the garments of those taking the cross as a reminder of their pledge; others had crucifixes tattooed on their bodies.

Franks who formed the core, Englishmen, Scots, Irishmen, Spaniards, Italians, Germans, and Greeks joined the marching armies. As strange as these diverse peoples were to one another, one thing united them, captured by the following anecdote relayed by a contemporary: "I heard that some barbarian people from I don't know what land were driven to our harbor [in France], and their language was so incomprehensible that, when it failed them, they made the sign of the cross with their fingers; by these gestures they showed what they could not indicate with words, that because of their faith they set out on the journey."[19]

Something new was happening; the Europeans who had fought and died against Islam in the preceding centuries had bought the continent the necessary time to mature in strength and confidence. In 1095, coastal Europe had long ceased to be the hunting grounds for slavers; once worthy of song, repelling Muslim invaders was now no great feat. Everywhere knights and men of war—not just the Franks but the even more martial Normans, or "North Men"—vied with each other in deeds of valor. The latter, Christianized descendants of Vikings who settled on the continent, had already defeated and expelled the Muslims from Sicily in 1091—then a major victory over Islam. In other words, when Urban made his call in 1095, Christians everywhere felt ready to take the war to—instead of always receiving it from—the ancient foe.

LOVE AND JUSTICE, SIN AND HELL

Having discussed the doctrine of jihad and its motivations at some length (see Introduction) here it is necessary to compare and contrast the motivations behind the crusades. Shocking as it may seem, love—not of the modern, sentimental variety, but a medieval, muscular one, characterized by Christian altruism, *agape*—was the primary driving force behind the crusades. As foremost crusade historian Jonathan Riley-Smith puts it, "The crusaders, moved by love of God and their neighbor, renouncing wives, children, and earthly possessions, and adopting temporary poverty and chastity, were described as going into a voluntary exile."[20]

Despite popular depictions of crusaders as prototypical European imperialists cynically exploiting faith, recent scholarship has proven the opposite,[21] that every crusader "risked his life, social status, and all his possessions when he took the cross."[22] Nor was it "those with the least to lose who took up the cross, but rather those with the most."[23] Great lords of vast estates—not dispossessed "second sons," as once believed—parted with their wealth and possessions upon taking the cross.*

"It was a miraculous sight," wrote one contemporary. "Everyone bought high and sold low; whatever could be used on the journey was expensive, since they were in a hurry; they sold cheaply whatever items of value they had piled up; what neither prison nor torture could have wrung from them just a short time before they now sold for a few paltry coins."[24] But it was worth it all[†] for the "message was clear," writes Thomas Madden: "Christ was crucified again in the persecution of his faithful and the defilement of his sanctuaries."[25] Both needed rescuing; both offered an opportunity to fulfill one of Christ's two greatest commandments: "Love God with all your heart" and "love your neighbor as yourself" (Luke 10:27).

The warrior-monks of the military orders that later developed and who were dedicated to protecting Christian pilgrims to the Holy Land especially conformed to these muscular notions of love. A few years after the founding of the Knights Templar in 1120, Pope Innocent II praised them thusly: "Like true Israelites and warriors most versed in holy battle, on fire with the flame of true love, you carry out in your deeds the words of the Gospel,

---

* Godfrey of Bouillon, a major leader of the First Crusade, sold much of his property and settled several ongoing disputes to his disadvantage in order to raise the sums necessary to fund his contingent of knights. The powerful magnate Raymond IV of Toulouse—whose resources were greater than those of most kings—divested himself of all properties, took the cross, and set off for the Holy Land, where he fought and died (see Stark 2009, 130; Rubenstein 2008, 93; Madden 2007, 23).

† While rebuking the cynical Europeans of his time who "with insolent lips . . . blame this novel enterprise," the crusades, Ekkehard of Aurach (d. 1126), a German abbot, elaborated: "They, like the Epicureans, prefer the broad way of pleasure to the narrow way of God's service. To them love of the world [is] wisdom and those who despise it are fools . . . I, however . . . exalt the glorious men of our time who have overcome the kingdoms of this world and who, for the sake of the blessed Shepherd who sought the hundredth sheep that was lost, have left wife and child, principalities and riches, and have taken their lives in their hands" (J. Robinson 1904, 316–318).

in which it is said, 'Greater love has no man than this, that a man lay down his life for his friends [John 15:13].'" Similarly, the Knights Hospitaller, originally dedicated to the service of the sick and needy, soon found that "the warfare in which their order was engaged had a symbiotic relationship to the care of the sick poor."[26]

Much of this is incomprehensible to the modern West, including (if not especially) its Christians. How could the crusaders be motivated by love and piety, considering all the brutal violence and bloodshed they committed? Not only is such a question anachronistic—violence was part and parcel of the medieval world—but centuries before Islam, Christian theologians had concluded that "the so called charity texts of the New Testament that preached passivism and forgiveness, not retaliation, were firmly defined as applying to the beliefs and behavior of the private person" and not the state, explains historian Christopher Tyerman. Christ himself distinguished between political and spiritual obligations (Matt. 22:21). He praised a Roman centurion without calling on him to "repent" by resigning from one of the most brutal militaries of history (Matt. 8: 5–13). When a group of soldiers asked John the Baptist how they should repent, he advised them always to be content with their army wages (Luke 3:14). Paul urged Christians to pray for "kings and all that are in authority" (1 Tim. 2:2). In short, "there was no intrinsic contradiction in a doctrine of personal, individual forgiveness condoning certain forms of necessary public violence to ensure the security in which, in St. Paul's phrase, Christians 'may lead a quiet and peaceable life in all godliness and honesty' (1 Tim. 2:2)."[27] Or as that chief articulator of "Just War" theory, Saint Augustine (d. 430), concluded, "It is the injustice of the opposing side, that lays on the wise man the duty to wage war."[28] Riley-Smith elaborates:

> What was evil in war itself? Augustine had asked. The real evils were not the deaths of those who would have died anyway, but the love of violence, cruelty, and enmity; it was generally to punish such that good men undertook wars in obedience to God or some lawful authority. . . . So the case for each expedition had to be a good one and

a feature of papal general letters was the care taken in arguing it as cogently as possible. Expeditions to the Levant, North Africa, or the Iberian Peninsula could be justified as responses to present Muslim aggression or as rightful attempts to recover Christian territory which had been injuriously seized in the past.[29]

But it was not all justice and altruism; another form of love—that of eternal self-preservation—motivated those who took the cross.* "Whoever shall set forth to liberate the church of God at Jerusalem for the sake of devotion alone and not to obtain honor or money will be able to substitute that journey for all penance," Pope Urban had decreed at Clermont.[30] It is scarcely possible for modern Western people to appreciate the significance of such a claim. Medieval Christians, Catholic and Orthodox, truly believed in sin; they were "used to dwelling on their behavioral shortcomings, and convinced that their spiritual welfare depended on taking positive action."[31]

> The expectation of eternal punishment, comprising pain far greater than any sensation felt during this life, was widespread and potent. Belief in the physical reality of the agonies of Hell reinforced the idea that penitential acts, such as pilgrimage or crusading, should likewise require endurance and suffering. . . . The idea that one's actions in this life affected one's eternal fate was the central plank of crusade ideology.[32]

There was another, related boon: Western knights were constantly sinning by engaging in violence against fellow Christian knights. But what could they do? Theirs was a martial culture; they were born in and bred on war; it is what they did—and arguably liked—best. Yet some were

---

* "It is no exaggeration to say that a crusade was for an individual only secondarily about service in arms to God or the benefiting of the church or Christianity; it was primarily about benefiting himself, since he was engaged in an act of self-sanctification" (Riley-Smith 2008, 33).

guilt-ridden at constantly breaking Christ's commands for love and peace. The case of Tancred (1075–1112), a young Norman knight whose exploits in the First Crusade were celebrated during his own (short) lifetime, is instructive. His friend, Ralph of Caen, records Tancred's inner turmoil at trying to reconcile his disposition for war with his devotion to Christ, a dilemma that was solved at Clermont:

> As an adolescent he excelled young men in his skill at arms, while surpassing old men in the seriousness of his behavior. . . . A careful student of God's commandments, he strove to listen to what he was told. . . . He deemed it wrong to disparage anyone, even when they disparaged him. . . . He preferred vigils to sleep, labor to rest, hunger to satiety, struggle to pleasure, the essential to the sumptuous. Fame and glory alone moved his young mind. But the deeds that acquired honor for him also inflicted on him a deep and damaging mood. For he spared neither his own blood nor an enemy's. Turning these points over in his mind, he would burn with anxiety, for he understood that his military engagements contradicted the Lord's command. The Lord orders that if one cheek is struck, the other is to be offered to the attacker, but the military life does not spare even family blood. The Lord admonishes us also to give a coat to one asking for a tunic, but military necessity urges that both these things and anything else beyond them must be taken as plunder. If a moment of rest were ever permitted to this wise man [Tancred], the opposition between his two callings would sap him of his boldness. But after Pope Urban's proclamation assigned remission of sins to any Christian who would fight against the gentiles [Muslims], then the strength of the man was seemingly roused from its slumber, his power returned, his eyes opened, his bravery redoubled. Previously, as noted, his mind had been of two parts, uncertain which path to follow—the Gospel or the world? But now that his skill as a soldier turned to the service of Christ the twofold reason for fighting enthused the man greater than you could believe.[33]

Cognizant of the innate bellicosity of Western knights,* Urban offered them a proper way to indulge it: "Let those who are accustomed to wage private wars wastefully even against Believers," he said "go forth against the Infidels in a battle worthy to be undertaken now and to be finished in victory. Now, let those who until recently existed as plunderers, be soldiers of Christ; now, let those who formerly contended against brothers and re-lations, rightly fight barbarians."[34] In short, "Soldiers of Hell, become sol-diers of the living God!"[35]

THE CRUSADERS' VIA DOLOROSA

Because the First Crusade became a mass movement from many corners of Christendom, different groups set off at different times. Many enthused peasants—men, women, and children—armed only with faith, or by today's standards, fanaticism, were first to set off. Such "popular" or "people's" crusades often ended in disaster. The charismatic preacher Peter the Her-mit and some twenty thousand marching peasants reached Constantinople in late 1096. Emperor Alexios, taking pity on the bedraggled throng and cognizant that faith alone would not suffice against the Turks, urged them to wait for their professional counterparts, the knights. The people refused and crossed the Hellespont, the last water barrier between Constantinople and Muslim-occupied Asia Minor.

Landing in the Nicaean inland, they "fell into the Turkish ambuscade and were miserably slaughtered," recollected Alexios's daughter, Princess Anna Comnena: "So great a multitude of Kelts and Normans died by the Ishmaelite sword that when they gathered the remains of the fallen, lying on every side, they heaped up, I will not say a mighty ridge or hill or peak, but a mountain of considerable height and depth and width, so huge was the mass of bones."[36]

Those captured underwent another trial: "Some of the prisoners were

---

* Decades before Urban, "the popes had been attempting to achieve a 'truce of God' among the feudal nobility, many of whom seemed inclined to make war, even on their friends, just for the sake of a good fight. After all, it was what they had trained to do every day since early childhood" (Stark 2009, 4).

challenged about their faith, and ordered to renounce Christ, but they proclaimed Christ with steady heart and voice, and were decapitated," writes
Guibert of Nogent (b. 1054). The fate of those kept alive—as usual, the
young and comely—was often worse:

> The Turks divided up among themselves some of the captives, whose
> lives they had spared—or rather reserved for a more painful death—
> and submitted them to dismal servitude at the hands of cruel mas-
> ters. Some were exposed in public, like targets, and were pierced
> by arrows; others were given away as gifts, while others were sold
> outright . . . [and taken to Khorasan and Antioch where] they would
> endure wretched slavery under the worst masters imaginable. They
> underwent a torture much longer than that endured by those whose
> heads were severed swiftly by the sword.[37]

How the Islamic lords of Asia Minor must have laughed! The indigenous Christian population of Anatolia having been annihilated in the years
following Manzikert, foreign Christians were now marching straight to the
Muslims for the same treatment.

A year later, in 1097, the crusading militias began arriving at Constantinople. Alexios received and generally treated them well, before ferrying
them to the lions' den. Once there, they were met by a frightful sight: "Oh,
how many severed heads and bones of the dead lying on the plains did we
then find beyond Nicomedia near the sea!" wrote Fulcher. They had come
upon the remains of the People's Crusade. "Moved to compassion by this,
we shed many tears there."[38]

Following their dirge, the Western knights viciously besieged the walls
of Nicaea, now the Seljuk capital. A month later, on June 19, 1097, it capitulated (not to the heavily armored newcomers but to the more diplomatic Alexios, who had followed the crusaders with his own army). The
crusaders continued their southward march through Anatolia. Bohemond,
a larger-than-life Norman,* and his nephew, the aforesaid Tancred, led the

---

* Byzantine princess Anna Comnena's vivid description of the man is worth relaying:
Bohemond was "a marvel for the eyes to behold, and his reputation was terrifying . . . he

van; Godfrey, lord of Bouillon and descendant of Charlemagne, and Raymond, count of Toulouse and veteran fighter against Muslims in Spain, brought the rear. Suddenly, some thirty thousand Muslim horsemen, out to avenge Nicaea, ambushed Bohemond. There, at Dorylaeum, the Westerners got their first real taste of nomadic warfare: "The Turks, with clashing of weapons and shrieking,[†] fiercely let loose a shower of arrows," writes Fulcher. "Stunned and almost dead and with many injured, we straightway turned our backs in flight. Nor is this to be wondered at since such fighting was unknown to any of us."[39]

Bohemond dispatched a messenger to Godfrey and Raymond in the rear: "If they would like to see the beginnings of the battle with the Turks, what they want is now here: come quickly." They rushed forth and, "when our men saw the enemy army face-to-face, they wondered where in the world such an infinite number of people had come from. Turks, Arabs, and Saracens stood out among the others," writes Guibert. The Muslims were intent on annihilating the insolent newcomers. Crusade leaders exhorted their men to "surrender your minds and bodies to the faith of the Lord of the Cross, and take up arms against this pile of husks, these little creatures who are hardly men at all." The heartened men "drew up their battle lines in an orderly fashion" and gave battle. Now it was the Muslims' turn to become acquainted with Western warfare; shocked and awed by the heavy cavalry charges, they galloped off, notwithstanding their vast numbers. Many thousands from both sides were slain.[40]

Turks and Franks would eventually become intimately acquainted with each other's arms and fighting style. The arrow and horse remained supreme for the former. Though the following account describes an encounter that occurred several decades later, it reflects what the First Crusaders must have experienced: "The Turks shot at us with such rapidity as to darken the

---

was so tall in stature that he overtopped the tallest by nearly one cubit, narrow in the waist and loins, with broad shoulders and a deep chest and powerful arms. . . . A certain charm hung about this man but was partly marred by a general air of the horrible" (Ross 1977, 325).

† Guibert of Nogent notes that "they shouted their war-like battle-cry in the horrible tones of their language," an apparent reference to the ancient battle cry of jihad— "Allahu Akbar"—which was (then) unrecognizable to Western ears (2008, 58).

heavens as neither rain nor hail could do, so that we suffered many casualties; and when the first had emptied their quivers and shot their bolts the second wave, in which there were yet more horsemen, came after them and began to shoot faster than could be believed."[41] Muslim sources also boast of the devastation caused among the crusaders by "clouds" or "showers" of arrows.[42] One tells of how "in one charred [Frankish] corpse more than forty arrows were found"; another says "dead horses [were seen] bristling like hedgehogs with the arrows sticking out of them."[43]

Even so, "in hand-to-hand conflict, horseman against horseman, foot-soldier against foot-soldier, the Europeans and Byzantines had the better of the Turks."[44] Muslims also conceded this point;* to them the Western knights were fearless mountains of steel, seen as "'leftovers from the race of Ad' [meaning giants] or not men at all. They carried stout broad-headed lances or spears of tempered steel."[45]

After Dorylaeum, the crusaders marched largely unopposed for three months until they reached Antioch. But where the Turks had failed, nature took over: starvation, thirst, disease, exhaustion, and delirium plagued the marching warriors. Many died: "You could see the many cemeteries where our pilgrims were buried along the footpaths, on the plains, and in the woods."[46] Some abandoned the quest; others persisted to the bitter end.

Indigenous Eastern Christians marveled at the sight of these foreign titans who, with the crucifix etched on them, had come to fight and kill the enemies of Christ: "When we passed by the villages of the Armenians," Fulcher writes, "it was astonishing to see them advance toward us with crosses and standards, kissing our feet and garments most humbly for love of God, because they had heard there that we would defend them from the

---

* Usamah bin Muniqdh (b. 1095) tells of a crusader who once came across eight Arab warriors. He demanded their camels; they refused and mocked him. One by one the knight proceeded to kill or incapacitate four of them. Then he again demanded the camels of the remaining four, "Otherwise I shall annihilate you!" The Muslims passively stood there as he harnessed and led off four of their camels, "under our very eyes, for we were helpless with regard to him. . . . Thus he returned with his booty; and he was only one while we were eight men!" (Wheatcroft 2005, 168).

Turks under whose yoke they had been oppressed for a long time."⁴⁷ Such greetings occurred frequently.†

ANTIOCH: HERE "THE NAME CHRISTIAN WAS" BORN

By October 1097, the crusaders were besieging the walls of Antioch. Formerly one of Christendom's oldest and greatest cities, Antioch was now a shadow of its self. Its Turkic ruler, Yaghi-Siyan, had long oppressed its Christian *dhimmis*, including by demanding an increase of *jizya* tribute, launching sporadic persecutions, forcing Christians on pain of death to convert to Islam, and converting Antioch's main cathedral into a horse stable.⁴⁸ When Yaghi-Siyan learned that the crusaders were approaching, he duped the Christian males outside and locked the city's gates, lest they turn on him during the siege. When they begged entry to take care of their women and children, the Turk promised he would take care of them himself.

Such is the Muslim account. Fulcher of Chartres relates something different: "Alas! How many Christians, Greeks, Syrians, and Armenians, who lived in the city, were killed by the maddened Turks. With the Franks looking on, they threw outside the walls the heads of those killed, with their *petrariae* [catapults] and slings. This especially grieved our people."⁴⁹

In response—and because the warrior aristocracy of Europe had no qualms about giving tit for tat—Bohemond "brought those [Muslims] he had captured back to the gate of the city, where, to terrify the citizens who were watching, he ordered that they be decapitated" and their severed heads catapulted over the city walls. European chroniclers had no illusions concerning who relied on and had perfected such terror tactics. After a Muslim cavalry sallied forth and was decimated, "they [Franks] cut off the heads of one hundred of those who had fallen in battle, and hung them before the walls of Antioch for the besieged Turks to look at," writes Guibert of Nogent, adding, "It is, of course, the custom of the Gentiles [meaning Muslims] to keep the decapitated heads and to display them as a sign of victory."⁵⁰

---

† In another instance, "when the Christians, evidently Greeks and Syrians . . . found that the Franks had come, they were especially filled with great joy" (Peters 1971, 72; cf. Stark 2009, 153, and Rubenstein 2008, 117).

Eight months into the siege, Antioch still withstood the crusaders. The latter, having long exhausted their provisions, were now starving and reduced to eating dogs, rats, and thistles; and despite rumors of a balmy Mediterranean clime, a particularly severe winter set in. Relief finally came by way of treachery. A Muslim tower captain—apparently an Armenian Christian who had converted to Islam during Yaghi-Siyan's persecutions—made a deal with Bohemond (which included (re)converting to Christianity). On June 3, the emaciated Europeans, having clandestinely entered under the cover of night, were running amok in the streets of Antioch, slaughtering anyone in sight. For, "as they recalled the sufferings they had endured during the siege, they thought that the blows that they were giving could not match the starvations, more bitter than death, that they had endured."[51] The result was a bloodbath not unlike those visited upon Christian cities all throughout Anatolia and Armenia at the hands of the Turks throughout the preceding decades. Reported one eyewitness: "All streets of the city on every side were full of corpses, so that no one could endure to be there because of the stench, nor could anyone walk along the narrow paths of the city except over the corpses of the dead."[52] Some Muslims, including Yaghi-Siyan, managed to escape; local Christians tracked, killed, and brought their former persecutor's head back to Bohemond, whose standard was by now firmly planted in Antioch.

On the very next day, Kerbogha, the *atabeg,* or Turkish lord, of Mosul, arrived with an enormous relief force—some thirty-five thousand fighters and their entourage, described by awestruck Europeans as an opulent city on horseback. Antioch was quickly blockaded and they who only yesterday were the besiegers became the besieged. Another famine struck—by the time the crusaders took Antioch, most of its stores had been depleted by the besieged Muslims—and the holed-up crusaders were again reduced to eating filth and shoes, and drinking horse blood.

After marching thousands of miles and suffering thousands of difficulties, they were granted nary a day to celebrate the liberation of, and recuperate in, Antioch. Was God *not* on their side? These were times to try men's souls. Morale reached a new low, as captured in the lament of Guy,

Bohemond's brother, who was not with them but heard of the plight of the crusaders:

> All powerful God, whose judgement never errs, who never permits the unjust to triumph over the just, why have you betrayed those who, out of love for you, have given themselves over to daily torment and death, who have left their relatives, wives, sons, the greatest honors, their native land, and why have you exposed them, without the aid of your protection, to be cut down by the swords of abominable men? . . . But so be it. It may be that you want them to die for you, and that you will crown them with glory and honor, yet. . . . You have plunged the entire Christian world into the depths of despair and incredulity, and you have provoked the worst men [Muslims/Turks] to display relentless aggression against your people. From this day forth no man will expect anything great from you, since those who believed themselves dearer to you than all other mortals have been subjected to such an unworthy fate. Therefore, O most gracious one, from now on why should they call upon you, when your own people will expect such a death?[53]

There was nothing the famished, desperate, and outnumbered crusaders could do but sally forth and meet the hordes besieging them. But before doing so, they resorted to a final effort at "dialogue" (such as it was then between Christians and Muslims).

Peter the Hermit, the fugitive leader of the People's Crusade who had managed to escape the slaughter and later joined the main army, was summoned and told to explain "to this contemptible contingent of Turks" why (in keeping with Just War theory) Christians were justified in taking Antioch, whereas Muslims were not. Peter set out with a delegation and interpreters. Once brought before Kerbogha, the hermit began:

> Our leaders and elders are greatly astonished that you would boldly and arrogantly enter into Christian land and their land. We think

and believe—possibly—that you have come here because you want to become Christians. Or maybe you have come here because you want to wrong the Christians in every way possible. All the same, our leaders ask that you at once leave God's land and the Christians' land. . . . And they will allow you to take all of your possessions with you.[54]

The proud Muslim was outraged: "We neither desire your God nor want your Christianity, and we spit on them and you!" In a rant laden with Islamic notions concerning when war is and is not justified—including references to "loyalty and enmity"—he continued:

Go back right away and tell your elders that if they desire to become Turks [synonymous for Latin writers with "Muslim"] in all things and if they wish to renounce your God whom you submissively worship and to repudiate your laws, then we will give them this land and more than enough from our land, including cities and castles such that . . . all of you will become knights and be like us, and we will always hold them to be the closest friends. Otherwise, let them know that they will all be punished by death, or else led to Khorasan where they will be forever throughout all time the captive slaves of us and our children.[55]

Peter returned to Antioch and relayed the message. So it would be war. But first, a three-day fast was ordered; the little food available was given to the horses. Then everyone, lord and commoner, "marched through the city squares, stopping at churches and calling on God's aid, barefoot and crying, beating their breasts, so grief stricken that father would not greet son, brother would not look at brother," to quote Raymond of Aguilers, who would later ride out with the army. On the morning of June 28, 1098, "everyone received the Eucharist and offered themselves to die for . . . God, if He should wish."[56] Then some twenty thousand knights—the entire crusading army minus two hundred left to defend Antioch—issued out of its gates.

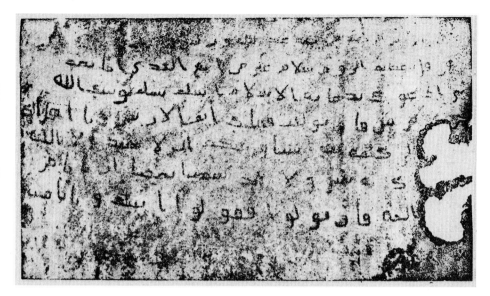

Image of Prophet Muhammad's purported letter ordering Emperor Heraclius to "submit [to Islam] and have peace" (c. 628). The missive was rejected and jihad unleashed on Christendom via Koran 9:29. Largely ignored by Western historiography, it remains an important point of reference for Muslims.

Greek (or Sea) Fire played a pivotal role in saving Constantinople from the Arabs during the First (674-678) and Second (717-718) Sieges.

A monument of Pelayo at Covadonga, where he inflicted the first major defeat of the invading Muslim armies in 722. Earlier he proclaimed that "Christ is our hope that through this little mountain, which you see, the well-being of Spain . . . will be restored." Though it took centuries of wars, Pelayo's prediction proved true. *Photograph by Tony Rotondas.*

Battle of Tours, France, where Charles Martel—who "as a hammer of iron" that "dashed and smote . . . his enemies"—and his Franks "wrought a great slaughter upon the enemies of Christian faith" in 732.

A painting depicting and titled, "The Harem." Fair (skinned, haired, and/or eyed) concubines and slaves were highly valued in the Islamic world and a primary motivation behind countless Muslim raids on Europe, which saw more than five million Christians enslaved.

A prototypical crusader and avowed enemy of Islam, Emperor Nikephoras II Phokas (912-969) brought "frightful and heavy slaughter upon Muslims" in his bid to reclaim former Christian territory. Under his rule the Byzantine Empire made an unprecedented comeback against Islam, since its domino-like collapse following the Yarmuk disaster in 636.

Aftermath of the Battle of Manzikert (1071). A shackled Romanus IV Diogenes (1030-1072)—the first Roman emperor to be captured in over a thousand years—is hauled off to the sultan's tent.

A medieval French illustration of Sultan Muhammad triumphing over Romanus.

The crusader siege of Antioch (1097-98). Due to Antioch's symbolic significance—"it was here that the name Christian was first employed" the crusaders later reminisced—and the desperate odds stacked against the Europeans, its capture held special significance for them.

Bohemond (1054-1111) was crowned prince of Antioch due to his role in its capture. A giant and imposing figure, the Norman was "a marvel for the eyes to behold, and his reputation was terrifying," wrote Anna Comnena. Although "a certain charm hung about this man," it "was partly marred by a general air of the horrible."

The crusader entry into Jerusalem, July 15, 1099. After the massacre of their enemies, "going to the Sepulchre of the Lord and His glorious Temple, the clerics and also the laity, singing a new song unto the Lord in a high-sounding voice of exultation, and making offerings and most humble supplications, joyously visited the Holy Place as they had so long desired to do."

A portrait of Saladin (1137-1193) made during his lifetime. Emboldened by his decisive victory at Hattin, the sultan—who "spoke of nothing else [but jihad]"—entertained hopes of invading Europe "so as to free the earth of anyone who does not believe in Allah, or die in the attempt."

The Battle of Hattin (July 3-4, 1187) marked the beginning of the end of the crusader presence in the Mideast. Surrounded by an ever shrinking ring of fire and foes, the crusaders were strangled into defeat.

A fifteenth century manuscript illustrates the execution of Raynald of Châtillon (1125-1187)—that most "powerful and violent infidel"—following his defiant refusal to renounce Christ and embrace Islam at the hands of Saladin.

An early image of an Almoravid, a reminder that the jihadi Africans were radically different—from race to saddle—than the Christian Spain they invaded in three major waves.

As highlighted in this painting, the turning point at Las Navas de Tolosa (1212) came when the giant king, Sancho VII of Navarre, smashed through the Muslim line and routed the African slave soldiers chained around Caliph Muhammad's tent.

Uzbek Khan (r. 1313-1341), who did much to Islamize the Mongols, condemns Grand Prince Mikhail Yaroslavich (1271-1319)—later canonized by the Russian Orthodox Church—to a slow and painful death.

After the Turkic victory at Nicopolis (1396), as many as ten thousand crusader prisoners were stripped naked and ritually beheaded after refusing to convert to Islam on Ottoman sultan Bayezid's orders.

Emperor Manuel II Palaiologos (1350-1425) spent his entire life theologically and militarily resisting the Turks. When in 2006 Pope Benedict passingly quoted Manuel's observation that Muhammad brought "things only evil and inhuman, such as his command to spread by the sword the faith he preached," Muslim riots erupted, churches were burned, and an Italian nun was murdered in Somalia.

An Ottoman miniature of the *devshirme*. Balkan Christian subjects were compelled to make an annual "blood tribute" payable in their sons. The best of these would be marched off "just as if they were so many sheep," and "either persuaded or forced to be circumcised and made Muslim." Those who survived a Spartan "training system" that partially consisted of "moral degradation and humiliation," often emerged as the most fearsome and fanatical of all jihadis, Janissaries.

Following his capture at the battle of Ankara (1402), the once unstoppable sultan and scourge of Christendom, Bayezid (1354-1403), was imprisoned and continuously humiliated by his host, Timur, another "Sword of Allah." "Within eight months he was dead from an apoplectic seizure— or perhaps by his own hand."

In his bid to conquer Constantinople, the relentless Muhammad II (1432-81) ordered teams of engineers, hundreds of men, and thousands of oxen to haul Ottoman warships out of the Bosporus, over a hill, and back down the opposite slope into the Golden Horn, thereby bypassing the harbor chain.

Ottoman sultan Muhammad II triumphantly enters Constantinople. Soon afterwards, "this forerunner of Antichrist mounted upon the Holy Table [of Hagia Sophia] to utter forth his own prayers," thereby "turning the Great Church into a heathen shrine for his god and his Mahomet."

The Cathedral of Otranto, Italy, houses the remains of 800 Christians ritually beheaded (their archbishop was sawed in half) for refusing to renounce Christ for Muhammad following an Ottoman invasion in 1480. *Photograph by Laurent Massoptier.*

Ivan III, Grand Prince of Moscow and "Gatherer of Russian Lands," spurns Ahmed Khan's demand for jizya through his emissaries, leading to the Great Stand on the Ugra in 1480 and Russian liberation from the Tatar Yoke.

The capitulation of Granada to King Ferdinand and Queen Isabella in 1492. "After so much labor, expense, death, and shedding of blood," the monarchs later wrote, "this kingdom of Granada which was occupied for over seven hundred and eighty years by the infidels," was now liberated.

After withstanding, up till then, history's most sustained bombardment—130,000 Ottoman cannon balls were fired in total—the Knights of Saint John, led by Jean Parisot de Valette, give thanks for the delivery of Malta, which by then looked worse than "the image of hell" itself.

Serbian Orthodox bishop Theodore of Vršac being skinned alive—a popular form of execution among the Turks—in 1594. Presaging the battle of Lepanto (1571), Famagusta fort's captured commander, Marco Antonio Bragadin, was skinned alive after refusing Islam.

The largest Muslim army ever to invade European territory—consisting of some 300,000 people and led by the "fanatically anti-Christian" Kara Mustafa (whose pavilion with Islamic standard appears)—came as late as 1683, engulfing and besieging Vienna.

Vienna was finally relieved on September 12 by another Holy League led by Polish king Jan Sobieski. "It is not a city alone that we have to save," he earlier argued, "but the whole of Christianity, of which the city of Vienna is the bulwark. The war is a holy one." Here Sobieski appears with his winged Hussars, who "struck fear in the hearts" of the jihadis.

The price of failure: on Christmas Day, 1683, Kara Mustafa—"who thought to have invaded the Western Empire, and carried everywhere fear and terror"—was strangled to death and his head sent to Sultan Muhammad IV, who months earlier had placed "the standard of the Prophet . . . into his hands for the extirpation of infidels, and the increase of Muslemen."

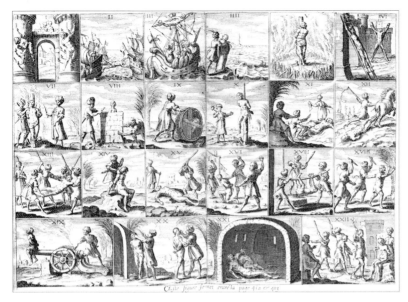

An etching from Father Pierre Dan's book on Barbary (1636) depicting twenty-two ways Muslim masters tortured their Christian slaves, including impalement, drowning, burning, dismembering, and crucifixion. As John Foxe explained in his *Book of Martyrs*, "In no part of the globe are Christians so hated, or treated with such severity, as at Algiers." Captain O'Brian's message to Thomas Jefferson that "our sufferings are beyond our expression or your conception" was, obviously, no exaggeration.

Before it could even elect its first president, the newborn United States was attacked on the high seas, leading to its first war, on Barbary. When Jefferson and Adams asked Barbary's ambassador why they were attacking Americans, "The ambassador answered us that it was founded on the laws of their Prophet, that it was written in their Koran, that . . . it was their right and duty to make war upon them [all non-Muslims] wherever they could be found, and to make slaves of all they could take as prisoners, and that every Musselman who should be slain in battle was sure to go to Paradise."

Remnants of the first Serbian uprising of 1809 can still be seen in the fifteen-foot-high "Skull Tower" erected in Niš by the Turks. It originally contained 952 decapitated heads of Serbian fighters. *Photograph by Chele Kula*

"The Bulgarian Martyresses," a Russian painting (1877) depicting Ottoman Bashi-Bazouks raping Christian women in 1876. American journalist MacGahan explained the ritual: "They would seize a woman, strip her carefully to her chemise, laying aside articles of clothing that were valuable, with any ornaments and jewels she might have about her. Then as many of them as cared would violate her, and the last man would kill her or not as the humor took him. . . . When a Mohammedan has killed a certain number of infidels he is sure of Paradise, no matter what his sins may be. . . . [T]he ordinary Mussulman takes the precept in broader acceptation, and counts women and children as well. . . . the *bashi bazouks*, in order to swell the count, ripped open pregnant women, and killed the unborn infants."

Diddling the time away by playing chess in his tent, the overly confident Kerbogha was taken unawares: "Didn't you tell me that there were few Franks and that they would never fight against me?" he barked at a subordinate. A wild battle commenced: the Muslims threw everything they had—even fire—at the crusaders; the desperate knights fought with a feral fury. "Accounts told of knights bristling like porcupines with arrows, darts, and javelins, but still moving forward and fighting ferociously."[57] Their discipline, orderliness, and remarkably tight formations eventually caused the Muslim horsemen—accustomed as they were to overwhelming their enemies with darts—to panic and retreat en masse. Next, a scene reminiscent of when Muslims and Franks first fought 366 years earlier at Tours unfolded. The crusaders "spent the night there and, always on watch, guarded themselves well. For on the following day they thought the fighting would be renewed by the Saracens, but these, exceedingly terrified, had fled on the same night," much to the surprised relief of Charles Martel's descendants.[58]

All medieval chroniclers portray the victory as a miracle; were not angelic hosts, led by Saint George, patron saint of Christian warriors, espied by many fighting alongside the knights? However one wishes to interpret such visions, the fact remains: "Modern military historians have attempted to come up with a more rational explanation for the Franks' success, but the task is difficult. How did a force as spent and starved as the crusaders manage to overcome a superior, well-fed, and well-rested adversary?"[59] Even some Muslims gnashed their teeth in frustration: "The Muslims were completely routed without striking a single blow or firing a single arrow," disgustedly wrote historian Ibn al-Athir (b. 1160). "The only Muslims to stand firm were a detachment of warriors from the Holy Land, who fought to acquire merit in Allah's eyes and to seek martyrdom. The Franks killed them by the thousand and stripped their camp of food and possessions, equipment, horses and arms, with which they re-equipped themselves."[60] Unsurprisingly, then, Antioch came to take pride of place in crusading lore.

The crusaders remained and recuperated in the ancient Christian city for the rest of the year. They sent a letter to Pope Urban, chronicling their tragedies and triumphs and invited him to Antioch, stressing that "it was here that the name Christian was first employed."[61]

Meanwhile, Muslim elites—long used to seeing Christian infidels at their feet—raged and fumed. Mu'izzi, an otherwise urbane court poet in distant Persia, sought to incite a leading grandson of the great Sultan Muhammad (Alp Arslan) to root out every last vestige of Christianity from the region: "For the sake of the Arab religion, it is a duty, O ghazi* king, to clear the country of Syria of patriarchs and bishops, to clear the land of Rum [Anatolia] from priests and monks. You should kill those accursed dogs and wretched creatures. . . . You should take the Franks prisoner and cut their throats. . . . You should make polo-balls of the Franks' heads in the desert, and polo sticks from their hands and feet."[62]

MISSION ACCOMPLISHED

In early 1099, the remaining crusaders—many were now dead, either by famine or foe, while others remained in Antioch under Bohemond's rule—resumed their march to the ultimate goal: Jerusalem. On their way they captured the northern Syrian town of Bara, which they "completely depopulated by the slaughter of its citizens." Then they reached and besieged Ma'ra (or Marrat), but it would not fall. As the days passed, starvation, dehydration, and the Syrian sun plagued them in ways even worse than at Antioch; bestial desperation set in: "I shudder to tell that many of our people," confessed Fulcher of Chartres, "harassed by the madness of excessive hunger, cut pieces from the buttocks of Saracens already dead there, which they cooked, but when it was not yet roasted enough by the fire, they devoured it with savage mouth. So the besiegers rather than the besieged were tormented."[63]

When they finally managed to scale the walls of Ma'ra, the by now maddened crusaders looked more beast than man: "Their appearance in the city terrified the Muslims, who shut themselves up in their houses," writes Ibn al-Athir. "For three days the slaughter never stopped; the Franks killed

---

* See footnote on p. 207 for a discussion of the word *ghazi* and its cognates.

more than 100,000 men and took innumerable prisoners."[64] The crusaders recouped inside Ma'ra for a month before they set off for the final phase of their journey.

Finally, on June 7, 1099, the crusaders—now a fraction of their original numbers—stood before the walls of Jerusalem. They wept with joy and wasted no time in besieging the city. It held out; great thirst set in— the Muslims had earlier poisoned or blocked the local wells—and tempers flared. The Westerners eventually agreed to launch an all-out assault on July 14. Before that day came, and on the advice of a "certain man of God," they "embrace[d] a painful regime of fasting and of continual prayers of devotion."[65] The Muslim defenders atop the walls watched in astonishment as the army that had only recently besieged them became a large, barefoot, and unarmed procession. With crosses held high, the knights marched around the walls of Jerusalem—in conscious emulation of the ancient Hebrews' procession around Jericho before God delivered it to them—before congregating at the Mount of Olives, where they heard impassioned sermons.

Safe behind their walls, the Muslims jeered; they shot arrows at and killed several Europeans during the procession. And "to further provoke Christians to rage, Saracens [atop the walls] subjected crucifixes to ridicule and shame," wrote a contemporary.[†] "They spat on them and did not even refrain from urinating on them in the sight of all." As Anastasius of Sinai had more than four centuries earlier called the invading Arabs "friends of demons" for desecrating Christian symbols and sacraments, so now the "enemies mocking us in the city" were seen as "limbs of those other enemies [demons], lesser and weaker versions of their masters." The crusaders were exhorted to ignore the sacrilege and "think on Christ, who until today has been outlawed and crucified in this city!"[66]

The final siege began on the night of July 13–14. "This side worked willingly to capture the city for [love of] their God," wrote Raymond of

---

† Islam's perennial contempt for Christian symbols, particularly the cross, appears regularly in the sources. In another instance, "Muslims put holy pictures [icons] to an insulting use, subjected images to various insults and dragged a crucifix through the streets at the tail of an ass. . . . Christian children who were captured . . . were made Muslim and taught to spit on the crucifixes" (Daniel 1962, 111).

Aguilers, while "the other side under compulsion resisted because of Muhammad's laws."[67] Siege towers were placed around different strategic points of the wall. The men on Godfrey's tower—he himself was perched atop it and wrought great havoc with his crossbow against the defenders—managed to capture a part of the wall, whence scaling ladders were quickly dropped and ascended by crusader after crusader. Some fought their way to and opened the city gates to the main force outside. They wildly stormed the city and massacred everyone in sight, mostly Muslims and Jews, but also a few indigenous Christians (most of whom had been expelled from the city before the siege, as at Antioch).[68]

Young Tancred, who was among the first to enter, hacked his way till he reached the Dome of the Rock, a mosque erected high above and looking down on the Sepulchre of Christ and decorated with Koran verses denouncing Christian truths: its "entryway was firm and inflexible, made of iron, but Tancred, harder than iron, beat at it, broke it, wore it down, and entered." He slaughtered his way into the building until he came face to face with a strange idol (possibly an elaborate candelabrum containing oriental images foreign to the Frank). Was it a Roman god, thought the bewildered man. No, it could only be one: "Wicked Mahummet! Evil Mahummet!" he cried while smiting it. "If only his companion were here now, the one to come! At this moment my feet would stomp on both Antichrists."[69]

Unlike Islam's longtime neighbors, the Byzantines, the newly arrived Westerners held vague (but negative) views concerning Muhammad. Even so, one theme was consistent and managed "to sum up his [Muhammad's] teachings," writes Guibert of Nogent, who was already middle-aged when Urban spoke at Clermont: "He gave them [his followers, Muslims] free reign for every shameful behavior."[70] As with the evolution of Eastern Christian views on Islam, so Western Christian views became more precise—and more hostile—over the following centuries of interaction with Islam.*

---

* Thus, for William of Tyre (b. 1130), who was born and raised in Jerusalem, the Arabian prophet was the "first-born of Satan," who "seduced" men with his "pestilent" teachings (Daniel 1962, 185). Saint Thomas Aquinas (d. 1274) best represents educated

When the smoke had cleared and the bloodletting subsided at Jerusalem, the surviving crusaders did what they had abandoned all and endured
years of deprivation and disease to do—that is, they did what must seem
amazing to modern sensibilities: they cleansed and dressed themselves in
white, removed their shoes, held crosses, and "going to the Sepulchre of
the Lord and His glorious Temple, the clerics and also the laity, singing a
new song unto the Lord in a high-sounding voice of exultation, and making
offerings and most humble supplications, joyously visited the Holy Place as
they had so long desired to do."[71]

Though deemed most worthy of the honor, Godfrey rejected the title of
King of Jerusalem—refusing to "wear a golden crown in the place where
Christ was crowned with thorns"[72]—and was instead coronated "Advocate
[meaning Defender or Guardian] of the Holy Sepulchre." The Syrian and
Armenian Christians who were ejected before Jerusalem's capture were
returned to repopulate the city. Jews and Muslims were also later invited
back.

MUSLIM REACTIONS

Local Muslims largely responded with apathy to the Frankish conquest
of Jerusalem. In all the surviving literature, only one source indicates that
there were any calls to jihad. Ali bin Tahrir, a Damascene cleric wrote *Kitab
al-Jihad,* another unoriginally titled rehashing or "Book of Jihad" in 1105.
He argued that if Muslims are obligated to go on regular jihads "to plunder the wealth, the women, and the property of the unbelievers," how much
more must Muslims respond with jihad when the infidels themselves take
the offensive against Islam? Instead it was the newly arrived crusaders who

---

Medieval views: "He [Muhammad] seduced the people by promises of carnal pleasure
to which the concupiscence of the flesh urges us . . . and he gave free rein to carnal
pleasure. In all this, as is not unexpected, he was obeyed by carnal men. As for proofs
of the truth of his doctrine. . . . Muhammad said that he was sent in the power of his
arms—which are signs not lacking even to robbers and tyrants [i.e., the "proof" that
God was with him is that he was able to conquer and plunder others]. . . . Muhammad
forced others to become his followers by the violence of his arms" (*Summa Contra
Gentiles,* book 1, chapter 6, art. 4; Thomas Aquinas 1975, 73).

had "zealously practiced jihad against Muslims," complained the scholar, while Muslims "brought only listlessness and disunity to war, each striving to leave this duty to others." Ali's conclusion? "Devote yourselves to the duty of jihad!"[73] These early calls largely fell on deaf ears for obvious reasons.

As seen in Chapter 4, centuries before the crusaders came, the Islamic world was racked with division. Shia Fatimids and Sunni Abbasids—the latter effectively ruled by semi-savage Turks—were at constant war. That petty chieftains, *atabegs* and emirs with no allegiance and less religion everywhere sought to carve their own kingdoms did not help matters. Nor did the arrival of the crusaders create Muslim unity: "While the Franks—Allah damn them!—were conquering and settling in a part of the territories of Islam," fumed Ibn al-Athir, "the rulers and armies of Islam were fighting among themselves, causing discord and disunity among their people and weakening their power to combat the enemy."[74] In this context, the pure doctrine of jihad—warfare against infidels, against the *other*—was lost to the average Muslim, who watched and suffered as Muslim empires, sects, and principalities collided.

Nor was there anything particularly strange about the latest conquerors. Muslims originally conflated Franks with Byzantines—both cross-carrying infidels. "Following a tradition attributed to the Prophet—'unbelief is one nation'—no particular need was felt to differentiate one infidel from another or to distinguish crusading from other forms of Christian warfare."[75] Thus, in 1099, it mattered little to local Muslims who lorded over them—so many different dynasties and sects, each more oppressive than the other, had come and gone in recent memory. After the initial massacres at Jerusalem and elsewhere—which the locals were accustomed to from Shia and Sunni infighting—the new rulers allowed Muslims to return, granted them freedom of worship (forced conversions to Christianity were expressly forbidden), lowered taxes, and enforced law and order.

As Riley-Smith puts it, "The Westerners appear to have constituted for most Muslims little more than an irritant, although Arab writers loved to dwell on traditional stereotypes: that they were unhygienic, dull, coarse, sexually lax, gullible, and hypocritical."[76] The records of Ibn Jubayr, an Andalusian Muslim who passed through the crusader kingdom in the early

1180s while on pilgrimage to Mecca, are typical. He denounced the apparent penchant for the "base and lower orders" of Franks to "revile" Muhammad, "the absence of cleanliness, the mixing with the pigs, and all the other prohibited matters too numerous to be related or enumerated."[77]

Less prosaically, Jubayr exhibited a certain ambivalence concerning life under Christian rule. He noted that Muslims "live in great comfort under the Franks; may Allah preserve us from such a temptation . . . [Muslims] are masters of their dwellings, and govern themselves as they wish. This is the case in all the territory occupied by the Franks."[78] But it was the seduction of life without the draconian dictates of sharia that most obsessed Jubayr (a concern that continues to plague pious Muslims living in modern Western societies). After describing a Christian marriage celebration in minute detail—"an alluring worldly spectacle" with pomp, fanfare, and musical instruments and a "proud" bride walking "like a dove, or in the manner of a wisp of cloud"—the amazed Muslim implored Allah to "protect us from the seduction of such a sight." In short: "Beware, beware of entering their lands."[79]

Speaking of Frankish women, one Muslim opinion, first formulated in the context of more proximate Byzantine women, remained fixed. Thus, Muhammad bin Hamed al-Isfahani (b. 1125), a celebrated Persian court scholar, once saw a ship containing "three hundred lovely Frankish women, full of youth and beauty" arrive by sea. As with Muslim descriptions of Eastern European women, the flattery ended there, and the rest of Muhammad's account reads like a fevered reflection of his own pornographic fantasies:

> They glowed with ardour for carnal intercourse. They were all licentious harlots, proud and scornful, who took and gave, foul-fleshed and sinful . . . making love and selling themselves for gold . . . with nasal voices and fleshy thighs, blue-eyed and grey-eyed. . . . They dedicated as a holy offering what they kept between their thighs. . . . They maintained that they could make themselves acceptable to God by no better sacrifice than this. . . . They made themselves targets for men's darts.[80]

On and on he goes. He was particularly fixated on one young woman who "walked proudly with the cross on her breast," since this only proved that she "longed to lose her robe and her honor." Just as the early Arabs had associated sexual immorality with Christian piety, so the Persian wrote, "Now among the Franks a woman who gives herself to a celibate man [monk] commits no sin, and her justification is even greater in the case of a priest, if chaste men in dire need find relief in enjoying her."[81]

THE JIHAD REAWAKENS

The crusaders ruled for some forty-four years after capturing Jerusalem with little interference from surrounding—and largely still disunited—Muslim rulers. Finally, with the rise of Imad al-Din Zengi (r. 1127–1146)—a particularly ruthless Turkish warlord and *atabeg* of Mosul and Aleppo—the old duty of jihad reawakened.* Having set his sights on the crusader kingdom of Edessa, Zengi "sent to summon the aid of the Turcomans, in fulfillment of their obligations in the jihad":

> Large numbers answered his appeal and they completely surrounded the city, intercepting all supplies and reinforcements. It was said that even the birds dared not fly near, so absolute was the desolation made by the besiegers' weapons and so unwinking their vigilance. Catapults drawn up against the walls battered at them ceaselessly, and nothing interrupted the remorseless struggle.[82]

After four months of this, on Christmas Eve, 1144, Edessa fell again to Islam. "The enemy rushed together from all directions, entered the city, and put all whom they encountered to the sword," writes William of Tyre (b. 1130). "Neither age, condition, nor sex was spared."

Thirty thousand souls were killed. Women, youths, and children

---

* A madrasa in Damascus bears an inscription from 1138 calling Zengi "the fighter of jihad, the defender of the frontier [*ribat*], the tamer of the polytheists [Christians] and destroyer of heretics [Shia]" (Lindsay and Mourad 2015, 54).

to the number of 16,000 were carried into slavery, stripped of their clothes, barefoot, their hands bound, forced to run beside their captors on horses. Those who could not endure were pierced by lances or arrows, or abandoned to the wild animals and birds of prey. Priests were killed out of hand or captured; few escaped. The Archbishop of the Armenians was sold at Aleppo. . . . The whole city was given over to looting, "for a whole year," resulting in "complete ruin." From this disaster the Christian community of Edessa never recovered.[83]

The jihad—not just beating but humiliating infidels—was back in all its glory. Edessa, the first of four established crusader kingdoms, was also the first to fall—and what a fall! Its conquest had a profound impact on Christian and Muslim alike. Although the Second Crusade was called to avenge it, the invincible aura of Frankish mettle, which two generations of Muslims had been born into believing, was virtually shattered overnight.

Two years later, Zengi was killed by one of his slaves—a long tormented Frank—and was thus transformed into a "martyr for the faith." A "holy man" saw the dead Zengi in a dream and inquired how it went with him: "Allah has pardoned me, because I conquered Edessa,"[84] responded the shade (thereby confirming the prophet's claim that fighting and killing infidels blots away all sins). Another contemporary martyr appeared in dreams proclaiming that "Allah has pardoned me" and that he is enjoying eternal bliss "stretched on couches" with houris.[85] Indeed, the theme that jihadis "sell" or "loan" their lives as part of a "bargain" or "transaction"—whereby Allah forgives all sins and showers them with celestial delights (see Introduction)—permeates Muslim sources from this era. Thus, when a "very old" Muslim man came to fight the crusaders, the emir sought to dissuade him on account of his age. The sheikh refused: "I have offered myself for sale, and He has bought me. By Allah, I neither agreed nor asked that the contract should be annulled!"[86]

Zengi's son and successor, Nur al-Din (b. 1118)—who "held the sharia in the deepest respect and applied its precepts"[87]—founded numerous madrasas, mosques, and Sufi orders all devoted to propagandizing the virtues of jihad and martyrdom.* Islamic zeal (or "radicalization") reached a fever pitch during his reign, and he made much use of it, fighting the crusaders for twenty years with mixed fortunes until his death in 1174.

It was then that a Kurd from Tikrit, who would forever alter the course of crusader history, emerged on the scene. Salah al-Din—the "Righteousness of Islam," more commonly, Saladin (b. 1137)†—formerly one of Nur al-Din's viziers, conquered Fatimid Egypt in 1171, effectively ending more than two and a half centuries of Shia rule and becoming Egypt's first sultan. On his master's death, he quickly moved and added more Muslim territories to his growing empire, thereby realizing the crusaders' greatest fear: a united Islamic front. He made an attempt against the crusader kingdom of Jerusalem as early as 1177, was routed near Ramallah, barely escaped on a swift camel back to Cairo, and bided his time. Saladin continued annexing Muslim-held territories, including Damascus and Aleppo, over the next decade, while sponsoring jihadi propaganda against the crusaders begun by his predecessors. According to Baha' al-Din, one of the sultan's many contemporary biographers/propagandists, Saladin was a pious Muslim—he loved hearing Koran recitals, prayed punctually, and "hated philosophers, heretics, and materialists and all opponents of the sharia."[88] Above all else he was a devotee of jihad:

> The sacred works [Koran, hadith, etc.] are full of passages referring
> to the jihad. Saladin was more assiduous and zealous in this than in

---

* He also commissioned Ibn 'Asakir (d. 1176), a Muslim scholar celebrated in his own time, to author a concise manual on jihad for distribution to all Islamic institutions. His book, *The 40 Hadiths for Inciting Jihad*, merely reproduced the 40 best *sahih*, or authenticated, hadiths already contained in books such as Abdullah bin Mubarak's (d. 797) original *Kitab al-Jihad* (see p. 66). They reinforced all the old themes: "Lining up for battle in the path of Allah [jihad] is worthier than 60 years of worship," said Muhammad. If the *mujahid* "dies or is killed, all his sins are forgiven. . . . He will be wedded to the virgins of paradise, and the crown of dignity will be placed on his head." Naturally, "he will also be saved from the torment of the grave . . . and saved from the terror" of judgment day. Those who shirk the duty of jihad "will be tortured like no other sinful human," etc. (see Lindsay and Mourad 2015, 151, 163, 161, 155).

† Although *al-din* literally means "the religion," in Islamic usage—particularly in Saladin's era when virtually every Muslim of rank had *al-din* in his name—"the religion" is synonymous with Islam.

anything else. . . . Jihad and the suffering involved in it weighed heavily on his heart and his whole being in every limb; he spoke of nothing else, thought only about equipment for the fight, was interested only in those who had taken up arms, had little sympathy with anyone who spoke of anything else or encouraged any other activity.[89]

Saladin added Mosul to his domains by spring of 1186, and in so doing became the supreme Muslim power of the Middle East. The time was right: "We should confront all the enemy's forces with all the forces of Islam," he told his subordinates.[90] But an existing truce with the crusader kingdoms still had three years to expire. A pretext to renege came a month after Saladin took Mosul. Raynald of Châtillon and Lord of Karak (b. 1125)—Saladin's longtime nemesis‡ and "Islam's most hated enemy" to contemporary Muslims[91]—raided a Muslim caravan traveling from Cairo to Damascus. Although he had not agreed to the crusader truce with Saladin—"Ask your Muhammad to deliver you!" he barked at his prisoners when they cited it— the sultan cried foul.[92] King Guy of Jerusalem (b. 1150) urged Raynald to return the plunder; the latter shot back that he was lord of his own domains and not the one who made a treaty with the enemy. "So Saladin," writes Ibn al-Athir, "was free to besiege and pillage, burn and ravage the whole region, which he did."[93]

The crusader kingdoms marshaled all their forces and set out to meet him near Nazareth in the summer of 1187. Although Saladin had more men—approximately 30,000, half of whom were light cavalry and many of whom were slave soldiers—the Christians had assembled the largest

‡ The two had been antagonists for years. In summer of 1181, Raynald broke a preexisting truce with Saladin by raiding weapon-bearing caravans traveling through his crusader kingdom east of the Jordan. Although Saladin had provoked Raynald into breaking the truce—which had indicated that arms could not be conveyed across the latter's land—the sultan cried foul and, portraying himself as the avenger of Islam, launched a reconnaissance-in-force mission in 1182. Cognizant of and seeking to counter Saladin's self-serving portrayals as defender of Islam, Raynald launched a fleet down the Red Sea that same year; his men sacked Medina and threatened to invade Mecca—the prophet's two holiest cities. Compelled to avenge this insult, Saladin marched a vast host toward Jerusalem in 1183. The crusader armies issued forth to meet and faced the Muslims for some days in the Valley of Jezreel. Saladin eventually withdrew; conditions were still not ideal for the subtle sultan.

army since capturing Jerusalem, consisting of some 20,000 knights, including 1,200 heavy horse. King Guy's strategy was simple: sit and wait for Saladin's light horsemen to hurl themselves and thus crumble against this Frankish wall of steel, as happened centuries earlier at Tours. Saladin, also cognizant that his men could not achieve victory through a head-on assault, suddenly withdrew his forces. The crusaders assumed he had permanently withdrawn (as he had done under similar circumstances in 1183); in fact, he had gone to and was besieging the nearby crusader kingdom of Tiberias.

Guy held a war council. All agreed to march to the relief of Tiberias except for the lord of Tiberias himself, Raymond, Count of Tripoli, who suggested a sit-and-wait approach. That he had once made a secret truce with Saladin—allowing the latter to make incursions into Christian territory that resulted in the slaughter of many knights of the military orders—did not sit well with the war council, especially the Templar Grand Master, nor lend much credence to Raymond's counsel. "You have tried hard to make us afraid of the Muslims," scoffed Raynald. "Clearly you take their side and your sympathies are with them, otherwise you would not have spoken this way. As for the size of their army, a large load of fuel will be good for the fires of hell!"[94]

THE BATTLE OF HATTIN

On the following morning, July 3, the crusaders set out for Tiberias. Some twenty miles of stony, parched land—with no natural water sources or wells—stood between them and their destination. Looking "like mountains on the march," a Muslim chronicler remarked that the "hardened warriors" moved "as fast as if they were always going downhill," despite being "loaded down with the apparel of war."[95] When Saladin learned that the crusaders were marching to relieve Tiberias—that is, when he learned that they had fallen for his trap—he rubbed his hands with glee: "This, indeed, is what we wished for most!"[96] He immediately dispatched his light cavalry to harry the crusaders. Guy hurried the march—the real battle, and water, lay in Tiberias—but then learned that his force's rear, now surrounded by swarms of archers, had been compelled to stop and engage the enemy. The king responded by ordering the entire army to halt and fight near a parched and ominous double hill formation, known as the Horns of Hattin. "This was on a burningly hot day," writes the Muslim chronicler, "while they themselves were burning with wrath."[97] According to Ernoul, a squire who was present:

> As soon as they [Franks] were encamped, Saladin ordered all his men to collect brushwood, dry grass, stubble and anything else with which they could light fires, and make barriers which he had made all round the Christians. They soon did this, and the fires burned vigorously and the smoke from the fires was great; and this, together with the heat of the sun above them caused them discomfort and great harm. . . . When the fires were lit and the smoke was great, the Saracens surrounded the host and shot their darts through the smoke and so wounded and killed men and horses.[98]

This continued into nightfall. No one slept; from the surrounding darkness, the Muslims, who by now "had lost their first fear of the enemy and were in high spirits," made a great din. "They could smell victory in the air, and the more they saw of the unexpectedly low morale of the Franks the more aggressive and daring they became."[99] Out of the smoke-filled darkness and into the crusader camp came volley after volley of arrows, accompanied by cries of "Allahu Akbar" and triumphant iterations of the *shahada*. As an infernal gloom from the surrounding brushfires choked them, the crusaders, utterly tormented by thirst, thought they had already died and were in hell.

Matters only worsened with the breaking of dawn, July 4: seventy camels laden with water and arrows had arrived during the night to refresh and replenish the Muslim camp; and because Saladin's archers could now see, even more precise shafts continued to rain on the crusader camp. The sadistic sultan also ordered "water pots placed near the [crusader] camp" and "then emptied in view of the Christians so that they should have still greater anguish through thirst, and their mounts too."[100] Driven to the brink of madness, the crusaders charged at their tormenters. And so, to quote Ibn al-Athir:

> The two armies came to blows. The Franks were suffering badly from thirst, and had lost confidence. The battle raged furiously, both sides putting up a tenacious resistance. The Muslim archers sent up clouds of arrows like thick swarms of locusts, killing many of the Frankish horses. The Franks, surrounding themselves with their infantry, tried to fight their way toward Tiberias in the hope of reaching water, but Saladin realized their objective and forestalled them by planting himself and his army in the way. He himself rode up and down the Muslim lines encouraging and restraining his troops where necessary.[101]

Saladin was no fearer of death. During an earlier battle, when an advisor had urged him not to expose himself to danger, the sultan asked, "What is the most noble death?" "Death in the path of Allah," responded his aid (meaning martyrdom during jihad). "Well then"—concluded Saladin, citing jihad's win-win rationale—"the worst that can befall me is the most noble of deaths!"[102]

As the battle raged, Muslim reserves "created more brushfires and the wind carried the heat and smoke down on to the enemy. They had to endure thirst, the summer's heat, the blazing fire and smoke and the fury of battle." Yet the desperate crusaders fought on: "Terrible encounters took place on that day," writes al-Isfahani; "never in the history of generations that have gone have such feats of arms been told."[103] Many crusaders "burned and glowed in a frenzied ferment"; knowing that "the only way to save their lives was to defy death," they "made a series of charges that almost dislodged the Muslims from their position in spite of their numbers, had not the grace of Allah been with them. As each wave of attacks fell back they left their dead behind them; their numbers diminished rapidly, while the Muslims were all around them like a circle about its diameter."[104]

Then the inevitable began: Frankish ranks broke; panic set in and men fled to the hills. King Guy and his guard had brought and now planted the

True Cross in the ground and prepared to make their final stand around it. Morale and courage was restored by this sight; all, including those who had just retreated, hacked their way to the sacred emblem, where they fought tooth and nail. But Saladin would not relent: charge after charge of Muslim horsemen, and volley after volley of Muslim arrows descended on the crusader army—which by now consisted of a confused mass of desperate men stumbling over the bodies of their dead; forests of prickly shafts appeared everywhere—in man, beast, and earth. With arms raised high and eyes full of tears, thousands implored the Cross for deliverance—only to see Muslims hack their way to and seize Christendom's most prized relic: "Its capture was . . . the gravest blow that they sustained in that battle," writes the Muslim chronicler. "It seemed as if, once they knew of the capture of the Cross, none of them would survive that day of ill-omen."[105]

Encircled by an ever-shrinking ring of fire and Islamic horsemen, tormented by arrows and thirst, the Fighters of Christ finally succumbed. The rout was complete, the gloating great: "This defeat of the enemy, this our victory occurred on a Saturday, and the humiliation proper to the men of Saturday [Jews] was inflicted on the men of Sunday [Christians], who had been lions and now were reduced to the level of miserable sheep."[106] In the end, single Muslim soldiers were seen dragging as many as thirty crusaders with one rope, any of whom would once have terrified the same—so maddened with thirst and reduced to delirium were the Europeans. Saladin "dismounted and prostrated himself in thanks to Allah, weeping for joy."[107]

THE JIHAD TRIUMPHS OVER THE CROSS

Great was the carnage surrounding the Horns of Hattin: "The dead were scattered over the mountains and valleys, lying immobile on their sides," writes al-Isfahani. "I passed by them and saw the limbs of the fallen cast naked on the field of battle, scattered in pieces over the site of the encounter, lacerated and disjointed, with heads cracked open, throats split, spines broken, necks shattered, feet in pieces, noses mutilated, extremities torn off, members dismembered, parts shredded, eyes gouged out, stomachs disemboweled. . . . A lesson to the wise."[108]

King Guy and other captured nobles—including that most "powerful and violent infidel" Raynald—were hauled to Saladin's tent to await their doom.[109] The sultan was magnanimous to Guy, explaining that "a king does not slay a king," and saved his invective for the Arabic-speaking Count of Châtillon. Always willing to place advantage before revenge—and thereby further winning the reputation of magnanimity—the shrewd sultan invited Raynald to convert to Islam and reap its rewards.

"Your Christ has deceived you," Saladin said in the rather straightforward "interfaith dialogue" of the day. "If you do not deny him, he will not be able to free you this day from my hand!" "Christ deceives no man," responded Raynald, "but that man is deceived who does not believe in him." Then, knowing his fate was sealed, the Frank made public confession: "I adore him, I confess him, I declare his name to you! If you believed in him, you would be able to escape the punishment of eternal damnation, which—doubt not!—has been prepared for you. But why are you delaying what you are about to do? I know that you thirst for nothing other than Christian blood!"* Saladin instantly drew out his scimitar and struck the defiant infidel—before his henchmen pounced on, decapitated, and triumphantly paraded Raynald's head around the Muslim camp. Thus ended that "most dangerous enemy of Islam."†

He was only the first; every other dedicated foe of Islam was denied ransom and consigned to slaughter. Saladin commanded that all captive Templars and Hospitallers‡—at least one hundred warrior-monks sworn to

---

* Peter of Blois (b. 1135) is the source of this little known dialogue. He precedes it by saying, "I am changing absolutely nothing of the words of" Raynald, but recording them as "they were related and written down to the lord pope and many then present," including Aimery of Lusignan. Special thanks go to historian Paul F. Crawford, an expert on the apparently much misunderstood Raynald. [Peter of Blois, *Passio Raginaldi*, unpublished translation-in-progress by Paul F. Crawford and Sarah J. Downey, all rights reserved to the translators, used here by express permission.]

† Baha' al-Din records a similar exchange, though without giving voice to the defiant Christian: "'Here I [Saladin] am, having asked victory through Muhammad, and Allah has given me victory over you.' He offered him [Raynald] Islam but he refused. The sultan then drew his scimitar and struck him, severing his arm at his shoulder. Those present finished him off and Allah speedily sent his soul to Hell-fire" (2001, 75).

‡ Minus Templar Grand Master Gerard de Ridefort, whom Saladin kept hostage as a bargaining tool for some time.

defend the Sepulchre of Christ to their dying breath—be brought before him. After boasting "I shall purify the land of these two impure races," the sultan "ordered that they should be beheaded, choosing to have them dead rather than in prison," explains the Muslim chronicler: "With him was a whole band of scholars and Sufis and a certain number of devout men and ascetics; each begged to be allowed to kill one of them, and drew his scimitar and rolled back his sleeve. Saladin, his face joyful, was sitting on his dais."[110]

The rest of the crusaders who could not purchase freedom—which included the overwhelming majority of the thousands captured—were sold into slavery. "That night was spent by our people in the most complete joy and perfect delight . . . with cries of 'Allahu Akbar' and 'There is no god but Allah,' until daybreak on Sunday."[111]

All that is known of the True Cross's fate is that Saladin ordered it to be paraded upside down in the streets of Damascus. From there, the Cross—discovered under Constantine, seized by Persians but recovered by Heraclius, smuggled to Constantinople during the Islamic siege of Jerusalem in 637 but then sent back to the Holy City when it was restored to Christendom—disappears from history and enters legend.[§]

JERUSALEM LOST

Because so many professional fighting men were lost at Hattin, the crusaders' kingdoms were left vulnerable. By July 10—a mere six days after the battle—the indefatigable sultan had speared through and captured Jaffa, Caesarea, Haifa, Sidon, and Acre. By September, Saladin stood before the strong walls of Jerusalem, now swollen with Christian refugees, "each one of whom would choose death rather than see the Muslims in power in their city," to quote Ibn al-Athir; for "the sacrifice of life, possessions and sons was for them a part of their duty to defend the city." The Muslims "began their battery of the walls, from which the Franks replied with other machines that they had constructed there. Then began the fiercest struggle

---

§ In the years that followed, several leading Europeans—including King Richard and Byzantine Emperor Isaac II—sought to ransom the True Cross but Saladin would not relent.

imaginable; each side looked on the fight as an absolute religious obligation."[112] Eventually coming to terms with reality, the city offered terms of
surrender, which Saladin spurned: "Neither amnesty nor mercy for you!"
replied he. "Our only desire is to inflict perpetual subjection upon you; tomorrow will make us your masters by main force. We shall kill and capture
you wholesale, spill men's blood and reduce the poor and the women to
slavery."[113]

With nothing to lose, the desperate, holed-up crusaders declared that,
if death was to be their lot, they would first have vengeance: they would destroy the Dome of the Rock, slaughter thousands of Muslim prisoners held
in the city, kill their own children, destroy their own possessions, and set
the city ablaze. Saladin would win nothing: "What advantage do you gain
from this ungenerous spirit of negation," they asked, "you who would only
lose everything by such a gain?"[114] The practical sultan saw the wisdom
in this: large ransoms, freed Muslims, intact possessions, and undamaged
mosques were preferable to yet another bloodbath of infidels. Those who
could ransom their lives were permitted to do so, and Jerusalem's gates
were opened to the conquering hero of Islam.

Now "a great cry went up from the city and from outside the walls,
the Muslims crying the Allahu Akbar in their joy, the Franks groaning in
consternation and grief," wrote Ibn al-Athir. "So loud and piercing was the
cry that the earth shook."[115] Saladin reestablished sharia; churches were
pillaged and vandalized; their bells were silenced, their crosses broken off.
The Church of the Holy Sepulchre was spared but sealed off. Like the True
Cross before it, a large golden cross fixed atop the Dome of the Rock was
removed, spat on, and dragged through the sewers. The Al Aqsa Mosque,
for decades the headquarters of the now massacred Knights Templar, was
purged and the muezzin's call to prayer heard again. "The Koran was raised
to the throne and the [Old and New] Testaments cast down," as Saladin
"purified Jerusalem of the pollution of those races, of the filth of the dregs
of humanity."[116] Muslims appreciated the continuity: "This noble act of
conquest was achieved, after Omar bin al-Khattab [the caliph who first conquered Jerusalem from Christendom in 637]—Allah have mercy on him!—
by no one but Saladin, and that is a sufficient title to glory and honour."[117]

Although many Christians were able to purchase their freedom and quit Jerusalem unmolested, much more could not. Saladin clemently granted freedom to the aged and infirm; the rest, approximately fifteen thousand, were sold into slavery. "Women and children together came to 8,000 and were quickly divided up among us, bringing a smile to Muslim faces at their lamentation," writes Muhammad al-Isfahani, who was present at the taking of Jerusalem. There follows yet another sadomasochistic tirade extolling the sexual debasement of European women at the hands of Muslim men:

> How many well-guarded women were profaned, how many queens were ruled, and nubile girls married, and noble women given away, and miserly women forced to yield themselves, and women who had been kept hidden [nuns] stripped of their modesty . . . and free women occupied [meaning "penetrated"], and precious ones used for hard work, and pretty things put to the test, and virgins dishonoured and proud women deflowered . . . and happy ones made to weep! How many noblemen [Muslim lords] took them as concubines, how many ardent men blazed for one of them, and celibates were satisfied by them, and thirsty men sated by them, and turbulent men able to give vent to their passion. How many lovely women were the exclusive property of one man, how many great ladies were sold at low prices . . . and lofty ones abased . . . and those accustomed to thrones dragged down![118]

Elated by his ongoing victories, the triumphant sultan began to entertain dreams of graduating from the merely *defensive* jihad to the more glorious and original *offensive* jihad begun by the prophet and his successors: "I think that when Allah grants me victory over the rest of Palestine," he confided to an associate, "I shall divide my territories, make a will stating my wishes, then set sail on this [Mediterranean] sea for their far-off lands [in Western Europe] and pursue the Franks there, so as to free the earth of anyone who does not believe in Allah, or die in the attempt."[119]

Meanwhile, just as Caliph Omar II had renewed the persecution of Christian *dhimmis* under his authority following the failed siege of

Constantinople in 718, so Saladin "retaliated" against the crusaders by collectively punishing their vulnerable coreligionists already under his control.* He had Coptic Christians tortured and crucified, commanded "whoever saw that the outside of a church was white, to cover it with black dirt," and ordered "the removal of every cross from atop the dome of every church in the provinces of Egypt."[120] And yet just as Alp Arslan was depicted by Christians as magnanimous but by Muslims as supremacist, so have Western historians long portrayed Saladin as a chivalrous knight, even though the "portrait of him drawn by" his Muslim biographers "is that of the pious [Muslim] leader rather than of a gallant knight, and it fails to explain the fascination" surrounding him.[121]

At any rate, Saladin was unable to realize his dreams of pursuing the Franks in order to convert or exterminate them. Word of Hattin and the fall of Jerusalem reached and rocked Western Christendom—the pope "died of grief when he heard the news"—and a new wave of crusaders came for the sultan.[122] This Third Crusade, spearheaded by England's King Richard, marked the high point of crusading and saw some of the fiercest fighting between Muslim and Christian, often to the latter's favor. After that came "thousands, maybe tens of thousands of crusades."[123] The vitriol reached new heights: whereas Peter the Venerable (b. 1092) could once say, "I approach you [Muslims], I say, not as our people often do, with arms but with words, not by force but by reason, not in hatred, but in love," for Benedict of Alignon (d. 1268), Muslims were unworthy of debating with, "but rather to be extirpated by fire and the sword."[124]

It mattered not; Jerusalem was forever lost to Christendom. In 1291,

---

* The continuity of Islamic collective punishment is evident in a 2011 report: "Life on any given day for Pakistani Christians is difficult. But members of Pakistan's Christian community say now they're being persecuted for U.S. drone attacks on Islamic militants hiding on the border with Afghanistan. The minority, which accounts for an estimated one percent of the country's 170 million [mostly Muslim] population, says because its faith is strongly associated with America, it is targeted by Muslims." "When America does a drone strike, they come and blame us," said one Christian. "They think we belong to America. It's a simple mentality" (http://www.foxnews.com/world/2011/04/23/pakistani-deprived-christian-community-say-theyre-persecuted.html).

the final crusader stronghold, Acre, was captured after arguably the most savage and desperate fighting since the crusades began nearly two centuries earlier, and the Western knights were finally expelled. A Dominican monk present at Acre's fall "was forced to see Christian women and children sold into slavery after being paraded through streets, watch nuns become concubines, hear the Christians being taunted that their Jesus could not help them against Muhammad."[125] "With these conquests," boasted a contemporary Arab historian, "the whole of Palestine was now in Muslim hands."[126] And though "the urge to regain the Holy Places of Christendom remained as strong as ever,"[127] in the coming centuries, a resurgent Islam coupled with an increasingly divided Christendom forced crusading energy to go on the defensive.

Although Hattin ranks among the most decisive battles between Muslim and Christian—particularly as it led to the loss of the focal point of all crusading, Jerusalem—from a macrohistorical perspective, it was far less significant than the original Arab conquest of the Holy Land in 637. Whereas the latter had a permanent, decisive quality, the crusader achievement was to recover Jerusalem—only to lose it again to Islam less than a century later, eventually leading back to the status quo first achieved by Muslims in the seventh century.

That said, the crusades had an enormous if instrumental impact on subsequent developments. "The spirit of adventure, released by the crusades, began to trace out the filaments of travel and discovery . . . and led to traders, notably the Venetian Polos, penetrating as far east as the Great Wall of China. These men, by discovering Asia, fired the economic imagination which eventually led to the discovery of the New World."[128] Even the world-changing voyages of Christopher Columbus were motivated by the recovery of Jerusalem.

Yet perhaps the most unforeseen and ironic aspect of the crusades is that a distorted and demonized version of them was eventually disseminated in and continues to haunt the West—while exonerating ongoing Muslim aggression as "payback"—to this very day. But that is another story.

CHAPTER 6

THE CRUSADE VICTORIOUS: THE BATTLE OF LAS NAVAS DE TOLOSA, 1212

I will not associate with the Arabs in friendship nor will I submit to their authority. Christ is our hope that through this little mountain, which you see, the well-being of Spain and the army of the Gothic people will be restored.

—Pelayo, c. 717, first Christian king after Islam conquered Spain[1]

It pleased our Lord, to give us a complete victory over the king and the Moors of Granada, enemies of our holy Catholic faith. . . . After so much labor, expense, death, and shedding of blood, this [last Muslim] kingdom of Granada which was occupied for over seven hundred and eighty years by the infidel . . . [has been conquered].

—Ferdinand and Isabella, 1492[2]

M ORE THAN THREE CENTURIES BEFORE POPE URBAN II CALLED for crusades against the Muslim East, and more than three centuries after Hattin, Spain was and continued to be—for a total of almost eight hundred years—a microcosm of the perennial war between Islam and Christianity. There, all aforementioned aspects of Christian-Muslim hostilities coalesced in sharp display.

Last we left him in 712, Musa bin Nusayr had followed his general, Tarek, and "entered the long plundered and godlessly invaded Spain to destroy it," says the *Chronicle of 754*. "He ruined beautiful cities, burning

them with fire; condemned lords and powerful men to the cross; and butchered youths and infants with the sword. . . . He terrorized everyone." Unable to describe the totality of ruin visited upon Spain, the chronicler—like
John of Nikiû and Matthew of Edessa on the Muslim invasions of Egypt
and Armenia, respectively*—concludes in dismayed resignation: "Who
can relate such perils? Who can enumerate such grievous disasters? Even
if every limb were transformed into a tongue, it would be beyond human
nature to express the ruin of Spain and its many and great evils."† Native
Spaniards had two choices: acquiesce to Arab rule or "flee to the mountains
where they risked hunger and various forms of death."³

A MUSTARD SEED

One of those who initially submitted to Muslim rule, experienced first-
hand treachery, and then fled to the northern mountains of Asturia was
destined to initiate what became a 781-year-long struggle against Islam:
Pelagius, better known as Pelayo (685–737), a Visigothic noble and sword-
bearer to King Roderick at the Battle of Guadalete (Chapter 3). After defeat, Pelayo (and others) fled north where Muslim rule was still tenuous.
There he eventually consented to become a vassal of Munnuza, a local
Muslim chief. Then, through some "stratagem," says the *Chronicle of Alfonso III*, Munnuza "married" Pelayo's sister—a matter that the sword-
bearer "by no means consented to." So Muslims were sent "to apprehend

---

* See pp. 33 and 106.

† Other early sources corroborate the devastation. The oldest account, the *Tempore
belli*, a Latin church hymn written soon after the fall of the Visigoths, "describes an
'implacable enemy,' 'full of enthusiasm in the exercise of war,' 'forcing Christian
troops to turn around and flee in panic,' sacking Christian temples and homes, burning
the cities of those who resisted, and taking their young women as sexual slaves, all creating an 'indescribable terror.'" Alfonso X's *History of Spain,* Archbishop Rodrigo of
Toledo's tenth-century history, and the *Chronicon Mundi* respectively tell of how "the
Muslim conquerors killed the men, burned cities, wasted the land, took young women
as sexual slaves"; "cut down fruit trees, destroyed churches, regarded sacred music as
blasphemy, and profaned chalices"; "changed the towers of ancient cities [to mosques];
destroyed castles . . . [and] monasteries; burned the books of the sacred law, and committed many bad deeds" (Fernandez-Morera 2016, 39–40).

him treacherously" and bring him back "bound in chains." Unable to fight them "because they were so numerous," Pelayo "climbed a mountain" and "joined himself to as many people as he found hastening to assemble." There, in the deepest hollows of the Asturian mountains—the only free spot left in Spain—the assembled fugitives hailed Pelayo their new king.[4]

"Hearing this, the king [i.e., governor of Cordoba], moved by an insane fury, ordered a very large army from all over Spain to go forth" and bring the insolent rebels to heel. With them went one Oppa, a bishop of noble birth who appears to have willingly acquiesced to Muslim rule. As the invaders surrounded Pelayo's mountain, Oppa met and tried to reason with him at the mouth of a deep cavern: "If when the entire army of the Goths was assembled, it was unable to sustain the attack of the Ishmaelites [at Guadalete], how much better will you be able to defend yourself on this mountaintop? To me it seems difficult. Rather, heed my warning and recall your soul from this decision, so that you may take advantage of many good things and enjoy the partnership of the Chaldeans [Arabs]."[5]

"I will not associate with the Arabs in friendship nor will I submit to their authority," asserted Pelayo.[6] Then the rebel made a prophecy that would be fulfilled over the course of nearly eight centuries: "Have you not read in the divine scriptures that the church of God is compared to a mustard seed and that it will be raised up again through divine mercy?" Oppa affirmed it was so; the fugitive continued: "Christ is our hope that through this little mountain, which you see, the well-being of Spain and the army of the Gothic people will be restored. . . . Now, therefore, trusting in the mercy of Jesus Christ, I despise this multitude and am not afraid of it. As for the battle with which you threaten us, we have for ourselves an advocate in the presence of the Father, that is, the Lord Jesus Christ, who is capable of liberating us from these few."[7]

There, at Covadonga—meaning "Cavern of the Lady"—battle commenced in the summer of 722.[*] A shower of rocks rained atop the Muslims in the narrow passes, where their numbers counted for nothing and

---

* Some sources place the date at 718.

only caused confusion. Then Pelayo and his band of rebels rushed forth from their caves and hiding-places and made great slaughter among them; those who fled the carnage were tracked and mowed down by other, now emboldened, mountaineers. Thus, "a decisive blow was dealt at the Moorish power.[†] The advancing tide of conquest was stemmed. The Spaniards gathered heart and hope in their darkest hour; and the dream of Moslem invincibility was broken."[8] For centuries thereafter, "Covadonga became the symbol of Christian resistance to Islam and a source of inspiration to those who, in words attributed to Pelayo, would achieve the *salus Spanie,* the salvation of Spain."[9] The earliest chroniclers often stress this existential struggle with Islam.[‡]

Several Muslim attempts were made to conquer the mountainous kingdom of Asturia (ruled by Pelayo until his death in 737) but the "mustard seed" continued to grow. To it "came all who were dissatisfied with Moorish dominion, all who clung to the hope of a Christian revival, all who detested Mahomet."[10] By 750, the entire northwest of Spain was back under Christian control.

The prize for such freedom was a barrage of nonstop jihads; the "Christians of the North scarcely knew the meaning of repose, security, or any of the amenities of life."[11] An environment similar to and created by the eastern caliphates' perennial war on Byzantium prevailed. A scorched no-man's-land, roughly along the Duero River, separated Muslim-ruled Spain (al-Andalus), from the northern rebels. After explaining how the Muslims intentionally devastated the region[§]—they later

---

† "Moor(s)," the name Spaniards gave and knew the Muslim invaders by, is etymologically related to Mauretania (and later Morocco), whence came blacks, Berbers, and Arabs.

‡ According to the ninth-century *Chronicle of Albelda,* "The Christians are waging war with them [the Muslims] by day and night and contend with them daily until divine predestination commands that they be driven cruelly thence. Amen!" The ninth-century *Prophetic Chronicle* looked forward to the day when "Divine Clemency may expel the aforesaid [Muslims] from our provinces beyond the sea and grant possession of their kingdom to the faithful of Christ in perpetuity. Amen!" (O'Callaghan 2004, 5–6).

§ As Ibn Hudayl of Granada explained, "It is permissible to set fire to the lands of the enemy, his stores of grain, his beasts of burden—if it is not possible for the Muslims to

named it "the Great Desert"—French historian Louis Bertrand (b. 1866) elaborates:

> To keep the Christians in their place it did not suffice to surround them with a zone of famine and destruction. It was necessary also to go and sow terror and massacre among them. . . . If one bears in mind that this brigandage was almost continual, and that this fury of destruction and extermination was regarded as a work of piety—it was a holy war against infidels—it is not surprising that whole regions of Spain should have been made irremediably sterile. This was one of the capital causes of the deforestation from which the Peninsula still suffers. With what savage satisfaction and in what pious accents do the Arab annalists tell us of those at least bi-annual raids. A typical phrase for praising the devotion of a Caliph is this: "he penetrated into Christian territory, where he wrought devastation, devoted himself to pillage, and took prisoners". . . . At the same time as they were devastated, whole regions were depopulated. . . . The prolonged presence of the Musulmans, therefore, was a calamity for this unhappy country of Spain. By their system of continual raids they kept her for centuries in a condition of brigandage and devastation.[12]

For Muslims, the frontier zone became "a territory where one fights for the faith and a permanent place of the ribat."[13] Military manuals compiled along the original *ribats* of Anatolia—chief among them Abdallah bin Mubarak's *Kitab al-Jihad*—were republished in Spain. There "they enjoyed uninterrupted popularity, even more than in their homelands. . . . Above all, interest in historical narratives of sira and maghazi [the biography and jihad

---

take possession of them—as well as to cut down his trees, to raze his cities, in a word, to do everything that might ruin and discourage him, provided that the imam deems these measures appropriate, suited to hastening the Islamization of that enemy or to weakening him. Indeed, all this contributes to a military triumph over him or to forcing him to capitulate" (Bostom 2005, 419).

campaigns of Muhammad respectively] remained strong in al-Andalus."[14] Because "service in the holy war, according to Muhammad, was the most meritorious of all works," the "opportunity to participate in the holy war in Spain and to obtain religious merit and even entrance into paradise drew many volunteers to the peninsula." Indeed, men such as governor Uqba bin al-Hajjaj (r. 734–740)—described by a tenth-century Arab chronicler as "a courageous champion of jihad, frontier warrior [*murabit*], intrepid and valiant, burning in his desire to hurt the polytheists [trinitarian Christians]"[15]—were common.

"THE ENEMIES OF THE CROSS"

As in the Middle East, "hurt[ing] the polytheists" in Spain manifested in familiar ways: from seizing and violating the sacred things of Christianity— churches, icons, crosses, and relics—to seizing and violating the sacred persons (or bodies) of the infidels. Due to some widespread and entrenched myths concerning the purported tolerance and enlightenment of al-Andalus, here it is necessary to document the reverse and establish context for the forthcoming centuries of war.

For starters, the destruction and spoliation of churches was hardly limited to the initial conquest years (711–715). It was a constant—and deliberate—affair. Once Abd al-Rahman I (d. 788) became emir of Cordoba, all churches still standing "were immediately pulled down," writes al-Maqqari.[16] He also "would take all the bodies which Christians honor and call saints, and he would burn them," adds al-Razi, another Muslim writer; "and he would burn their beautiful churches; and in Spain there were many and very magnificent churches, some built by the Greeks and some by the Romans." After him, "churches were destroyed as part of the persecution of Christians under the Umayyad ruler Muhammad I (reigned 852–886)." Caliph al-Mansur (d. 1002) was also "a notorious burner of Christian churches."[17]

Even the ancient Visigothic church of Saint Vincent, the main basilica of Cordoba, which the invaders initially vouchsafed to Christians on condition of surrender, was coercively "purchased," razed to the ground, and its precious materials cannibalized to construct the Great Mosque of Cordoba—on the heads of northern Christian slaves no less.* This transformation of churches into mosques grieved medieval Christians to no end. Mark of Toledo (b. 1193) lamented that where "formerly many priests offered the divine obsequy to God, now villainous men devoted supplications to the execrable Muhammad."[18]

As in the East, the intentional destruction or mutilation of churches into mosques was meant to highlight Islam's supremacy. As Dario Fernandez-Morera, author of *The Myth of the Andalusian Paradise,* writes: "Whenever Muslim chroniclers make reference to Christian churches in Spain, it is to boast of their transformation into mosques or their outright destruction as symbols of Islamic dominance over the mushriks ('polytheists')—as Christians were called . . . Muslim historians emphasize that, like the jizya, the destruction of Christian churches, statues, and relics was intended to humiliate the 'People of the Book' and affirm Islamic hegemony."[19]

Little wonder the ranks of the free northwest continued to swell with Christian refugees. As al-Razi notes, "Seeing this [the targeting of churches], the Christians, when they could, would take their sacred things, and would flee to the mountains."[20]

None of this is to suggest that all Muslim rulers were committed to the destruction of churches and degradation of Christians; several governors, particularly those closer to the Christian frontier, permitted obedient Christian subjects to keep their sacred sites. What it does suggest, however, is that, as in other Muslim-occupied territories, whether the next ruler would be "radical" or "moderate"—to use an anachronistic but familiar dichotomy—was always a coin flip away. The archeological facts speak for themselves: although churches dotted Spain's landscape when Islam came in 711, "today, the remains of even small 'Mozarabic' [*dhimmi*] churches

---

* That faith persevered in even the most desperate of times is evident in that "there has been found on a wall [of the Cordoban mosque] the form of a cross, rudely carved by one of these unfortunates" (Bertrand 1952, 70).

can be found only outside the former 'al-Andalus,' and none of them in major urban centers."[21]

Similarly, the intentional desecration of Christian sacraments and symbols—particularly the cross—earned Muslims the sobriquet "Enemies of the Cross" among the Peninsula's Christians. Alfonso III's *Chronicle* tells how Muslim vandals "threw out from the churches the crosses and altars, the holy oils and the books and the things which were honored by Christendom, all was scattered and discarded."[22] During the siege of Lisbon (1147) Muslims displayed "with much derision the symbol of the cross. They spat upon it and wiped the feces from their posteriors with it.[†] At last they urinated on it, as on some despicable thing, and threw our cross at us."[23] One of the standard prayers Christians recited before battle suggests such scenes were common: "Grant that, by the power of your name and the most victorious Cross, the people of the Moors, who everywhere always humiliate it, may powerfully be conquered."[24]

Muslim sources confirm this hostility. One popular anti-Christian treatise published in al-Andalus was titled "Hammers [for breaking] the Crosses."[25] As the Umayyad caliphate had effaced the image of the cross from Byzantine coins in the eighth century, so Ibn Rushd al-Jadd (d. 1126), a prominent Andalusian jurist, said that golden "crosses must be broken up before being distributed" as plunder. "As for their sacred books [Bibles], one must make them disappear," added the jurist (later clarifying that unless all words can be erased from every page in order to resell the blank book, all Christian scripture must be burned).[26] This systematic erasure of Spain's Christian heritage—this attempt to make churches, crosses, and even the very printed words of the Gospel "disappear"—prompted men such as Pedro II, who "accepted the material sword to punish evildoers" in 1204, to describe Muslims as they who "wished to abolish the memory of the Christian name."[27]

[†] At Lisbon they "also continuously attacked Blessed Mary, the mother of God, with insults and with vile and abusive words, which infuriated us. They said that we venerated the son of a poor woman" (Allen 2010, 306).

AN EMPORIUM OF WHITE FLESH

Another motivation that fueled the Eastern caliphates' jihad on Byzantium—the seizure of slaves, particularly women and children—continued to fuel the jihad on Christians in Spain. As seen, from the moment Muslims landed in 711, Tarek sought to entice his men by citing the waiting women of Europe's westernmost peninsula. Afterward, when Caliph Al-Walid in Damascus saw the great plunder harvested, he was delighted by "the resources of all the people of Spain . . . its riches and the beauty of its young girls."[28] Because the "Umayyads particularly valued blond or red-haired Franc or Galician women as sexual slaves,"[29] which were harder to acquire from better fortified Byzantium, "al-Andalus became a center for the trade and distribution of slaves."[30] In exchange for peace, north Christians sometimes even had to make annual tributes "not of money, or horses, or arms, but of a hundred damsels (all to be distinguished for beauty) to ornament the harems."[31]

To maintain the slave emporium reputation of Cordoba, merchants "would put ointments on slave girls of a darker complexion to whiten their faces; brunettes were placed for four hours in a solution to make them blond ('golden'); ointments were placed on the face and body of black slaves to make them 'prettier.'" As for the sexual objectification of European infidels—which, as seen, meant portraying them as promiscuous by nature—slavers played up this fantasy in order to facilitate sales. According to a twelfth-century document: "The merchant tells the slave girls to act in a coquettish manner with the old men and with the timid men among the potential buyers to make them crazy with desire . . . [and] he dresses them all in transparent clothes."[32]

Forced or indoctrinated into being promiscuous, some of these hapless women appear to have done their job well. Due to Cordoba's status as a slave epicenter—practically every Muslim emir was born to a pale concubine—large numbers of sex slaves and forced prostitutes were always on public display trading their wares. Ibn Hazm may have had them in mind, and not the average cloistered female Muslim, when he wrote that women "have nothing else to fill their minds, except loving union [sex] and what brings it about, flirting and how it is done, intimacy and the various ways of achieving it. This is their sole occupation, and they were created for nothing else."[33]

Something of this fantasy—where half-naked women lounge about in caliphal harems pining for their turn to see and please their masters—eventually passed into the West's popular imagination. But it is more a product of fiction along the lines of the *Arabian Nights* than reality. Consider the life and times of Abd al-Rahman III (r. 929–961), the caliph most associated with al-Andalus's "golden age." According to Muslim records, he once "threw himself upon" one of his Christian concubine's "face to kiss and bite her, and she got disgusted by this and turned her face away"; this "so provoked his anger that he ordered the eunuchs to seize her and put a candle to her face, burning and destroying her beauty."[34] Similarly, when Abu Imran the executioner was summoned, he found his master "in the company of a girl, beautiful like an oryx, who was being held by his eunuchs in a corner of the room, who was asking for mercy." The caliph gave none: "Take that whore, Abu Imran, and cut her neck." The executioner obliged: "With one blow I made her head fly." The caliph gifted Imran with her jeweled necklace, adding, "May Allah bless it to you."[35] When a thirteen-year-old Christian slave boy rejected his repeated sexual advances, Abd al-Rahman III had him slowly tortured and then beheaded.[36*]

Finally, it bears mentioning that disdain for Christian churches, coupled with desire for European women, coalesced into a familiar stereotype. As Mideast Muslims had portrayed Christian churches and monasteries as places where naturally promiscuous women fornicate, so Ibn 'Abdun (b. 1050), an Andalusian judge, proclaimed:

---

* Considering that Rahman had 3,750 slaves and 6,300 concubines, it is likely that he dehumanized thousands more, especially those unfortunate enough to attract his attention. More generally, if this is how the one Muslim ruler most celebrated by Western academics as the epitome of "tolerant" and "enlightened" rule in almost eight centuries of Muslim history in Spain behaved, what might be surmised of other rulers? Ibn Hazm alludes to the answer by referring to him as "one of a number of depraved caliphs" (Fernandez-Morera 2016, 130).

Muslim women shall be prevented from entering their [Christians']
abominable churches, for the priests are evil-doers, fornicators, and
sodomites. Frankish [generic for Spanish, Christian] women must be
forbidden to enter the church except on days of religious services or
festivals, for it is their habit to eat and drink and fornicate with the
priests, among whom there is not one who has not two or more women
with whom he sleeps. This has become a custom among them, for they
have permitted what is forbidden and forbidden what is permitted.[37]

The aforementioned hostility and contempt were hardly limited to obvious enemies such as the free infidels of the north but extended to those
Christians and Jews who acquiesced to Muslim rule as *dhimmis*. In keeping
with the Koran's command to make infidels feel "humbled" (9:29), *jizya*
collectors were advised to hold the infidel by the throat during payment
and yell, "Oh dhimmi, enemy of Allah, pay the jizya that you owe us for
the protection and tolerance we grant you!" An Andalusian *muhtasib*—a
police figure who seeks to "promote virtue and prevent vice," an office that
still exists in Muslim nations such as Saudi Arabia—said a "Muslim must
not massage a Jew or a Christian nor throw away his refuse nor clean his
latrines. The Jew and the Christian are better fitted for such trades, since
they are the trades of those who are vile." Nor were Jews and Christians
permitted to dress in a dignified manner but, "on the contrary be abhorred
and shunned and should not be greeted* with the formula, 'Peace be with
you.'"[38]

Being made to feel inferior was one thing; many *dhimmis* learned to live
with it. But two other sharia provisions created—and continue to create†—
deep frustrations. The first, still colloquially known as Islam's "blasphemy" law, banned on pain of death any speech that could be interpreted

---

* In keeping with Muhammad's command: "Do not initiate the Salam [peace greeting]
to the Jews and Christians, and if you meet any of them in a road, force them to its narrowest alley" (Ibrahim 2013, 152).

† For a comprehensive look into and many modern-day examples of the effects of Islam's apostasy, blasphemy, and proselytism laws, especially as they apply to Christians,
see Ibrahim 2013, 95–145.

as offensive to Muhammad and/or Islam (including preaching the Gospel, which contradicts—and thus makes a liar of—Muhammad). The second, Islam's apostasy law, also bans on pain of death any Muslim attempts to leave Islam (which, then and now, is particularly evident when a Muslim actively converts to and practices another religion, usually Christianity, as opposed to merely being indifferent to Islam). These laws had a suffocating effect on freedom of thought, speech, and even conscience, and led to frequent uprisings by Christian *dhimmis* and recent/nominal converts—followed by brutal Muslim suppressions and wholesale massacres.

Though perhaps superfluous, it is briefly worth noting that both Christians and Muslims saw and disliked each other through distinctly ideological prisms. Like their Eastern coreligionists, many Spanish Christians believed that Muhammad was, to quote a seventh-century document, a "son of darkness."[39] "Inspired by a malign spirit, he invented an abominable sect consonant with carnal delights . . . of carnal men," wrote another;[40] Muslims "were ordered to rob, to make prisoner and to kill the adversaries of God [Allah] and their prophet, and to persecute and destroy them in every way." Christians remained scandalized by Islamic sexuality, wondering "what will paradise be, but a tavern of unwearied gorging and a brothel of perpetual turpitude?"[41]

For Muslims, Christians remained contemptible infidels who dared associate a man (Jesus) with Allah—that is, "Allah's enemies," to be fought to the death or submission. The mention of a Christian king's name was always followed by "May Allah curse [or damn] him!"[42] Whereas the Muslims of the East dubbed the Byzantine emperor "Dog of the Romans," the Muslims of Spain made use of Islam's other unclean animal: the pig, as one emir so named King Alfonso VI of Castile-Leon.

"THE VICTORIOUS" JIHADI

Such is the backdrop of the events to be narrated. After the founding of the Christian kingdom of Asturia (c. 720), a number of other northern Christian kingdoms, including Galicia, Leon, Castile, Navarre, Aragon, and Catalonia—whose significance and names morphed and changed with the vicissitudes of time—evolved from and alongside the "mustard seed." Though largely free, they spent more than three centuries on the defensive and were sometimes almost snuffed out—for instance in 793, when Cordoban Emir Hisham I (b. 757) declared jihad against the north. One hundred thousand jihadis, coming from as far as Arabia, answered his call: "For several months he [Hisham's general Abd al-Malik] traversed this land in every direction, raping women, killing warriors, destroying fortresses, burning and pillaging everything, driving back the enemy who fled in disorder," writes Ibn al-Athir. "He returned safe and sound, dragging behind him Allah alone knows how much booty." Although the chronicler refers to this as "one of the most famous expeditions of the Muslims of Spain," it was also one of countless.[43]

But it would be left to Muhammad bin Abi Amir (938–1002)—originally a student of sharia in Cordoba—to crush the northern kingdoms once and for all. Once he proclaimed jihad—and because "every young Moor of ambition, every aspirant for a paradise, either in this world or the next . . . when seized with the spirit of adventure, or an excess of devotion, or inspired by greed of land, or in quest of social distinction, sought his career and his field in Christian Spain"[44]—they flocked to his banner in droves. With these hordes, Muhammad "made war, summer and winter, against the Christians," boasts a Muslim chronicler;[45] he launched and participated in fifty-seven jihads, all successful, earning him the appellation of Almanzor (from Arabic al-mansur), "the Victorious." He sacked, burned, and terrorized the Christian regions of the north—destroying their churches so that "not a trace remained"[46]—including in the burgeoning kingdoms of Leon, Castile, and Barcelona, and ritually massacred or enslaved tens of thousands. Unlike others, his jihad appears to have been motivated by sincere piety and not just a pious pretext for war, rapine, and plunder: he always carried a Koran, "over which he meditated endlessly"[47]; and, because "the martyr should be buried with his body unwashed . . . and still in his bloodstained clothes, since the mode of his suffering and death has already purified him,"[48] the Victorious Muhammad saved a "great coffer" of "dust which covered his boots and clothes in the course of his campaigns against the Christians." This he ordered sprinkled atop his grave when he died, so that Allah might be pleased with him on judgment day.[49]

In 997 Almanzor reached the northwestern corner of Spain—now deep into Christian territory—and sacked Santiago de Compostela, a pilgrimage site second only to Rome. It contained the remains of Saint James the Greater, the nation's patron saint—later dubbed Santiago Matamoros, or Saint James the Moor-Slayer, for reportedly appearing on a snow-white charger and helping Christians slaughter thousands of Muslims in 844 at Clavijo. Because Almanzor held a "special grudge against this fighting saint," he razed his shrine to the ground; its icons, statues, and crosses were "overthrown and mutilated"; the church bells of Compostela were sent to and used as lamps at the Great Mosque of Cordoba. The monks who took up arms to defend the sanctuary were slaughtered; only the saint's tomb was spared, supposedly by "divine splendor," which "dazzled the eyes of the audacious invaders."[50] The attack backfired; "news of the desecration of the sanctuary far from arousing fear and dismay, or causing disaffection, aroused extraordinary indignation and renewed fervor. The cause of James the Apostle became the cause of the whole of Christendom."[51]

Almanzor himself sensed the coming storm. In 1002, as he lay dying from a mortal wound sustained during another campaign on a Christian site, this Islamic cleric turned emir lamented his failure to extirpate the northern infidels: "Had I laid waste all the territories subdued by my arms, had I by ruin and destruction made a desert of at least ten days' march between our extreme frontier and that of the Christians, we might then have averted the approaching tempest."[52]

Whether these words were posthumously attributed to Almanzor or not, they would prove true. By 1031 Muslim infighting caused the Cordoban caliphate to crumble into some thirty petty Muslim states. So began the First Taifa (Arabic for "sect"), which is reminiscent of the First Fitna and other Muslim civil wars: as Muslim chieftain fought Muslim chieftain, the pristine notion of jihad on infidels lost meaning, giving the northerners a respite to regroup and respond. By the 1050s, Ferdinand I of Leon-Castile could reverse the tables on and weaken neighboring Muslim kingdoms by exacting tribute and financially bleeding them. His son, Alfonso VI, followed the same policy; his ambassador explained the logic: "Al-Andalus originally belonged to the Christians. Then they were defeated by the Arabs. . . . Now that they are strong and capable, the Christians desire to recover what they have lost by force. This can only be achieved by weakness and encroachment. In the long run, when it [al-Andalus] has neither men nor money, we'll be able to recover it without any difficulty."[53]

Having fiscally bled the enemy dry, Alfonso VI drove the Muslims out of Toledo, the Visigoths' ancient capital in 1085—the formal start date of the Reconquista. This highly symbolic victory "made a great noise throughout Christendom. Loud was the lamentations among the Mahommedans."[54] Alfonso explained his motivation:

> The city, by the hidden judgment of God, for three hundred and seventy-six years had been held by the Moors who commonly blasphemed the name of Christ. . . . In the place where our holy fathers adored the God of faith, the name of the cursed Muhammad was invoked . . . I took up arms against the barbarous peoples. . . . I directed my army against this city . . . thinking that it would be pleasing in the sight of the Lord, if I, Alfonso, the emperor, under the leadership of Christ, were able to restore to the devotees of his faith, the city which wicked people under the evil guidance of their leader Muhammad had taken from the Christians.[55]

RECONQUEST?

Here it is necessary to pause and evaluate the very theme of *reconquest* in light of the fashionable view that Christian claims to reconquer Spain from Muslim invaders were largely manufactured during the crusading era as a pretext—or myth—to justify what were merely territorial wars.[56] Academics who hold this view argue that because Christians and Muslims sometimes allied together against their own coreligionists, religion was always an alibi, never the real reason behind wars in Spain.

Reality is more complex. Having broken away from Cordoban authority and the demands of its fanatical *ulema*,* the Taifa kings soon found
the duties of annual jihad burdensome, cooled on their Islam, and coop-
erated with whoever best met their interests. For Muslim kingdoms adjacent to Christian powers this often meant Christians. A racial factor was
also involved. As seen, most of the Muslim aristocracy was born to European slave mothers; many emirs had fair hair, eyes, and complexions; they
looked more like—and felt an affinity to—their Christian neighbors, than
the more African and Arab populations of the south.†

Still, beneath the convenient veneer of Muslim-Christian cooperation
lay that old, existential hate, flaring out whenever opportune. Thus, when
Cordoban emir Abdullah bin Muhammad (d. 912) took Polei castle, which
was defended by both Muslim and Christian soldiers, he pardoned the Muslims while executing one thousand Christians for refusing to convert to
Islam (minus one who complied). As one Reconquista historian writes:

> The reconquest can best be understood as an ongoing process, which,
> though often interrupted by truces, remained the ultimate goal to-
> ward which Christian rulers directed their efforts over several centu-
> ries. Claiming descent from the Visigoths, they argued that they had
> a right, indeed an obligation, to recover the lands of the Visigothic
> kingdom; once Christian, those lands were now believed to be held
> unjustly by the Muslims. Thus the struggle for territory was placed
> in a religious context and the reconquest became a religious war be-
> tween Christians and Muslims.[57]

---

* Contrary to popular belief, "in no other place within the Islamic empire was the influence of Islamic clerics on daily life as strong as in al-Andalus" (Fernandez-Morera
2016, 91).

† Abd al-Rahman III "had white skin, a pink face, and blue eyes, and he tinted his
blond hair black to appear more 'Arabic' to his subjects." Because each successive
caliph mated almost exclusively with white Christian slave girls, the "Arab" gene was
successively reduced in half, so that the last Umayyad caliph, Hisham II (d. 1013) was
approximately only .09 percent Arab (Fernandez-Morera 2016, 162–163).

The claim that the Reconquista was an ideological pretext for generic war further ignores what those Christians who withdrew to Spain's northwest quadrant always said—that is, ignores the primary sources of history. Even if Pelayo's boast that "through this little mountain, which you see, the well-being of Spain and the army of the Gothic people will be restored" was posthumously attributed, that still means the idea of reconquest is at least as old as Alfonso III, the Asturian (b. 848), who lived centuries before "pretexts" for twelfth- and thirteenth-century crusades on Andalusian Muslims were needed (the account was recorded during his reign).

Similarly, from Pelayo on, nothing earned Christian kings as much praise from the chroniclers as recapturing territory from Muslims. Phrases such as "extended the kingdom," "expanded the land of the Christians," "liberated from Moors," or "liberated from Arabs" highlight the reigns of the earliest fighting kings. "Killing all the Arabs with the sword, he led the [freed] Christians back with him to his country," is Alfonso I's (r. 739–757) claim to fame.[58] Fernando I (1016–1065)—praised for having "expelled the madness of the Moors from Portugal"[59]—succinctly explained the matter to a Muslim delegation:

> We seek only our own lands which you conquered from us in times past at the beginning of your history. Now you have dwelled in them for the time allotted to you and we have become victorious over you as a result of your own wickedness. So go to your own side of the straits [of Gibraltar, to Africa] and leave our lands to us, for no good will come to you from dwelling here with us after today. For we shall not hold back from you until God decides between us.[60]

No one deemed such "separatist" sentiments unjust. A century before Islam invaded Iberia, Saint Isidore of Seville (d. 636), like Augustine before him, had explained that "a war is just which is carried on after a declaration to recover property or to repel enemies."[61] "There is war between Christians and Moors and there will be until the Christians have recovered the lands that the Moors have taken from them by force," prince Juan Manuel

(d. 1348) once observed before highlighting the difference between Just War and just plain old jihad: "There would not be war between them on account of religion or sect, because Jesus Christ never ordered that anyone should be killed or forced to accept his religion."[62] As for the popes in Rome, they regularly exhorted the kings of Spain "to expel them [the Muslims] and drive them far from the lands which the Christian people had cultivated for a long time before."[63]

In short, the idea that the Reconquista was later manufactured is rooted to the demonstrably false claim that the crusades were unprovoked wars of conquests on Muslims, and so both needed pretexts. That said, Europeans *did* see a connection between Jerusalem and Spain: both were Christian centuries before Islam invaded and conquered them; in both Christians continued to be abused; and thus both needed liberating.

THE SECOND ISLAMIC INVASION OF SPAIN

With the recapture of Toledo in 1085, Christians held nearly half of the Peninsula's territory. Muslims began to perceive the despised "swine" that had been holed up in the north for centuries as a real threat. In a recurring theme that continues to manifest to this day, they blamed their woes on the libertine, un-Islamic behavior of the Taifa rulers who had failed to enforce the totality of sharia. One chronicler captures popular sentiment: Muslims were on the retreat "because of the lack of care of their kings, because of their abandonment of [Islamic] ruling, because of their abandonment of war [periodic jihad] . . . and because of their indolence and their liking for good living, since the only preoccupation of each one of them was the wine they drank, the female singers they listened to, and the amusements in which they spent their days."[64]

Pressured by their subjects, the Taifa kings made the fateful decision of summoning a jihadi regime from Africa to their aid. The Almoravids— from Arabic *al-murabitun,* "those who man the *ribat*"—were austere and pious (today "radical") Islamic zealots who, as their name denotes, devoted their lives to waging jihad along the frontiers of the Niger and Senegal rivers. Outraged to learn that Christian infidels were lording over Andalusian

Muslims, they eagerly accepted the invitation and entered southern Spain en masse. In 1086, one year after Alfonso's recapture of Toledo, the African tribesmen met and—through the old nomadic feigned cavalry retreat followed by outflanking tactic—crushed the Christian hero at the battle of Sagrajas (or Zallaqa)—"one of the most bloody ever fought between Christian and Moor."[65] The king himself barely escaped the carnage with severe wounds. Afterward, the foreign victors erected a mountain from some 2,400 Christian heads, whence triumphant cries of "Allahu Akbar" rang.[66] Unlike the racially and religiously watered-down Muslims of al-Andalus, this was a new—or rather old—breed of Muslims: in appearance and behavior they resembled those Africans that first invaded the Peninsula in the eighth century under the leadership of Tarek and Musa; and in certain respects this was the second mass invasion of Spain in the name of Islam.

Over in Rome, Pope Urban II perceived this latest jihad as a "threat not only to Christian Spain but also to southern France." In 1089 he exhorted the region's nobles and bishops to refortify and arm Tarragona, near the Pyrenees border, "so that city . . . may be celebrated as a barrier and bulwark against the Saracens for the Christian people." Anticipating his call at Clermont in 1095 by six years, Urban decreed that Christians fighting and dying against Muslims in Spain earned remission of sins.[*] He even forbade enthusiastic Spanish knights from joining the crusades in the East: "For there is no virtue in delivering Christians from Saracens there while exposing Christians here to the tyranny and oppression of the Saracens,"[67] explained the pope.[†]

The Almoravid chief, Yusif bin Tashufin (r. 1061–1106), could not press his victory at Sagrajas due to rebellions in North Africa, which he

---

[*] He was not alone: After Urban II, "Paschal II, Gelasius II, Calixtus II, Eugenius III, and Anastasius IV all emphasized that anyone engaged in the struggle against Islam in Spain merited the remission of sins given for the oriental crusade" (O'Callaghan 2004, 48).

[†] Similarly, in 1101 Pope Paschal II forbade Christians from leaving Spain—"which the ferocity of the Moabites [Almoravids] so frequently assails"—to crusade in the Holy Land. "For we are not a little fearful of the tyranny [of the Muslims] in the western regions if you depart. . . . We command you to stay in your country; fight with all your strength against the Moabites and the Moors" (O'Callaghan 2004, 34).

returned to quell. He returned in 1089 "with a large body of Africans and proclaimed a jihad, or holy war, calling upon all the Mahommedan princes of Andalusia to join his standard. But whether by reason of their own dissensions, or from an apprehension which proved to be well founded," the Taifa kings, "who by this time had discovered the Africans to be rude barbarians" with an "excess of religious zeal, responded but languidly to the appeal."[68] Yusif attacked Toledo without them; although he ravaged much of the surrounding countryside, he failed to take the city. The "moderate" Muslim aristocracy was again blamed: "In the Muslim cities the ordinary people, in an attack of religious fervor fueled by their enthusiasm for military victory, supported the fierce, sanctimonious power of the Almoravids. The old emirs of al-Andalus were considered corrupt libertines . . . and were sent off into exile."[69]

Andalusia's new masters kept the Christian line from advancing south but spent most of their energy reabsorbing the Taifa states. With the fall of Saragossa in 1102, the Almoravids consolidated the remainder of Muslim Spain under their rule and enforced strict sharia, which saw the renewed persecution of Christian *dhimmis* and razing of their churches.

An indecisive tug of war ensued over the following years between Muslim and Christian. Then, in 1118, another Alfonso (b. 1074)—surnamed the "Battler" or "Warrior"—took charge of and spearheaded the Reconquista. Described as the "quintessential crusader devoted to the destruction of Islam until his dying day," this founder of the new kingdom of Aragon attacked the Ebro River Valley and, with the aid of Frankish veterans from the First Crusade, retook Saragossa in 1118.[70] This was the first major Christian victory over Islam since Toledo thirty-three years earlier. The Battler continued his relentless drive into Almoravid territory, often returning with thousands of rescued Christian *dhimmis*. Because that which does not kill makes one stronger, they were ideal for and volunteered to repopulate and man the devastated frontier zone again Islam. Muslim leaders responded with the usual: collective punishment. Bertrand summarizes these times:

From the outset of the Almoravid invasion the destruction of Christian churches had begun. . . . The *faquis* [or *fuqaha'*, experts in sharia] commenced to persecute the Christian *Mozarabs* [*dhimmis*] so intolerably that they begged the king of Aragon, Alfonso the Warrior, to come and deliver them. The Aragonese did not succeed in taking Granada. When they retreated, the faquis avenged themselves on the Mozarabs in the most ruthless fashion. Already ten thousand of them had been compelled to emigrate into the territory of Alfonso to escape their enemies' repression. The remainder were deprived of their property, imprisoned, or put to death. Many of them were deported to Africa . . . where oppression of all kinds compelled them to embrace Islam. Ten years later there was a fresh expulsion. The Christians were again deported to Morocco *en masse*. Here, then, were cities and whole districts depopulated by massacres and proscriptions.[71]

In 1134, Alfonso the Battler—"reckoned among the greatest warriors of the age, who contributed materially to the extension of the frontiers of Christian Spain"[72]—died in battle. Christians everywhere feared the future: men shaved their heads and rent their clothes; woman scratched their faces bloody. All lamented: "O best defender, who have you named to defend us? For the Almoravids will now invade the kingdom that by royal power you ripped from the hands of the Saracens, and we will be captured without a defender."[73]

But by now crusading fervor had reached a fever pitch in Europe—especially in that centuries-old microcosmic field of battle, Spain; other battlers and warriors were on the move. In 1138, Alfonso VII of Leon, while ravaging northern Andalusia, "destroyed their synagogues [mosques] and burned the books of Muhammad's law with fire. All the learned men of sharia, wherever they were found, were put to the sword," lamented Ibn al-Hayyan.[74] In 1139, Afonso Henriques defeated the Almoravids at Ourique, "undoubtedly one of the severest blows ever inflicted on the Moorish dominion,"[75] and became the first king of the newborn nation of Portugal.

By 1146, the Christians were making unprecedented advances south, even taking Cordoba for a brief time. In 1147, with the aid of Second Crusaders—English, Scottish, Anglo-Norman, and Flemish men who had come to fight "the infidels and enemies of the cross of Christ"[76]—Lisbon, Tortosa, and Almeria were recaptured. Such are some of the fruits borne of the Second Crusade, which is generally dismissed as ineffective due to its failures in the East.

THE THIRD ISLAMIC INVASION OF SPAIN

In response to this barrage of Christian victories, history repeated itself: "Just as the Almoravides, fresh from the desert and mountains, had prevailed over the effeminate Andalusians, so a fresh burst of fanatical warriors from regenerate Islam was to supersede the Almoravides."[77] The discontent Muslim masses now accused the Almoravids of impiety and summoned the aid of another even more "radical" North African regime: the Almohads, from Arabic *al-muwahidun,* those who profess *tawhid,* the absolute unity of Allah, and relentless jihad on anyone who associates anything with the deity—which always included Trinitarian (that is, "polytheistic") Christians.

The origins of the Almohads trace to Ibn Tumart (1082–1130). A Berber from the Atlas Mountains, he traveled to the great madrassas of the East before returning to Morocco in 1118 as an accomplished master of sharia. Well liked and respected for his learning and piety, Tumart's megalomaniacal designs became apparent when he began to present himself not just as the Mahdi—a "guided one" of mystical pedigree who sets wrongs to rights in Islamic eschatology—but as the prophet Muhammad himself reincarnated. Of the throngs of African tribesmen he seduced, al-Marrakushi (b. 1185), a Muslim scholar well acquainted with Almohad origins, writes:

> Their enchantment with him grew, their respect for him was confirmed, so that at last they came to the point where if he ordered one of them to murder his own father or brother or son, he would have hastened to do so without the least hesitation. This would have been

facilitated by the natural lightness with which these people shed blood; this is a thing which is one of the inborn traits of their nature, and to which the climate of their region predisposes them. . . . As to the alacrity with which they shed blood, I myself during my stay in the Sus [south of Morocco] saw some astonishing examples.[78]

In 1123, Tumart "raised a considerable army" of Africans and told them: "March against these heretics and perverters of religion who call themselves the al-Murabits [Almoravids], and call them to put away their evil habits, reform their morals, renounce heresy, and acknowledge the sinless Imam Mahdi," that is, himself. To press home that he was Muhammad made manifest again, he commanded them with the same words and formulations the prophet had used: "If they [Almoravids] respond to your call, then they are your brothers; what they have will be yours, and what you owe they will owe. And if they do not, then fight them, for the Sunna makes it lawful for you."* His followers began raiding far and near, "cutting off provisions and communications, killing and pillaging without sparing anyone," including fellow Muslims not deemed Islamic enough. And, as happened four centuries earlier—when the Berbers had concluded that if they could not beat the jihad they might as well join it—"great numbers of people recognized their authority and joined them."[79]

Once they had overthrown the Almoravid base in North Africa, the Almohads—"the fiercest and most fanatical of all the Mahommedan hordes which had yet visited the country"[80]—began pouring into Spain in 1146. As their barges touched land, trains of camels carrying veiled emirs marched out, "causing consternation among the Christians,"[81] who were unused to the uncouth desert dromedaries.

So began Spain's third Islamic invasion. The Almohads scored several

---

* Compare with the prophet's injunctions in a canonical hadith: "When you meet your enemies who are polytheists, invite them to three courses of action. If they respond to any one of these, you also accept it and withhold yourself from doing them any harm. Invite them to (accept) Islam; if they respond to you, accept it from them and desist from fighting against them. . . . If they refuse to accept Islam, demand from them the jizya. If they agree to pay, accept it from them and hold off your hands. If they refuse to pay the tax, seek Allah's help and fight them" (*Sahih Muslim* 19:4294).

initial victories against the Christian kingdoms, stopped the frontier from moving south, and "began an intense persecution of the Christians still under Muslim rule."[82] By 1164, whatever Christian *dhimmi* population was left in Granada was exterminated.

Pope Adrian IV in Rome urged Christians to subdue these "barbarous peoples and wild nations, that is, the madness of the Saracens who are a most destructive pestilence."[83] As an immediate defense against this latest jihad, Christian kingdoms expanded the roles of the military orders, including by establishing native orders to garrison strongholds and safeguard their borders. Living in castles along the Christian-Muslim frontier, these warrior-monks served as the first and sturdiest line of defense. As in Outremer, they were Spain's answer to Islam's *ribat,* and were augmented by the Almogavers: Christian volunteers (originally farmers, shepherds, and escaped *dhimmis*) clad in rough garments and armed with daggers who lived in the forests along the frontier and made it their business to raid or repel Muslims—the Reconquista's Robin Hoods.[84]

In 1184, Almohad caliph Abu Yaqub, renowned for his successful jihads on the Christians, died from battle wounds against them; in 1185, Afonso I of Leon-Castile—"the Conqueror," another "intrepid extirpator of the enemies of the Christian name"[85]—followed the caliph to the grave. A lull set in; treaties were made and the Reconquista forestalled. Soon the Spaniard kings began quarreling among themselves, even as the Muslims began to advance, including with notable victories against Portugal in 1190. Three years later, Pope Celestine III—outraged[†] that Christian kings were signing treaties advantageous to the Almohads while weakening each other through infighting—ordered Spain's prelates to make peace between the monarchs and terminate all truces with the Almohads.

Once accomplished, a coalition of Christian forces, augmented by volunteers from around Christendom, was ordered to assemble under the leadership of King Alfonso VIII of Castile (1155–1214), surnamed "the Noble" for his widely acknowledged just and pious rule.[‡] Instead of waiting for

---

[†] That countless other Christians had just sacrificed their lives fighting Muslims in the brutal Third Crusade (1189–1192) did not help his mood.

[‡] After quoting one chronicler who referred to Alfonso VIII in effusive terms—"the

reinforcements, he rashly decided to engage the numerically superior Muslim army, led by Caliph Abu Yusuf (r. 1184–1199) and stationed at Alarcos, just south of Toledo.

On seeing infidels advance, the Muslims were exhorted by the jihad's win-win rationale: "fight in the service of Allah . . . after which shall follow either a glorious martyrdom and the joys of paradise, or victory and rich spoils."[86] Then on July 18, 1195, "the Almohads, well-rested and organized in tribal groups each with its own standards, initiated the combat. The Christians, disconcerted, charged in a disorderly manner, dispersing some of the volunteers who had come to participate in the holy war."[87]

At one point the Muslim line feigned retreat; when Alfonso gave chase, the Almohads outflanked and encircled the Christians. All was lost. Alfonso sought to "plunge [himself] into the midst of the Moors and redeem his lost honour" by fighting to the death, but was forcefully prevented by his retreating nobles. Alarcos went down "in the annals of Spain as one of the most calamitous reverses ever sustained by the Christian armies—a victory for the Mussulmans so complete as to promise to bring back the days of Almanzor."[88]

And it was all Alfonso's fault, for spurning reinforcements and rashly engaging the caliph. The indignity rankled, but the forty-year-old king had time.

Because insurrections in North Africa were a constant and required his attention, Abu Yusuf was unable to press his advantage and made a truce with the kings of Castile, Leon, and Navarre—who anyway had begun fighting each other once again.

In May 1211, Almohad caliph Muhammad al-Nasir (r. 1199–1213), known to Christians as Miramamolin,* left Africa for Spain intent on destroying Alfonso VIII, still seen by Andalusian Muslims as the nearest and

---

best king who had ever been in Christendom, the light of Spain, the shield and sustenance of Christianity, a king most loyal and truthful, in all things straightforward and pious, and perfect in all good manners"—the normally skeptical nineteenth-century Henry E. Watts conceded that Alfonso "seems to have deserved this flattering character better than any of his predecessors" (1894, 112).

* A corruption of the Arabic emir al-mu'minin ("Commander of the Faithful"), a title first adopted by history's second caliph, Omar bin al-Khattab).

strongest infidel. In July the caliph besieged Salvatierra Castle, which stood eighteen miles south of and protected the road to Toledo, whence the king reigned. After enduring a fifty-one-day siege, the knights surrendered. Exultant, the caliph boasted he had cut off "the right hand of the king of Castile" and cited Alfonso's absence as "the clearest proof of his weakness."

Things continued to worsen for the disgraced king of Alarcos infamy. Weeks later, his oldest son and heir, Infante Fernando—who had dedicated "the first fruits of his knighthood to Almighty God by driving the enemies of the Christian name from the bounds of his inheritance which they impiously occupied"—died at age twenty-two.[89] With the jihad fast approaching, and while mourning his beloved son, Alfonso made ready for the siege of Toledo—or, in his words, made ready to "be counted among the martyrs."[90]

Also noting that Alfonso was preparing "to die rather than witness the ruin of the Christian people," Pope Innocent III declared a crusade and, in the words of the *Anales Toledanos I,* granted "such liberty throughout the whole world that all should be absolved from their sins, and this pardon was [granted] because the king of Morocco said that he would fight against those who adored the cross throughout the world." Innocent exhorted the Spaniard kings to keep the peace, stay focused, and aid each other "against the enemies of the cross of the Lord who not only aspire to the destruction of the Spains, but also threatened to vent their rage on Christ's faithful in other lands and, if they can—which God forbid—oppress the Christian name."[91]

That the caliph sought to extirpate Christianity by fire and sword is documented in other sources. In a widely circulated letter attributed to Muhammad al-Nasir himself, he boasted that Muslims had "cleansed Jerusalem of the filthiness of the Christians," and that the latter should "submit to our empire and convert to our [sharia] law." Otherwise "all those who adore the sign of the cross . . . will feel our scimitars."[†]

Troubadours everywhere sought to rile Christians: "Saladin took Jerusalem," they sang in verse, and "now the king of Morocco announces that

---

[†] After pointing out that "the letter's language is quite unlike that of authentic Almohad letters," one authority concludes that, "though, if asked, al-Nasir would likely have subscribed to the sentiments expressed" (O'Callaghan 2004, 68).

he will fight against all the kings of the Christians with his treacherous Andalusians and Arabs," who "in their pride think the world belongs to them."
Even so, "with Him [God] you will conquer all the dogs and renegade turncoats that Muhammad has bamboozled." The religious divide was heightened by a racial one: "Firm in the faith, let us not abandon our heritage to
the black dogs from oversea."[92]

THE BATTLE OF LAS NAVAS DE TOLOSA

Finally, between May 13 and 20, "the faithful of Christ gathered at Toledo
from all parts of the world . . . to give battle in support of Christendom in
Spain." On May 16, fasting men and women made barefoot processions
around the Lateran Basilica in Rome and prayed "that God might be pro-
pitious to those engaged in battle"; similarly, "litanies and prayers were
offered in France for the Christians who were about to fight in Spain."[93]

Alfonso VIII hosted an impressive array of crusaders in Toledo. Pedro II of Aragon, and the titan-like Sancho VII of Navarre,* were present
with their men. The king of Leon failed to appear, but many of his subjects
came. Thousands of Frankish knights, Catalan warriors, free Christians,
and fighting clergymen from everywhere were there. The military orders
were present and eager for battle. To support such a vast force—including
two thousand knights and their squires, ten thousand cavalrymen, and up
to fifty thousand infantrymen—Alfonso strained his resources to the limit,
dispensed with "gold as though it were water," and commanded the Spanish
church to submit half of its resources to the war effort.[94]

On June 20, "Alfonso—may Allah curse him—left Toledo with a vast
army and proceeded to Calatrava, which he besieged," writes contemporary Muslim chronicler al-Marrakushi:

> The castle had been in Muslim hands since al-Mansur Abu Yusuf
> conquered it following the great victory [of Alarcos]. The Muslims

---

* According to a study published in 1952 by Luis del Campo, who examined Sancho's
remains, the king of Navarre was apparently over seven feet tall. (https://dialnet.unirioja
.es/servlet/articulo?codigo=2253697)

surrendered it to Alfonso after he had given them a safe conduct. Thereupon, a large number of the Christians [Franks] withdrew from Alfonso (may Allah curse him!), when he prevented them from killing the Muslims who were in the castle. They said, you have only brought us along to help you conquer the country, and forbid us to plunder and kill the Muslims.[95]

Archbishop Rodrigo of Toledo confirms that "only Spaniards and a few northerners" saw the crusade to its end.[96]

By July 6 the crusader army had taken several other Muslim strongholds and was now deep into hostile and unfamiliar territory, suffering from lack of water. A mysterious shepherd guided them through a "relatively easy passage" until they reached Las Navas de Tolosa,[†] over one hundred miles south of Toledo—precisely where Caliph Muhammad al-Nasir, who had left Seville to meet the Christians two days after they had left Toledo, was currently situated.[97]

The army he brought with him "was a very large, heterogeneous force, made up of Berbers, tough black slave warriors (the 'imesebelen,' who were chained together as an unbreakable guard around the Almohad caliph's tent), Arabs, Turkic mounted archers, Andalusian Muslim levies . . . mujahidin (volunteer religious fighters—jihadists—from all over the Islamic world), and even Christian mercenaries and defectors."[98]

"When the Saracen army realized" Christian fighters were approaching, "they advanced in order to stop camp from being established," Alfonso wrote in his journal. "Our men, even though few, defended themselves bravely." Recalling his rashness at Alarcos, he and his men "waited, fully armed . . . on the crest of the mountain, until the whole army of the Lord safely" arrived on Saturday, July 14. "Very early next day, Sunday, the Saracens came up with their huge army arrayed in battle-lines."[99]

The two forces could not have looked any more different: most of the approximately twelve thousand Spaniards were heavily armored; knights

---

† There is reason to believe that the battle took place seven miles north of its place name, in the mountainous region between Santa Elena and Miranda del Rey.

carried three-foot-long double-sided swords. In comparison, most of the African Muslims were near naked, their shields made of hippo hides. But their numbers—thirty thousand—and unbridled ferocity made up for it.

The Christians spent the rest of that Sunday recuperating and preparing, including spiritually. On their knees, tearful men beat their chests and implored God for strength. Militant clergymen—all of whom were determined "to rip from the hands of the Muslims the land they held to the injury of the Christian name"—roamed the camp, administered the Eucharist, heard the confessions of and exhorted the crusaders to fight with all their might. Then, about midnight, "the voice of exultation and confession sounded in the Christian tents and the voice of the herald summoned all to arm themselves for the Lord's battle."[100] A contemporary summarizes:

> After hearing the solemnities of masses, and being renewed by the life-giving sacrament of the Body and Blood of Jesus Christ, our God, they fortified themselves with the sign of the cross. They quickly took up their weapons of war, and with joy rushed to the battle as if they were invited to a feast. Neither the broken and stony places, nor the hollows of the valleys nor the steep mountains held them back. They advanced on the enemy prepared to die or to conquer.[101]

Such determination was especially evident in King Alfonso. For nearly twenty years, his disastrous defeat at Alarcos had festered; then, he had sought to die in battle but was prevented the honor. Now, aged fifty-seven and at the head of a mighty host, he would either be avenged or die trying. Everyone's eyes were on him that eve of battle; a homilist foretold the fated king that the ignominy and opprobrium he had incurred at Alarcos "would be purged on that day [of battle, tomorrow] by the power of our Lord Jesus Christ and his most victorious cross, against which the king of Morocco had blasphemed from his filthy mouth."[102]

Even so, the fey king appeared pessimistic; to Rodrigo he said, "Archbishop, you and I will die here." The heavily armored clergyman replied, "Never, for you will overcome your enemies here." After some talk of military strategy, Alfonso, looking on the enemy hordes, became dismal again: "Archbishop, here we will die"—though a "death in such circumstances is not unworthy."* "If it please God," Rodrigo concluded, "let it not be death, but the crown of victory; but if it should please God otherwise, we are all prepared to die together with you."[103]

With the crack of dawn, battle commenced on July 16. King Pedro commanded the Christian left and King Sancho the right. In the center stood the battle-hardened military orders and Castilians, with Alfonso overseeing everything from the rear. The Muslim front lines consisted of the usual light cavalry; behind them came the rest of the diverse forces, ordered by tribe; in the very rear was Caliph Muhammad's tent, surrounded by a bodyguard of black slave-warriors chained together. The Almohad army appears to have made good use of the terrain: "The enemy occupied certain eminences, very steep places and difficult to climb by reason of the woods which lay between us and them, and by reason of some very deep gorges cut by streams, all of which formed a major impediment to us and was a great help to the enemy," noted Alfonso.[104]

For long the battle was something of a stalemate: "Those lined up in the first ranks discovered that the Moors were ready for battle," writes a contemporary: "They attacked, fighting against one another, hand-to-hand, with lances, swords, and battle-axes; there was no room for archers. The Christians pressed on; the Moors repelled them; the crashing and tumult of arms was heard. The battle was joined, but neither side was overcome, although at times they pushed back the enemy, and at other times they were driven back by the enemy."[105]

Determined to penetrate the Muslim host, "our front ranks," wrote Alfonso, "and some of the middle ranks . . . cut down many lines of the enemy who were stationed on the lower eminences. When our men reached the last of their lines, consisting of a huge number of soldiers, among whom was the king of Carthage [Muhammad], there began desperate fighting among

---

* "This kind of language appears throughout the twelfth- and thirteenth-century sources and testifies to Christian awareness of a mortal struggle against Islam" (O'Callaghan 2004, 202).

the cavalrymen, infantrymen, and archers, our people being in terrible danger and scarcely able to resist any longer."[106]

For every Muslim line the Christians broke through, others instantly formed—so great were the ranks of Islam. "At one point certain wretched Christians who were retreating and fleeing cried out that the Christians were overcome." When King Alfonso, "who was prepared rather to die than to be conquered [again], heard that cry of doom," he and his knights "hasten[ed] quickly up the hill where the force of the battle was."[107] "Then we," continues Alfonso, "realizing that the fighting was becoming impossible for them [retreating Spaniards], started a cavalry charge, the cross of the Lord going before [us] and our banner with its image of the holy Virgin and her Son imposed upon our device." They fought valiantly, but the Africans continued to close in on them.[108]

Then something of a miracle happened: "Since we had already resolved to die for the faith of Christ, as soon as we witnessed . . . the Saracens" attacking the cross and icons "with stones and arrows," the furious crusaders "broke their line with their vast numbers of men, even though the Saracens resisted bravely in the battle, and stood solidly around their lord."[109] Christians in the rear saw the cross appear as if miraculously and remain aloft behind enemy lines. Inspired beyond hope, the native sons of Spain broke through the Muslim center, slaughtering "a great multitude of them with the sword of the cross." Sancho, the giant king of Navarre, followed by his men, was first to bulldoze through and rout the African slave soldiers chained around the caliph's tent.

Instantly mounting a horse, Caliph Muhammad "turned tail and fled. His men were killed and slaughtered in droves, and the site of the camp and the tents of the Moors became the tombs of the fallen. Those who escaped from the battle wandered scattered about the mountains like sheep without a shepherd," though not for long[110]: "We followed up the pursuit till nightfall, and killed more in that rout than we had in battle."

"In this way the battle of the Lord was triumphantly won, by God alone and through God alone," concluded the once ill-starred but now redeemed king.[111]

THE BEGINNING OF THE END FOR ISLAM

The outcome of battle was a shock to all. Muslim chroniclers offered a plethora of excuses for defeat, from claiming that Alfonso "launched a surprise attack on the Muslims, who were not prepared for battle," to indifference and disaffection among the jihadis, whose "payment was in arrears."[112] Apparently the rugged and closed terrain, which was not conducive to large-scale cavalry maneuvering or archery, also worked against the Muslim way of war. Be that as it may; as with the crusader victory at Antioch in 1098—another engagement where the odds were stacked against the Christians—Las Navas de Tolosa was seen as a miracle by pope and peasant. Not only was the full might of the hitherto unbeatable[*] caliph decimated; but whereas tens of thousands of Muslims died,[†] only some two thousand Christians—mostly the warrior-monks of the military orders who were always wherever fighting was thickest[‡]—perished.

Alfonso ordered a church built on the field of battle to honor the fallen; the miraculous cross of victory was displayed in it. The tapestry covering the entrance of the caliph's tent was sent as a trophy to the monastery of Las Huelgas, where it still hangs as a reminder of when Christian kings met and defeated the combined forces of Muhammad. The lance, silk tent, and gold-worked standard of the caliph—who had only recently vowed to "lodge his horses in the portico of St. Peter's Church and to fix his standard [declaring "There is no god but Allah and Muhammad is his messenger"]

---

[*] "Our father, the king and lord, conquered Miramamolin in a pitched battle," wrote Alfonso's daughter Berenguela to her sister: "we believe this to be a signal honor, because until now it was unheard of that the king of Morocco should be overcome on the battlefield" (O'Callaghan 2004, 72).

[†] "The Saracen horsemen had numbered 185,000," wrote Alfonso, "as we afterwards learned in a true account from certain servants of the sultan, whom we took prisoner; the foot soldiers were uncountable. . . . On their side there fell in the battle 100,000 armed men, perhaps more, according to the estimates of Saracens we captured later" (Allen 2010, 312–313). While Muslim sources are even more extreme—claiming that "only 600 out of 600,000 Almohad soldiers survived the battle"—they reflect the magnitude of the loss in Muslim eyes (O'Callaghan 2004, 144).

[‡] The masters of the orders of Santiago and the Knights Templar both fell on that day; the permanent wounds of the master of Calatrava were so debilitating that he had to resign his commission.

on top of it"—were the only things sent to and hung in St. Peter's in Rome.[113]

Back in Seville, the disgraced caliph downplayed the disaster: "He argued that the consequences for the Christians were bad, while the Muslims remained under divine protection, hardly suffering any harm; nor were their numbers diminished. After admonishing his hearers not to be sad because he was not, he assured them that Allah would not abandon them and would not open a path for the 'infidels.' In essence, the caliph tried to pretend that a great disaster had not occurred."[114]

Muhammad al-Nasir died unlamented on Christmas Day the following year. And he was wrong: "The Christian victory at Las Navas marked the end of Muslim ascendancy in Spain and helped to undermine the Almohad empire, which now entered a period of rapid decline," explains one Reconquista authority. "The balance of power was now tipped decisively in favor of the Christians, thus making possible the subjugation of the greater part of al-Andalus in the next forty years."[115]

One by one, Muslim cities fell to Christians hands. That Muslim leaders were fighting each other did not help. Arguing that the "gate is indeed open and the way clear," because "the Moors"—guided by "the unfaithful and damned apostate, Muhammad"—are undergoing "discord and capital hatreds, divisions, and quarrels," Ferdinand III of Castile (r. 1217–1252) vigorously resumed the Reconquista and in 1236 conquered Cordoba, for centuries the capital of Muslim Spain.[116]

The city "was cleansed of all filthiness of Muhammad," writes a contemporary Spanish chronicler[117]; its Great Mosque, which centuries earlier had been "built with the materials of demolished churches brought to Cordoba on the heads of Christian captives, thus exalting the true religion and trampling polytheism"—as a Muslim historian had once boasted[118]—was reconsecrated as a church.*

---

* Although it has been the Cathedral of Cordoba for nearly 800 years, and was a Christian church before it became a mosque, many in and out of Spain still call it the "Mosque of Cordoba"—as if by rights it was always a mosque, appropriated by Christians, and not vice versa.

Then Ferdinand "ordered the cross to be put upon the chief tower [minaret] where the name of the false Muhammad was wont to be called upon and praised," continues the Spanish chronicler. The sight of the crucifix atop the church-turned-mosque-turned-church again "caused confusion and ineffable lamentation among the Saracens and, on the contrary, ineffable joy to the Christians."[119] Ferdinand—"the tyrant, the accursed one," as he was known to Muslims—also found and returned the bells of Saint James to his sanctuary in Compostela, whence 250 years earlier Almanzor had seized and sent them to the Cordoban mosque as trophies.[120]

As al-Andalus's greatest cities continued to fall to Christian arms—Valencia in 1238, Seville in 1248—similar scenes unfolded: "While the victors customarily guaranteed religious freedom to the vanquished, they also took over the principal mosques and transformed [or retransformed] them into churches." Just as Muslims had for centuries purified captured Christian towns and churches "from the filth of idolatry and . . . from the stains of infidelity and polytheism," so now, tit for tat, Christian conquerors and clergymen engaged in elaborate ceremonies whereby mosques and cities were "cleansed of the filthiness of Muhammad"—a ubiquitous phrase in the chronicles concerning what transpired after Muslim cities were conquered[121]—even as Muslims lamented "over dwellings emptied of Islam" and "mosques . . . wherein only bells and crosses may [now] be found."[122]

Because of the victory at Las Navas de Tolosa, the kings of thirteenth-century Spain all but finished what Pelayo and his Asturian mustard seed began in the eighth century. Christians noted and appreciated the continuity of events: if "miserable Spain was almost entirely devastated" following defeat at Guadalete in 712, five hundred years later, on July 16, 1212, "victorious Spain not only won out against the Ishmaelites, but also vigorously beat them down"[123]; and "the famous city of Cordoba . . . which for such a long time had been held captive, that is, from the time of Rodrigo, king of the Goths, was now restored to the Christian[s]."[124] Las Navas de Tolosa was Christendom's response to Hattin, and for centuries thereafter, July 16 was celebrated as the "Triumph of the Holy Cross" in the Spanish calendar (until Second Vatican abolished it).[125]

As Ferdinand III of Castile lay in his deathbed in 1252, he explained to his son, Alfonso X, what mattered most:

> My lord, I leave you the whole realm from the sea hither that the Moors won from Rodrigo, king of Spain [500 years earlier]. All of it is in your dominion, part of it conquered, the other part tributary. If you know how to preserve in this state what I leave you, you will be as good a king as I; and if you win more for yourself, you will be better than I; but if you diminish it, you will not be as good as I.[126]

The remote Muslim kingdom of Granada, at the very southern tip of the Peninsula, was the only region left to "win more" from. Although it was quickly subjected to tributary status, conquering this final bastion of Islam was stalled for over two centuries. Surrounded by mountainous terrain and with the sea behind it, Granada was well fortified, inaccessible, and isolated from the rest of Iberia. Moreover, Christian infighting habitually flared out, as Castile, Aragon, and Portugal increasingly jockeyed for power. In 1469, King Ferdinand of Aragon and Queen Isabella of Castile were wed, thereby beginning the unification of Spain. It was not long before the monarchs— particularly the queen, a committed Catholic—began eyeing this holdout emirate.

When, on Christmas Day, 1481, Granadan Muslims stormed a Christian fortress in nearby Zahara and slaughtered all present, Ferdinand and Isabella declared war, so that "Christendom might be delivered from this continued threat at the gates," as they wrote the pope, and "these infidels of the kingdom of Granada [might be] ejected and expelled from Spain" once and for all.[127] After a decade of military campaigns and sieges, Granada finally surrendered on January 2, 1492.

"After so much labor, expense, death, and shedding of blood," the monarchs announced, "this kingdom of Granada which was occupied for over seven hundred and eighty years by the infidels" had been liberated.[128] "Church bells pealed across Europe in celebration when Granada fell. That door through which Islam had entered Europe through the West was finally shut after a span of over seven hundred years."[129]

For centuries thereafter, the liberation of Spain was celebrated by parading an effigy of Islam's prophet—the "Mahoma"—before it exploded in fireworks. Although Vatican II formally banned the ritual, it continues to this day in smaller villages.

TAQIYYA: JIHAD GOES UNDERGROUND

Although Islam ceased to be a political power in Spain after the fall of Granada, many Muslims remained—meaning a different type of war was soon underway. From the start, Christian monarchs had generally given newly conquered Muslim populations two options: depart unmolested or remain under the king's protection, which was often enforced with rigor.* Some Muslims stayed and converted to Christianity. Others, known as *mudejares*—from an Arabic word meaning "tamed" or "domesticated"— remained as Muslims and were subjected to the same *dhimmi* stipulations imposed on Christians under Islam. Still others—Muslim purists—not deigning to be ruled by infidels, left for Muslim-held territories, which, after 1252, always meant Granada.

When it surrendered in 1492, Granada's nearly half-million Muslim population had nowhere else to go—except the deserts of Africa—and so chose to remain. Although they were initially granted lenient terms, including the right to travel abroad and practice Islam freely, these *mudejares* proved far from "tamed." They launched many hard-to-quell uprisings— several "involving the stoning, dismembering, beheading, impaling, and burning alive of Christians"[130]—and regularly colluded with foreign, mostly Muslim, powers (first North Africans, later Ottoman Turks) in an effort to subvert Spain back to Islam.†

---

* James I of Aragon executed his own men when they violated the terms of Valencia's surrender (Constable 1997, 211).

† A letter sent by an anonymous Granadan to Ottoman sultan Bayezid II is typical of how Muslims in Spain sought to rile foreign Muslim powers to their aid in the name of Islam: "Alas for the exchanging of Muhammad's religion for that of the Christian dogs, the worst of creatures! . . . Alas for those minarets in which the bells [of the Christians] have been hung in place of the Muslim declaration of the shahada!" The towns "have become strongholds for the worshipers of the Cross, and in them the latter are [horror of horrors] safe against the occurring raids [jihads]" (Allen 2010, 367).

A final "Muslim uprising in 1499, and the crushing of this revolt in 1501, led to an edict that Muslims had to convert to Christianity or leave the peninsula."[131] Contrary to popular belief, the motivation was less religious and more political; it was less about making Muslims "good Christians" and more about making them "good citizens." So long as they remained Muslim, they would remain hostile and disloyal to Christian Spain; and because secularism, atheism, and multiculturalism were not options then, the only practical way Muslims could slough off their tribalism was by embracing Christianity.

Under such circumstances, sharia is clear: Muslims should try to emigrate. But there has always been one important caveat: whenever Muslims find themselves under infidel authority, they may say and do almost anything—denounce Muhammad, receive baptism and communion, venerate the cross, all anathema to Islam—so long as their hearts remain true to Islam. Such is the doctrine of *taqiyya*,* which has traditionally defined Islam's modus operandi under non-Muslim authority. Even the fanatical and uncompromising *ribat* warriors (*al-murabitun*) who devoted their lives to waging jihad on the Eastern Roman Empire were not above such dishonorable tactics, as relayed by the Baghdadi jurist Abd al-Jabbar: "Border warriors and those who resided many years in Constantinople, both as captives

---

* Koran 3:28 is one of the primary verses that sanction *taqiyya*: "Let believers [Muslims] not take infidels [non-Muslims] for friends and allies instead of believers. Whoever does this shall have no relationship left with Allah—except when taking precaution against them in prudence." Al-Tabari (d. 923), author of a mainstream Koran commentary, offers the following exegesis of 3:28: "If you [Muslims] are under their [non-Muslims'] authority, fearing for yourselves, behave loyally to them with your tongue while harboring inner animosity for them . . . [know that] Allah has forbidden believers from being friendly or on intimate terms with the infidels rather than other believers—except when infidels are above them [in authority]. Should that be the case, let them act friendly towards them while preserving their religion." Another mainstream authority on the Koran, Ibn al-Kathir (d. 1373) writes of 3:28, "Whoever at any time or place fears . . . evil [from non-Muslims] may protect himself through outward show." As proof, he quotes Muhammad's close companion Abu Darda: "Let us grin in the face of some people while our hearts curse them." Another companion said, "Doing *taqiyya* is acceptable till the Day of Judgment [i.e., in perpetuity]" (Ibrahim 2010, 3–13). For more, see Raymond Ibrahim, "How Taqiyya Alters Islam's Rules of War," *Middle East Quarterly* 17:1 (2010): 3–13.

and as free men . . . feigned conversion to Christianity out of *taqiyya* and spread out among the Christians and mixed with them."[132]

Moreover, "Sunni Muslims had invoked *taqiyya* to justify dissimulation under Christian domination in other periods and regions, including Sicily after the Norman conquest in 1061–91 and the Byzantine Marches," particularly during the eras of Nikephoros II Phokas and John Tzimiskes, when "large Muslim populations came under Christian rule."[133]

Unsurprisingly, then, *taqiyya* defined Islam in post-Reconquista Spain.[†] Once the edict to convert or emigrate appeared, virtually the entire Granadan population—hundreds of thousands of Muslims—openly embraced Christianity but remained crypto-Muslims. Publicly they went to church and baptized their children; at home they recited the Koran, preached undying hate for the infidel and their obligation to liberate al-Andalus.[‡] That these "Moriscos"—that is, self-professed Muslim converts to Christianity who were still "Moorish," or Islamic—went to great lengths to foist their deception cannot be doubted: "For a Morisco to pass as a good Christian took more than a simple statement to that effect. It required a sustained performance involving hundreds of individual statements and actions of different types, many of which might have little to do with expressions of belief or ritual per se. Dissimulation [*taqiyya*] was an institutionalized practice in Morisco communities that involved regular patterns of behaviour passed on from one generation to the next."[134]

Despite this elaborate masquerade, Christians increasingly caught on: "with the permission and license that their accursed sect accorded them," one frustrated Spaniard remarked, "they could feign any religion outwardly and without sinning, as long as they kept their hearts nevertheless devoted

† One authority refers to a 1504 fatwa promoting *taqiyya* among Spain's subject Muslims as "the key theological document for the study of Spanish Islam" (Harvey 2005, 60). Even so, as a frontier society, where the vicissitudes of war frequently saw Muslims come under Christian authority, al-Andalus's jurists had written about and promoted *taqiyya* from the start.

‡ According to sharia, once a region has been conquered by—or literally "opened" to the light of—Islam, it remains a part of the Abode of Islam forever; if infidels reconquer it, Muslims are obligated to reconquer it.

to their false impostor of a prophet. We saw so many of them who died while worshipping the Cross and speaking well of our Catholic Religion yet who were inwardly excellent Muslims."[135]

Christians initially tried to reason with the Moriscos; they reminded them how they became Muslim in the first place: "Your ancestor was a Christian, although he made himself a Muslim" to avoid persecution or elevate his social status; so now "you also must become a Christian."[136] When that failed, Korans were confiscated and burned; then Arabic, the language of Islam, was banned. When that too failed, more extreme measures were taken; it reached the point that a Morisco could "not even possess a pocketknife for eating with that did not have a rounded point, lest he savage a Christian with it."[137]

A Muslim chronicler summarizes these times: "Such of the Muslims as still remained in Andalus, although Christians in appearance, were not so in their hearts; for they worshipped Allah in secret. . . . The Christians watched over them with the greatest vigilance, and many were discovered and burnt."[138] Such are the origins of the Spanish Inquisition.[*] For no matter how much the Moriscos "might present the appearance of a most peaceful submission," writes Bertrand, "they remained nevertheless fundamental Musulmans, watching for a favourable opportunity and patiently awaiting the hour of revenge, promised by their prophecies."[139]

Thus, when a rumor arose in 1568 that the Ottoman Turks had finally come to liberate them, formerly "domesticated" and "tamed" Muslims near Granada, "believing that the days under Christian rule were over, went berserk. Priests all over the countryside were attacked, mutilated, or murdered; some were burned alive; one was sewed inside a pig and barbequed; the

---

[*] Despite popular belief, many more Muslim Moriscos were tried and executed during the Inquisition than Jewish Marranos (Stark 2012, 347). Moreover, Christian hostility for Jews was fiercely exacerbated by the Christian conflation of Jews with the chief enemy, Muslims. As Daniel Pipes summarizes in his review of *The Jew as Ally of the Muslim: Medieval Roots of Anti-Semitism* (1986): "(1) Medieval Christians feared and hated Muslims. (2) Medieval Christians saw Jews as the allies of Muslims. (3) Therefore, medieval Christians feared and hated Jews. . . . This is a radical new approach" and "makes great sense; indeed, it adds a whole new dimension to our comprehension of the way Christian-Jewish relations developed."

pretty Christian girls were assiduously raped, some sent off to join the harems of Moroccan and Algerian potentates."[140]

In the end, if Muslims could never be loyal to infidel authority—constantly colluding and subverting, including with foreign Muslims—and if conversion to Christianity was no solution due to the dispensation of *taqiyya*, then only one solution remained: between 1609 and 1614, all Moriscos were expelled from the Peninsula to Africa, at which point the nearly one-thousand-year-old war for Spain was truly at an end.†

---

† Although Christian Spain is often vilified for resorting to this last recourse, it had, in fact, merely followed another page from the Islamic playbook: for both the Almoravids and Almohads had deported tens of thousands of Christian *dhimmis* to Africa on the claim that they posed a fifth column that could potentially help their northern coreligionists. Muslims were also first to introduce inquisitions in Spain, trying and torturing new converts.

CHAPTER 7

MUHAMMAD'S DREAM:
THE SIEGE OF CONSTANTINOPLE, 1453

Don't you believe that what I fear could happen, namely that by the just judgment of God this fire [Turkish conquests in Balkans] shall advance so far that it could occupy the border of [Western] Christians? What then are those wretched Christians doing now? What are their princes doing? What about the pastors of the Church? Do they not sleep or do they suffer instead from lethargy so that they simply await Christendom to be consumed bit by bit? They play around—or rather hurt themselves—with lances and dances! And in the meantime, the Turk snuffs out the name of Christ and has already sworn, has already vowed himself to his own God, not to remain at peace under any agreement, unless he hears the praises of Muhammad sung. . . . O where now is . . . Godfrey, Bohemond, Baldwin, and the rest of the princes who . . . liberated the sepulcher of Jesus Christ from the hands of the infidel? . . . Where is that noble Charles [Martel], king of the Franks?

—Bartolomeo de Giano, c. 1438[1]

A MONGOL STORM

DURING THE FINAL YEARS OF THE CRUSADER PRESENCE IN THE Middle East, an unprecedented storm of violence overtook the region: the Mongols—or "Tatars"—had come from the farthest east to conquer. A nomadic people who, like their Turkic cousins, were born and raised on horse and bow, furiously rode westward, leaving smoke, ruins, and millions of corpses in their wake.

204

On the easternmost fringes of Christendom, Russia was virtually annihilated between 1237 and 1241; "both Moscow and Kiev, the modern
and the ancient capitals, were reduced to ashes."[2] Two-thirds of the Russian population perished, and "Christian blood flowed like a great river,"
writes Bishop Serapion of Vladimir, who witnessed the Mongol onslaught[*]:
"Thus . . . fell upon us a merciless people who devastated our land, took entire cities off to captivity, destroyed our holy churches, put our fathers and
brothers to death, and defiled our mothers and sisters."[3]

The Mongol monsoon continued westward and struck southern Poland,
Hungary, and even Austria; victory was added to victory, and none could
halt their advance. "The Latin world was darkened by this cloud of savage
hostility," writes Edward Gibbon: "A Russian fugitive carried the alarm
to Sweden; and the remote nations of the Baltic and the ocean trembled at
the approach of the Tatars, whom their fear and ignorance were inclined
to separate from the human species. Since the invasion of the Arabs in
eighth-century Europe had never been exposed to a similar calamity."[4] And
Europe was right to fear, for Ögedei Khan, the famous Genghis Khan's
(d. 1227) son and successor, had ordered his men to conquer all lands unto
the "Great Sea," or Atlantic Ocean. Only a chance of fate saved Europe:
as Ögedei's westbound hordes[†] were preparing to storm Vienna, the Great
Khan died in 1241, prompting his chieftains to abandon their western advance and rush back to Mongolia.

---

[*] Several other contemporary accounts capture the devastation wrought upon Russia.
According to an Italian traveling to Kiev in 1246, the Mongols "attacked Russia, where
they made great havoc, destroying cities and fortresses and slaughtering men; and they
laid siege to Kiev, the capital of Russia; after they had besieged the city for a long time,
they took it and put the inhabitants to death. When we were journeying through that
land we came across countless skulls and bones of dead men lying about on the ground.
Kiev had been a very large and thickly populated town, but now it has been reduced
almost to nothing, for there are at the present time scarce two hundred houses there and
the inhabitants are kept in complete slavery. Going on from there, fighting as they went,
the Tartars destroyed the whole of Russia" (Dawson 2005, 29–30).

[†] Though the word today seems to have derogatory connotations, its etymology is Tur-
kic-Mongol—*orda* or *ordu*—and means camp or army.

Like Russia, the eastern lands of Islam—particularly Persia and Mesopotamia—were devastated by the Mongols. Baghdad, the opulent capital of the Abbasid caliphate for half a millennium, was torched in 1258, its population decimated, and the last caliph rolled in a carpet and stomped on till dead by Mongol horsemen.[*]

Islam's salvation came at the hands of slaves. Like his predecessors, Saladin and his immediate successors, the Ayyubids, had extensively relied on slave soldiers, mostly Turkic peoples from around the Black Sea. And, in a repeat of history, these slaves eventually overthrew their masters. Thus, at the height of the Mongol invasions, around 1250, the Mamluk sultanate— *mamluk* is Arabic for "owned," belying its slave origins—was born in Egypt. In 1260 the Mamluks met and defeated the invaders at Ayn Jalut (near Galilee). Although a spectacular victory over the hitherto unstoppable Mongol war machine, the damage was done in the eastern domains of Islam. "There is no doubt," wrote Persian historian Hamdallah Mustawfi (b. 1281), "that the destruction which happened on the emergence of the Mongol state and the general massacre that occurred at that time will not be repaired in a thousand years, even if no other calamity occurs and the world will not return to the condition in which it was before that event."[5] His seven-hundred-year-old prediction remains to be gainsaid.

RECHARGING THE JIHAD ON CHRISTENDOM

One consequence triggered by the Mongol eruption onto world history had unforeseen repercussions for the perennial war between Muslim and Christian: their invasion into eastern Anatolia prompted a mass migration of Turks, many of them slaves or mercenaries bought or brought by the Seljuk sultanate, to the western regions of that peninsula, near the frontier with the Eastern Roman Empire (which, during the crusades, had managed to recapture key cities of western Anatolia).

---

[*] Ibn al-Kathir portrays this last Abbasid caliph, Musta'sim, as something of an indifferent sensualist. "The Tatars . . . rained arrows on it [caliphal palace] from every side until a slave-girl was hit while she was playing before the Caliph and amusing him" (Lewis 1987, 82).

As this was for centuries the *ribat* par excellence, countless newcomers were assimilated into the ethos of jihad, not least because it complemented their tribal ways. Historian Patrick Balfour (aka Lord Kinross) explains:

> These were a people driven instinctively by an inherited impulse as nomads to move onward, over a deliberately planned westerly route in search of pastures new. Since their conversion to Islam, this search was sanctified and further inspired by their religious duties as Ghazis, under the holy law [sharia], to seek out and fight the infidel in the Abode of War, or *Dar el-Harb*: to raid and occupy his lands, seize his possessions, kill or carry into captivity his people, and subject their communities to Moslem rule.[6]

They were further confirmed into this way of life "by 'holy men,' sheikhs and dervishes[†] . . . who had fled from Turkestan and Persia into Asia Minor and who rekindled Turkish enthusiasm for war against the infidel."[7]

Some twenty years after the Seljuk sultanate centered in Konya (central Anatolia) was subjugated by the Mongols in 1243, a dozen or so independent Turkish kingdoms arose in the west, each ruled by a chieftain (a *bey* or emir) and each dedicated to the *ghazwa* (or *ghaza*)—an Arabic word for "raid" that is so laden with connotations of jihad as to be virtually synonymous with it.[‡] Accordingly, because they all "considered themselves ghazis, or warriors of Islam . . . from the 1260s, they mounted regular raids into Byzantine territory."[8]

---

† Contrary to contemporary portrayals of otherworldliness and/or moderation, "Sufis played a key part in preaching the jihad." The sheikh of a "whirling dervish" once presented a Turkish bey with a war-club, which the latter solemnly placed on his head and pledged to do the Greater and Lesser jihads: "With this club will I first subdue my passions and then kill all the enemies [i.e., deniers] of the faith" (Riley-Smith 1995, 250).

‡ Most of Muhammad's raids are called *ghazawat* (*ghazwa,* singular) in the oldest Arabic biographies of the prophet, appropriately titled the *maghazi*. "The Gazi is the sword of Allah," wrote one Muslim chronicler (ca. 1400), "he is the protector and refuge of the believers. If he becomes a martyr in the way of Allah, do not believe that he has died—he lives in beatitude with Allah, he has eternal life" (Crowley 2014, 31).

One of these westernmost chiefdoms founded by and named after Osman Ghazi (d. 1324), "the Ottomans were utterly devoted to frontier warfare—here known as ghaza—for the sake of plunder, territorial expansion, glory, and religion all at once," writes another Western authority.[9] Because Osman's *ribat* abutted Byzantine territory, all who wanted "to take part in the jihad and find booty or martyrdom" flocked to his banner—not least because his effective leadership brought more of the former.[10]

That "an ideology of warfare, and specifically of holy warfare against Christians, provided the raison d'etre of the Ottoman state from its beginning and formed the basis of its identity and cohesion"[11] has repeatedly been stressed by Muslim and non-Muslim historians, past and present.[*] After all, they were not mere *mujahidin,* "jihadis"; they were *murabitun,*[†] the greatest of all jihadis, frontier warriors fighting Islam's archenemy, the Eastern Roman Empire, along the *ribat.*

More propagandistically, not only did the Ottomans portray themselves as the descendants of the once great Seljuks—the first Muslim Turks to humiliate the Byzantines—but, like the Seljuks, they presented themselves as the "spiritual descendants" of those seventh- and eighth-century Arab heroes who lived along the *ribats* of Anatolia and perfected the jihad, thereby "establish[ing] continuity with the Arab Muslim past in the same geographical area."[12] Because nothing bestowed Islamic legitimacy as jihadi bona

---

[*] Thus one fourteenth-century Muslim moralist "attributes to the Ottoman sultans as their major quality their prosecution of the holy war"; a fifteenth-century writer refers to the Ottoman sultans as "the pre-eminent ghazis and mujahids after the apostle of Allah and the rightly-guided caliphs" (Hillenbrand 2007, 167–168). Turkish professor Inalcik writes that "the ideal of Gaza, Holy War, was an important factor in the foundation and development of the Ottoman state. . . . Gaza was a religious duty, inspiring every kind of enterprise and sacrifice" (Fregosi 1998, 211). Bernard Lewis says, "The classical jihad against Christendom was resumed by the Ottomans—of all major Muslim dynasties, the most fervently and consistently committed to the Muslim faith and to the upholding and enforcement of the Holy Law. In the early centuries of Ottoman history, jihad forms a major theme in their political, military, and intellectual life alike" (2003, 237).

[†] As such, "the ghaza of the Turks in Anatolia at the turn of the fourteenth century had a certain amount in common with the ribat of the Almoravids some two centuries previously in North Africa" (Bonner 2006, 153). After all, the word "Almoravid" is simply a transliteration of *al-murabitun*, they who fight along the *ribat.*

fides,‡ the Ottomans' chief contenders, the Mamluks in Egypt, also engaged in mass jihadi rhetoric—followed by action—so that, writing around 1317, William of Adam lamented that "the entire region is occupied by the hostile sword of either the Saracens of Egypt or the Turks of Asia Minor."[13]

THE OTTOMAN WAR MACHINE

In 1323, as Osman lay peacefully dying in bed, he enjoined his son and successor, Orhan, "to propagate religion [Islam] by thy arms."[14] By 1326, after a multiyear siege, Orhan took Bursa, one of Byzantium's greatest strongholds, and transformed it into the first Ottoman capital. All churches were cleansed and transformed into mosques and madrassas,[15] whence the indoctrination and finer points of jihad spread.§ As for the bey, he was forever living the jihad. The traveler Ibn Batutua, who once met Orhan in Bursa, observed that, although the *ghazi* had captured some one hundred fortresses, "he had never stayed for a whole month in any one town," because he "fights with the infidels continually and keeps them under siege."[16] Christian cities fell like dominos: Smyrna in 1329, Nicaea in 1331, and Nicomedia in 1337. By 1340, the whole of northwest Anatolia was again under Muslim control, thanks to the Ottomans.

Thus, "the foes of the cross, and the killers of the Christian people, that is, the Turks, [were] separated from Constantinople by a channel of three or four miles."[17]¶ Although its two waterway entry points, the Bosporus

---

‡ The Ottomans further emulated the Seljuks by maintaining close ties with the Sunni *ulema*, "who wrote prolifically in support of the ruling dynasty" (Hillenbrand 2007, 167). So did the Mamluks: Ibn Taymiyya (d. 1328), one of the great Muslim doctrinaires of his era, whose writings continue to inform and inspire "radical" Muslims, worked for these slaves-turned-sultans: "He taught that Christians and open heretics [e.g., Shias] were not the only targets for jihad, for the pious also had a duty to resist those rulers who professed themselves to be Muslims, but who failed to apply the sharia in all its rigour. For a ruler or a soldier to abandon the jihad was the greatest sin a Muslim could possibly commit" (Riley-Smith 1995, 247).

§ For example, the sheikhs taught Orhan that "if a town or district had resisted him and was taken by force of arms, the Christians had no rights. One-fifth of the population might be enslaved, the men sent to work on the conquerors' land, and the boys trained for the army" (Runciman 2004, 34–35).

¶ Already by 1341, Turkish bey Omar of Aydin, "the Lion of Allah," could terrorize

and the Dardanelles, were well guarded—the latter by the fortified town of Gallipoli, the former by Constantinople itself—on March 2, 1354, a massive earthquake leveled Gallipoli, causing its survivors to withdraw. Citing it as the work of Allah, Suleiman, a son of Orhan, "at once—apparently on the same day—crossed the Dardanelles with his army to occupy the ruins of Gallipoli. The Ottomans had their first foothold in Europe."[18] The energetic *ghazi* prepared to go to work, but first things first: "Where there were churches he destroyed them or converted them to mosques," writes an Ottoman chronicler: "Where there were bells, Suleiman broke them up and cast them into fires. Thus, in place of bells there were now muezzins."[19]

Cleansed of all Christian "filth," Gallipoli became, as a later Ottoman bey boasted, "the Muslim throat that gulps down every Christian nation—that chokes and destroys the Christians."[20] From this dilapidated but strategically situated fortress town, the Ottomans "launched a campaign of terror" throughout the countryside, always convinced they were doing God's work.[21] "They live by the bow, the sword, and debauchery, finding pleasure in taking slaves, devoting themselves to murder, pillage, spoil," explained Gregory Palamas, an Orthodox metropolitan who was taken captive in Gallipoli, adding, "and not only do they commit these crimes, but even—what an aberration—they believe that God approves them!"[22]

After Orhan's death in 1360 and under his son Murad I—the first of his line to adopt the title "Sultan"—the westward jihad began in earnest. Wisely ignoring the high walls of Constantinople for the time being, the sultan first set about "striking terror into the hearts of the infidels" (to quote Koran 8:12) of the surrounding Thracian countryside. Thus, "at Chorlu the massacre of the garrison and the decapitation of its commandant were calculated to spread terror of the Turkish invaders throughout the Balkans."[23] It worked: Adrianople, Byzantium's second most important city after Constantinople, surrendered in 1369 "rather than risk the fate of Chorlu."[24] It replaced Bursa as the Ottoman capital, whence the jihad resumed.

---

the Christian Aegean with 350 ships and 15,000 men from a captured port in Smyrna (Madden 2004, 180).

Ottoman successes lay in the evolution of their war making. From the start, Turkic *ghazis* were formidable raiders and fought in the manner of other nomadic peoples, including their Mongol cousins and Seljuk predecessors. Horse and bow, speed and ruse, were their chief weapons, and they used them to great effect.* Beginning with Orhan, but more so under Murad, the Ottomans were transformed into a highly disciplined and efficient war machine—so that by the fifteenth century, a Burgundian traveler observed, "They can start suddenly, and a hundred Christian soldiers would make more noise than ten thousand Osmanlis. When the drum sounded they put themselves immediately in march, never breaking step, never stopping till the word is given. Lightly armed, in one night they travel as far as their Christian adversaries in three days."[25]

The frontlines of a typical Ottoman army consisted of unpaid irregulars, or *bashi bazouks* (literally, "Crazy Heads")—vagabonds who subsisted entirely on pillage and plunder, whatever they could grasp. As their name denotes, they were undisciplined and reckless, and as such were often sent ahead of the main force to harass and sow confusion among the enemy. While most were infantry, some (the *akinji*) were light cavalry. Behind these came the professional soldiery, including cavalrymen (*sipahi*) and infantrymen, the dreaded Janissaries.

CHRISTIAN SLAVE BOYS TURNED JIHADIS EXTRAORDINAIRE

The earliest Janissaries—or *yeniçeri,* meaning "new soldier"—consisted of enslaved Christians who were taken as the sultan's share of human booty, converted to Islam and indoctrinated in jihad, and then set loose on their former Christian kin (thereby perpetuating the cycle of conquest, enslavement, and conversion, always to Christendom's demographic loss and Islam's demographic gain).

---

* Being "originally of the stock of the Mongolian steppe-dwellers," the Turks "upheld the use of the arrow as a divine gift with which Allah and his Prophet had furnished man" (Atiya 1978, 80).

When already-enslaved Christians were not enough to satisfy the sultan's war-making needs, he instituted the *devshirme*. From the late fourteenth century on, all subject Christian families from the Balkan region—Greeks, Serbs, Bulgarians, Albanians, Macedonians, and others— were compelled, on pain of death, to make an annual "blood tribute," payable in their own flesh, that is, their sons, some as young as eight.*

It was collected variously. Sometimes Ottoman officials would go door to door, other times fathers were ordered to bring their sons to the public squares. After the boys were examined, the very best—the handsomest and halest—were hauled off, often torn from the grips of their hysterical mothers.[†] Any father who dared offer resistance was executed on the spot, and armed revolts against the levy-collectors were not unknown.[‡]

Many parents did what they could to prevent the snatching of their sons' bodies—which could further "end up as victims of Turkish pederasty,"[26] or the "Turkish Disease"—and souls.[§] Some parents mutilated their boys in ways that would make them useless to their new masters. Sometimes

---

* While this was hardly a novel enterprise for Islam—during the initial seventh-century conquests Arabs took the sons of subjugated infidel populations in lieu of tribute (e.g., p. 36)—for the ever-expanding Ottoman war state, the blood levy was preferred.

† A sixteenth-century European manuscript recounts the "sorrow the Greeks bear, the fathers and mothers who are separated from their children at the prime of life. Think ye of the heart-rending sorrow! How many mothers scratch out their cheeks! How many fathers beat their breasts with stones! What grief these Christians experience on account of their children who are separated from them while alive and how many mothers say, 'It would be better to see them dead and buried in our church, rather than to take them alive in order to become Turks and abjure our faith. Better that you had died!'" (Bostom 2005, 558).

‡ For example, in 1565 in Epirus and Albania.

§ For "West Europeans," the "lusty Turk" was "a picture of lechery"; they were "particularly aghast at the open homosexuality and possibly envious of stories from the harem. Venice forbade lads under fourteen from visiting Constantinople [then Istanbul] for fear that they would be afflicted with the 'Turk disease'" (Akbar 2003, 90). In his sweeping survey of Christian views on Islam Norman Daniel writes: "The accusation was, as it still is, very frequently made, that Islam either permits, or else that it encourages, unnatural intercourse between people of the same or opposite sexes, and, indeed, any sexual act whatsoever, for its own sake." The reason for this was the belief that "Islam positively exploited universal human weakness" (1962, 141, 147).

"the children ran away on their own initiative, but when they heard that the authorities had arrested their parents and were torturing them to death, returned and gave themselves up." In one instance, "a young Athenian who returned from hiding in order to save his father's life . . . chose to die himself rather than abjure his faith."[27]

In general, however, the Turks got whichever Christian boy they set their eyes on. Gianfrancesco Morosini, a sixteenth-century Italian diplomat, describes how the Turks herded and marched off these children, "just as if they were so many sheep." On reaching their new dwelling places in Ottoman territory, the boys were "either persuaded or forced to be circumcised and made Muslim." Nor were these merely symbolic or superficial acts: "The first thing they are made to learn is the Turks' false religion, which they know so well as to put us to shame."[28]

Having learned to submit, they were next subjected to a draconian training system not unlike the ancient Spartan *agoge*: "They make them drudge day and night, and they give them no bed to sleep on and very little food." They were allowed to "speak to each other only when it is urgently necessary" and were made to "pray together without fail at four prescribed times every day." As "for any little offense, they beat them cruelly with sticks, rarely hitting them less than a hundred times, and often as much as a thousand. After punishments the boys have to come to them and kiss their clothing and thank them for the cudgelings they have received. You can see, then," concluded the Italian observer, "that moral degradation and humiliation are part of the training system."[29]

Ironically, however—and as with other historically Muslim institutions that have been whitewashed⁋—this abduction, forced conversion, and jihadi indoctrination of Christian children is portrayed by several leading

---

⁋ For instance, many Mideast academics, such as John Esposito, insist that *jizya*, "entitled them [*dhimmis*] to Muslim protection from outside aggression and exempted them from military service"—without pointing out that the "protection" Christians and Jews bought was actually from the Muslims themselves, and that *dhimmis* were "exempted . . . from military service" because, as infidels, they themselves were the enemy and had to remain separate and subjugated. (http://raymondibrahim.com/2015/05/28 /islamic-jizya-fact-and-fiction/)

214 Sword and Scimitar

academics "as the equivalent of sending a child away for a prestigious education and training for a lucrative career."[30]

What *is* true is that whoever survived the indoctrination and dehumanization of this ordeal of fire emerged with a fanatical appetite for war on infidels and became the most feared element of the Ottoman army: a Janissary, a "new soldier." That they exhibited a "dog-like devotion to the sultan," the man responsible for abducting them from their families and faith, and engaged in "wild behavior" against his enemies[31]—that is, against their former families and faith—is further proof that they are among recorded history's earliest victims of Stockholm Syndrome.*

"THE FIELD OF BLACKBIRDS"

Under Murad I, who perfected the *devshirme,* the Ottoman drive into the Balkans began in earnest and was unstoppable. By 1371 he had annexed portions of Bulgaria and Macedonia to his sultanate, which now so engulfed Constantinople that "a citizen could leave the empire simply by walking outside the city gates."[32] Unsurprisingly, then, when Prince Lazar of Serbia (b. 1330) defeated Murad's invading forces in 1387, "there was wild rejoicing among the Slavs of the Balkans. Serbians, Bosnians, Albanians, Bulgarians, Wallachians, and Hungarians from the frontier provinces all rallied around Lazar as never before, in a determination to drive the Turks out of Europe."[33]

Murad responded to this effrontery on June 15, 1389, in Kosovo. There, a Serbian-majority coalition augmented by Hungarian, Polish, and Romanian contingents—twelve thousand men under the leadership of Lazar—fought thirty thousand Ottomans under the leadership of the sultan himself. Despite the initial downpour of Turkic arrows, the Serbian heavy cavalry

---

* Defined by *Merriam-Webster* as "the psychological tendency of a hostage to bond with, identify with, or sympathize with his or her captor." Others who managed to safeguard their soul seem to have been permanently scarred by the trauma of their youth. According to a sixteenth-century European observer, "They gather together and one tells another of his native land and of what he heard in church or learned in school there, and they agree among themselves that Muhammad is no prophet and that the Turkish religion [Islam] is false" (Bostom 2005, 558).

plummeted through the Ottoman frontlines and broke the left wing; the Ottoman right, under Murad's elder son Bayezid, reeled around and engulfed the Christians. The chaotic clash continued for hours.

On the night before battle, Murad had beseeched Allah "for the favour of dying for the true faith, the martyr's death."[34] Sometime near the end of battle, his prayer was granted. According to tradition, Miloš Obilić, a Serbian knight, offered to defect to the Ottomans on condition that, in view of his own high rank, he be permitted to submit before the sultan himself. They brought him before Murad and, after Miloš knelt in false submission, he lunged at and plunged a dagger deep into the Muslim warlord's stomach. The sultan's otherwise slow guards responded by hacking the Serb to pieces. Drenched in and spluttering out blood, Murad lived long enough to see his archenemy, the by now captured Lazar, brought before him, tortured, and beheaded. A small conciliation, it may have put a smile on the dying martyr's face.

Murad's son Bayezid (b. 1360, r. 1389–1403) instantly took charge: "His first act as Sultan, over his father's dead body, was to order the death, by strangulation with a bowstring, of his brother. This was Yaqub, his fellow-commander in the battle, who had won distinction in the field and popularity with his troops."[35] Next Bayezid brought the battle to a decisive end; he threw everything he had at the enemy, leading to the slaughter of every last Christian—but even more of his own men in the process. So many birds flocked to and feasted on the vast field of carrion that posterity remembered Kosovo as the "Field of Blackbirds." Though essentially a draw—or at best a Pyrrhic victory for the Ottomans—the Serbs, with less men and resources to start with in comparison to the ascendant Muslim empire, felt the sting more.

A THUNDERBOLT STRIKES AN EAGLE

Back in Adrianople, the sheikhs, citing Islamic logic—that the murder of one is preferable to societal schisms, *fitna*—and quoting the Koran (e.g., 9:47), exonerated Bayezid of murdering his own brother, thereby establishing the "practice of imperial fratricide which was to root itself all too

permanently in the history of the Ottoman dynasty."[36] The tone was set for
the new sultan's life, which, like many other Muslim leaders before and after
him, was at once pious and depraved, with no apparent conflict between the
twain. In between jihads, "Bayezid, living idly and wantonly, never ceased
from lascivious sexual acts, indulging in licentious behavior with boys and
girls." But he also "had a contrasting religious side to his nature, building
for himself a small chamber on the top of his mosque in Bursa, where he
would . . . confer with the theologians of his Islamic establishment."[37]

Such ostensible contradictions in his lifestyle are resolved on the reali-
zation that Islamic piety (or lack thereof) for Islamic heads of state was best
reflected by their adherence to jihad. In this light, Bayezid—whose moniker
was *Yildirim,* or "Thunderbolt," due to "the fiery energy of his soul and rapidity of his destructive march"[38]—was certainly pious. Or, in the words of
Doukas, a contemporary Greek historian:

[Bayezid] was a feared man, precipitate in deeds of war, a persecutor of Christians as no other around him, and in the religion of the
Arabs a most ardent disciple of Muhammad, whose unlawful commandments were observed to the utmost, never sleeping, spending his
nights contriving intrigues and machinations against the rational flock
of Christ. . . . His purpose was to increase the nation of the Prophet
and to decrease that of the Romans. Many cities and provinces did he
add to the dominion of the Muslims.[39]

In short, as a *ghazi* devoted not only to conquering New Rome—on
Muhammad's promise that doing so would wipe away all sins—but also
Old Rome, where he promised to "feed his horse with oats on the altar of
St. Peter's," Bayezid could simply do no wrong.[40]

Before he could enact his pious intentions against the infidels, Bayezid
spent the first years of his reign consolidating power and authority over the
Turks in Anatolia. Taking advantage of this, Byzantine Emperor John V (b.
1332) condescended to become Bayezid's vassal;* he sent his forty-year-old

* The prudent Ottomans often tried to seduce those worthy opponents whom they
could only defeat at great cost: instead of fighting *against,* they were invited to fight *for*

son, Manuel II Palaiologos (b. 1350)—whose family crest memorably depicted the double-headed eagle—as a ward/hostage of the thirty-year-old sultan in 1390.

At the latter's courts, Muslim clerics regularly accosted Manuel about his Christian faith; he boldly responded in like manner, at one point arguing: "Show me just what Mohammed brought that was new, and there you will find things only evil and inhuman, such as his command to spread by the sword the faith he preached."[†] (When, in 2006, Pope Benedict quoted this assertion in the context of Manuel's greater point, that "to act unreasonably is foreign to God," anti-Christian riots erupted around the Muslim world, churches were burned, and an Italian nun who had devoted her life to serving the sick and needy of Somalia was murdered there.[41])

Meanwhile, the jihad leader of the *ghazi* state never seemed to miss an opportunity to humiliate the heir apparent of the ancient capital of Christendom. Bayezid even sadistically forced Manuel to accompany the Turks and witness the final destruction of Philadelphia,[‡] the last Christian bastion in Asia Minor, which had hitherto survived by paying *jizya* to the Turks. Manuel later wrote of "the intense suffering he endured at the sight of destroyed Christian cities. Above all, it was the thought that they were actually helping their archenemy that sickened him. In one of his letters he

---

the Turks as subordinates. Since the former often led to death and destruction, whereas the latter often led to security and prosperity, some—especially whenever annihilation was certain—opted for vassalage. As with the alliances of convenience between Muslims and Christians in Spain, these exceptions to the rule are now often cited as "proof" that religion was only a pretext for war between Turks and Europeans.

† As a man who spent his entire life both orally and militarily resisting Turks—whom he described as "barbaric and ignorant" for they "delighted in bloodshed and massacres"—Manuel II was well acquainted with Islam. He understood the three choices it imposed on non-Muslims: "[1] they must place themselves under this law [sharia, meaning become Muslims], or [2] pay tribute and, more, be reduced to slavery [an accurate depiction of *jizya* and *dhimmi* status], or, in the absence of wither, [3] be struck without hesitation with iron." In the context of proving that irrational teachings cannot emanate from God, he argued that these three options are "extremely absurd," particularly the notion that, if being a non-Muslim is so bad, why should money, *jizya*, allow one to "buy the opportunity to lead an impious life"? (Quotes from Demetracopoulos n.d., 270, and Manuel 2009).

‡ That this same Philadelphia is mentioned in the Book of Revelation gave this event an apocalyptic veneer.

remarked bitterly, 'but one thing is unbearable for us: we are fighting with them and for them [Muslims] and it means that we increase their strength and decrease ours.'"[42]

Emperor John V thought to make use of this time of relative peace by refortifying Constantinople with marble from the many ruined churches lying outside the city wall. Once the laborious project was complete, Bayezid ordered him to raze it—or else he would blind his captive son and heir. Although the dejected emperor complied, "this frightful humiliation proved the final blow for John. Prematurely aged and broken by his long miseries . . . the old Emperor retired to the gloom of his palace" and died, "not yet having reached his sixtieth birthday."[43]

When word of his father's death reached Manuel in early 1391, "he succeeded in fleeing from the sultan and arrived in Constantinople, where he was crowned emperor." Fearing "the popularity of Manuel," Bayezid "regretted not having murdered him during his stay at his court," but sent a tempered message to his former "ward," now safe behind the walls: "If you wish to execute my orders, close the gates of the city and reign within it; but all that lies outside belongs to me."[44]

The more Manuel sought to placate Bayezid, the more the sultan saber-rattled. In the early 1390s he felt secure enough to resume the Balkan jihad, and by 1393 had conquered the whole of Bulgaria and its capital Trnovo. Emboldened by his fresh victories, not only did the sultan demand an increase in *jizya* from the increasingly impoverished Constantinople—taxing even the vineyards and vegetables outside the city walls—but he demanded "the establishment of a kadi, or judge, in Constantinople, for its Muslim population." For, explained Bayezid, "it is not good or consonant with the Prophet's ordinances that the children of Muslims be nurtured and educated by *gavurs* [*kafirs,* or infidels]."[45]

This demand was soon followed by the arrival of an Ottoman army before the wall, slaughtering or enslaving on its way such Greeks in southern Thrace as were still Christians. Thus the first Ottoman siege of Constantinople began. The city was closely invested for seven months. Bayezid then raised the siege on stiffer terms than those initially agreed. The Emperor Manuel was forced to agree to the establishment within the walls of an Islamic tribunal, and the cession of a quarter in the city to Moslem settlers. . . . Henceforward, from the minarets of two mosques the Moslem call to prayer echoed through the city, which the Ottomans now called Istanbul, a corruption of the Greek *is tin poli,* "to the city."⁴⁶

Bayezid felt unstoppable: "The Ottomans, having subdued Wallachia, Bulgaria, Macedonia and Thessaly and pushed the Wallachians back north of the Danube, conquered Thessalonica in 1394. A new wave of terror ensued."⁴⁷

By a ruse, Bayezid gathered in one place the representatives of the aristocratic families of the Palaiologoi, with Manuel at their head, and the Slavic princes. He apparently planned to do away with them all, so that, as Manuel later quoted him, "after the land had been cleared of thorns, by which he meant us [Christians], his sons [Muslims] might dance in the Christian land without fearing to scratch their feet." But instead of purging these archons, he "spewed forth his wrath by means of the outrages he committed upon our followers, cutting out the eyes of our admirals, and cutting off hands, and bringing some of those in authority into great disgrace," before ignominiously dismissing his Christian subordinates with arbitrary threats.⁴⁸

No sooner had the emperor arrived home when another summons from Bayezid came. Enough was enough: "Manuel had come to the inevitable conclusion: no further trust could be placed in a course of vassalage to the Turks. . . . The policy inaugurated by John V, reluctantly accepted and continued by Manuel II, had finally ceased to work. Appeasement had failed."⁴⁹ The emperor responded by shutting his gates and preparing Constantinople for war, which duly came some months later, when a large Ottoman army arrived before and besieged the city in 1394.

DISASTER AT NICOPOLIS

In that same year, the Ottomans "were doing great injury to Hungary," and caused its young king, Sigismund (1368–1437), to appeal "to Christendom for assistance."[50] Western aid would not merely be altruistic but self-benefiting. For not only had Bayezid been making the old Muslim boast of feeding his horse on the altar of Saint Peter in Rome, but French king Charles VI received word that the ambitious sultan intended to "come to France after he had finished with Austria."[51] Considering the Thunderbolt's legendary speed and restlessness, such threats were not lightly dismissed.

Sigismund's appeal further came at an opportune time. The hitherto quarreling English and French had made peace in 1389, and a "crusade against the Turks furnished a desirable outlet for the noble instincts of Western chivalry." That "men of all kinds"—pilgrims, laymen, and clergymen returning from the Holy Land and Egypt—told of "the miseries and persecutions to which their Eastern co-religionists were subjected by the 'unbelieving Saracen,' and . . . appeal[ed] with all the vehemence of piety for a crusade to recover the native land of Christ," further settled matters.[52]

Western knights everywhere—mostly French but also English, Scottish, German, Spanish, Italian, and Polish—took up the cross in one of the largest multiethnic crusades against Islam. Their ultimate goal, according to a contemporary, was "to conquer the whole of Turkey and to march into the Empire of Persia . . . the kingdoms of Syria and the Holy Land."[53] A vast host of reportedly some one hundred thousand crusaders—"the largest Christian force that had ever confronted the infidel"[54]—reached Buda in July 1396.

But numbers could not mask the disunity, mutual suspicions, and internal rancor that was evident from the start. The French spurned Sigismund's suggestion that they forego the offensive and take a defensive posture. When the king suggested that his Hungarians were more experienced with and thus should lead the attack on the Turks, the Frenchmen accused him of trying to steal their glory and set out to take the field before him. They easily took two garrisons before reaching and besieging Nicopolis, an Ottoman stronghold on the Danube. Victories and still no response from Bayezid led to overconfidence and complacency; dissolution set in and some sources say the camp became all but a brothel.

Suddenly, on September 25, 1396, as the Western leaders were feasting in a tent, a herald burst in with news that the Thunderbolt, who only three weeks earlier was far away besieging Constantinople, had come. Without waiting for Sigismund's Hungarians, who were still trailing behind, the Westerners instantly formed rank and made for the first, visible line of the Ottoman force, the *akinjis,* or irregular light cavalry. Although they made quick work of them, the Muslim horsemen had "veiled from the sight of the enemy a forest of pointed stakes, inclined towards the Christians, and high enough to reach the breast of a horse." Many charging steeds were impaled and fell—as volleys of arrows descended upon man and beast, killing many of both.[55]

"So considerable was the loss inflicted on the Christians." A young French knight called on the men "to march into the lines of the enemy to avoid a coward's death from their arrows and the Christians responded to the marshal's call." Although the Muslim archers harrying them were scattered along a sloping hill, the unhorsed and heavily armored crusaders marched to it on foot. As they ascended, "the Christians struck vigorously with axe and sword, and the Ottomans retaliated with sabre, scimitar and mace so valiantly, and packed their lines so closely, that the issue remained at first undecided. But as the Christians were mailed, and the Ottomans fought without armour, the bearers of the Cross . . . butchered 10,000 of the infantry of the defenders of the Crescent, who began to waver and finally took to their heels."[56]

As the latter fled, another, larger host of horsemen became visible. The unwavering crusaders "hurled themselves on the Turkish horse, effected a gap in their lines, and, striking hard, right and left, came finally to the rear," where they hoped to find and kill Bayezid with "their daggers [which they used] with great effect against the rear." Startled at this unusual way of fighting—reportedly another five thousand Muslims were slaughtered in the melee—"the Turks sought safety in flight and raced back to Bayezid beyond the summit of the hill."[57]

At this point, the Western leaders called on their knights to stop, recover, and regroup. Yet despite "their exhaustion, the weight of their armour, and the excessive heat of an Eastern summer day," the berserkers pursued "the fugitives uphill in order to complete the victory." There, atop the hill, the full might of the Muslim host finally became visible: forty thousand professional cavalrymen (*sipahi*), with Bayezid grinning in their midst.

Instantly and to the clamor of drums, trumpets, and wild ejaculations of "Allahu Akbar!" they charged at the outnumbered and now exhausted Christians. The latter valiantly fought on, "no frothing boar nor enraged wolf more fiercely," writes a contemporary.[58] One veteran knight, Jean de Vienne, "defended the banner of the Virgin Mary with unflinching valour. Six times the banner fell, and six times he raised it again. It fell forever only when the great admiral himself succumbed under the weight of Turkish blows." His "body was found later in the day with his hand still clutching the sacred banner."[59]

Still, no amount of righteous indignation or battle fury could withstand the rushing onslaught. Some crusaders broke rank and fled; hundreds tumbled down the steep hill to their deaths; others hurled themselves in the river and drowned; a few escaped and got lost in the wood (a handful made it home from their odyssey years later, in rags and unrecognizable).[60]

The Hungarians arrived only to witness the grisly spectacle of a vast Muslim army surrounding and massacring their Western coreligionists. Sigismund boarded and escaped on a ship in the Danube. "If they had only believed me," reminisced the young king (who lived on to become Holy Roman Emperor thirty-seven years later); "we had forces in plenty to fight our enemies." He was not alone in blaming Western impetuosity: "If they had only waited for the king of Hungary," wrote Froissart, a contemporary Frenchman, "they could have done great deeds; but pride was their downfall."[61]

Though it failed, the crusade caused considerable damage to Bayezid's forces: "for the body of every Christian, thirty Muhammadan corpses or more were to be found on the battlefield."[62] But the Islamic warlord would have his vengeance:

On the morning after the battle the sultan sat and watched as the surviving crusaders were led naked before him, their hands tied behind them. He offered them the choice of conversion to Islam or, if they refused, immediate decapitation. Few would renounce their faith, and the growing piles of heads were arranged in tall cairns before the sultan, and the corpses dragged away. By the end of a long day, more than 3,000 crusaders had been butchered, and some accounts said as many as 10,000.[63]

Whether because hours of this "hideous spectacle of mutilated corpses and spilt blood horrified [even] Bayezid," or whether because his advisors convinced him that he was needlessly provoking the West, "he ordered the executioners to stop."[64]

When news of this disaster spread throughout Europe, "bitter despair and affliction reigned in all hearts," writes a chronicler. Never again would the West unite and crusade in the East. "Henceforward it would be left to those whose borders were directly threatened to defend Christendom against the expansion of Islam."[65] All of this was a sign of the times, of a burgeoning secularization in the West that prioritized nationality over religion. As historian Aziz Atiya notes in his seminal study of the battle:

The Christian army consisted of heterogeneous masses, which represented the various and conflicting aspirations of their countries and nascent spirit of nationality therein. The sense of unity and universality that had been the foundation of Empire and Papacy in the early Middle Ages was passing away, and in its place the separatism of independent kingdoms was arising. This new separatist tendency demonstrated itself amidst the crusading medley before Nicopolis. There was no unity of purpose, no unity of arms and companies, and no common tactics in the camp of the Christians. The Turkish army was, on the other hand, a perfect example of the most stringent discipline, of a rigorous and even fanatic unity of purpose, of the concentration of supreme tactical power in the sole person of the Sultan.[66]

For an increasingly isolated Constantinople, such developments boded ill.

A NEW "SWORD OF ALLAH" INTERVENES

After Nicopolis, the Thunderbolt instantly shot back to the siege of Constantinople, taking Athens and central Greece along the way. Bayezid seemed invincible. Because a "sultan's role as ghazi in the jihad, waged against the infidel in general and Christians in particular"[67] was the primary way of garnering Islamic legitimacy, his fame grew rapidly in the East: "Muhammadan potentates and even the formidable [Mamluk] Sultan of Egypt himself, began to entertain vague suspicions and fears of the ever-rising power of the Ottoman monarch."[68]

Emperor Manuel was now in the West, making stops in Italy, France, England, and elsewhere in an effort to rally support and raise recruits for his beleaguered kingdom. His hosts were "impressed by the dignity of his demeanor" and erudition; but they were more "moved to pity for him; for he had come as a beggar, in a desperate search for help against the infidel who encompassed his empire." He cut a tragic figure during a banquet with King Henry IV of England, or so thought Adam of Usk: "I reflected, how grievous it was that this great Christian prince should be driven by the Saracens from the furthest East to these furthest Western islands to seek aid against them. . . . O God, what dost thou now, ancient glory of Rome."[69]

By 1402 the siege had gone on and off for nearly a decade. Food reserves were exhausted, and many had died of famine and disease; others in maddened desperation had climbed over the walls and surrendered themselves to the Turks. Yet others persevered. When Bayezid sent a haughty message demanding surrender, Manuel's nephew and regent, John VII, told the envoys to "tell your master that we are weak, but that we trust in God, Who can make us strong and can put down the mightiest from their seats. Let your master do as he pleases."[70]

God answered Constantinople's prayers in the unlikeliest of forms: Timur, the latest self-styled "Sword of Allah," notorious for building massive pyramids from the decapitated heads of those who resisted him. Long known in the West as "Tamerlane" (1336–1405), this Mongol-Turkic emir ruled over an extensive central Asian empire that abutted the Ottomans' easternmost domains. Because "Timur was impatient of an equal, and Bayezid was ignorant of a superior," a battle of egos in the guise of territorial and other disputes inevitably began in words. In a letter chastising the sultan, Timur contemptuously asked:

> What is the foundation of your insolence and folly? You have fought some battles in the woods of Anatolia; contemptible trophies! You have obtained some victories over the Christians of Europe; your sword was blessed by the apostle of Allah; and your obedience to the precept of the Koran, in waging jihad against the infidels, is the sole consideration that prevents us from destroying your country, the frontier and bulwark of the Moslem world. Be wise in time; reflect; repent; and avert the thunder of our vengeance, which is yet suspended over your head.[71]

Such an epistle did not sit well with the hubristic Turk. Bayezid responded in like manner: "Your armies are innumerable: be they so; but what are the arrows of the flying Tartar against the scimitars and battle-axes of my firm and invincible Janizaries?" But then the Turk went one further and mocked the sixty-six-year-old Mongol in the persons of his wives and concubines, thereby crossing the line of acceptable bluster in the East.[72]

War it would be. Bayezid recalled all his available men from Europe— thus finally raising the siege of Constantinople—and on July 20, 1402, met Timur in Ankara, where one of history's wildest battles ensued. Turkish historians attribute great valor to "the Thunderbolt [who] continued to wield a heavy battle-axe. As a starving wolf scatters a flock of sheep, he scattered the enemy." Even so, he was overwhelmed, captured, bound, and dragged to Timur's feet.[73]

To the jeers of Asia, the once proud conqueror and scourge of infidels was placed in a cage like a wild beast, and stories of his ill use abound: "that he was kept in chains by night; that he was made to serve as Timur's footstool; that in appropriating Bayezid's harem Timur humiliated his Serbian wife, Despina,* by obliging her to serve naked at the table before her former lord and his conqueror. His sufferings broke Bayezid's spirit and finally his mind. Within eight months he was dead from an apoplectic seizure—or perhaps by his own hand."[74]

As the Eastern Roman Empire had experienced centuries earlier when Emperor Romanus Diogenes was captured at Manzikert, so now the Ottoman Empire—which had hitherto never had a sultan captured—received a massive blow to its prestige. Everywhere Anatolian beys declared independence of the Ottomans; civil war erupted. Though it irked him to no end,[†] Timur had unwittingly gone from being the "Sword of Allah" to being the "Sword of God" that saved Constantinople.

Manuel took advantage of this reprieve by refortifying its walls and liberating Thessalonica and other Greek regions from the distracted Ottomans. Finally, having spent a lifetime fighting (and theologically debating) Turks, the wearied emperor, now aged seventy-two, retired to a monastery, where he died in 1425.[‡]

That same year Sultan Murad II (r. 1421–1451), a grandson of Bayezid, suddenly appeared and heavily besieged the walls of Constantinople, which were desperately manned by every citizen, including women and children. The siege failed but it was obvious to all that the Turks were on the warpath again.

---

* After the battle of Kosovo, the slain prince Lazar's daughter was sent to adorn Bayezid's harem; he later made her one of his four wives to cement Serbian vassalage.

† In one version, Timur tells the captured sultan: "I knew that your troops were always at war with the infidels . . . and my intention was, if you had hearkened to my counsels, and consented to a peace, to have given you powerful succours, both of money and troops, to carry on the war for religion with greater vigour, and to exterminate the enemies of Mohammed" (Marozzi 2004, 336). After all, "Timur was, or claimed to be, a pious Muslim, and despite enormous destruction was careful to show due deference to the places and personnel of the Islamic faith" (Lewis 2003, 103).

‡ That Manuel's life knew no repose comes out in one of his later writings: "When I had passed my childhood and not yet reached the age of man, I was encompassed by a life full of tribulation and trouble; but according to many indications, it might have been foreseen that our future would cause us to look at the past as a time of clear tranquility" (Vasiliev 1952, 629).

"EVIL AND ILL-FATED FIRST-FRUITS"

In 1430, Murad re-invaded Thessalonica. To ensure the capture of the city, he incited his men by guaranteeing them the keeping of whatever they could grab—a sort of tax-free jihad.[§] The city was quickly stormed; men were massacred, women and children raped. After the bloodbath subsided, a mad rush to collect as much booty as possible followed. The invaders fettered and hurriedly dragged the Christians "like senseless animals" to their colleagues waiting in tents before rushing back to search for more plunder, animate and inanimate. In the end seven thousand women and children were hauled off. Before the plunderers were finished, even churches and buildings had been stripped of their marble. "This was the evil and ill-fated first-fruits of future calamities destined to befall the imperial city," wrote Doukas (b. 1400), a contemporary court historian at Constantinople.[75]

Bartolomeo de Giano, an Italian Franciscan writing from Constantinople in 1438, also documented the "calamitous and lamentable slaughter that we see in these days." Raiding every corner of the Balkans, the *ghazis* erected "great mountains of [Christian] heads," and "so great a quantity of bodies lay consumed, partially rotted, partially devoured by dogs, that it would seem unbelievable to anyone who had not seen it with their own eyes."[76] Survivors were either enslaved to "serve their [masters'] wicked and filthy pleasures" and/or forced into becoming "Saracens [Muslims] who will later be enemies of the Christians."

From Hungary, three hundred thousand were enslaved and "carried off in just a few days"; from Serbia and Transylvania one hundred thousand were hauled off.[♩] "The massive enslavement of slavic populations during this period gave rise, in fact, to our word 'slave': in Bartolomeo's time, to be a slave was to be a Slav."[77] Further telling is that "the Turkish word *kiz*,

---

§ Booty was generally collected and later divvied up, with at least a fifth—which often included the crème de la crème—going to the leader (based on Koran 8:41).

♩ As impossible as these numbers sound, Ottoman chroniclers writing of these raids often make complementary statements, for example, that "the number of captives surpassed that of the combatants" (Bostom 2005, 91).

meaning 'girl,' 'slave girl,' and 'sexual slave girl' (or 'concubine') came to mean also 'Christian woman' in Islamic usage."[78]

Young and old everywhere were seen being "led away in iron fetters tied to the backs of horses," continues Bartolomeo, and "women and children were herded by dogs without any mercy or piety. If one of them slowed down, unable to walk further because of thirst or pain, O Good Jesus! she immediately ended her life there in torment, cut in half."[79] The slave markets of Adrianople were so inundated with human flesh that children sold for pennies, "a very beautiful slave woman was exchanged for a pair of boots, and four Serbian slaves were traded for a horse."[80]

So "strengthened by their victories and afire with such a great lust for gain," the Turks "believe without doubt that they are going to destroy the entirety of Christendom in a short time." Every day in Christian lands under Ottoman rule, "the most holy name of Christ is denied and Muhammad, the son of the devil, exalted," fumed the Franciscan; everywhere churches, crosses, and chalices are "cast down and trampled underfoot!"[81]

But it was to no avail. Whatever unity Christendom once had was gone:

> When, oh when, therefore, [continued Bartolomeo] shall these miserable [Western] Christians be roused [to action]? . . . Where is the glorious kingdom of the Franks now, which in ancient times drove the Saracens from Hispania? Where is the great power of the English? These two have been consumed [fighting] against one another. Where now is the king of Aragon, terror of the infidel? Where are the other powers and Christian princes? The Germans are hateful to the Hungarians and Bohemians, the Hungarians fight with the Poles. The pastors of the Church are at odds with the pastors, the barons with the barons, and cities use themselves up against other cities, so that even if no other persecution is inflicted from the outside, they are more than enough for their own ruin.[82]

At the Council of Florence, Manuel's eldest son, Byzantine Emperor John VIII, had even gone as far as to convert to Catholicism and submit to papal primacy—to great censure from his Orthodox subjects—as the price for Western aid. This culminated in the creation of a crusader coalition consisting primarily of Hungarians, Poles, and Wallachians. In 1444 they met and fought Murad II in what became known as the Crusade of Varna, and suffered a crushing defeat. Ottoman power was henceforth uncontested. Sparks of resistance continued and national heroes—Hungary's John Hunyadi, Albania's Skanderberg, and later Wallachia's Vlad the Impaler ("Dracula")—valiantly fought the Turks till their dying breath, but the writing was on the wall.

THE ONE FORETOLD: MUHAMMAD'S NAMESAKE

In 1451, Murad II died and was succeeded by his nineteen-year-old son by a "slave girl of undetermined but probably Christian origin." This was Muhammad II (r. 1451-1481),* "the mortal enemy of the Christians," to quote a contemporary prelate.[83] On becoming sultan his first order was to have his nineteen brothers, including an infant, strangled, and three concubines pregnant by his brothers decapitated. Like that of his great grandfather Bayezid I, young Muhammad's life exhibited those seemingly contradictory qualities of piety and depravity. "His passions were at once furious and inexorable. . . . In the palace, as in the field, a torrent of blood was spilt on the slightest provocation" and "the noblest of the [male] captive youth were often dishonored by his unnatural lust."[84]

But Muhammad was also deeply instructed in Islam. When only two, Murad—who wanted young Muhammad to receive an education steeped in the Koran and sharia—sent him to Amasya, a renowned "religious center . . . for the Islamic establishment." When the youth laughed at one Ahmed, a formidable cleric hired to instruct him, "the mullah launched upon him such a shower of blows that from then onward he treated his teacher with considerable respect, soon learning from him the whole of the Koran."[85]

Citing his namesake's prophecy—that the greatest of all Muslims would be he who takes Constantinople—on becoming sultan, Muhammad "declared that he would be that prince, triumphing over the infidel in the

---

* Pronounced in Turkish and often transliterated in English as "Mehmet."

name of Islam."[86] At first, few Christians acknowledged this; they banked on a cessation of hostilities due to his youth and inexperience. Moreover, when Constantinople sent a diplomatic embassy to congratulate him on ascending the Ottoman sultanate, he "swore by the god of their false prophet, by the prophet whose name he bore," a bitter Doukas retrospectively wrote, that "he was their friend, and would remain for the whole of his life a friend and ally of the City and its ruler Constantine [XI]."[87] Although the Christians believed him, Muhammad was taking advantage of "the basest arts of dissimulation and deceit" afforded by Islam.* "Peace was on his lips while war was in his heart."[88]

What was in his heart became apparent a year later. In early 1452, Sultan Muhammad took a thousand skilled masons and laborers to the European side of the Bosporus, thus blockading Constantinople. His "labourers began to demolish the churches and monasteries nearby, collecting from them such pieces of masonry as could be used again" to build a fortress.[89] "This aroused the religious zeal of the inhabitants of Constantinople, and an expedition set out to stop the Turks; but they were taken and put to the scimitar."[90] When the emperor sent messengers to remind Muhammad of their recently signed peace treaties, he had them beheaded. Once erected, "Cut Throat Castle"—so named as a possible solution to the old charge that Constantinople was a "bone in the throat of Allah"[91]—severed all communications between the city and the Black Sea, whence its corn supply came. When a Venetian ship refused to stop, it was sunk. The half-drowned crew

---

* According to sharia, circumstance is the deciding factor of when peace treaties with infidels should be made: when strong, Muslims should maintain the offensive; when weak, they should sue for peace—including, as seen in Chapter 6, by feigning conversion, or *taqiyya*. More generally, the use of deceit to gain advantage over infidels is based on the prophet's famous dictum that "war is deceit" (*Sahih Bukhari* 52:269), which he said while encouraging a recent convert to lie to his tribesmen for Islam's benefit. Muhammad also permitted another young convert to deceive an elderly Jewish poet (who had mocked the prophet) into thinking the Muslim was his friend; once the Jew dropped his guard and took the Muslim youth into his confidences, the latter assassinated him (Ibn Ishaq 1997, 367–368). In short, and as one Arabic legal manual devoted to jihad as defined by the four schools of law concludes, "The ulema agree that deception during warfare is legitimate . . . deception is a form of art in war" (Karima 2003, 304; for more on "war is deceit" see Ibrahim 2007, 142–143).

was beheaded, their bodies unceremoniously cast aside; their captain was slowly impaled,[†] his body left along the roadside as proof that Muhammad meant business.[92]

The sultan then appeared at the head of fifty thousand men, quietly reconnoitering Constantinople's walls, before withdrawing to Adrianople in late September 1452, where few saw him and even less knew his designs. Sources speak of an obsessed sultan who spent sleepless nights roaming his city in disguise and stabbing to death anyone foolhardy enough to recognize and salute him.

After Muhammad spurned or executed more delegations, Emperor Constantine XI Palaiologos (b. 1405), Manuel's son, sent a final message: "As it is clear that you desire war more than peace . . . so let it be according to your desire. I turn now and look to God alone. . . . However I release you from all your oaths and treaties with me, and, closing the gates of my capital, I will defend my people to the last drop of my blood."[93] And so it was: the city went into besieged mode; bridges were destroyed, and the barrier chain made taut to prevent enemy vessels from entering the Golden Horn harbor.

Constantine next appealed to Rome for aid; the pope said the decree of union signed by his elder brother, the late John VIII at the Council of Florence, must be proclaimed in Constantinople. The emperor complied, but no one came. Christian kings and principalities everywhere cited their own problems. Insult was added to injury: "Looking bitterly down on the vast sea of their enemies and knowing that the Latin Mass was being proclaimed in their beloved Orthodox churches, the Byzantines could ruefully reflect that they had paid the price of union without reaping its rewards."[94]

But if kings failed, individual heroes came of their own accord. Among these was Giovanni Giustiniani (b. 1418), a Genoese nobleman and siege

---

[†] Jacopo de Campi, a Genoese merchant well acquainted with Ottoman ways, described the procedure: "The Grand Turk [makes] the man he wishes to punish lie down on the ground; a sharp long pole is placed in the rectum; with a big mallet held in both hands the executioner strikes it with all his might, so that the pole, known as a *palo,* enters the human body, and according to its path, the unfortunate lingers on or dies at once; then he raises the pole and plants it in the ground; thus the unfortunate is left in extremis; he does not live long" (Crowley 2014, 153).

expert. He personally financed and led seven hundred highly trained soldiers—four hundred of which were fully armored—to Constantinople. "One of the most noted soldiers of his age," Giovanni was "a skillful leader and a man of outstanding energy, audacity, and courage. When he offered his sword to the emperor [in early 1453], Constantine made him commander-in-chief of the defence forces of the city, and endowed him with all but dictatorial powers. From his arrival a spirit of hope swept Constantinople."[95]

Yet no sooner did Giovanni arrive, than another seven hundred men aboard Italian vessels slipped out of Constantinople in fear of the impending siege.[96] A Venetian colony, already there and embarrassed to flee, agreed to fight, "for the honour of God and the honour of all Christendom."[97] "There were also some worthless, cowardly noblemen and inhabitants of the City who fled with their households, as they feared war and our adversaries," writes Georgio Sphrantzes (b. 1401), another court historian and confidant of Constantine XI. "When this was reported to the emperor, he took no action against them, but sighed deeply."[98] These were times that showed what individual men were made of.

In the end, less than seven thousand fighters, two thousand of whom were foreigners, made ready to protect fifteen miles of walls, while twenty-six Christian ships patrolled the harbor. The rest of Constantinople's population—women and children, the elderly and sick, monks and nuns—would help as best they could, repairing walls, clearing moats, carrying food and water to their defenders, and collecting and melting down gold and silver objects from churches to pay mercenaries.

Against this small but committed defense, the Ottoman Empire would soon belch forth all it had. Throughout the spring of 1453—and in the context of earthquakes and torrential rains which seemed to presage "the coming of Anti-Christ"—the city watched helplessly as battalion after battalion made its way to and surrounded Constantinople by land and sea. One contemporary remarked that Muhammad's "army seemed as numberless as grains of sand, spread . . . across the land from shore to shore."[99] In the end, some one hundred thousand fighters and one hundred warships came.

"Yet, for all the feeling of despair, there was no lack of courage."[100] After all, Constantinople had withstood a millennium's worth of sieges not because of its manpower but because of its strategic location and foundation: by land it was surrounded by layers of walls and ditches; by sea its harbor, the Golden Horn, was sealed off by a barrier chain three hundred yards long (each link of this ponderous boom was some twenty inches long).

Jihadi fervor ran high in the Ottoman camp. "Discipline was good, and the morale of the troops very high. Every Moslem believed that the Prophet himself would accord a special place in Paradise to the first soldier who should force an entry into the ancient Christian capital," Runciman writes. "Of the sultan's own enthusiasm there could be no doubt. Many times he was heard to declare his determination to be the prince who should achieve this supreme triumph for Islam."[101]

Daily he prayed before his men on a carpet facing Mecca. Wandering dervishes recited all the appropriate hadiths and prophecies, including that "in the jihad against Constantinople, one third of Muslims will allow themselves to be defeated, which Allah cannot forgive; one third will be killed in battle, making them wondrous martyrs; and one third will be victorious" and enjoy the fruits of victory.[102] The win-win nature of jihad offered something for everyone. "The religious merit of subduing the city of the Caesars attracted from Asia a crowd of volunteers," writes Gibbon, "who aspired to the crown of martyrdom; their military ardour was inflamed by the promise of rich spoils and beautiful females."[103]

In all of this, nothing was new: for over eight hundred years, Muslims, beginning with their prophet, had been clamoring about the need to conquer the ancient Christian capital and the rewards it would bestow on its conquerors. Muslims—first Arabs, now Turks—had besieged it with vast forces. The mighty walls of Constantinople always repulsed them. But when Sultan Muhammad came with his hordes in 1453, he brought something new: cannons, built by a well-paid Hungarian or German artillery expert named Urban, one of several European turncoats.* The most monstrous of

---

* "The sultan had a redoubtable 'fifth column' at his disposal. . . . Many of his followers were already well trained in espionage, sabotage and betrayal" (Cardini 2001, 127).

these—twenty-seven feet long and capable of firing 1,300-pound balls to the distance of a mile—required sixty oxen to transport it from the foundries of Adrianople.

THE FINAL SIEGE OF CONSTANTINOPLE

Muhammad commenced bombardment on April 6. Although a hole was early made in the wall, Giovanni and his men atop it "opened a terrific fire from hand guns, wall guns, bows, crossbows, and catapults and swept the leading ranks of the attackers back into the ditch." By evening the breach was repaired. Around the same time, Loukas Notaras, Grand Duke of Constantinople, defeated a naval assault on the harbor chain. It was not an auspicious start for the sultan. "So furious was Mahomet at his ill-success that his generals had the greatest difficulty in persuading him not to load his trebuchets with his own dead and to hurl them over the walls of the city."[104] He soothed his nerves by instead bombing and taking two nearby Thracian castles and impaling all seventy-six survivors, including those who surrendered.[105]

For the next several weeks cannons continued to fire at the walls; but because they took hours to reload, could only shoot a handful of balls a day, were imprecise, collapsed from their own recoil, and often malfunctioned for days or weeks, at best they usually created holes in the wall toward nighttime—at which point the defenders would emerge under the cover of dark and refortify the breach as best they could. Oftentimes the makeshift walls they re-erected from the rubble absorbed cannon fire even better than when standing perpendicularly.

On April 18, an all-out assault was ordered on an area of the wall deemed sufficiently weak. To the sound of drums, cymbals, and Islamic war cries, throngs of Ottomans rushed the walls with ladders, hooks, fire, and sword. "The reports of muskets, the ringing of bells, the clashing of arms, the cries of fighting men, the shrieks of women and the wailing of children, produced such a noise, that it seemed as if the earth trembled," remembered an eyewitness. "Clouds of smoke fell upon the city and the camp, and the combatants at last could not see each other."[106] After four hours of brutal fighting some two hundred Muslims were dead, but no Christians.

Muhammad's patience again began to wear thin. Two days later, on April 20, after Baltoghlu, his naval commander, failed to bypass the harbor chain—and, adding insult to injury, failed to prevent three Genoese ships from fighting their way into the Golden Horn—the enraged sultan ordered him impaled. His advisors begged mercy, and he relented: instead of torturous death, Muhammad ordered four slaves to hold the hapless commander down while he personally scourged him with a whip; Baltoghlu was then plundered of his possessions, titles, and lands, and banished into obscurity.[107] "Once more the sultan became depressed and kicked the ground in desperation, and bit his own hands like a dog," notes Sphrantzes.[108]

That the naval clash saw four Muslims die for each Christian demonstrated "the superiority of Christian seamanship" and boosted morale in Constantinople.[109] "They prayed to their prophet Muhammad in vain," writes Nicolo Barbaro (b. 1420), another eyewitness, "while our Eternal God heard the prayers of us Christians, so that we were victorious in this battle."[110]

Muhammad turned to more extreme measures. In a grueling project recommended by "a Christian traitor," teams of engineers, hundreds of men, and thousands of oxen physically hauled Ottoman warships out of the Bosporus, transported them up and over a hill, and then back down the opposite slope into the Golden Horn, thereby bypassing the guardian chain.[111]

Thus, sometime in late April, Christian sailors found seventy warships descending on them to cries of "Allahu Akbar."[112] Fierce fighting followed, and ships foundered. When forty half-drowned Christian sailors managed to swim to shore, "by the Sultan's orders these were fixed by the fundament [anus] upon sharp stakes, which pierced them to the top of their heads," wrote an eyewitness.* "The stakes were planted, and they were left to die in full view of the guards on the walls."[113] Constantinople responded by marching all 260 of their Ottoman prisoners to the walls and executing them before the sultan. He cared little, for his venture had paid off: the

---

* See footnote on p. 231 for an eyewitness description of this ghastly form of execution.

Ottomans finally had a foothold in the harbor, thereby further isolating the city from the flow of food and supplies.

Things were looking bleak for the defenders behind the wall; demoralization crept in. Along with worrying about the Ottomans, they now had to worry about finding food for themselves and their families. Tempers flared; Genoese and Venetians accused each other of complicity. "I beg you, my brothers, keep the peace among you," Emperor Constantine intervened; "we have enough fighting originating from the outside. Do not quarrel with each other for the mercy of God!"[114] Some implored the emperor to quit the city; he could fight the Ottomans more effectively without than within his walls, they argued, and possibly get aid. "I thank all for the advice which you have given me," he responded after patiently listening, but "how could I leave the churches of our Lord, and His servants the clergy, and the throne, and my people in such a plight? What would the world say about me? I pray you, my friends, in future do not say to me anything else but 'Nay, Sire, do not leave us!' Never, never will I leave you! I am resolved to die here with you!" Adds the chronicler: "And saying this the Emperor turned his head aside, because tears filled his eyes; and with him wept the Patriarch and all who were there."[115]

Meanwhile, assaults on the wall continued—cannons fired day after day—but seven weeks after the siege began, no Muslim had managed to set foot in the city. So "the sultan resorted to other tricks."[116] Just as he had gone around the impassable harbor chain, so now he would go over the obstinate walls. Around May 19, a massive wooden tower, a *helepolis,* or "city-taker," was rolled up to the trenches; being higher than the wall, it spewed a deadly fire onto the besieged while providing cover for Ottoman diggers to fill the ditch. Giovanni blew it up by rolling powder kegs into the fosse. Such successes kept spirits alive. "What would I not give to win that man over to my side!" exclaimed Muhammad. "He attempted to bribe him; but to no avail."[117]

If he could not go through or over the walls, he would go under them, concluded the determined sultan. Between mid-May to May 25, the Ottomans made several attempts to undermine fourteen separate areas of the wall; each was frustrated by Johann Grant, a German countermining expert. "Either he blew up the Turkish miners or smoked them out, suffocated them by stink-pots or drowned them by letting in water, or else met them underground and fought them with knife, axe and spear."[118]

Muhammad was at his wit's end and held council with his senior officers. There was some discussion of withdrawing; in the end, Muhammad decided on vomiting forth every last man he had against the walls in one last-ditch effort. But first he would need to inflame his men. On the evening of May 28, he assembled and exhorted them along familiar lines: "As it happens in all battles, some of you will die, as it is decreed by fate for each man. Recall the promises of our Prophet concerning fallen warriors in the Koran: the man who dies in combat shall be transported bodily to Paradise and shall dine with Mohammed in the presence of women, handsome boys, and virgins."[119]

But just like his namesake (the prophet of Islam), Sultan Muhammad knew that rewards in the now were always more attractive than promises in the hereafter. As Sheikh Akshemsettin had earlier told him, "You well know, that most of the soldiers have in any case been converted [to Islam] by force. The number of those who are ready to sacrifice their lives for the love of Allah is extremely small. On the other hand, if they glimpse the possibility of winning booty they will run towards certain death."[120] Nor did the sultan forget what happened when his father, Murad II, had promised his men three days of uninterrupted looting if they took Thessalonica: the city was seized in three hours.

And so the "Sultan swore by their immortal god [Allah], by the four thousand prophets, by Mahomet, by the soul of his father and by the sword with which he was girded, that his warriors would be granted the right to sack everything, to take everyone, male or female, and all property or treasure which was in the city; and that under no circumstances would he break his oath," writes Leonard of Chios, a Catholic prelate who was present (other contemporary Byzantine records confirm this point). "He asked nothing for himself, except the buildings and walls of the city; all the rest, the booty and the captives, would be theirs." Any Muslim still uninspired by the boons of the here or hereafter was left with a final thought: "But if I see any man lurking in the tents and not fighting at the wall," warned the sultan, "he will not be able to escape a lingering death," that is, impalement.[121]

Muhammad's "announcement was received with great joy," and from thousands of throats came waves of thundering cries of "Allahu Akbar!" and "There is no god but Allah and Muhammad is his prophet!"[122] "Oh! If you had heard their voices raised to heaven," wondered Leonard behind the wall,* "you would have been struck dumb with amazement. . . . We . . . were amazed at such religious fervor, and begged God with copious tears to be well disposed towards us."[123] All this "most terrible shouting," confirms Nicolo, "was heard as far as the coast of Anatolia twelve miles away, and we Christians were very fearful."[124]

The all-out assault was set for May 29. Atonement, ablutions, prayers, and fasting, "under penalty of death," were ordered for May 28.[125] Fanatics of all sorts were loosed in the camp to regale the men with tales of the win-win jihad. Wandering "dervishes visited the tents, to instill the desire of martyrdom, and the assurance of spending an immortal youth amidst the rivers and gardens of paradise, and in the embraces of the black-eyed virgins [houris]."[126] They quoted all the "relevant verses from the Koran and Hadith" and reminded the men that "they were following in the footsteps of the companions of the Prophet killed at the first Arab siege of Constantinople" between 674 and 678. Criers swept throughout the camp to horn blasts: "Children of Muhammad, be of good heart, for tomorrow we shall have so many Christians in our hands that we will sell them, two slaves for a ducat, and will have such riches that we will all be of gold, and from the beards of the Greeks we will make leads for our dogs, and their families will be our slaves. So be of good heart and be ready to die cheerfully for the love of our [past and present] Muhammad."[127]

As fanaticism was being whipped up in the Muslim camp, fatalism was

---

* Others heard but did not understand: "The enemy's cries, like the roar of the stormy sea, were heard inside our City, and we were wondering what was happening in their camp" (Sphrantzes 1980, 120).

besetting the beleaguered city, and omens boded ill.[†] Constantine's ministers again implored the exhausted emperor to quit the city; he collapsed during their harangue; when he revived he cried out, "Remember the words I said earlier! Do not try to protect me! I want to die with you!" to which they replied, "All of us will die for God's church, and for you!"

On May 27—as Constantinople was being "engulfed by a great darkness" that "hovered above the city" and "shocked and horrified" the people[128]—Constantine learned that, contrary to hopeful rumor, no relief forces were coming. He turned away from the messenger and leaning against a wall "began to weep bitterly for grief."[129]

The city was truly alone.

On May 28—even as the Ottoman camp was being whipped into a jihadi frenzy—large-scale religious processions were ordered; all churches were packed with petitioners; barefoot and weeping, carrying crosses and icons and chanting "*kyrie eleison*"—"Lord have mercy"—clergy led women and children along the walls, "begging God not to deliver us" to this "most wicked of all" enemies.[130]

Thus, both Christians and Muslims spent that last night calling on their deities: the besieged implored their god of love for safety, while the besiegers implored their god of war for victory.

The spent emperor delivered a defiant speech before his assembled officials, lay and clergy: "You know well the hour has come: the enemy of our faith wishes to oppress us . . . with the entire strength of his siege force, as a snake about to spew its venom. . . . For this reason I am imploring you to fight like men with brave souls, as you have from the beginning unto this day, against the enemies of our faith." "This wretch of a sultan," Constantine continued, sought to transform their churches "into shrines of his blasphemy, shrines of the mad and false prophet, Mohammed, as well as into stables for his horses and camels."[131]

---

† A full moon on May 24 was blackened by a three-hour eclipse. Then on May 27 a strange fog enveloped the city, and when it lifted, a weird light was seen, including from the Ottoman camp, flickering about Hagia Sophia before fizzling; it was heralded as the departure of the Divine Presence. Icons and crosses inexplicably fell.

The emperor then went into Hagia Sophia "and devoutly received, with tears and prayers, the sacrament of the holy communion."[132] He proceeded to the palace, begged pardon of any he might have offended during his life, bid his wife farewell (he had no children) and returned to the wall.

Finally, on May 29, around two a.m., Muhammad shattered the quiet of night by unleashing all hell against Constantinople: to blasting sounds of trumpets, cymbals, and Islamic war-cries, cannon fire lit the horizon as ball after ball came crashing into the wall. Adding to the pandemonium rang church bells and alarms.* The cacophony was maddening. After the initial wave of cannon fire, the sultan implemented his strategy: "I have decided to engage successively and without halt one body of fresh troops after the other," he had told his generals, "until harassed and worn out the enemy will be unable further to resist."[133] On and on, wave after wave, the hordes came, all desirous of booty or paradise—or merely evading impalement.

First came thousands of *bashi bazouks,* the irregular "Crazy Heads"; they were followed by "the sultan's military police and court officials [who] beat them back with iron clubs and whips" whenever they wavered. With ladders and hooks, they fought, clawed, and clambered onto the wall. "Who could narrate the voices, the cries of the wounded, and the lamentation that arose on both sides?" recollected Sphrantzes. "The shouts and din went beyond the boundaries of heaven."[134]

After two hours of this, thousands of the vagabond raiders lay dead beneath the wall. Having served their purpose of wearying the defenders down, Muhammad—now mounted near the wall and directing traffic with a mace in his hand—ordered another wave of fresh Anatolian Turks to crash against the wall. The jihadis built and clawed atop human pyramids of their own wounded and dead, all while cannon balls careened and crashed— to no avail. Having the high ground, the Christians slew countless. "One could only marvel at the brutes," conceded Leonard of Chios. "Their army was being annihilated, and yet they dared to approach the fosse again and again."[135]

---

* "When the Turks heard the ringing of the bells," one source notes, "they ordered their trumpets, flutes, and thousands of other musical instruments to sound out" and drown the hateful chimes (Dmytryshyn 1991, 216).

By four a.m. cannon fire had made several breaches, which the Janissaries charged, even as their former kin and coreligionists held firm. Michael Kritoboulos (b. 1410) offers a snapshot:

> [Giovanni] Giustiniani with his men and the Romans . . . fought bravely with lances, axes, pikes, javelins, and other weapons of offense. It was a hand-to-hand encounter, and they stopped the attackers and prevented them from getting inside the palisade. There was much shouting on both sides—the mingled sounds of blasphemy, insults, threats, attackers, defenders, shooters, those shot at, killers and dying, of those who in anger and wrath did all sorts of terrible things. And it was a sight to see there: a hard fight going on hand-to-hand with great determination and for the greatest rewards, heroes fighting valiantly, the one party [Ottomans] struggling with all their might to force back the defenders, get possession of the wall, enter the city, and fall upon the children and women and the treasures, the other party bravely agonizing to drive them off and guard their possessions, even if they were not to succeed in prevailing and in keeping them.[136]

Then two things happened in quick succession: Giovanni—that indefatigable hero whom everyone including the emperor looked to for inspiration—was shot through the breastplate and severely wounded. He begged to be removed from action but Constantine pleaded: "Do not abandon me at this moment of danger. It is on you that the salvation of this city depends."[137] The deeply anguished man would not relent and was finally carried through the city to a waiting Genoese ship, demoralizing all who saw him.[†]

As this was happening, a small detachment of Turks entered the city through a minor doorway the defenders had left open during the melee. They quickly planted the Islamic flag, causing consternation among the defenders. Playing on their worst fears, the sultan cried aloud, "The city is

---

[†] Giovanni withdrew to Chios, "where he died," writes a contemporary chronicler, "either from shame at having left the battle at such an inopportune moment, or because his wound was mortal" (Melville-Jones 1973, 123).

ours!" and ordered his best Janissaries to charge. One Hassan—"a giant of a beast"—slew all before him and inspired other Turks to press in behind him. When a well-aimed stone took him down, he continued swinging his scimitar on one knee until riddled and "overwhelmed by arrows" he was welcomed into paradise by the houris. "By then, the whole host of the enemy were on our walls and our forces were put to flight." Thousands of invaders flooded in and slaughtered the outnumbered defenders; others were trampled underfoot and "crushed to death" by the press of men.[138]

Crying, "The City is lost, but I live," Constantine, seized by a fey madness, stripped and flung off his royal regalia and "spurred on his horse and reached the spot where the Turks were coming in large numbers." With his steed he "knocked the impious from the walls" and with "his drawn sword in his right hand, he killed many opponents, while blood was streaming from his legs and arms."* Inspired by their lord, men shouting "Better to die!" rushed into and were consumed by the oncoming throng.[139] "The Emperor was caught up among these, fell and rose again, then fell once more."[140] Thus "he died by the gate with many of his men, like any commoner, after having reigned for three years and three months."[141]

And on that May 29, 1453, the 2,206-year-old Roman state died with him,† and "the saying," observed another contemporary, "was fulfilled: 'It started with Constantine [the Great] and it ended with Constantine [XI].'"[142]

THE DENOUEMENT OF JIHAD

It was not long before seventy thousand Muslims were inside the city, "raging and pressing on each other like wild beasts" and "with such force that it seemed a very inferno." They "went rushing about the city, and anyone they found they put to the scimitar, women and men, old and young, of any condition. This butchery lasted from sunrise, when the Turks entered the

---

* Some Ottoman chroniclers tersely confirm that "the ruler of Istanbul [Constantinople] was brave and asked for no quarter" (Crowley 2014, 231).

† Although it was founded in 325, to both those who lived in and those who attacked it, Constantinople was the literal continuation of the Roman Empire founded in 753 BC, a fact often forgotten due to frequent if not exclusive use of the word "Byzantine" (as discussed in the Introduction).

city, until midday," writes Nicolo Barbaro.[143] "They killed so as to frighten all the city—and to terrorize and enslave all by the slaughter," adds Kritoboulos.[144] "In many places the ground could not be seen, as it was covered by heaps of corpses," concludes Sphrantzes.[145]

As usual, those massacred during the initial onslaught—including the elderly who "were slain without mercy" and "new-born babes [who were] thrown in the streets"[146]—were among the fortunate ones. For, once the bloodletting had subsided, the invaders, variously described as "running furiously like dogs," or "like wild animals," "swarmed about the place, and gave vent to their natural cruelty and inhumanity with every cruel and lustful act."[147]

Everywhere "women were raped, virgins deflowered and youths forced to take part in shameful obscenities."[148] The victims—which included grown men—were not only gang-raped but subjected to perverse and degrading acts: "Women had to redeem themselves with their own bodies, men by fornicating with their hands or some other means.‡ Whoever was able to pay the assessed amount could remain in his faith and whoever refused had to die."[149] Another account says the victims were forced to endure "strange and horrible unions."

The old Muslim conflation of Christian piety with sexual promiscuity was on display, particularly against nuns who appear to have been doubly targeted for debasement. "They sought out the monasteries, and all the nuns were led to the fleet and ravished and abused by the Turks, and then sold at auction for slaves throughout Turkey," notes Nicolo.[150] "The nuns," confirms Leonard, "were disgraced with foul debaucheries."[151]

Because thousands of citizens had fled to and were holed up in Hagia Sophia, it offered an excellent harvest of slaves once its doors were axed down. "One Turk would look for the captive who seemed the wealthiest, a second would prefer a pretty face among the nuns. . . . Each rapacious Turk was eager to lead his captive to a safe place, and then return to secure a second and a third prize. . . . Then long chains of captives could be seen

---

‡ Forced to perform masturbation on their conquerors (and/or other sordid activities)?

leaving the church and its shrines, being herded along like cattle or flocks of sheep." The slavers sometimes fought each other to the death over "any well-formed girl,"[152] even as many of the latter "preferred to cast themselves into the wells and drown rather than fall into the hands of the Turks."[153]

Having taken possession of one of Christendom's greatest and oldest basilicas—nearly a thousand years old at the time of its capture—the invaders "engaged in every kind of vileness within it, making of it a public brothel."[154] On "its holy altars" they enacted "perversions with our women, virgins, and children,"[155] including "the Grand Duke's daughter who was quite beautiful." She was forced to "lie on the great altar of Hagia Sophia with a crucifix under her head and then raped."[156] Ottoman chronicles confirm these Christian accounts, if rather tersely: "They made the people of the city slaves and killed their emperor, and the gazis embraced their pretty girls."[157]

Finally, in keeping with Islam's perennial threat and primordial boast, they used Hagia Sophia and many other churches as "a stable for their horses," which they fed from toppled altars turned into troughs. Indeed, lest the jihadi pedigree of the sack be missed, the invaders everywhere set to desecrating and mocking all vestiges of Christianity—a sort of "Islam was here." Thus, "they paraded the [Hagia Sophia's main] Crucifix in mocking procession through their camp, beating drums before it, crucifying the Christ again with spitting and blasphemies and curses. They placed a Turkish cap . . . upon His head, and jeeringly cried, 'Behold the god of the Christians!'" They "gouged the eyes from the [embalmed] saints" and dumped their corpses "in the middle of the streets for swine and dogs to trample on . . . and the images of our Lord Jesus Christ and His Saints were burned or hacked to pieces."[158]

Many other churches in the ancient city suffered the same fate.* "The crosses which had been placed on the roofs or the walls of churches were

---

* Much gloating followed this "cleansing" of Constantinople: "For the evil-voiced clash of the bells of the shameless misbelievers was substituted the Muslim call to prayer," notes one sixteenth-century Ottoman historian, "and the ears of the people of jihad were filled with the melody. . . . The churches were emptied of their vile idols, and cleansed from their filthy and idolatrous impurities" (Hillenbrand 2007, 175).

torn down and trampled." The Eucharist was hurled to the ground; holy icons were stripped of gold, "thrown to the ground and kicked." Bibles were stripped of their gold or silver illuminations before being burned. "Icons were without exception given to the flames."[159] Patriarchal vestments were placed on the haunches of dogs; priestly garments were placed on horses.

Thus was the prophecy penned some 762 years earlier, the *Apocalypse,* fulfilled—or at least reenacted for the umpteenth time.[†]

"Everywhere there was misfortune, everyone was touched by pain" when Sultan Muhammad finally made his grand entry into the city. "There were lamentations and weeping in every house, screaming in the crossroads, and sorrow in all churches; the groaning of grown men and the shrieking of women accompanied looting, enslavement, separation, and rape."[160] The sultan rode to Hagia Sophia, dismounted, and went in, "marveling at the sight" of the grand basilica. Espying a Turk wildly hammering at the marble floor, he inquired what he was doing. "It is for the Faith!" replied the fanatic. Muhammad struck him down with his scimitar: "Be satisfied with the booty and the captives; the buildings of the city belong to me."[161]

Like other grand churches that came under Muslim control—such as John the Baptist's basilica, now the Great Mosque of Damascus—Hagia Sophia's lot was not destruction but transformation into a mosque. Cleansed of its crosses, statues, and icons—the sultan himself knocked over and trampled on its altar[162]—Muhammad ordered a muezzin to ascend the pulpit and sound "their detestable prayers. Then this son of iniquity [the sultan], this forerunner of Antichrist, mounted upon the Holy Table to utter forth his

---

† Probably written in Syria c. 691, the anonymous author predicts that "Greece will go to destruction, and those who dwell in it to captivity and to sword. Romania [Anatolia] will go to perdition and slaughter. . . . They will slaughter the priests after defiling them within the sanctuaries and go to bed with women in venerable and holy places. . . . And they will put them [holy vestments] on their horses and spread them over their beds. They will stable their flocks in the tombs of the saints. . . . The fire of testing comes to the race of Christians" (Pseudo-Methodius 2012, 43–49; a different translation appears on p. 124). Incidentally, it should not be imagined that the atrocities committed during the Islamic sack of Constantinople were significantly worse than those of earlier Islamic conquests. Rather, the former's records are much more detailed and, written in the fifteenth century, much better preserved than those from earlier centuries.

own prayers," thereby "turning the Great Church into a heathen shrine for his god and his Mahomet."[163]

Like others before and after him, Muhammad found no conflict in moving from piety to perversion. Drunk that night at his victory banquet, he sent word to Grand Duke Loukas Notaras—whose aforementioned daughter was gang-raped on the altar of Hagia Sophia—commanding him to surrender his youngest son to the sultan's sexual gratification. "When the boy's father heard this, his face turned ashen as though he had been struck dead." He replied that "it would be far better for me" to die than "hand over my own child to be despoiled by him." On hearing this, Muhammad, "in a rage," ordered Loukas executed. Before being killed, the Grand Duke—citing "Him Who was crucified for us, died and arose"—exhorted his terrified sons to reject Muhammad's advances and not fear the outcome. Encouraged, they too "were ready to die," and were executed.[164] The sultan stabbed to death another fourteen-year-old Christian boy who "preferred death to infamy."[165]

During the same festivities, "and as he had promised his viziers and his other officers," Muhammad had the "wretched citizens of Constantinople" dragged before them and "ordered many of them to be hacked to pieces, for the sake of entertainment."[166] The rest of the city's population—as many as forty-five thousand—were hauled off in chains to be sold into Eastern slavery.

Only one thing was needed to make the sultan's triumph complete: the head of his archenemy, Constantine XI. So a noggin claimed to be that of the fallen emperor was rushed to him and nailed onto a column. Standing before it, the sultan exulted: "Fellow soldiers, this one thing was lacking to make the glory of such a victory complete. Now, at this happy and joyful moment of time, we have the riches of the Greeks, we have won their empire, and their religion is completely extinguished. Our ancestors* eagerly desired to achieve this; rejoice now since it is your bravery which has won

---

* Which for the Ottoman Turks meant not only their predecessors and kin, the Seljuk Turks, but the Arab *murabitun* who had centuries earlier dedicated their lives to waging jihad on Constantinople.

this kingdom for us." Muhammad then ordered the severed head skinned, stuffed with bran, and "sent as a symbol of victory to the governors of Persia and Arabia"—a reminder to the two older Muslim peoples that it was a Turk who did what for centuries they could not.[167]

The news spread like wildfire across the lands of Islam. For unlike Manzikert, which was more a Turkic victory, the conquest of Constantinople held great significance for all Muslims. Even in Egypt, where the Ottomans' chief rivals the Mamluks reigned, the "good tidings were proclaimed, and Cairo decorated" to celebrate "this greatest of conquests." The Sharif of Mecca wrote to Muhammad, calling him "the one who has aided Islam and the Muslims, the Sultan of all kings and sultans," and— further underscoring the idea that conquest over infidels is the epitome of Islamic piety—"the resuscitator of the Prophet's sharia." But above all, it was the very fact that Constantinople—long "known for being indomitable in the eyes of all," as the Meccan put it—*had* fallen, that the prophet's centuries-old prophecy *had* come true, that struck the *umma* with shocked euphoria.[168]

Such a reaction is indicative of Constantinople's role when it stood. For when Islam overwhelmed and conquered the great cities and regions of Christendom during its first century of existence, it was New Rome that continued to defy the scimitar—even after the caliphate hurled all it had against its walls in not one but two all-out sieges. Had Constantinople fallen when an inchoate "Dark Age" Europe was already being bombarded from every side by the caliphate's allies and potential allies—Muslim Moors from the south, slave-trading Vikings from the north, and Hunnish Magyars from the east—Western Europe would have been faced with a grim prospect: the full, unhampered might of the caliphate—not across the (Mediterranean) sea, not behind impassable mountain ranges (of the Pyrenees)—but right smack in the continent, at its eastern backdoor, ready, eager, and willing to sweep through and mop up the rest of Christendom.

As it happened, however, Constantinople *did* withstand Islam. Even in the decades before its fall, when the city was a shadow of its former self, it remained a thorn in the Ottomans' side; for no matter how far into the

Balkans they advanced, so long as Constantinople stood, the Muslim rear remained vulnerable. In short, and as Byzantine historian John Julius Norwich puts it, "Had the Saracens captured Constantinople in the seventh century rather than the fifteenth, all Europe—and America—might be Muslim today."[169]

Now that it had fallen in 1453, pressing questions remained: Was Western Europe still weak and divided? Would Muhammad—in the person of his latest namesake—take Rome next? Or had its eastern and now dead counterpart bought the rest of Europe the needed time to mature against the forthcoming jihad?*

---

* Men cognizant of Christendom's history with Islam—such as Pope Pius II (r. 1458–1464), who was adamant about recovering Constantinople—appreciated such questions: "In the past we received our wounds in Asia and in Africa—in foreign countries. This time, however, we are being attacked in Europe, in our own land, in our own house. You will protest that the Turks moved from Asia to Greece a long time ago, that the Mongols established themselves in Europe and the Arabs occupied parts of Spain, having approached through the straits of Gibraltar. We have never lost a city or a place comparable to Constantinople" (Cardini 2001, 128).

CHAPTER 8

THE RISE AND FALL OF ISLAM: THE SIEGE OF VIENNA, 1683

Mahomet will never lay down his arms until he is either wholly victorious or completely vanquished.

—Pope Pius II, 1459[1]

Awake, Saladin. We have returned. My presence here consecrates the victory of the Cross over the Crescent.

—French General Henri Gouraud, Damascus, 1920[2]

VICTORY ON THE PERIPHERY

IF THE FIFTEENTH CENTURY WITNESSED ISLAM FINALLY ACHIEVE ITS eight-hundred-year-old goal of conquering Constantinople, so did it witness two different Christian civilizations—one Catholic and at Europe's westernmost border with Islam, the other Orthodox and at its easternmost—complete their centuries-long wars of liberation against Muslim occupation.

In Spain, the "capture of Granada [in 1492] produced an extraordinary effect throughout the Christian world and was viewed as a fitting revenge for the fall of Constantinople thirty-nine years earlier."[3] And though "what Constantinople was to the Ottoman sultan, Granada was to Ferdinand and Isabella,"[4] the war with Islam was hardly over from Spain's perspective. No sooner was Granada conquered when the two monarchs funded the ambitious voyage of one Christopher Columbus in an effort to launch "a final and definite Crusade against Islam by way of the Indies"[5] (which culminated in the incidental founding of the New World).

Many Europeans were convinced that if only they could reach the peoples east of Islam—who if not Christian were at least "not as yet infected by the Mahometan plague," to quote Pope Nicholas[6]—together they could crush Islam between them.* This comes out clearly in Columbus's own letters: in one he refers to Ferdinand and Isabella as "enemies of the wretched sect of Mohammet" who are "resolve[d] to send me to the regions of the Indies, to see" how the people thereof can help in the war effort;[7] in another written to the monarchs after he reached the New World Columbus offers to raise an army "for the war and conquest of Jerusalem."[8]

Nor were Spain and Columbus the first to implement this strategy; once Portugal was cleared of Islam in 1249, its military orders launched into Muslim Africa. "The great and overriding motivation behind [Prince] Henry the Navigator's [b. 1394] explosive energy and expansive intellect was the simple desire to take the cross—to carry the crusading sword over to Africa and thus to open a new chapter in Christendom's holy war against Islam."[9] He launched all those discovery voyages because "he sought to know if there were in those parts any Christian princes," who "would aid him against the enemies of the faith."[10]

But the fifteenth century also saw the liberation from Islamic domination of Christendom's easternmost nation, Orthodox Russia. Due, however, to a number of reasons—from the geographical to the geopolitical—its history remains the least known in the West.†

---

* The plan was centuries old and connected to the legend of Prester John, a supposedly great Christian monarch reigning in the East who would one day march westward and avenge Christendom by destroying Islam.

† Orthodox Russia has always seemed foreign, more "Eastern," and thus not part of the same "story" or legacy of the West. This sentiment was only exacerbated following the Cold War and persists until now. Moreover, the Mongol conversion to Islam, which occurred decades after the Tatars conquered Russia, is often dismissed by academics as skin deep at best, a superficial formality that had little impact on the everyday lives of Mongol masters and Russian subjects. As Bernard Lewis explains, "In addition to the Moors and Turks, there was a third Muslim advance into Europe [the Mongol/Tatar], often overlooked by Western historians but deeply burned into the consciousness

MONGOLS TURNED MUSLIMS

Although pagan when they conquered Russia around 1240, by 1300 the Mongols were thoroughly Islamized. Arabic was adopted, "the entire Muslim religious establishment of qadis, muftis, and the like arose in Sarai, the Horde's capital on the lower Volga," and "sharia, Muslim religious law," reigned supreme. "With this the Russo-Tatar conquest society entered the mainstream of Medieval Christian-Muslim frontier life," that is, it entered into a familiar paradigm. The building of churches "virtually came to a halt for a hundred years," and a host of "ransoms" and "irregular taxes, essentially extortions"—in a word, *jizya*—were exacted "to ensure the constant flow of wealth from Russia to the steppe."[11]

The Mongols' religious tolerance (or indifference) disappeared on their conversion to Islam. Whereas many Mongol leaders had originally favored their Christian subjects due to "their modesty and other habits of this kind," to quote Syriac bishop Bar Hebraeus (d. 1286), "their love has turned to such intense hatred . . . because they have all alike become Muslims."[12] Matters especially came to a head when the khan, Mahmud Ghazan, converted to Islam in 1295 and yielded to "popular pressure which compelled him to . . . persecute Christians," and culminated in the following ordinance: "The churches shall be uprooted, and the altars overturned, and the celebrations of the Eucharist shall cease, and the hymns of praise, and the sounds of calls to prayer shall be abolished; and the heads of the Christians, and the heads of the congregations of the Jews, and the great men among them, shall be killed."[13]

Empowered by this ordinance and believing "that everyone who did not abandon Christianity and deny his faith should be killed," Muslim mobs ran amok, slaughtering and wreaking havoc among Christian populations. In Mongol-controlled Armenia, church services were banned and local authorities ordered to pluck out the beards of and inflict other humiliations on every adult Christian man. "When few Christians defected [to Islam] in

---

of the East" (1994, 12). Elsewhere Lewis writes: "The Muslim attempt to conquer Europe falls into three main phases—those of the Arabs, the Tatars, and the Turks" (2004, 124).

response to these measures, the Khan then ordered that all Christian men be castrated and have one eye put out—which caused many deaths in this era before antibiotics, but did lead to many conversions" to Islam.[14]

A similar animus animated Mongol-Russian relations. At the peak of the Golden Horde's power in 1327, Uzbek Khan's cousin Shevkal—"the destroyer of Christianity," according to a Russian chronicle—asked the khan to "allow me to go to Rus to destroy their Christian faith, to kill their princes and to bring you their wives and children." Uzbek consented. At the head of a vast horde, Shevkal invaded Russia "with great haughtiness and violence. He inaugurated great persecution of the Christians, [using] force, pillage, torture, and abuse."[15] Nor were Russians ignorant of the reason behind their (renewed) sufferings: everywhere in their chronicles "they appear as defenders of the faith battling to save Christianity from marauding infidels driven by religious animosity," and "Mongol atrocities" are always recorded "as incidents in a continuous religious war."[16]

That the Mongols would convert to Islam was by no means evident from the start. Genghis's grandson Hülegü—who taunted Muslims by portraying himself as the "scourge of Allah" before annihilating the Abbasid caliphate—was notoriously hostile to Muhammad's creed and lenient to Christian and Jewish *dhimmis*.[*] When Hülegü's brother, Kublai Khan, discovered that a Muslim vizier, one "Achmath" (probably Ahmed), was using his high office to exploit the khanate's largely non-Muslim subjects, Kublai's "attention [went] to the doctrines of the Sect of the Saracens," wrote Marco Polo,[†] "which excuse every crime, yea, even murder itself,

---

[*] Hülegü once announced that "all Christians are to be freed from servitude and taxes [*jizya*] in Muhammadan lands. . . . No one is to molest their goods and those of their churches which have been destroyed are to be rebuilt." Similarly, in 1259 Hülegü commanded that "every religious sect should proclaim its faith openly, and that no Moslem should disapprove. On that day there was no single Christian," remarked a disappointed Muslim, "who did not put on his finest apparel" (Lamb 1927, 223). Of course, "the Mongols had not in fact lavished particular benevolence on the Christians during their occupation of Syria. They had merely implemented their traditional even-handed approach towards all religions and their adherents," which, considering what *dhimmi* Christians were accustomed to, must have seemed benevolent (Morgan 1988, 155).

[†] In fact, the Venetian traveler had much to say about Islam, most of which agreed

when committed on such as are not of their religion. And seeing that this doctrine had led the accursed Achmath and his sons to act as they did without any sense of guilt, the Khan was led to entertain the greatest disgust and abomination for it. So he summoned the Saracens and prohibited their doing many things which their religion enjoined."[17]

Still, as nomads, the Mongols shared much in common with other tribal peoples before them—Arabs, Berbers, Turks—who submitted to and found Islam compatible with their way of life. Their enemies were always the "other"—anyone and everyone outside their tribe (or in an Islamic context, infidels outside the *umma*).[‡] Christian Just War theory was utterly unintelligible to them: a people's refusal to submit to Mongol rule was all the reason needed to massacre and/or enslave them.[§] Once subjugated, only tribute (or in an Islamic context, *jizya*) could purchase their victims' lives.[¶]

---

with what other Europeans had noted: "According to their doctrine, whatever is stolen or plundered from others of a different faith, is properly taken, and the theft is no crime; whilst those who suffer death or injury by the hands of Christians, are considered as martyrs." The *hashashin*—whence the English word "assassin"—or Nizari Ismailis (a Shia sect) sold their lives in desperate assassination attempts to enter "paradise, where every species of sensual gratification should be found, in the society of beautiful nymphs [houris]." The Muslim ruler of Baghdad's "daily thoughts were employed on the means of converting to his religion those who resided within his dominions, or, upon their refusal, in forming pretences for putting them to death"; and Muslims "utterly detest the Christians" (Marco Polo 2001, 32, 47, 28–29, 264).

‡ Fra Carpini, a Western traveler sent "to exhort the pagan conquerors to cease the slaughter of Christian peoples," said: "They are irritable and disdainful to other men, and beyond belief deceitful. Whatever mischief they intend they carefully conceal, that no one may provide against it. And the slaughter of other people they consider as nothing." "The Tartars," he adds, "fight more by stratagem than by sheer force" (Lamb 1927, 73–74, 219).

§ In 1246, Pope Innocent IV wrote to Guyak Khan imploring him to "desist . . . from the persecution of Christians," adding: "I am surprised that you have seized all the lands of the Magyar and the Christians. Tell us what their fault is." The khan replied to the notion that people must somehow be at "fault" before they are attacked with confusion: "These words of yours I have also not understood. The eternal God has slain and annihilated these lands and peoples, because they have neither adhered to Genghis Khan, nor [to] the khagan [current supreme ruler]" (Allen 2010, 391–392).

¶ "The purpose of the taxes imposed on the conquered populations was quite simply the maximum conceivable degree of exploitation. There was little pretence that in Mongol eyes their subjects had any justification for their existence except as producers of revenue" (Morgan 1988, 102). One is reminded of the early caliphate's characterization

Even the career of the great Genghis Khan mirrors Muhammad's: they both unified the hitherto infighting tribes of Mongolia and Arabia; their successors redirected the combined might of their nations against the lands of the "other," the infidel. As head chief, Genghis, like Muhammad, formulated a code of law, the Yassa, which "was ever afterwards treated by his people with the veneration due a divine ordinance."[18] Because the Yassa, like the Koran, was authored in a nomadic setting, it echoes the Muslim doctrine of "loyalty and enmity": it exhorts Mongols "to aid one another—and destroy other people"; they are "forbidden" from making peace with any "people who have not submitted"; and non-Mongol subjects (like *dhimmis*) are "forbidden . . . to hold honorary titles" or "take a Mongol for servant or slave."[19]

In short, and as contemporary European observers had long said of the Turks, "the Tartars had [also] adopted Islam because it was the easy religion, as Christianity was the hard one," to quote Ricoldo of Monte Croce (d. 1320).[20] Whereas Islam complemented their preexisting way of life, Christianity only challenged it.

OVERTHROWING THE TATAR YOKE

The Golden Horde's infrastructure began to fracture from internal discord in 1359. Taking advantage of this, the principality of Moscow (or Muscovy) began to defy its overlords. So Khan Mamai, seeking to squash the rebels and "impose Islam on the Russians," made for Moscow with some one hundred thousand Turco-Tatars in 1380.[21] Boasting that they would put their swords "to the test for the Russian land and the Christian faith" against "the armor of the Moslems," the Russians accepted the challenge.[22] Under the general leadership of Grand Prince Dmitri Ivanovich of Moscow, some fifty thousand Russians went out and met the khan at Kulikovo Field, near the Don River and other tributaries. The opposing armies were so vast as to be spread out over eight miles. The Christians strategically positioned

---

of *dhimmi* populations in Egypt and elsewhere as "milk camels" (see pp. 34, 56).

themselves between rivers and dense forests, thereby limiting the Tatar horsemen's maneuvering and flanking abilities.

"I will neither protect my face nor hide in the rear, but let us all brothers fight together," Dmitri said in response to his *voivodes'* (or warlords') pleas to stay out of harm's way: "I want to die for Christianity ahead of anyone else, with deed as well as word, so that all others who see it will become bold."[23] More practically, explained the grand prince, "it is better that we fall in battle than become slaves of these infidels."[24]

Once battle commenced on September 8, 1380, "there was such a great massacre and bitter warfare and great noise, such as there never had been in Russian principalities," writes the chronicler; "blood flowed like a heavy rain and there were many killed on both sides."[25] Although outnumbered two-to-one, the Russians, "seek[ing] revenge for Tatar offenses," fought with a savage fury.[26] True to his word, Dmitri was seen at the front "striking to the right and to the left, killing many; he himself was surrounded by many [Tatars] and was hit many times on his head and his body."[27] After hours of fierce fighting and despite heavy casualties, the Russians, with the aid of hidden cavalry that had charged out of the surrounding thick woods, managed to rout the Muslims.

And so Grand Prince Dmitri—who, on learning the Mongols had fled, instantly collapsed from heavy loss of blood—led the first major Russian victory against their Tatar oppressors in 150 years.

Although the Battle of Kulikovo shattered the myth of Mongol invincibility and bestowed great honor on Moscow, full liberation was still a century away. For in 1382, the regrouped and recovered Tatars invaded Moscow, nearly burning the entire city to the ground and leaving some twenty-four thousand corpses in their wake.

But the resilient duchy continued to be the chief Russian thorn in the Horde's side.[28] By 1409, Emir Edigei was warning Grand Prince Vasily Dmitrivich to stop withholding full payment of *jizya*—"lest evil befall your domain, and Christians meet their final doom, and our anger and war be upon you!"[29] The warning ignored, Edigei came slaughtering, pillaging, and burning, including in Moscow, though he failed to take it. For what was done at the Kulikovo Field could not now be undone; over the next few decades, Moscow continued to grow in strength and prestige even as the Horde continued to diminish in both.

In 1478, Ivan III, Grand Prince of Moscow and "Gatherer of Russian Lands," defiantly refused payment of *jizya* to Ahmed Khan. Despite the Tatar's raging and howling—for Ahmed was reputed to be a "savage and fighter-of-Allah"[30]—Moscow's archbishop and all boyars "pleaded with the Grand Prince to remain firm against Islam on behalf of Orthodox Christianity." Two years later Ahmed set out for Moscow with a massive host. All Russian men were exhorted to "make all necessary sacrifices in order to put an end to the burning and pillaging of your homes, the killing of your children, the abusing of your wives and your daughters—things that other great lands are now suffering from the Turks, such as Bulgaria, Serbia, Greece" (a reference to the ongoing havoc the Ottoman Turks were wreaking in the Balkans just then).[31]

With Ivan at their head, the Russians went to confront Ahmed's hordes. In early October, 1480—one hundred years after the battle of Kulikovo— the two armies found themselves on the opposite banks of the Ugra River. Arrows and insults were hurled over the river, but when it froze and became passable, both Christians and Muslims withdrew, and "thus ended the Horde tsars," concludes a grateful chronicler. As with the fall of Granada, that this great liberation came only twenty-seven years after the fall of Constantinople further heightened its significance. "And then in our Russian Land we were freed from the burden of submission to the Muslim and began to recover," sang another chronicler, "as if from winter to clear spring."[32]

As shall be seen, however, this encomium should not be taken too literally. For as liberating as it was not to be formally subjugated and paying tribute to the khanate, devastating slave raids on Russia continued for centuries. One recorded by a chronicler nearly seventy years after the Great Stand on the Ugra documents how Tatar raiders were still "spilling the blood of Christians, desecrating and ruining the churches";[33] another notes that they "raped the young nuns" and "cut off the nose, ears, hands and feet of those whom they did not take away into captivity."[34]

MUHAMMAD'S JIHAD CONTINUES

Although Christendom scored decisive victories against Islam along its western and eastern borders, the Ottoman advance toward the heart of Europe continued unabated. Still only twenty-one years old when he sacked Constantinople in 1453, Muhammad II had many good decades of jihading before him. He subdued Serbia once and for all and most of Greece in 1459. That same year, Pope Pius II convened the Council of Mantua. Frustrated that none of the invited Western heads of state came, he warned that no one was out of reach of the Turkish scimitar:

> [For] can we expect peace from a nation which thirsts for our blood, which has already planted itself in [the southern portions of] Hungary after having subjugated Greece? Lay aside these infatuated hopes. Mahomet will never lay down his arms until he is either wholly victorious or completely vanquished. Each success will be only a stepping-stone to the next until he has mastered all the Western Monarchs, overthrown the Christian Faith, and imposed the law of his false prophet on the whole world. . . . Oh, that Godfrey, Baldwin, Eustace, Hugh, Bohemund, Tancred, and those other brave men who re-conquered Jerusalem were here! Truly they would not need so many words to persuade them.[35]

Little came from his pleas. As for Muhammad, in his bid to feed his horses on the altar of Saint Peter's basilica—did not the prophecies claim that "we will conquer Constantinople before we conquer Rome"?—he invaded Italy and captured Otranto in 1480.[36] More than half of its twenty-two thousand inhabitants were massacred, five thousand led away in chains. On a hilltop (subsequently named "Martyr's Hill") another eight hundred Christians were ritually beheaded for refusing to convert to Islam, and their archbishop sawed in half.

Now it was Pope Sixtus IV's turn to chastise an indifferent West: "Let them [Western Europeans] not think that they are protected against invasion, those who are at a distance from the theatre of war! They, too, will bow the neck beneath the yoke, and be mowed down by the sword, unless they come forward to meet the invader. The Turks have sworn the extinction of Christianity. A truce to sophistries! It is the moment not to talk, but to act and fight!"[37]

Less than a year later, Sultan Muhammad II died aged forty-nine, likely poisoned by his son and successor, Bayezid II. If he could not attain the same quantity of victories as his father, Bayezid's were every bit as atrocious in quality, as evidenced by the extant documentation of his conquest of Methone, Greece:

Then Sultan Bayezid came inside; he entered and prayed in the Frankish church which he converted into a mosque, as it remains to the present day. [Other churches were burned.] They butchered the pitiable Christians. They say that the slaughter was so great that blood ran into the sea and stained it red. From there, after Bayezid had prayed, he . . . ordered all Methonians captured alive, young and old, to be brought before him. He ordered the execution of all those who were ten years or older; and so it happened. They gathered their heads and bodies, put them together, and built a big tower outside the city, which can still be seen nowadays. This happened in 1499.[38]

Around that same time, German satirist Sebastian Brant published what became a popular poem on the gradual nature of Islam's advances vis-à-vis a "sleeping" Christendom:

> *Our faith was strong in th' Orient*
> *It ruled in all of Asia*
> *In Moorish lands and Africa*
> *But now [since the seventh century] for us these lands are gone . . .*
> *We perish sleeping one and all*
> *The wolf has come into the stall*

And steals the Holy Church's sheep
The while the shepherd lies asleep
Four sisters of our Church you find
They're of the patriarchic kind
Constantinople, Alexandria, Jerusalem, Antioch
But they've been forfeited and sacked
And soon the head [Rome] will be attacked.[39]

As the poem's continuity suggests, learned Europeans saw the Ottoman scourge as the latest in a continuum of Islamic terror: for whereas the Arabs were "the first troops of locusts" that appeared "about the year 630," wrote a contemporary English priest, "the Turks, a brood of vipers, [are] worse than their parent . . . the Saracens, their mother."[40]

A "MAGNIFICENT" GHAZI AND THE SUNDERING OF CHRISTENDOM

All such warnings and laments continued to fall on deaf ears when the next sultan, Selim I (r. 1512–1520), turned his back on Europe and successfully spent his energy against the Ottomans' longtime rival, the Mamluk sultanate. As a result, by 1517, the Ottoman Empire's domains included Anatolia, the Balkans, the Levant, Islam's three holiest cities (Mecca, Medina, and Jerusalem), Egypt, and practically all of North Africa. "Now that the terrible Turk has Egypt and Alexandria and the whole of the Roman eastern empire in his power," lamented Pope Leo X, "he will swallow not just Sicily and Italy but the whole world!"[41]

Three years later, the tenth and longest-reigning Ottoman sultan, twenty-six-year-old Suleiman I—known as "the Magnificent" among Europeans but "the *ghazi*" among Turks—came to power, murdered his brothers,* and made ready to employ the full resources of his

---

* As Austria's ambassador to the Ottoman Empire during the reign of Suleiman once mused: "It is an unfortunate thing to be a son of [Ottoman] emperors. It is because when one of them succeeds to the throne, the others then wait for their death" (https://www.dailysabah.com/feature/2015/08/07/the-history-of-fratricide-in-the-ottoman-empire—part-1).

six-hundred-thousand-square-mile empire against Europe.[42] He moved quickly, capturing Belgrade in 1521 and Rhodes in 1522, both of which even his great grandfather, Muhammad II the Conqueror, could not.

Four years later Suleiman smashed the "shield of Christianity," the hitherto mighty kingdom of Hungary, at the pivotal battle of Mohacs. At the head of seventy thousand Muslims—many self-proclaimed devotees of "jihad and martyrdom," eager for "a perpetually happy life" with "the houris"[43]—he annihilated the Hungarian army, built a massive pyramid of heads, and returned to Constantinople with one hundred thousand slaves.

By 1529 the sultan was laying siege to the gates of Vienna; but because it was a somewhat impromptu invasion that came at the end of campaigning season—and was accompanied by bad weather, bogged-down and abandoned siege engines, and camp disease—Suleiman lifted the siege after less than three weeks.

Suleiman's unprecedented advances into Europe could not have come at a worse time; for the last, worst, and most acrimonious sundering of Christendom—"the ultimate effect of which was to benefit the Muslims"[44]—began in 1517, the same year the Ottomans had absorbed the vast domains of the Mamluk sultanate. A Catholic clergyman named Martin Luther (1483–1546) had initiated history's Protestant Reformation. Whatever else can be said of him, Luther unwittingly did much to weaken European unity against invading Islam. Although he maintained the traditional Christian view on Islam—denouncing the Koran as a "cursed, shameful, desperate" book filled with "dreadful abominations"—he condemned the concept of crusading and originally preached passivity[45] against the Muslim invaders,* saying that, although the sultan "rages most intensely by murdering Christians in the body . . . he, after all, does nothing by this but fill heaven with saints."[46]

---

* Concerning "Luther's contention that those who make war on the Turks rebel against God, who is punishing our sins through them," Erasmus quipped: "If it is not lawful to resist the Turks, because God is punishing the sins of his people [Christians] through them, it is no more lawful to call in a doctor during illness, because God also sends diseases to purge his people of their sins" (Allen 2010, 415).

Perhaps worst of all, by portraying the Catholic pope as more of an "Antichrist" than the Ottoman sultan—an office held by Muslim leaders responsible for the slaughter and enslavement of hundreds of thousands of Christians—Luther and other Reformation leaders[†] ushered in a sort of relativism that prevails to this day, one that cites (often distorted) episodes from Catholic history to minimize ongoing Muslim atrocities.[‡]

The Catholic Church responded with its own invective "and frequently tried to discredit Protestant doctrine by likening it to Islam—Muhammad was an early Protestant and the Protestants were latter day Saracens."[47] It finally got to the point that both Catholics and Protestants began "heaping praise upon the infidel" in an effort to portray each other as unparalleled evil.[48] All the while, Muslims sat back and laughed to the exasperation of sensible men like the humanist Erasmus: "While we have been endlessly fighting among ourselves," he grumbled, "the Turks have vastly extended their empire or, rather, their reign of terror."[49]

This "reign of terror" was especially evident along Europe's Mediterranean coast. When Suleiman became sultan, pirates from Algiers—known as the "Barbary" corsairs (betraying their Berber roots)—were already terrorizing the Christian Mediterranean, their boats and ranks swollen with vengeful Moriscos recently expelled from Spain. Other pirates were European "renegades," that is, apostates to Islam; "most of them were captives seized as children," and a sort of "janissary-institute-for-piracy" developed as "the bolder and handsomer boys were often picked out by the penetrating eye of the reis [leader], and once chosen the young captive's career was

---

[†] John Calvin went as far as to say that the Islamic prophet and Catholic pope were "the two horns of Antichrist." (See Rev. Francis Nigel Lee's "Calvin on Islam.") For the record, that "the Reformation produced . . . a definite boost to the positive evaluation of Islam, and therefore to the birth and development of an often conventional and mannered pro-Islamic stance" (Cardini 2001, 150), should not be interpreted as an attack on Protestantism or a defense of Catholicism, as it says nothing about the theological merits, or truths, of either. Rather, the point here is that the actions of fallible men, of both religious persuasions, had unforeseen consequences.

[‡] For example, "the prevailing image of the Spanish Inquisition as a monstrously bloody and brutal institution is a fiction mainly reflecting Protestant (especially British) hostility towards Catholicism" (Stark 2012, 5).

established."[50] They too were indoctrinated in and emboldened by Muhammad's promises: "A campaign by sea is like ten campaigns by land," said the prophet, "and he who loses his bearings at sea is like one who sheds his blood in the path of Allah."[51] And so the piratical lust for booty was heightened by dreams of martyrdom.

Around 1520 Suleiman took the most notorious of these Barbary pirates, Khair al-Din Barbarossa, into his service and helped him prosecute the sea jihad on Europe. The ensuing reign of terror forced Europeans along the Mediterranean coast to relive the days of their ancestors in the centuries before the crusades, when the Middle Sea was first inundated with jihad and slave raiding (see Chapter 3). Over the following two decades, hundreds of thousands of Europeans were enslaved, so that, by 1541, "Algiers teemed with Christian captives, and it became a common saying that a Christian slave was scarce a fair barter for an onion."[52]

CHINKS IN THE ARMOR: MALTA AND LEPANTO

Despite the seaborne jihad's successes, "You will do no good," a seasoned corsair counseled Suleiman, "until you have smoked out this nest of vipers," a reference to the Knights Hospitaller, now the Knights of Saint John headquartered in Malta.[53] Suleiman had evicted them from Rhodes in 1522—whence for two hundred years they had frustrated all Ottoman naval attempts—and Holy Roman Emperor Charles V had bequeathed the island of Malta to the homeless Hospitallers in 1530. They were the emperor's response to the sultan's corsairs—and, for more than three decades, a thorn in Suleiman's side.* Having finally decided to eliminate this "headquarters of infidels," in March 1565 one of the largest fleets ever assembled—carrying some thirty thousand Ottomans—was dispatched to take the tiny island, which had a total fighting population of eight thousand.

Pope Pius IV implored the kings of Europe to Malta's aid, to no avail: the king of Spain "has withdrawn into the woods," complained the pope,

---

* Although the Knights of Saint John sought to respond in kind by enslaving Muslim enemies wherever possible, slaving around the Mediterranean was by far "a prevalently Muslim phenomenon" (R. Davis 2003, 9).

"and France, England and Scotland [are] ruled by women and boys." Only the viceroy of neighboring Sicily responded, but he needed time to raise recruits. Jean Parisot de Valette (1494–1568), the Grand Master of the Knights—"his disposition is rather sad," but "for his age [seventy-one], he is very robust" and "very devout"—made preparations for the forthcoming siege, including by explaining to his men what was at stake:[54] "A formidable army composed of audacious barbarians is descending on this island," he warned; "these persons, my brothers, are the enemies of Jesus Christ. Today it is a question of the defense of our Faith as to whether the book of the Evangelist [the Gospel] is to be superseded by that of the Koran? God on this occasion demands of us our lives, already vowed to His service. Happy will those be who first consummate this sacrifice."[55]

The Ottomans commenced their arrival in late May with a nonstop bombardment of St. Elmo, one of Malta's key forts. "With the roar of the artillery and the arquebuses, the hair-raising screams, the smoke and fire and flame," a chronicler writes, "it seemed that the whole world was at the point of exploding." The vastly outnumbered and soon wearied defenders, who were ordered to "fight bravely and sell their lives to the barbarians as dearly as possible,"[56] did just that; and for every Christian killed defending the fort, numerous Muslim besiegers fell. After withstanding all that the Ottomans could throw against it for a month, on June 23, St. Elmo, by now a heap of rubble, was finally stormed and captured.

Virtually all 1,500 defenders were slaughtered. The same grisly fate Saladin had centuries earlier consigned to Islam's staunchest enemies—the Knights Templars and Hospitallers—was now meted out to their heirs. The Knights of Saint John "were hung upside down from iron rings . . . and had their heads split, their chests open, and their hearts torn out."[57] Ottoman commander Mustafa ordered their mutilated corpses (along with one Maltese priest) nailed to wooden crosses and set adrift in the Grand Harbor in order to deride and demoralize the onlooking defenders. It failed: the seventy-one-year-old Valette delivered a thundering and defiant speech before the Christians, beheaded all Muslim prisoners, and fired their heads from cannon at the Turkish besiegers.

The Ottomans proceeded to subject the rest of the island to, at the time, history's most sustained bombardment (some 130,000 cannonballs were fired in total). "I don't know if the image of hell can describe the appalling battle," wrote a contemporary: "the fire, the heat, the continuous flames from the flamethrowers and fire hoops; the thick smoke, the stench, the disemboweled and mutilated corpses, the clash of arms, the groans, shouts, and cries, the roar of the guns . . . men wounding, killing, scrabbling, throwing one another back, falling and firing."[58]

Although the rest of the forts were reduced to rubble, much Muslim blood was spilled for each inch gained; for "when they got within arms' reach the scimitar was no match for the long two-handed sword of the Christians."[59] Desperate fighting spilled into the streets, where even Maltese women and children participated. It was now late August and the island was still not taken; that, and mass casualties led to mass demoralization in the Ottoman camp. Embarrassed talk of lifting the siege had already begun when Sicily's viceroy Garcia de Toledo finally arrived with nearly ten thousand soldiers at St. Paul's Bay.

There, where the apostle was once shipwrecked, the final scene of this Armageddon played out as the fresh newcomers routed the retreating Ottomans, who finally fled on September 11. "So great was the stench in the bay," which was awash with countless bloated Muslim corpses, "that no man could go near it."[60] As many as twenty thousand Ottomans and five thousand defenders died.

After forty years of successful campaigning against Europe, Suleiman I finally suffered his first major defeat. One year later he succumbed to death, aged seventy-one. More importantly for Europe, a chink in the Ottoman armor was perceived through the inspiration of Malta. Accordingly, when in 1570 Ottoman forces invaded the island of Cyprus, the pope easily managed to form a "Holy League" of maritime Catholic nation-states, spearheaded by the Spanish Empire, in 1571.

Before they could reach and relieve Cyprus, its last stronghold at Famagusta was taken through treachery. After promising the defenders safe passage if they surrendered, Ottoman commander Ali Pasha—known as

Müezzinzade ("son of a muezzin") due to his pious background—had reneged and launched a wholesale slaughter.

He ordered the nose and ears of Marco Antonio Bragadin, the fort commander, hacked off. Ali then invited the mutilated infidel to Islam and life: "I am a Christian and thus I want to live and die," Bragadin responded. "My body is yours. Torture it as you will." So he was tied to a chair, repeatedly hoisted up the mast of a galley and dropped into the sea, to taunts: "Look if you can see your fleet, great Christian, if you can see succor coming to Famagusta!" The mutilated and half-drowned man was then carried near to St. Nicholas Church—by now a mosque—and tied to a column, where he was slowly flayed alive. The skin was afterward stuffed with straw, sown back into a macabre effigy of the dead commander, and paraded in mockery.[61]

News of this and other ongoing atrocities and desecrations of churches in Cyprus and Corfu enraged the Holy League as it sailed east. A bloodbath followed when the two opposing fleets—carrying a combined total of 600 ships and 140,000 men, more of both on the Ottoman side—finally met and clashed on October 7, 1571, off the western coast of Greece, near Lepanto. According to one contemporary:

> The greater fury of the battle lasted for four hours and was so bloody and horrendous that the sea and the fire seemed as one, many Turkish galleys burning down to the water, and the surface of the sea, red with blood, was covered with Moorish coats, turbans, quivers, arrows, bows, shields, oars, boxes, cases, and other spoils of war, and above all many human bodies, Christians as well as Turkish, some dead, some wounded, some torn apart, and some not yet resigned to their fate struggling in their death agony, their strength ebbing away with the blood flowing from their wounds in such quantity that the sea was entirely coloured by it, but despite all this misery our men were not moved to pity for the enemy. . . . Although they begged for mercy they received instead arquebus shots and pike thrusts.[62]

The pivotal point came when the flagships of the opposing fleets, the Ottoman *Sultana* and the Christian *Real,* crashed into and were boarded by one another. Chaos ensued as men everywhere grappled; even the grand admirals were seen in the fray, Ali Pasha firing arrows and Don Juan swinging broadsword and battle-axe, one in each hand. In the end, "there was an infinite number of dead" on the *Real,* whereas "an enormous quantity of large turbans, which seemed to be as numerous as the enemy had been, [were seen in the *Sultana*] rolling on the deck with the heads inside them."[63]

The don emerged alive but the pasha did not. When the central Turkish fleets saw Ali's head on a pike in the *Sultana* and a crucifix where the flag of Islam once fluttered, mass demoralization set in and the waterborne melee was soon over. The Holy League lost twelve galleys and ten thousand men, but the Ottomans lost 230 galleys—117 of which were captured by the Europeans—and thirty thousand men.

It was a victory of the first order, and all of Christendom—Catholic, Orthodox, and Protestant—rejoiced. Practically speaking, however, little changed. Cyprus was not even liberated by the Holy League. "In wrestling Cyprus from you we have cut off an arm," the Ottomans painfully reminded the Venetian ambassador a year later. "In defeating our fleet [at Lepanto] you have shaved our beard. An arm once cut off will not grow again, but a shorn beard grows back all the better for the razor."[64] Even so, the twin victories of 1565 and 1571 proved that the relentless Turks could be stopped. If Malta showed that a tiny but dedicated force could hold out against them, Lepanto suggested that the Turks could even be defeated in a head-on clash—at least by sea, which of late had been the Islamic powers' latest hunting grounds. As Miguel Cervantes, who was at the battle, has the colorful Don Quixote say: "That day . . . was so happy for Christendom, because all the world learned how mistaken it had been in believing that the Turks were invincible by sea."[65]

But defeat at sea, no matter how spectacular, could not shake what was first and foremost a land power.

EYEING THE "GOLDEN APPLE"

It is commonly affirmed that after Lepanto the Ottoman Empire went into steady decline. Certainly a number of unworthy sultans followed Suleiman the Magnificent Ghazi—such as Selim "the Sot"—and setbacks were not uncommon. Even so, the greatest extent of the Ottoman Empire did not come until the 1670s; by then Crete and large areas of the Ukraine were added to its domains. Soon, Vienna—the "Golden Apple" that had evaded even Suleiman's grasp in 1529—was being eyed again.

Like Constantinople before it, symbolic and practical reasons made Vienna especially enticing to Ottoman eyes: it was the Austrian capital of the Holy Roman Empire, the Turks' Christian archenemy for a century and a half; and it was a strategic gateway into the heart of Europe; from it, Italy (and Rome) to the south and the disunited German kingdoms to the north could easily be invaded. Furthermore, as the cultural center of Europe and opulent seat of empire, Vienna was a cornucopia of animate and inanimate delights of the kind to entice even the most sated Muslim lord.

Such a lord was Kara—meaning "black"—Mustafa (so known for his swarthy complexion). In 1676, at age forty-two, he became Ottoman Grand Vizier, second only to the sultan. His military ambition was rivaled only by his "insatiable avarice": he owned three thousand female slaves and concubines, seven hundred black eunuchs, and thousands of wild and exotic animals. He paid for this ostentatious lifestyle by doing "favors" for those willing to buy them, and "spared nothing to satisfy his avarice. So it may be said," writes Sieur La Croix (or Le Croy), a diplomat stationed at the Ottoman Empire's French embassy, "that the Vizier had more ready money than his master."[66]

This "fanatically anti-Christian" Grand Vizier[67]—who in 1674 captured a Polish town, flayed his prisoners alive, and sent their stuffed hides to the sultan—burned to achieve what even the Magnificent Ghazi could not: the conquest of Vienna. Unfortunately for the Holy Roman Empire, it had two other enemies besides the scimitar-rattling Turks: the French, in the megalomaniacal guise of Louis XIV, and Protestant rebels in north

Hungary, then under Austrian rule, continued to make common cause with the Ottomans against their mutual enemy.* When a Hungarian Protestant count, Imre Thokoly, called on the Turks for military aid against the Austrians—thereby providing the necessary pretext for the Ottomans to mobilize and march for war—the French promised the Turks they would in no way impede their progress to Vienna.

Citing that "they ought to take advantage of the disorders of the Christians by the siege of the place [Vienna], the conquest of which would assure that of all Hungary, and open 'em a passage to the greatest victories,"[68] Mustafa spent the early months of 1683 marshalling what would arguably be the largest Muslim army ever to invade Christian territory.

During an elaborate pre-jihad ceremony, Sultan Muhammad IV, "desiring him [Mustafa] to fight generously for the Mahometan faith," placed "the standard of the Prophet . . . into his hands for the extirpation of infidels, and the increase of Muslemen."[69] The vainglorious vizier responded by making that old Muslim boast: not only would he take Vienna, but soon thereafter he would stable his horses at St. Peter's in Rome before turning on his French "ally."[70]

Once the Ottoman army reached Belgrade on the feint of aiding Thokoly against two Austrian strongholds, Mustafa made his true intentions known in a war council: to march directly on and take Vienna, the head of the infidel snake, so that "all the Christians would obey the Ottomans." Although a welcome proposition in theory, wiser minds counseled

---

* As northern Protestants and southern Muslims had the same common enemy between them—Catholic Christendom, particularly in the guise of the Holy Roman Empire—the principle that "the enemy of my enemy is my friend" was on constant display from the start. By 1535, "it was one of the bitterest truths . . . that the Catholic King [Charles V] would spend more time, money, and energy fighting the French and the Protestants than he ever devoted to the war with Suleiman" (Crowley 2009, 58). Such factors place the sultan's supposedly intrinsic successes in a different spotlight. Similarly, Protestant queen Elizabeth I of England (r. 1558–1603) formed an alliance with the Muslim Barbary pirates—who during her reign had enslaved hundreds of thousands of Europeans—against Catholic Spain, prompting that nation's papal nuncio to lament that "there is no evil that is not devised by that woman, who, it is perfectly plain, succored Mulocco [Abd al-Malek] with arms, and especially with artillery" (Brotton 2016, 80).

prudence. In typical oriental fashion, Ibrahim, the sage-like pasha of Buda, spoke in parables: the only way to pick up a treasure in the center of a poisoned carpet without walking on it is by rolling up the carpet toward the apple—that is, by first subduing all obstacles along the way. "You are an old man of eighty—your mind is defective" was all the pasha got for his trouble from Mustafa, for the latter "wou'd not hearken to anything but his own pride and obstinacy."[71]

In this manner, "the Grand Vizier, animated by so good a beginning, and by the accounts he had received of the weakness of the Christians, his principal design being the conquest of Vienna," explains La Croix, "pushed directly to Vienna" at the head of a vast multitude said to consist of three hundred thousand people[72]: nearly two hundred thousand combatants, the rest artisans, tradesmen, concubines, prostitutes, and camp stragglers of all kinds. The fighting men consisted mostly of Turks and Tatars. Two Christian vassals marched with the Ottoman host: the Lutheran count, Thokoly; and the Calvinist Transylvanian prince, Apafi.

Apprehensive of Turkish intentions in advance, Pope Innocent XI had been petitioning Catholics everywhere to unite in a formal crusade against the approaching infidels. Germans and Poles, moved by both pious and practical considerations—if Vienna fell, Rome and Catholicism would fall, and the Turks would be on their own borders—responded to the appeal and began making war preparations. (Needless to say, Catholic France ignored the summons and even exploited the situation by making militant inroads into the Holy Roman Empire's territory. Little wonder "the Crescent Moon climbs up the night sky, and the Gallic cock sleeps not" was a common saying in Austria.[73])

On July 7, 1683, rumor of the Ottoman frontrunners—a horde of thirty-five thousand Tatar horsemen who were burning and pillaging everything in their wake—sparked mass panic in and a general exodus out of Vienna. Even Holy Roman Emperor Leopold I (r. 1658–1705) abandoned his own capital and fled to Passau, Bavaria. But he left some twelve thousand soldiers to man the city's walls under the capable command of Count Ernst von Starhemberg, who instantly proceeded to level all buildings and structures outside Vienna's walls in order to deny the Ottomans any cover during the impending siege.

A week later, Mustafa and his vast forces—including by now "an infinite number of unfortunate slaves that had been forcibly carried away out of Austria"[74]—arrived around July 14. The camp they pitched, which completely surrounded Vienna, looked like a crescent-shaped city of canvas. Before unleashing hell against the city's thick walls and bastions, Mustafa followed protocol. Over one thousand years earlier, his prophet Muhammad had sent an ultimatum to Emperor Heraclius: *aslam taslam,* "submit [to Islam] and have peace." Much had changed in the millennium since: the Arabs had long ceased to lead Islam; the art of war and technology had advanced; nations and kingdoms had risen and fallen; even the appearance of Europeans (now wig-wearing and powdered) and Turks (colorfully and ostentatiously attired) had changed. But Islam's pre-battle ultimatum remained the same.

A message was delivered to Starhemberg that July 14: "We have come . . . with the intention of conquering this citadel and preaching the True Religion."[75] "Accept Islam, and live in peace under the sultan! Or deliver the city and live in peace as Christians under the sultan. If any man prefer, let him depart peaceably, taking his goods with him."[76] Starhemberg ignored the summons and continued with preparations. He knew that Mustafa had earlier passed through the neighboring city of Perchtoldsdorf and offered it identical terms—only to renege once the besieged Austrians opened their gates by massacring and enslaving them.[77] But if the military commander deigned not to respond, graffiti inside the city—including "Muhammad, you dog, go home!"—seems to capture its mood.[78] More eschatologically, "broadsheets with excerpts from the [seventh-century] *Apocalypse* were printed in Vienna during the Turkish siege of 1683" to reveal the who and why behind these apparent end times.[79]

THE WAR FOR VIENNA

Bombardment commenced on the next day. Like Suleiman before him, Mustafa had been unable to transport the heaviest cannons to the siege

and was forced to rely on light and medium artillery. Although they created much damage inside the city, they proved largely ineffective against
its walls. Mustafa responded by putting the camp's thousands of Austrian
captives to work digging trenches to and tunnels under the city's walls, in
an effort to use black powder to bring them down. That the trenches had to
be dug all the way from the Ottoman camp—Vienna's over three hundred
cannons kept its surrounding vicinity clear of hostile forces—made for a
slow and tedious procedure; and when the Turks finally got under the walls,
Viennese sallies and countermining operations frustrated their progress.
But because the best troops, the Janissaries, were in the trenches, where
Mustafa had "ordered each one of them to do his utmost to bring the enterprise to a successful conclusion, expending life and property for the true
faith," to quote an Ottoman historian, slow but steady progress was made.[80]

On August 12, nearly a month into the siege, a massive mine "said
to have shaken half the town" exploded, allowing the Muslims to reach
and entrench themselves along the outer fortifications.[81] Complementing
this victory outside the wall was the suffering behind it: without fresh
water—the Turks had cut off all external conduits—and with corpses, sew-
age, and rubble piling everywhere, an epidemic of dysentery—"the Turks'
strongest ally"—plagued Vienna. Hospitals and churches were overflowing
with sick and dying, and "there was great suffering just short of starvation, so that mostly older men and women died off."[82] Because death and
disease had also shrunken the professional soldiery's ranks, Starhemberg
ordered all able-bodied males in the city to report to wall duty; any shirk-
ing their responsibilities—including by falling asleep on duty even if from
exhaustion—were to be executed.[83]

Matters went from bad to worse when, on September 4, a massive det-
onation created a breach in the Burg, the strongest bastion; the Austrians
filled it in an effort to stop the oncoming rush of bodies and scimitars to
the cries of "Allah! Allah! Allah!"[84] After two hours of desperate fighting, the defenders managed to repulse the invaders and reclaim the Burg.
Though countless more Turks died, the two hundred Christian lives lost in
that critical encounter were keenly felt by their already paltry and steadily

dwindling numbers. An anonymous Englishman present during the siege summarized the situation: "The powerful enemy . . . since July 15 . . . had so vigorously attacked it [Vienna] with two hundred thousand men; and by endless workings, trenchings, and minings, reduced it almost to its last gasp."[85]

That last gasp came on September 8, when another all-out Muslim assault succeeded in capturing the Burg. Now the four thousand remaining defenders made ready to fight in the middle of the streets, a dismal prospect considering their vastly outnumbered status.[86] That same night, Starhemberg fired distress rockets into the night sky to give "notice to the Christian army"—that is, whatever relief force there may have been—"of the extremity whereto the city was reduced."[87] Understanding exactly what these rockets signified, cries of "Allahu Akbar!" followed them, as the Ottomans implored their deity to "obliterate the infidels utterly from the face of the earth!"[88]

It was then that it happened: "After a siege of sixty days," writes the anonymous Englishman, "accompanied with a thousand difficulties, sicknesses, want of provisions, and great effusion of blood, after a million of cannon and musket shot, bombs, granadoes, and all sorts of fire works, which has changed the face of the fairest and most flourishing city in the world, disfigured and ruined [it] . . . after," continues the verbose man, "a vigorous defense and a resistance without parallel, heaven favorably heard the prayers and tears of a cast down and mournful people."[89] For to the city's great joy, Starhemberg's distress rockets were answered by a hail of fireworks that lit the night sky.

The relief army had finally come.

Before the main Ottoman army had arrived, the bulk of the Holy Roman Empire's army did not remain with Starhemberg behind the walls but marched out to survey and possibly engage the Turks in the open. Initially with some twenty thousand Austrian men under his command—soon augmented by another twenty thousand Germans—Duke Charles of Lorraine, Emperor Leopold's brother-in-law, concluded there was little he could do but pull north of Vienna and await Polish reinforcements.

From the formation of this latest Holy League against Islam, the Poles seemed a wild and unpredictable lot: unlike the Germans—who in ethnicity, language, and culture were akin to the Austrians—the Poles were more like the Russians, common and crude, at least to the ultra-refined, wig-and-powder-wearing Viennese court of Leopold. But they were doughty fighters, and the Polish-Lithuanian Commonwealth was then one of Europe's largest and most powerful states. The military renown of Jan Sobieski—better known as John III, king of Poland and Grand Duke of Lithuania—against Turks and Tatars was widely acknowledged. But in 1683, he was fifty-four years old, obstinate, possibly complacent, and definitely fat. With much to lose—Protestant Hungarians threatened to attack Catholic Poland in his absence—and little to gain by marching, fighting, and dying for the Austro-Germans at a time when Christian infighting was rife, everyone wondered: would the Polish king honor his vow and come?

He did—to the ecstasy of Leopold, who flattered in a letter: "Your name alone, so terrible to the enemy, will ensure a victory."[90] Noting that "already the Ottoman fury is raging everywhere, attacking alas, the Christian princes with fire and sword," Sobieski set his affairs in order.[91] He wrote to Thokoly, the Hungarian troublemaker, "that if he burnt one straw in the territories of his allies, or in his own, he would go and burn him and all his family in his house."[92] Then on July 17, Sobieski left Warsaw and took the long southern road to Vienna.

He stopped at Krakow to rest and muster more men. During a church ceremony on August 10, "the nuncio published the Pope's indulgence for all men going out to battle in this Holy War. After hearing a powerful sermon on this same theme, the King moved down from his throne to the altar steps for the benediction, and was blessed by the nuncio," who "writing afterwards to Innocent, recalled the singing, his sense of the King's intense devotion, and the weeping of the Queen."[93] Hitting so close to home, this latest grand jihad had "stirred up his [Sobieski's] military ambition and his Christian fervor." As he himself put it, "It is not a city alone that we have to save, but the whole of Christianity, of which the city of Vienna is the bulwark. The war is a holy one."[94]

On September 6, Charles's forty-thousand-strong Austro-German army met and merged with Sobieski's twenty-five thousand Poles. This "union, so happily made, recovered the courage of the Germans, and gave them hopes to succor the place, and drive out the Turks."[95] It was then that Starhemberg's rockets were answered. Charles continued to lead the Austro-Germans, but overall command was given to the veteran Polish king. With an impressive total of almost seventy thousand fighters, the crusaders were still outnumbered by the Muslim invaders. But no one else would come and Vienna was on the verge of falling. It was now or never.

Because they could better survey the Ottomans' layout and possibly mount a surprise attack from there, the relief army made for the summit of Kahlenberg Hill, northwest of Vienna. During the arduous three-day ascent through the thick Vienna Wood, some heavy artillery was lost in the muddy and tortuous terrain. Once on top and looking down, the Holy League saw Vienna enveloped in fire, smoke, rubble, and trench-mazes; encroaching Turks and galloping hordes were everywhere. But when Sobieski espied how spread Mustafa's forces were and the lack of entrenchments facing the Kahlenberg—whence Mustafa never expected a serious offensive—the king grinned: "This man is badly encamped. He knows nothing of war; we shall certainly defeat him."[96]

But first things first: Friar Marco d'Aviano, Emperor Leopold's spiritual advisor who did much to keep the Holy League intact, conducted mass on the hilltop and, with large crucifix in hand, roused the army to war. Echoing words spoken a thousand years earlier by the banks of the Yarmuk and repeatedly thereafter, he stressed that they were not fighting for Vienna but for their wives and children—for Christendom itself. Surprised by the loud cries "of the Christian troops on an opposite hill, and in sight of the Turkish camp," Mustafa ordered a few more cannons and troops positioned against the Kahlenberg, though kept the best of both besieging Vienna, against the advice of his generals.[97] It would fall any moment now, the vizier insisted, and he was not about to quit. As an added precaution, he ordered all adult males among the thirty thousand Christian slaves in the Ottoman camp massacred—lest they somehow aid their coreligionists—while the Muslim fighters "ravish'd the young maids and women, and cut off the heads of the old men and women."[98]

Battle commenced in the early morning hours of September 12 with several exchanges of artillery fire, followed by the slow descent of the Austro-German troops. Skirmishes and cannon raged for hours amid the rocky crags and slopes. The Austro-Germans, out to avenge what Vienna had been subjected to, fought fiercely, but no matter how many Turks and Tatars they hewed, more appeared. By afternoon the wearied and would-be liberators paused. It was then that a large white banner emblazoned with a red cross appeared on the opposite slope: the Poles—loudly calling on divine aid and appearing to the Turks like "a flood of black pitch coming down the mountain consuming everything it touched"[99]—had finally appeared, fighting manfully and encouraging their Austro-German counterparts.

Soon an uncoordinated mass of horses, men, steel, and gunfire clashed and boomed around the ravines and rubble of the Kahlenberg*—even as the noose continued to tighten around Vienna. The status quo continued for some hours, and several battalions considered withdrawing for the coming night. But Sobieski and other war veterans insisted on victory or death. "I am an old man," an elderly Saxon fighter pointed out, "and I want comfortable quarters in Vienna tonight."[100] Fierce but indecisive fighting continued.

Meanwhile, and in the hopes of striking the Ottomans in the heart and bringing matters to a close, Sobieski, "who exposed himself like the meanest soldier," kept an eye on the hard-to-miss and ostentatious tent of Mustafa—which further stood out by the green flag of Islam the sultan had imparted him. Once it came within range, "he caused all his artillery to fire upon that pavilion."[101] Few Ottomans ever expected enemy fire to reach the very heart of their city-like camp, which was filled with civilians of all sorts, and panic ensued. In the chaos, Sobieski espied a weakness in the

---

* One knight later remarked that "there were places where the ground looked even, but on getting nearer we found very deep ravines, and vineyards surrounded by lofty walls"; another: "[we fought] from ridge to valley and from valley to ridge" (Stoye 1964, 259).

Muslim line and ordered history's largest cavalry charge straight through it and for the Grand Vizier's tent.

At the head of some twenty thousand Polish, German, and Austrian horsemen, Sobieski, with his young son by his side, crashed with thunderous violence into the Ottoman line. Wearing heavy armor with eagles' wings, carrying large lances, and astride even larger and heavily armored steeds of war, three thousand hussars—the elite cavalry of the Polish army that surrounded its king—were an especial sight to behold: to the besieged Viennese, some of whom were now sallying forth to join the fray, they looked like winged liberators; to the increasingly demoralized Muslims, they looked like avenging angels and "struck fear in the hearts of the Turks and their Tartar allies."[102]

"By Allah, the King is really among us?" blurted Murad Giray, the dismayed khan of Crimea, on seeing Sobieski present and fighting. When Mustafa ordered him to redouble his efforts, "the Tartar Prince replied, that he knew the King of Poland by more than one proof, and that the Vizier would be very happy if he could save himself by flight, as having no other way for his security, and that he was going to show him example."[103] And off scurried the khan with his hordes. Murad had never liked Mustafa—who from the start of the campaign had snubbed and rejected his counsel at every opportunity—and was not about to lose more men for a dying cause. Boiling with fury, Mustafa was finally forced to lift the siege and redirect all his forces and artillery against the relief army. But it was too late. Hundreds of Janissaries, now trapped between the onslaught of the liberators and besieged, were slaughtered where they stood. By sunset, some fifteen thousand Ottomans lay dead or dying on the ground. The rest—including Mustafa himself, this man "who thought to have invaded the Western Empire, and carried everywhere fear and terror"[104]—fled as best they could back to Ottoman territory.

While inspecting the now abandoned Ottoman camp—"as large as Warsaw or Vienna"—the liberators were amazed at Mustafa's "baths, fountains, canals, a garden, a kind of menagerie or place for strange beasts and birds, with dogs, rabbits and parrots." An ostrich of "admirable beauty" that had been plundered from one of Leopold's country houses was found decapitated rather than returned to its owner. Also telling was that "a great many French"—including a "French engineer" who "hath done very much hurt to this City"—were scattered among the dead Turks, the latter of which had "French silver and gold in their pockets."[105] But it was the "prodigious quantity of riches," including countless rubies and diamonds, that Sobieski wrote the queen about: "You will not tell me at my return, what the Tartarian women tell their husbands when they see them return from the army without booty: You are not a Man, seeing you return empty-handed."[106] In the end, "tents, baggage, artillery [including "120 great guns"], ammunition, and provisions enough to load eight thousand wagons, was divided among our army."[107]

But the joys of victory were tempered by a "lamentable spectacle," and Sobieski "was pierced . . . at the sight of an infinite number of slaves, whose throats the infidels had cut after their defeat, and whose bodies yet chained were extended confusedly amongst the dying and the wounded. The King was particularly touched with a child of about four years of age, who seemed to be admirably beautiful notwithstanding he was covered all over with blood from a wound he had received on his head." The victors did not tarry long in the camp, "it being impossible to remove in so short a time such a number of dead bodies, both Turks, Christians, and horses, whereof the stench was so great on the road, that it was enough to have caused an infection."[108]

Desolation was nothing less in the city of *Vienna,* where the King entered the day after the battle, and found heaps of ruines, rather than houses, and even the emperor's palace reduced to ashes, by the cannon and bombs: but he was eased of the grief which this dismal spectacle had occasioned, by the acclamations of the inhabitants, who thinking no more of their past calamities, were transported with joy for their unexpected deliverance: The city not being able to hold out two or three days more. Some kissed his hands, some his feet and others his robe. . . . They called him their Saviour.[109]

Although the above is from the Polish account, the anonymous Englishman confirms that "the King of Poland had the greatest share of the glory of this day which he best deserved: for he may be truly styled one of the greatest kings of Christendom, and the most valiant."[110] Sobieski wrote to Pope Innocent: "We came, we saw, God conquered!"[*] Acknowledging his role, the pontiff conferred the title "Defender of the Faith" on Sobieski and marked September 12 as the Feast of the Most Holy Name of Mary—as her appellation had been on countless Catholic lips, including Sobieski's, during the war.

Meanwhile, a "melancholy and restless" Kara Mustafa, holed up in Belgrade for the winter, paced "night and day in his chamber waiting his destiny, which pursuant to the usual custom of the Turks cou'd not but be very unfortunate."[111] In what was supposed to be a grand jihad, the Grand Vizier had been permitted to muster the largest Muslim force ever to march on Europe—and still botched it.[†] When Sultan Muhammad ordered his execution, Mustafa submitted, "as Allah pleases."[112] When those closest to him protested, he rebuked them: "People of little faith . . . Will you take from me the crown of a martyr, and deprive me of the felicity promis'd to those who render their lives with submission?"[‡] And so on Christmas Day, 1683, while Christendom rejoiced, Kara Mustafa was strangled to death and his head sent to Sultan Muhammad.[113]

---

[*] A modest take on Julius Caesar's more boastful, "I came; I saw; I conquered."

[†] Among Mustafa's blunders, he refused to launch an all-out assault on the city, choosing to tear and wear it down. Muslim leaders had an old tradition of guaranteeing their men all the booty they could grasp whenever an all-out assault on a fortified city—which required headlong, suicidal charges—was ordered. Both sultans Murad II and Muhammad II had done just that in order to take Thessalonica and Constantinople, respectively. But greedy Mustafa would not suffer his men to pick Vienna clean before him—hence the piecemeal siege. Moreover, though this process gave the Christian relief force the necessary time to arrive, Mustafa did virtually nothing to impede their progress, despite his generals' advice, confident that the Tatars would be enough to forestall any offensive, while devoting his army's energies on the siege.

[‡] "Any other but a *Turk* wou'd have laid hold on this occasion to have sold his life dearly," observed the Frenchman La Croix, "but as a blind obedience to the Emperor's [sultan's] commands, is one of the principal points of the *Mahometan* Law, the Grand Vizier otherwise seeing that it wou'd signify nothing to oppose so great a number that must overpower 'em, resolv'd to show his resolution, and make a virtue of necessity" (189).

The Holy League formed under Pope Innocent, spearheaded by Sobieski's Poles and the Austro-German forces, remained intact and went on the offensive against the Turks. Two years later, Orthodox Russia joined the Catholic league. Between 1683 and 1697, fifteen major battles were fought between the Turks and Christians, twelve won by the latter. By 1699, the Ottoman Empire—"which had terrified Christendom for over three hundred years"[114]—was reduced to signing the humiliating Treaty of Karlowitz, which required it to cede large territories back to its infidel enemies§ and thus marked the beginning of the end of Islamic power. As Bernard Lewis puts it, "The last great Muslim assault on Europe, that of the Ottoman Turks, ended with the second unsuccessful siege of Vienna in 1683. With that failure and the Turkish retreat that followed, a thousand years of Muslim threat to Europe came to an end."[115]

This is not entirely correct. For wherever and whenever Islamic empires waned but Muslims remained—recall Spain's morphing experiences with Islam after 1492—the jihad collapsed back to its more primordial, piratical form.¶

FROM EMPIRE BUILDERS TO
SLAVE-TRADERS

Even as the Ottoman Empire was beginning its slow retreat, an English naval captain complained that "the strength and boldness of the Barbary pirates is now grown to that height, both in the [Atlantic] ocean and the Mediterranean seas, as I have never known anything to have wrought a greater sadness and distraction . . . than the daily advance thereof."[116] Indeed, according to the conservative estimate of American professor Robert Davis,

---

§ Including Transylvania and most of Hungary to Austria; Podolia to Poland; and Azov to Russia.

¶ Thus, in 1683, when all of Europe was celebrating the deliverance of Vienna, "the Vicar Apostolic, Jean de Vacher, who was acting as [French] consul [to Algiers], and worked untiringly among the poor [European] captives for thirty-six years, was, by order of Mezzomorto [Hussein Pasha, an Ottoman admiral], with many of his countrymen, blown from the cannon's mouth; and the same thing happened to his successor in 1688, when forty-eight other Frenchmen suffered the same barbarous death" (Lane-Poole 1890, 262).

"between 1530 and 1780 there were almost certainly a million and quite possibly as many as a million and a quarter white, European Christians enslaved by the Muslims of the Barbary Coast." (With countless European women selling for the price of an onion, little wonder by the late 1700s, European observers noted how "the inhabitants of Algiers have a rather white complexion."[117]

A similar situation prevailed in the East. For three centuries after the Russians cast off the Tatar Yoke in 1480, the Crimean khanate—the longest lived successor state of the Golden Horde—continued to flourish as Islam's premiere slave emporium for white flesh. Described by Christians as the "heathen giant who feeds on our blood,"[118] the khanate is estimated to have enslaved and sold "like sheep" some three million Slavs—Poles, Lithuanians, Russians, and Ukrainians—between 1450 and 1783.[119]

Moreover, whereas the European transatlantic African slave trade was fueled by a racial bias, the Muslim slave trade of Europeans—which in the sixteenth century far exceeded the former—was fueled by that old sadistic contempt for infidels. This point comes out repeatedly in the sources. When French priest Jerome Maurand, who as part of the then Franco-Ottoman alliance, witnessed the Turks' conquest of the tiny Mediterranean island of Lipari in 1544, he failed to comprehend why the Muslims so wantonly tortured the now enslaved population—including by slowly gutting the old and weak with knives "out of spite." Unable to hold his tongue, he "asked these Turks why they treated the poor Christians with such cruelty, [and] they replied that such behavior had very great virtue; that was the only answer we ever got."[120] (The dumbfounded clergyman apparently failed to realize that "the honour of Islam lies in insulting *kufr* and *kafirs* [non-Muslims]," as prominent Indian cleric Sheikh Ahmed al-Sirhindi (d. 1624) once said.[121]

Considering that the blood of a non-Muslim was deemed "equal to that of a dog," to quote second caliph Omar—and in keeping with Islam's built-in tribalism whereby outsiders were deemed subhuman—the sadistic treatment of infidels was always par for the course. In his *Book of Martyrs,* John Foxe (d. 1587) wrote, "In no part of the globe are Christians so hated, or treated with such severity, as at Algiers," where the slaves were

regularly treated "with perfidy and cruelty."[122] Centuries later, Robert Playfair (d. 1899) agreed: "In almost every case they [European slaves in Al-
giers] were hated on account of their religion."[123] Eastern European slaves
of the Crimea fared no better: "The old and infirmed men, who will not
fetch much at a sale, are given up to the Tatar youths, either to be stoned,
or to be thrown into the sea, or to be killed by any sort of death they might
please."[124] In 1630 a Lithuanian wrote:

> Among these unfortunates [Slavic slaves] there are many strong ones;
> if they [Tatars] have not castrated them yet, they cut off their ears
> and nostrils, burned cheeks and foreheads with the burning iron and
> forced them to work with their chains and shackles during the day-
> light, and sit in the prisons during the night; they are sustained by
> the meager food consisting of the dead animals' meat, rotten, full of
> worms, which even a dog would not eat. The youngest women are
> kept for wanton pleasures.[125]

As Barbary slaving was a seafaring venture, nearly no part of Europe
was untouched. From 1627 to 1633, Lundy, an island off the west coast of
Britain, was actually occupied by the pirates, whence they pillaged England at will. In 1627 they raided Denmark and even far off Iceland, haul-
ing a total of some eight hundred slaves. Such raids were accompanied by
the trademark hate; one English captive writing around 1614 noted that the
Muslim pirates "abhor the ringing of the [church] bells being contrary to
their Prophet's command," and so destroyed them whenever they could.[126]

In 1631, nearly the entire fishing village of Baltimore and elsewhere
in Ireland were raided and "237 persons, men, women, and children, even
those in the cradle" seized.[127] Father Dan, who frequently visited Algiers
in his attempts to release and redeem slaves, including through ransom
money raised, described their fate in words that echoed through the centuries:* "It was pitiable to see them exposed for sale; for then they separated

---

* Nearly a century before Father Dan, French priest Jerome Maurand described in
near identical terms the fate of the Christians of the island of Lipari off Sicily after it

wives from their husbands, and infants from their fathers. They sold the husband to one and the wife to another, tearing the daughter from her arms, without any hope of ever seeing her again. . . . No Christian could witness what took place without melting into tears, to see so many honest girls and so many well brought up women abandoned to the brutality of these barbarians."[128]

If the baseline treatment of infidel slaves was marked by contempt and cruelty, the punishments they received for real or imagined offenses beggared description: "If they speak against Mahomet [blasphemy], they must become Mahometans, or be impaled alive. If they profess Christianity again, after having changed to the Mahometan persuasion [which some insincerely did in an effort to attain liberty], they are roasted alive [as apostates], or thrown from the city walls, and caught upon large sharp hooks, on which they hang till they expire."[129]

Any European rebuffing the homosexual advances of their masters—"male slaves were often used for sexual purposes"[130]—were especially brutalized by their disgraced would-be rapists:*

A young Christian on one occasion killed his master under provocation so gross as fully to justify the act [a subtle reference to attempted sodomy]. He was dragged to the place of execution over the rough and pointed stones, subjected to the insults of an excited and brutal crowd. On his arrival there each of the spectators seemed to take a pleasure in assisting at the work. He was crucified against the wall with four large nails; a red hot iron was thrust through his cheeks to prevent him from speaking, and, in this condition, he was slowly

was invaded by the Ottomans in 1544: "To see so many poor Christians, and especially so many little boys and girls [enslaved] caused a very great pity. . . . The tears, wailings and cries of these poor Lipariotes, the father regarding his son and the mother her daughter . . . weeping while leaving their own city in order to be brought into slavery by those dogs who seemed like rapacious wolves amidst timid lambs" (http://www.levantineheritage.com/pdf/PiccirilloAnthonyThesis.pdf).

* One contemporary observer noted how Christian slave boys between the ages of nine and fifteen "dared not go out of the house [of their master], for fear of being debauch'd by the Turks" (R. Davis 2003, 126).

burnt to death with fire brands. Such acts of cruelty were by no means uncommon.[131]

Missionaries often expressed their concern that "young men would allow themselves to be seduced sexually as well as religiously, to become catamites even as they became Muslims. Indeed, many clerics, insofar as they had any notions of Islam, acted as if the two forms of seduction were closely linked."[132] In other words, becoming Muslim and/or submitting to the sexual desires of one's Muslim master were seen as two sides of one coin that could potentially buy slaves leniency. Others simply "made themselves Muslims in despair."[133]

AMERICA AND ISLAM MEET: THE BARBARY WARS

By the mid-eighteenth century, the power and influence of the Muslim slaver states relative to Europe plummeted. Russia finally crushed and annexed the Crimea in 1783. As for Barbary, no longer able to acquire slaves from the European coastline—certainly not on the scale of previous centuries—its full energy was spent on raiding infidel merchant vessels. Instead of collectively invading and definitively neutralizing the Barbary Coast, European powers preferred to buy peace through tribute.[†]

Fresh and fair meat appeared on the horizon once the newly born United States[‡] broke free of Great Britain (and was therefore no longer protected by the latter's *jizya* payments). In 1785 Algerian pirates captured two American ships, the *Maria* and *Dauphin*; they enslaved and paraded the sailors through the streets to jeers and whistles. Considering the aforementioned treatment of Christian slaves, when the *Dauphin*'s Captain O'Brian later wrote to Thomas Jefferson that "our sufferings are beyond our expression or your conception," he was not exaggerating.[134]

---

† Others preferred to use the terrorists against their European competitors. France's Louis XIV, who had supported the Ottoman siege of Vienna, reportedly once said, "If there were no Algiers, I would make one" (Lane-Poole 1890, 256).

‡ Muslims had known about the New World since its discovery in the sixteenth century; then an Ottoman author expressed his "pious hopes that it would, in due course, be illuminated by Islam and added to the Ottoman realm" (B. Lewis 2003, 305).

Jefferson and John Adams—then ambassadors to France and England respectively—met with Tripoli's ambassador to Britain, Abdul Rahman Adja, in an effort to ransom the enslaved Americans and establish peaceful relations. In a letter to Congress dated March 28, 1786, the hitherto puzzled American ambassadors laid out the source of the Barbary States' unprovoked animosity:

> We took the liberty to make some inquiries concerning the grounds of their pretentions to make war upon nations who had done them no injury, and observed that we considered all mankind as our friends who had done us no wrong, nor had given us any provocation. The ambassador answered us that it was founded on the laws of their Prophet, that it was written in their Koran, that all nations who should not have acknowledged their authority were sinners, that it was their right and duty to make war upon them wherever they could be found, and to make slaves of all they could take as prisoners, and that every Musselman who should be slain in battle was sure to go to Paradise.[135]

Abdul had continued by smugly noting that Islam's "law" offers "as an incentive" more slaves to those who are first to board infidel vessels, and that the power and appearance of the seaborne jihadis—who always carried three knives, one in each hand and another in their mouths—"so terrified their enemies that very few ever stood against them."[136] One can only imagine what the ambassadors—who some years earlier had asserted in the U.S. Declaration of Independence that all men were "endowed by their Creator with certain inalienable rights"—must have thought of their Muslim counterpart's answer. At any rate, the ransom demanded to release the American sailors was over fifteen times greater than what Congress had approved, and little came of the meeting.

Back in Congress, some agreed with Jefferson that "it will be more easy to raise ships and men to fight these pirates into reason, than money to bribe them."[137] In a letter to a friend, George Washington wondered: "In such an enlightened, in such a liberal age, how is it possible that the great maritime powers of Europe should submit to pay an annual tribute to the little piratical States of Barbary? Would to Heaven we had a navy able to reform those enemies to mankind, or crush them into nonexistence."[138] But the majority of Congress agreed with John Adams: "We ought not to fight them at all unless we determine to fight them forever."[139] Considering the perpetual, existential nature of Islamic hostility, Adams was probably more right than he knew. Congress settled on emulating the Europeans and paying off the terrorists, though it would take years to raise the demanded ransom.

In 1794 Algerian pirates captured eleven more American merchant vessels. Two things resulted: the Naval Act of 1794 was passed, and a permanent standing U.S. naval force was established. But because the first war vessels would not be ready until 1800, American *jizya* payments—which took up 16 percent of the entire federal budget—began to be made to Algeria in 1795. In return, some 115 American sailors were released, and the Islamic sea raids formally ceased. American payments and "gifts" over the following years caused the increasingly emboldened pirates to respond with increasingly capricious demands.

One of the more ignoble instances occurred in 1800, when Captain William Bainbridge of the *George Washington* sailed to the Dey of Algiers (a Turkish honorific for the pirate lords of Barbary), with what the latter deemed insufficient tribute. Referring to the American crew as "my slaves," Dey Mustapha proceeded to order Bainbridge to transport the Muslim's own annual tribute—hundreds of black slaves and exotic animals—to the Ottoman sultan in Istanbul/Constantinople. Adding insult to insult, the Dey commanded the U.S. flag taken down from the *George Washington* and the Islamic flag hoisted in its place; and, no matter how rough the seas might be during the long voyage, Bainbridge was ordered to make sure the vessel faced Mecca five times a day for the prayers of Mustapha's ambassador and entourage.[140] Initially outraged, Bainbridge condescended to being the pirate's delivery boy.

Soon after Jefferson became president in 1801, Tripoli demanded an immediate payment of $225,000, followed by annual payments of

$25,000—equivalent today to $3.5 million and $425,000, respectively—or else. "I know," he argued, "that nothing will stop the eternal increase of demand from these pirates but the presence of an armed force." Jefferson refused the ultimatum. (Perhaps he had recalled Captain O'Brian's observation concerning his Barbary masters: "Money is their God and Mahomet their prophet."[141])

Having not receiving the demanded *jizya,* on May 10, 1801, the pasha of Tripoli proclaimed jihad on the United States. But by now, the latter had six war vessels, which Jefferson deployed to the Barbary Coast. Their initial show of force was enough to cause Tunis and Algiers, which were flirting with the idea of emulating Tripoli's demands on America, to think otherwise. For the next five years, the U.S. Navy warred with Tripoli, making little headway and suffering some setbacks—the most humiliating being when the *Philadelphia* and its crew were captured in 1803.

Desperate measures were needed: enter William Eaton. As U.S. consul to Tunis (1797–1803), he had lived among and understood the region's Muslims well. He knew that "the more you give the more the Turks will ask for,"[142] and despised that old and ubiquitous sense of Islamic superiority: "It grates me mortally when I see a lazy Turk reclining at his ease upon an embroidered sofa, with one Christian slave to hold his pipe, another to hold his coffee, and a third to fan away the flies."[143] Seeing that the newborn American navy was making little headway against the seasoned pirates, he devised a daring plan: to sponsor the claim of the Dey's brother, exiled in Alexandria; and then to march the latter's supporters and mercenaries, mostly Bedouins, through five hundred miles of desert, from Alexandria to Tripoli.

The trek was arduous—not least because of the Muslim mercenaries themselves. Eaton had repeatedly tried to win them over: "I touched upon the affinity of principle between the Islam and Americans [*sic*] religion."[144] But despite such ecumenical overtures, "We find it almost impossible to inspire these wild bigots with confidence in us," he lamented in his diary, "or to persuade them that, being Christians, we can be otherwise than enemies to Mussulmen. We have a difficult undertaking!"[145] (For all his experience with Muslims, Eaton was apparently unaware of the finer points of their law, namely, "loyalty and enmity.")

Finally, on April 27, 1805—in what became the United States' first historical victory as a nation—Eaton reached, attacked, and conquered Tripoli's coastal town of Derne. Soon thereafter, as he was preparing to march on to Tripoli itself, he learned that, as of June 10, the war was over: U.S. consul-general Tobias Lear had negotiated what was later deemed an ignoble peace treaty with Tripoli; it included the surrender of Derne back to the Barbary state and the American payment of $60,000 to ransom the *Philadelphia*'s crew.

Four months later, in October 1806, the first American edition of the Koran was printed in the United States. As the editor's note makes clear, its publication was not for the "cultural enrichment" of Americans—as is often claimed today—but to inform them why they had been at war for the last four years. After opening up by saying, "This book is a long conference of God, the angels, and Mahomet, which that false prophet very grossly invented," the editor concluded: "Thou wilt wonder that such absurdities hath infected the better part of the world, and wilt avouch, that the knowledge of what is contained in this book, wilt render that law [sharia] contemptible."[146]

Because "that law" commands Muslims to take the offensive against infidels whenever a favorable opportunity presents itself—including by breaking peace treaties*—when war between the United States and Britain broke out again in 1812, Barbary saw its chance and again began to raid American ships and enslave their crews. When peace with Britain was achieved in 1815, the United States decided to put an end to Barbary

---

* In a canonical hadith, Muhammad said, "If I take an oath and later find something else better, I do what is better and break my oath." He encouraged Muslims to do the same: "Whenever you take an oath to do something and later you find that something else is better than the first, then do the better one and make expiation for your oath" (*Sahih Bukhari* 8:78:618–619). If the default status between Islam and infidels is one of hostility, and the opportunity presents itself to (profitably) exercise this hostility, clearly that is "better" than maintaining a temporary peace treaty—hence why Barbary reneged on the United States during the latter's war with Britain in 1812. For more on Islam's elastic views on peace treaties with non-Muslims, see footnote on p. 200.

predations once and for all: what had become by now a massive navy (compared to Jefferson's original six vessels of 1801) was deployed to and made quick work of the Barbary Coast. This time the peace treaty was dictated by the United States: Algiers had to release all Americans, make no more claims for tribute, and even pay $10,000 in indemnities for ships and other stolen property. Tunis had to pay $60,000 and Tripoli $30,000 for the ships and properties they had stolen.

Thus the United States' first war—which erupted before it could even elect its first president and intermittently lasted some thirty-two years—was against Islam; and the latter had initiated hostilities on the same rationale that had been used to initiate hostilities for the preceding 1,200 years. Though most Americans are now unaware of their nation's first military conflict, references to it are common. The oldest paean of the U.S. armed forces, "The Marines' Hymn," boasts of fighting everywhere for "right and freedom"—including as far as "to the shores of Tripoli"; the oldest U.S. military monument was made to honor those Americans who fought and died in the Barbary Wars. According to its plaque, "'Millions for defense, but not one cent for tribute' became the rallying cry for this war." The turbaned heads of the vanquished enemy appear at the foot of the eagle-topped column. (Needless to say, although the United States' oldest monument was for decades located inside the Capitol Building, it now rests in the much less conspicuous faculty club of the Naval Academy in Annapolis.)

Even so, "to the United States of America belongs the honour," concedes British historian Stanley Lane-Poole, "of having first set an example of spirited resistance to the pretensions of the Corsairs."* Others followed suit: in 1816, British "Lord Exmouth went on to Tunis and Tripoli, and obtained from the two Deys the promise of the total abolition of Christian

---

* "It is not too much to say that the history of the foreign relations of Algiers and Tunis is one long indictment, not of one, but of all the maritime Powers of Europe, on the charge of cowardice and dishonour," remarks British historian Stanley Lane-Poole in words that may have contemporary relevance. "[It] seems absolutely incredible, and yet it is literally true. . . . Holland, Sweden, Demark, Spain, and the United States were tributaries of the Bey! . . . So flourished the system of the weak levying blackmail upon the strong" (Lane-Poole 1890, 258–259).

slavery."[147] When he asked the same of Algiers, "his proposals were indignantly rejected, and he was personally insulted; two of his officers were dragged from their horses by the mob, and marched through the streets with their hands tied behind their backs." The outraged Dey proceeded to order "extensive massacres of Italians living under British protection."[148] Exmouth returned that same year at the head of a large naval squadron and bombarded Algiers. According to his memoirs:

> The battle was fairly at issue between a handful of Britons, in the noble cause of Christianity, and a horde of fanatics assembled around their city, and enclosed within its fortifications, to obey the dictates of their despot. The cause of God and humanity prevailed; and so devoted was every creature in the fleet, that even British women served at the same guns with their husbands, and, during a contest of many hours, never shrank from danger, but animated all around them.[149]

The Muslims surrendered and "the whole of the slaves in Algiers . . . were at once set at liberty, and the Dey was made to refund the money, amounting to nearly four hundred dollars, which he had that year extorted from the Italian States."[150]

But, as the Americans had experienced, it was not long before the Algerians resumed "the same course of insolence and violence." "Free European girls were carried off by the Dey; the British consulate was forced open, and even the women's rooms searched" for fresh concubines. "Nothing," concludes the British historian, "but downright conquest could stop the plague, and that final measure was reserved for another nation than the English." On July 4, 1830—after the insufferable Dey smacked the French consul across his face during an altercation—a French fleet reached and placed Algiers under heavy, nonstop bombardment. A week later it "had seen the last of its Mohammedan rulers."[151]

The colonial age, which witnessed the meteoritic rise of European power and concomitant nose-dive of Muslim power, had begun.

WESTERN TRIUMPH

Although colonialism and "the whole complex process of European expansion and empire" is often presented today in a historic vacuum, it too "has its roots in the clash of Islam and Christendom," explains Bernard Lewis: "It began with the long and bitter struggle of the conquered peoples of Europe, in east and west, to restore their homelands to Christendom and expel the Muslim peoples who had invaded and subjugated them . . . .The victorious liberators, having reconquered their own territories, pursued their former masters whence they had come."[152]

Thus all throughout the latter half of the nineteenth and into the early twentieth century, Europeans subjugated one Muslim region after another. Certainly there was some spirited resistance: in Sudan and Somalia, another Mahdi and a "Mad Mullah" respectively screamed bloody jihad, fought heroically, and scored some notable victories, but were ultimately crushed by the British (the former in 1898 at Omdurman, the latter between 1904 and 1920). And as late as 1921, Islam managed to score one of its greatest victories in centuries, when over ten thousand Spanish soldiers were butchered at the Battle of Annual in Morocco.

Even so, after 1683, one can no longer speak of seismic battles of macrocosmic significance; nor was there any stopping the Western juggernaut. Along with Algeria, France took Syria, Lebanon, and Tunisia, sharing Morocco with Spain; Britain took Egypt, Sudan, Iraq, the Transjordan, Yemen, and Oman; Italy took Libya. Islamic power had so waned that "Muslims were treated as if they did not exist by the Europeans, who considered them as followers of a fanatical religion that would soon be totally eclipsed by the ineluctable march of progress and reason."[153]

As for the only remaining Muslim power of note, the increasingly shrinking Ottoman Empire, its chief antagonist came not from the West but from the East—from Russia. Centuries earlier in 1472, Constantine XI's niece, Zoe-Sophia Palaiologina, had married Ivan III, who went on to overthrow the Tatar Yoke in 1480. From then until the Bolshevik Revolution, Russia, and Moscow in particular, saw itself as the "Third Rome." As blood-descendants of the last Roman emperor who died fighting defending his city, its tsars (literally *Caesars*) claimed the mantle of defenders—if not avengers—of the twelve million Orthodox Christian subjects of the Ottoman Empire, and had a special interest in restoring Constantinople. They waged a series of wars on and made inroads into Ottoman territory.

A cycle soon developed: Russian encroachments emboldened Balkan Christians to seek liberation from their Islamic overlords. As *dhimmis* are only to be tolerated inasmuch as they meekly submit to Muslim authority, such agitation abrogated their protected status, making them no better than the invading Russians in Ottoman eyes. Retribution was swift and terrible. Remnants of the first Serbian uprising of 1809 can still be seen in the fifteen-foot-high "Skull Tower" erected by the Turks and originally containing 952 decapitated heads of Serbian fighters. After the Greeks sought liberation in 1821, contemporary reports told of attempts "to slaughter all the Christian subjects of the Ottoman empire" and Muslim mobs "attacking every Christian without distinction."[154] Such Ottoman reprisals led to renewed incursions by Russia, starting the cycle of rebellion and retribution anew.

By 1853, Tsar Nicholas I could realistically appeal to "the European powers to divide the Ottoman Empire by mutual agreement and turn Constantinople into a free city."[155] Instead, France and Britain, apprehensive of the Eastern Orthodox nation's growing might and influence, openly allied with the Turks against Russia in the scandalous Crimean War (1853–1856). Such realpolitik came under severe criticism once the full extent of Turkish atrocities became public.

Because it was well covered by Western journalists and contained the centuries-old hallmarks of sadistic contempt for infidels—including mutilations, crucifixions, systematic rapes, and the wanton desecration of Christian churches and symbols—the Ottoman response to the Bulgarian uprising of 1876 especially provoked outrage. Those educated in or experienced with Islam sought to enlighten their countrymen on the source of the animus, namely, that "most nauseous of all abominations, Mohammedanism," to quote a contemporary Anglican clergyman.[156] One of the most detailed and widely disseminated reports came from American journalist J. A. MacGahan:

They would seize a [Bulgarian] woman, strip her carefully to her chemise, laying aside articles of clothing that were valuable, with any ornaments and jewels she might have about her. Then as many of them
as cared would violate her, and the last man would kill her or not
as the humor took him. . . . [Skeletons of children were found] with
frightful saber cuts in their little skulls. The number of children killed
in these massacres is something enormous. They were often spitted
on bayonets, and we have several stories from eye-witnesses who saw
the little babes carried about the streets . . . on the points of bayonets. The reason is simple. When a Mohammedan has killed a certain number of infidels he is sure of Paradise, no matter what his sins
may be. . . . The ordinary Mussulman takes the precept in broader
acceptation, and counts women and children as well. The advantage
of killing children is that it can be done without danger, and that a
child counts for as much as an armed man [when it comes to earning
paradise]. Here in Batak [in Bulgaria] the *bashi bazouks*, in order to
swell the count, ripped open pregnant women, and killed the unborn
infants.[157]

Tens of thousands of Bulgarians were slaughtered, and those Turks
who butchered the most were decorated by Ottoman command.

Such revelations prompted public outrage against Britain's pro-
Ottoman policy and prompted Russia to wage yet another war on the unpopular Islamic empire in 1877, leading to the liberation of much of the
Balkans, including Bulgaria, Romania, Serbia, and Montenegro. The
Russians—who centuries earlier were led to Christianity by and now eagerly sought to liberate Constantinople—even nearly succeeded, when a
fleet of British warships came and lifted their siege of Istanbul.

That Catholic France and Protestant Britain sided with Muslim Turks
against Orthodox Russia—in certain respects yet another manifestation of
Christendom's schisms—is often cited as proof that Europe's wars with
the Ottomans, certainly in the nineteenth century, had little to do with a
Christian-Muslim divide and everything to do with realpolitik. This is only

partially true. The abolition of *jizya* and emancipation of formerly *dhimmi* subjects was one of the most embittering stipulations the Ottoman Empire had to accept to end the Crimean War in 1856. Then, "for the first time since 1453, church bells were permitted to ring . . . in Constantinople," writes M. J. Akbar. "Many Muslims declared it a day of mourning."[158] Indeed, because superior social standing was from the start one of the perks of conversion to Islam, resentful Muslim mobs rioted and hounded Christians all over the empire. In 1860 as many as thirty thousand Christians were massacred in the Levant alone.[*]

Even so, "when the Ottomans oppressed Greeks in the 1820s, Maronites around 1860, Bulgarians in the 1870s and Armenians in the 1890s, European diplomats had to come to the defense of these Christians because of feelings of Christian solidarity in their own countries. It was only in the twentieth century that Christian concerns began to disappear from international diplomacy."[159]

In short, although the realities of realpolitik were always present, the twin aims[†] of the First Crusade preached in 1095—liberating Christian lands and providing relief to fellow Christians—were still evident in Europe's dealings with Islam during the colonial era.[‡] As a contemporary

---

[*] None other than Mark Twain recounted what took place: "Men, women and children were butchered indiscriminately and left to rot by hundreds all through the Christian quarter . . . the stench was dreadful. All the Christians who could get away fled from the city, and the Mohammedans would not defile their hands by burying the 'infidel dogs.' The thirst for blood extended to the high lands of Hermon and Anti-Lebanon, and in a short time twenty-five thousand more Christians were massacred" (Twain 1869, 326).

[†] As British historian Derek Lomax put it, "The popes, like most Christians, believed war against the Muslims to be justified partly because the latter had usurped by force lands which belonged to Christians and partly because they abused the Christians over whom they ruled and such Christian lands as they could raid for slaves, plunder and the joys of destruction" (Stark 2009, 33).

[‡] "In a word we say that the Egyptian State was at the highest degree of justice and good order and arrangement," writes a Coptic Christian around the turn of the twentieth century concerning British rule. "And it removed religious fanaticism, and almost established equality between its subjects, Christian and Muslim, and it eliminated most of the injustice, and it realized much in the way of beneficial works for the benefit of all the inhabitants" (Patrick 1996, 134).

French historian and journalist remarked, the "conquest of Algiers in 1830 and our recent expeditions in Africa are nothing other than crusades."[160]

Nearly one hundred years later, another Frenchman—General Henri Gouraud, a veteran soldier who lost an arm fighting the Ottomans—conquered Damascus in 1920. He proceeded to the tomb of the jihadi victor of Hattin and kicked it, shouting, "Awake, Saladin. We have returned. My presence here consecrates the victory of the Cross over the Crescent."[*]

He was more right than he knew—at least in the socio-political if not the theological realm. For two years later, the Ottoman sultanate was abolished; two years after that, in 1924, the caliphate followed it into the dustbin of history—not at the hands of European imperialists but Muslim reformers seeking to emulate the former's nontraditional but victorious ways.

The perennial war between Islam and the West was over—or so it seemed.

---

[*] "Gouraud's triumphalism also reflected the view of Christians in many countries. For them the victory of the allied powers over the Ottoman empire represented a victory of Christianity over Islam, marking the end of what had been perhaps the longest conflict in human history" (Jamieson 2006, 8–9; quotation also in Sehgal 2003, 22).

MUSLIM CONTINUITY VS.
WESTERN CONFUSION

Every Muslim who is well aware of the history of Islam, knows that jihad against infidels is an integral part of Islam, and those who read history would know.

—Islamic State[1]

E VEN AS GENERAL GOURAUD WAS TRIUMPHING BEFORE SALADIN'S mausoleum, his contemporary, the Anglo-French historian Hilaire Belloc (b. 1870), was having misgivings:

Millions of modern people of the white civilization—that is, the civilization of Europe and America—have forgotten all about Islam. They have never come in contact with it. They take for granted that it is decaying, and that, anyway, it is just a foreign religion which will not concern them. It is, as a fact, the most formidable and persistent enemy which our civilization has had, and may at any moment become as large a menace in the future as it has been in the past.[2]

That the West has completely "forgotten all about Islam" can hardly be overstated and has since only become more pronounced. After all, if many academics are now defining the very word "jihad" itself as "being a better student, a better colleague, a better business partner. Above all, to control one's anger,"[3] surely all more subtle forms of continuity between the past and the present jihad are destined to be missed.

Thus, when the Islamic State declares that "American blood is best, and we will taste it soon," or "We love death as you love life," or "We will conquer your Rome, break your crosses, and enslave your women,"[4] virtually no one in the West understands that they are quoting the verbatim words—and placing themselves within the footsteps—of their jihadi forbears as recounted in the preceding history.[*]

When Muslim men sexually assault Western women while saying things like "You white women are good at it," or "German women are there for sex," or "All Australian women are sluts and deserve to be raped,"[5] very few understand that they are drawing on a long tradition of seeing pale infidels as the epitome of promiscuity, as recounted in the preceding history.

When Muslim migrants go on church-vandalizing sprees in the West—many hundreds of churches, crosses, and Christian statues have been respectively desecrated, broken, and beheaded in just Germany, France, and Austria[6]—very few understand that this modus operandi stretches back to and has been on continuous display since Islam's first contact with Christian civilization, as recounted in the preceding history.

Once upon a time, the Islamic world was a superpower and its jihad an irresistible force to be reckoned with. Over two centuries ago, however, a rising Europe—which had experienced more than one millennium of Muslim conquests and atrocities—eclipsed and defanged Islam. As Muhammad's civilization retreated into obscurity, the post-Christian West slowly came into being. Islam did not change, but the West did: Muslims still venerate their heritage and religion—which commands jihad against infidels—whereas the West has learned to despise its heritage and religion, causing it to become an unwitting ally of the jihad.

Hence the current situation: Islamic jihad is back in full vigor, while the West facilitates it in varying degrees; hence the irony: "At a time when the military superiority of the West—meaning chiefly the USA—over the

* See p. 21, p. 103, p. 160, and pp. 172–173.

Muslim world has never been greater," observes historian Alan G. Jamie-son, "Western countries feel insecure in the face of the activities of Islamic terrorists. . . . In all the long centuries of Christian-Muslim conflict, never has the military imbalance between the two sides been greater, yet the dominant West can apparently derive no comfort from that fact."[7]

In short, if Islam is terrorizing the West today, that is not because it can, but because the West allows it to. For no matter how diminished, a still swinging Scimitar will always overcome a strong but sheathed Sword.

NOTES

PREFACE

1. B. Lewis 1994, 127.
2. B. Lewis 2004, 375.
3. http://www.meforum.org/480/lessons
-from-the-prophet-muhammads-diplomacy.
4. For example, see "The Islamic State
and Islam" or "Beheading Infidels: How
Allah 'Heals the Hearts of Believers,'" at
www.RaymondIbrahim.com.
5. B. Lewis 1994, 180.

INTRODUCTION

1. *Sahih Muslim* 9:1:31.; cf. *Sahih
Bukhari* 2:24.
2. *Sahih Bukhari* 4:52:220.
3. Ibid., 147.
4. *Sahih Muslim* 31:5917. Author's
translation from original Arabic.
5. Cook 2005, 6.
6. Gibbon 1952, 244.
7. Ibn Ishaq 1997, 547.
8. Ibn Khaldun 1958, 252.
9. Bukay 2013, 13.
10. Santosuosso 2004, 75.
11. Lindsay and Mourad 2015, 147.
12. Ibrahim 2007, 143.
13. For houris in the Koran see 44:54,
52:20, 55:72, 56:22; for serving boys see
52:24, 56:17, and 76:19; for other aspects of
a corporeal heaven, see 35:33, 43:71, 47:15,
52:22.
14. Lindsay and Mourad 2015, 71.
15. Grant 1992, 52.
16. Bonner 2006, 72.
17. Akgündüz n.d.
18. Bostom 2005, 162.
19. Cardini 2001, 3.
20. B. Lewis 2004, 125.
21. Phaedo n.d., 109b.
22. Muir 1923, 200.
23. *Sahih Bukhari* 4:55:657.
24. Tabari 1993, 8:104–105.
25. Ibn Ishaq 1997, 533.
26. Bostom 2005, 385.
27. Theophanes 1963, 336.
28. Wolf 1990, 113.

CHAPTER 1

1. Tolan 2002, 65.
2. Donner 2008, 67.
3. Ibn al-Kathir n.d.
4. Tabari 1993, 102–104.
5. Ibid., 102; Glubb (1963) 1980, 112.
6. Baladhuri 1968, 178.
7. Ibid., 174.
8. Ibid., 182.
9. Kennedy 2007, 80.
10. Akram 1970, 406.
11. Waqidi 1997, 148.
12. Nicolle 1992, 12.
13. Waqidi 1997, 154.
14. Waqidi 1997, 166–169, 175.
15. Grant 1992, 57–58.
16. Santosuosso 2004, 91.
17. Butler 1992, 151.
18. Waqidi 1997, 144.
19. Ibid., 156–157.
20. Ibid., 157–159.
21. Bonner 2004, 243.
22. Waqidi 1997, 176.
23. Ibid., 176.
24. Ibid., 178.
25. Ibid., 171–173.
26. Akram 1970, 421.
27. Waqidi 1997, 185.
28. Ibid., 193.

29. Ibid., 193.

30. Ibid., 186, 195; Baladhuri 1968, 208; Akram 1970, 427. In the original, the word for "arm" could also be interpreted as the masculine genital appendage.

31. Waqidi 1997, 207.

32. Ibid., 185–186, 195.

33. Ibid., 194.

34. Santosuosso 2004, 96–97.

35. Kaegi 1995, 135–136.

36. Glubb (1963) 1980, 179.

37. Ibid., 146.

38. Butler 1992, 165.

39. Hoyland 1997, 72.

40. Bonner 2004, 116.

41. Hoyland 1997, 100–101; Waqidi 1997, 185.

42. Wheatcroft 2005, 44.

43. Theophanes 1997, 476.

44. Bostom 2005, 398.

45. See "The 60 Martyrs of Gaza and the Martyrdom of Bishop Sophronius of Jerusalem," by David Woods, in Bonner 2004, 429–450.

46. Bonner 2004, 445, 448.

47. Atiya n.d. 7.

48. Butler 1992, 522.

49. Hoyland 1997, 153.

50. Butler 1992, 299.

51. Ibid., 162.

52. Kennedy 2007, 153.

53. Muqaffa 1948, 230.

54. "The Destruction of the Library of Alexandria by the Arabs: The Account of the Arab Traveler Abd al-Latif al-Baghdadi." October 6, 2017. https://copticliterature.wordpress.com/2017/10/06/the-destruction-of-the-library-of-alexandria-by-the-arabs-the-account-of-the-arab-traveler-abd-al-latif-al-baghdadi/.

55. Kennedy 2007, 153.

56. Butler 1992, 291.

57. Ye'or 2010, 275–276.

58. Paul the Deacon 1907, bk. 5 ch. 13.

59. Scott 2012, 166.

60. Butler 1992, 192.

61. Ibrahim 2007, 80–81.

62. Guindy 2009, 14–15.

63. Ye'or 2010, 270–271.

64. Wolf 1990, 115.

65. Ramelah 2017, 5.

66. Butler 1992, 460; see also Guindy 2009, 14–18.

67. B. Lewis 1987, 22.

68. Ibrahim 2007, 200–201.

69. Muqaffa 1948, 237.

70. Butler 1992, 347–348; Guindy 2009, 14–16.

71. E.g., Maqrizi 1873, 91; cf. Little 1976, 567.

72. Kennedy 2007, 201–202.

73. Ibid., 206; Hakam 2010, 170.

74. Santosuosso 2004, 114.

75. Hakam 2010, 205.

76. Fernandez-Morera 2016, 13.

77. Kennedy 2007, 210.

78. Glubb (1963) 1980, 355.

79. Kennedy 2007, 124.

80. Fernandez-Morera 2016, 44.

81. Kennedy 2007, 222.

82. Santosuosso 2004, 116.

83. Fernandez-Morera 2016, 42–43.

84. Maqqari 1964, 251.

85. Ibid., 252.

86. Ibid., 253.

87. Paul the Deacon 1907, bk. 6 ch. 10.

88. Scott 2014, 42.

89. Donner 2008, 118–119.

90. Ibid., 117; for date and history see Griffith 2010, 34; see also Rubenstein 2015, 49.

91. Griffith 2010, 37 (eighth-century dating); Tolan 2002, 37 (seventh-century dating).

92. Kaegi 1995, 206.

93. Wolf 1990, 113–114.

94. Ibn Khaldun 1958, 229; see also Fernandez-Morera 2016, 47.

95. Donner 2008, 28.

96. Butler 1992, 258.

97. Glubb (1963) 1980, 13.

98. Belloc 1938, 58.

99. Donner 2008, 116.

100. Gabrieli 1968, 150.

CHAPTER 2

1. Gullen 2006, 192.

2. Donner 2008, 115.

3. Bonner 2004, 31.

4. Ibid., 241.

5. Ye'or 2010, 276–277.

6. Ibid.

7. Theophanes 1997, 493; Wolf 1990, 122.

8. Theophanes 1997, 494.

9. Ostrogorsky 1969, 125.

10. Bonner 2004, 248.

11. Cheikh 2004, 124.

12. Ibid., 125.

13. Cheikh 2004, 125–128.

14. Ibid., 126–127.

15. Scott 2014, 66–69.

16. Khan 2009, 323.

17. Scott 2014, 66–69.

18. Donner 2008, 122.

19. Ibid., 115.

20. Hoyland 1997, 57.

21. Ibid., 117, 119–121.

22. Bonner 2004, 217–226; Tolan 2002, 44.

23. Daniel 1962, 67.

24. Daniel 1962, 4.

25. All quotes from John of Damascus, in Bonner 2008, 217–226, and Sidway 2010, 187–194.

26. Theophanes 1997, 465.

27. Bonner 2004, 223.

28. Bar Hebraeus 1932, 10:115.

29. Bostom 2005, 391.

30. Wolf 1990, 130.

31. Theophanes 1997, 577.

32. Bar Hebraeus 1932, 10:115.

33. Theophanes 1997, 535.

34. Gibbon 1952, 290.

35. Brockelmann 2000, 91.

36. Guindy 2009, 182.

37. Bostom 2005, 391.

38. Tabari 1993, 2:1315.

39. Cheikh 2005, 63.

40. Wolf 1990, 134.

41. Jeffery 1944, 321.

42. Wolf 1990, 138.

43. Brooks 1899, 24.

44. Ibid, 25.

45. Ibid., 26.

46. Theophanes 1997, 545.

47. Tabari 1964, 2:1316.

48. Gibbon 1952, 291.

49. Theophanes 1997, 545.

50. Wolf 1990, 137.

51. Norwich 1997, 110.

52. Fuller 1987, 338.

53. Theophanes 1992, 90.

54. Theophanes 1997, 546.

55. Ibid., 546.

56. Gibbon 1952, 291.

57. Wheatcroft 2005, 49.

58. Bar Hebraeus 1932, 10:117.

59. Theophanes 1997, 550.

60. Bonner 2004, 228.

61. Bostom 2005, 398.

62. Jeffery 1944, 324.

63. Ibid., 329.

64. Ibid., 317.

65. Ibid., 328.

66. Ibid., 321.

67. Ibid., 330.

68. Suyuti 1970, 249.

69. Bonner 2004, xvii–xxxi.

70. Ibid., xxi.

71. See Bonner 2006, 136.

72. Lindsay and Mourad 2015, 25.

73. Bonner 2006, 97.

74. Bonner 2004, 423.

75. Cook 2005, 25.

76. Bury 1889, 405.

77. Vasiliev 1952, 236.

CHAPTER 3

1. Maqqari 1964, 275.

2. P. Davis 1999, 105.

3. Maqqari 1964, 253.

4. Ibid., 265.

5. Ibid., 259.

6. Ibid., 265.

7. Ibid., 266.

8. Ahmad 1987, 448.

9. Hakam 1969, 19–20; Hakam 2010, 206.

10. Maqqari 1964, 268.

11. Ibid., 271.

12. Ibid., 272.

13. Ibid., 273.

14. Hakam 2010, 208; cf. Hakam 1969, 22.

15. Maqqari 1964, 274.

16. Fernandez-Morera 2016, 12.

17. Maqqari 1964, 275.

18. Ibid., 275, 288.

19. Ibid., 275, 279–280.

20. Ibid., 283.

21. Ibid., 297.

22. Fregosi 1998, 99.

23. Wolf 1990, 132, 52.

24. Fernandez-Morera 2016, 40.

25. Wolf 1990, 142.
26. Maqqari 1964, 291.
27. Ibid., 288.
28. Ibid., 289.
29. Wolf 1990, 133.
30. Ibid., 135.
31. Tabari 1992, 179.
32. Santosuosso 2004, 55.
33. Wolf 1990, 138.
34. Ibid., 144.
35. Ibid., 143.
36. Ibid., 142.
37. Ibid., 143.
38. Fuller 1987, 342.
39. Gibbon 1952, 294.
40. W. Davis and West 1913, 363.
41. Creasy and Speed 1900, 165.
42. Gibbon 1952, 293–294.
43. Bostom 2005, 423.
44. Hanson 2002, 143.
45. P. Davis 1999, 104.
46. Hakam 1969, 33.
47. W. Davis and West 1913, 363.
48. P. Davis 1999, 104.
49. Fregosi 1998, 118.
50. Creasy and Speed 1900, 166.
51. P. Davis 1999, 105.
52. W. Davis and West 1913, 363.
53. Hanson 2002, 139.

54. W. Davis and West 1913, 364.
55. Hanson 2002, 140.
56. Gibbon 1952, 294.
57. Bede 1990, 323.
58. Hanson 2002, 144–145.
59. Santosuosso 2004, 126.
60. Einhard 2008, 19.
61. Tierney and Painter 1970, 140.
62. Pirenne 1974, 27.
63. B. Lewis 1993, 79.
64. Einhard 2008, 37.
65. Wheatcroft 2005, 157.
66. Cardini 2001, 19–23.
67. Fletcher 2004, 43.
68. Bostom 2005, 421.
69. Brownsworth 2009, 158.
70. Gibbon 1952, 349.
71. Bonner 2006, 171.
72. Donner 2008, 77–78.
73. Cardini 2001, 23.
74. Scott 2014, 16.
75. Scott 2014, 162.
76. Fuller 1987, 342.
77. Cowley and Parker 2001, xiii.
78. N. Robinson 1887, 84.
79. Bostom 2005, 419.
80. Maqqari 1964, 275.
81. Hakam 2010, 216–217.
82. Gibbon 1952, 255.

CHAPTER 4

1. Hillenbrand 2007, 159.
2. Bostom 2005, 598.
3. Treadgold 1997, 441.
4. Bostom 2005, 598.
5. P. Davis 1999, 118.
6. Leo the Deacon 2005, 98–100.
7. Matthew of Edessa 1993, 21.
8. Ibid., 21.
9. Leo the Deacon 2005, 82.
10. Brownsworth 2009, 190.
11. Ibid., 197.
12. Friendly 1981, 76.
13. Cheikh 2004, 169.
14. Ibid., 170.
15. Leo the Deacon 2005, 126.
16. Cheikh 2004, 170, 173.
17. Dennis 2008, 147.
18. Leo the Deacon 2005, 98.
19. Ibid., 90, 139–140.
20. Ibid., 146.
21. Leo the Deacon 2005, 138.
22. Ibid., 139.

23. Matthew of Edessa 1993, 28, 32, 34.
24. Jamieson 2006, 39.
25. Brownsworth 2009, 216.
26. Friendly 1981, 56.
27. Fuller 1987, 389.
28. Pipes 1981, 153.
29. Bostom 2005, 605.
30. Friendly 1981, 50.
31. Ibn Khaldun 1958, 252.
32. Friendly 1981, 38.
33. G. Lewis 1988, 118.
34. Ibid., 87.
35. Ibid., 11–12.
36. Quote from renowned Persian scholar, al-Ghazali, in Hillenbrand 2007, 147–148.
37. Friendly 1981, 26.
38. Crowley 2014, 24.
39. Matthew of Edessa 1993, 44.
40. Fuller 1987, 391.
41. Matthew of Edessa 1993, 76, 134–135.

42. Ibid., 95, 98.

43. Ibid., 95, 98, 99, 130.

44. Ibid., 64.

45. Ibid., 87–88.

46. Michael Psellus 1966, 158.

47. Friendly 1981, 95.

48. Fuller 1987, 393.

49. Friendly 1981, 149.

50. Hillenbrand 2007, 6.

51. Matthew of Edessa 1993, 131.

52. Friendly 1981, 142.

53. Matthew of Edessa 1993, 103.

54. Matthew of Edessa 1993, 103.

55. Hillenbrand 2007, 241.

56. Friendly 1981, 128.

57. Matthew of Edessa 1993, 127.

58. Hillenbrand 2007, 10.

59. Friendly 1981, 152.

60. Hillenbrand 2007, 249.

61. Michael Psellus 1966, 352.

62. Hillenbrand 2007, 260.

63. Friendly 1981, 149.

64. Matthew of Edessa 1993, 128–129.

65. Ibid., 132.

66. Ibid., 132.

67. Hillenbrand 2007, 53, 63, 69.

68. Michael Psellus 1966, 355.

69. Nicolle 2013, 65; Hillenbrand 2007, 251.

70. Hillenbrand 2007, 59.

71. Friendly 1981, 160.

72. Hillenbrand 2007, 234, 38.

73. Nicolle 2013, 62; Friendly 1981, 181.

74. Hillenbrand 2007, 231.

75. Ibid., 231.

76. Ibid., 55, 100.

77. Ibid., 28–29, 39, 68.

78. Ibid., 55, 69.

79. Fuller 1987, 402.

80. Hillenbrand 2007, 247.

81. Ibid., 101.

82. Ibid., 239.

83. Ibid., 247.

84. Ibid., 247.

85. Ibid., 250.

86. Friendly 1981, 191; Hillenbrand 2007, 235.

87. Hillenbrand 2007, 61, 102.

88. Hillenbrand 2007, 248.

89. Michael Psellus 1966, 356.

90. Nicolle 2013, 83.

91. Hillenbrand 2007, 73, 54; Friendly 1981, 146.

92. Hillenbrand 2007, 253.

93. Ibid., 70.

94. Nicolle 2013, 88.

95. Hillenbrand 2007, 36.

96. Ibid., 42, 72.

97. Ibid., 71.

98. Ibid., 29, 40, 39, 41, 57.

99. Michael Psellus 1966, 358–359.

100. Ibid., 365.

101. Skylitzes quoted in Friendly 1981, 202.

102. Hillenbrand 2007, 255.

103. Ibid., 244.

104. Friendly 1981, 203.

105. Matthew of Edessa 1993, 136.

106. Friendly 1981, 203.

107. Hillenbrand 2007, 137.

108. Ibid., 210.

109. Ibid., 235.

110. Nicolle 2013, 92.

111. Bostom 2005, 608.

112. Fuller 1987, 404.

113. Friendly 1981, 1.

CHAPTER 5

1. Quote from Donner 2008, 119; cf. Pseudo-Methodius 2012, 43–49; and cf. Griffith 2010, 32–35.

2. Brundage 1962, 18–19.

3. Frankopan 2013, 59–60.

4. Ibid., 61; see also Guibert of Nogent 2008, 33.

5. Ye'or 2010, 292.

6. Rubenstein 2015, 56.

7. Bostom 2005, 392.

8. Maqrizi 1873, 86.

9. Stark 2009, 85.

10. Brundage 1962, 18–19.

11. B. Lewis 2003, 235.

12. Donner 2008, 67.

13. Ibrahim 2013, 39–42; Stark 2009, 91.

14. Wheatcroft 2005, 159.

15. Frankopan 2013, 98.

16. Tyerman 2006, 49.

17. Peters 1971, 30.

18. Frankopan 2013, 96.

19. Guibert of Nogent 2008, 26; Frankopan 2013, 117.

20. Riley-Smith 2008, 32.
21. https://www.firstthings.com/article/2005/06/crusaders-and-historians
22. Rubenstein 2015, 13.
23. Madden 2007, 12.
24. Guibert of Nogent 2008, 42, 25.
25. Madden 2007, 9.
26. Riley-Smith 2008, 21–22.
27. Tyerman 2006, 30–31.
28. Riley-Smith 2008, 12.
29. Ibid., 13–16.
30. Rubenstein 2015, 62.
31. Riley-Smith 1995, 26.
32. Ibid., 27.
33. Rubenstein 2015, 74.
34. Peters 1971, 31.
35. Stark 2009, 4; see also, Guibert of Nogent 2008, 38.
36. Anna Comnena 1969, 312.
37. Guibert of Nogent 2008, 45.
38. Peters 1971, 42.
39. Ibid., 46.
40. Guibert of Nogent 2008, 58–61.
41. Friendly 1981, 127.
42. Gabrieli 1993, 58–59.
43. Ibid., 38–39.
44. Friendly 1981.
45. Shatzmiller 1993, 151.
46. Peters 1971, 43.
47. Ibid., 51.
48. Frankopan 2013, 91.
49. Peters 1971, 53–54.
50. Guibert of Nogent 2008, 68, 56, 75.
51. Ibid., 84.
52. Frankopan 2013, 163.
53. Guibert of Nogent 2008, 96.
54. Rubenstein 2015, 121.
55. Rubenstein 2015, 121.
56. Ibid., 121–123.
57. Wheatcroft 2005, 170.
58. Peters 1971, 82.
59. Rubenstein 2015, 122.
60. Gabrieli 1993, 9.
61. Peters 1971, 67.
62. Hillenbrand 2007, 151–152.
63. Peters 1971, 69.
64. Gabrieli 1993, 9.
65. Rubenstein 2015, 142.
66. Ibid., 143–144.
67. Ibid., 145.
68. Cardini 2001, 60.
69. Rubenstein 2015, 149.
70. Guibert of Nogent 2008, 28.
71. Peters 1971, 78.
72. Cardini 2001, 60.
73. Rubenstein 2015, 157–158.
74. Gabrieli 1993, 18.
75. Riley-Smith 2008, 71.
76. Ibid., 68–69.
77. Allen 2010, 111.
78. Stark 2009, 172.
79. Allen 2010, 111.
80. Gabrieli 1993, 204–207.
81. Ibid.
82. Ibid., 50.
83. J. B. Segal, quoted in Bostom 2005, 611.
84. Gabrieli 1993, 53.
85. Ibid., 62.
86. Ibid., 60.
87. Ibid., 70–71.
88. Ibid., 90.
89. Ibid., 99–100.
90. Ibid., 119.
91. Ibid., 123.
92. Allen 2010, 152.
93. Gabrieli 1993, 117.
94. Ibid., 120.
95. Allen 2010, 155.
96. Fuller 1987, 425.
97. Ibid., 155.
98. Ernoul n.d.
99. Gabrieli 1993, 121.
100. Ernoul n.d.
101. Gabrieli 1993, 121.
102. Ibid., 102.
103. Fuller 1987, 426.
104. Gabrieli 1993, 122, 132.
105. Ibid., 137.
106. Ibid., 134.
107. Ibid., 123.
108. Ibid., 135.
109. Ibid., 112.
110. Ibid., 138.
111. Baha' al-Din 2001, 75.
112. Gabrieli 1993, 140.
113. Ibid., 156.
114. Ibid., 157.
115. Ibid., 144.
116. Ibid., 164.
117. Ibid., 145–146.
118. Ibid., 163.
119. Ibid., 101.
120. Guindy 2009, 88.

121. Gabrieli 1993, xviii.
122. Ernoul n.d.
123. Andrea and Holt 2015, xvi.
124. Daniel 1962, 117, 113.

125. Akbar 2003, 62.
126. Madden 2007, 189.
127. Fletcher 2004, 131.
128. Fuller 1987, 436.

CHAPTER 6

1. Wolf 1990, 167.
2. O'Callaghan 2004, 214.
3. Wolf 1990, 132.
4. Ibid., 165
5. Ibid., 166.
6. O'Callaghan 2004, 5.
7. Wolf 1990, 167.
8. Watts 1894, 26.
9. O'Callaghan 2004, 5.
10. Watts 1894, 27.
11. Bertrand 1952, 87.
12. Ibid., 90–92.
13. O'Callaghan 2004, 12.
14. Bonner 2006, 111.
15. Fernandez-Morera 2016, 32.
16. Ibid., 121.
17. Ibid., 80.
18. Daniel 1962, 110.
19. Fernandez-Morera 2016, 80, 216.
20. Ibid., 79.
21. Ibid., 78.
22. Ibid., 48.
23. Allen 2010, 306.
24. O'Callaghan 2004, 186.
25. Constable 1997, 143.
26. Fernandez-Morera 2016, 41.
27. O'Callaghan 2004, 183.
28. Wolf 1990, 133.
29. Fernandez-Morera 2016, 162.
30. Ibid., 159.
31. Adam 1906, 132.
32. Fernandez-Morera 2016, 159.
33. Ibid., 160.
34. Ibid., 131.
35. Ibid., 131–132.
36. Ibid., 130, 158.
37. Constable 1997, 178.
38. Ibid., 178–179.
39. Fletcher 2004, 27.
40. Tolan 2002, 166.
41. Daniel 1962, 123, 149.
42. O'Callaghan 2004, 15.
43. Bostom 2005, 597.
44. Watts 1894, 9.
45. Bertrand 1952, 93.
46. Ibid., 94.
47. Ibid., 58.

48. Bonner 2006, 75.
49. Bertrand 1952, 59.
50. Watts 1894, 52.
51. Cardini 2001, 38.
52. Fernandez-Morera 2016, 136.
53. O'Callaghan 2004, 30.
54. Watts 1894, 66.
55. O'Callaghan 2004, 30.
56. Ibid., 3.
57. Ibid., 21.
58. Wolf 1990, 169.
59. O'Callaghan 2004, 24.
60. Ibid., 9.
61. Ibid., 178.
62. Ibid., 211.
63. Ibid., 60.
64. Fernandez-Morera 2016, 106.
65. Watts 1894, 67–68.
66. Fregosi 1998, 160.
67. O'Callaghan, 2004, 30–33.
68. Watts 1894, 68.
69. Cardini 2001, 43.
70. O'Callaghan, 2004, 48.
71. Bertrand 1952, 126–127.
72. Watts 1894, 105.
73. O'Callaghan 2004, 201.
74. Ibid., 204. Brackets in the original.
75. Watts 1894, 108.
76. O'Callaghan 2004, 46.
77. Watts 1894, 108–109.
78. Constable 1997, 187.
79. Ibid., 189.
80. Watts 1894, 109.
81. O'Callaghan 2004, 132.
82. Scott 2014, 84.
83. O'Callaghan 2004, 51.
84. Ibid., 129.
85. Ibid., 57.
86. Fregosi 1998, 188.
87. O'Callaghan 2004, 142–143.
88. Watts 1894, 113.
89. O'Callaghan 2004, 66–67.
90. Ibid., 67.
91. Ibid., 67–69.
92. Ibid., 68–69.
93. Ibid., 70.
94. Ibid., 71.

95. Smith 2014, 139.
96. O'Callaghan 2004, 71.
97. Allen 2010, 311.
98. Fernandez-Morera 2016, 54.
99. Allen 2010, 311.
100. O'Callaghan 2004, 81, 188.
101. O'Callaghan 2002, 49.
102. O'Callaghan 2004, 180.
103. Ibid., 190.
104. Allen 2010, 312.
105. O'Callaghan 2002, 50.
106. Allen 2010, 312.
107. O'Callaghan 2002., 50.
108. Allen 2010, 312.
109. Ibid., 313.
110. O'Callaghan 2002, 50.
111. Allen 2010, 312.
112. Smith 2014, 139–141.
113. O'Callaghan 2004, 69.
114. Ibid., 74.
115. Ibid., 76.
116. Ibid., 84.
117. Wheatcroft 2005, 92.
118. Fernandez-Morera 2016, 135.

119. Wheatcroft 2005, 92.
120. O'Callaghan 2004, 116.
121. Fernandez-Morera 2016, 204–206.
122. Constable 1997, 221.
123. O'Callaghan 2004, 74.
124. O'Callaghan 2004, 95.
125. Fernandez-Morera 2016, 54.
126. O'Callaghan 2004, 8.
127. Ibid., 214.
128. Ibid., 214.
129. Akbar 2003, 85.
130. Fernandez-Morera 2016, 55.
131. Constable 1997, 364.
132. Stewart 2013, 446.
133. Stewart 2013, 445–446.
134. Ibid., 482.
135. Ibid., 445.
136. Allen 2010, 338.
137. Wheatcroft 2005, 127.
138. Allen 2010, 339.
139. Bertrand 1952, 154.
140. Fregosi 1998, 314; cf. Baroja 2003, 177–186; and Dominguez et al. 1993, 40.

CHAPTER 7

1. Giano n.d., 6–10.
2. Gibbon 1952, 484.
3. Zenkovsky 1974, 6, 201, 247.
4. Gibbon 1952, 484.
5. Morgan 1988, 173.
6. Kinross 1979, 34, 19.
7. Ibid.
8. Madden 2004, 178.
9. Bonner 2006, 145.
10. Riley-Smith 1995, 250.
11. Bonner 2006, 145.
12. Hillenbrand 2007, 160.
13. William of Adam 2012, 63.
14. Kinross 1979, 30.
15. Brockelmann 2000, 261.
16. Dunn 2005, 152.
17. William of Adam 2012, 71.
18. Madden 2004, 182.
19. Bostom 2005, 63.
20. Doukas 1975, 144–145.
21. Wheatcroft 2005, 190.
22. Riley-Smith 1995, 250–251.
23. Kinross 1979, 46.
24. Wheatcroft 2005, 190.
25. Kinross 1979, 34.
26. Moczar 2008, 38–39.
27. Bostom 2005, 560.

28. Allen 2010, 405, 406.
29. Ibid.
30. Moczar 2008, 39.
31. Bostom 2005, 557.
32. Madden 2007, 195.
33. Kinross 1979, 57.
34. Ibid., 58.
35. Ibid., 61.
36. Ibid.
37. Doukas 1975, 88; Kinross 1979, 64.
38. Kinross 1979, 61.
39. Doukas 1975, 62, 139.
40. Kinross 1979, 66.
41. From Benedict's lecture: "Faith, Reason and the University: Memories and Reflections," at University of Regensburg, September 12, 2006.
42. Moczar 2008, 35.
43. Barker 1969, 80.
44. Vasiliev 1952, 629.
45. Kinross 1979, 65; Doukas 1975, 132.
46. Kinross 1979, 65.
47. Cardini 2001, 113.
48. Vasiliev 1952, 629.
49. Barker 1969, 118.
50. Allen 2010, 397.

51. Atiya 1978, 2.
52. Atiya 1978, 9, 19.
53. Ibid., 56, 32.
54. Kinross 1979, 67.
55. Atiya 1978, 86.
56. Ibid., 87, 91.
57. Atiya 1978, 91.
58. Tuchman 1980, 561.
59. Atiya 1978, 91.
60. Ibid., 91.
61. Kinross 1979, 69, 68.
62. Atiya 1978, 96.
63. Wheatcroft 2005, 192.
64. Madden 2007, 97.
65. Madden 2004, 185; Hillenbrand 2007, 169.
66. Atiya 1978, 71.
67. Hillenbrand 2007, 167.
68. Atiya 1978, 119.
69. Runciman 2004, 1.
70. Ibid., 40.
71. Gibbon 1952, 498.
72. Ibid.
73. Kinross, 1979, 76.
74. Ibid.
75. Bostom 2005, 614–615; Doukas 1975, 171–172.
76. Giano n.d., 3.
77. Ibid., 3, 6.
78. Fernandez-Morera 2016, 163.
79. Giano n.d., 3.
80. Bostom 2005, 569.
81. Giano n.d., 3.
82. Ibid., 8.
83. Kinross 1979, 87; Melville-Jones 1973, 15.
84. Gibbon 1952, 539.
85. Kinross 1979, 87–88.
86. Ibid., 101.
87. Melville-Jones 1973, 61.
88. Gibbon 1952, 540.
89. Runciman 2004, 66.
90. Melville-Jones 1973, 68.
91. Crowley 2014, 2.
92. Melville-Jones 1973, 71.
93. Kinross 1979, 102.
94. Brownsworth 2009, 293.
95. Fuller 1987, 512.
96. Norwich 1997, 373.
97. Runciman 2004, 83.
98. Sphrantzes 1980, 103.
99. Crowley 2014, 100.
100. Runciman 2004, 79.
101. Ibid.
102. Crowley 2014, 163.
103. Gibbon 1952, 508.
104. Fuller 1987, 513.
105. Crowley 2014, 111.
106. Fuller 1987, 513.
107. Ibid., 514.
108. Sphrantzes 1980, 108.
109. Runciman 2004, 103.
110. Crowley 2014, 139.
111. Melville-Jones 1973, 20.
112. Crowley 2014, 153.
113. Melville-Jones 1973, 5.
114. Sphrantzes 1980, 112.
115. Fuller 1987, 515.
116. Sphrantzes 1980, 104.
117. Fuller 1987, 516.
118. Fuller 1987, 517; Jones, 5, 17.
119. Sphrantzes 1980, 119.
120. Crowley 2014, 195.
121. Melville-Jones 1973, 33, 92, 49.
122. Sphrantzes 1980, 120.
123. Melville-Jones 1973, 33.
124. Nicolo 1969, 58–59.
125. Melville-Jones 1973, 6.
126. Gibbon 1952, 549.
127. Crowley 2014, 194, 200.
128. Dmytryshyn 1991, 217, 216.
129. Crowley 2014, 172.
130. Sphrantzes 1980, 120.
131. Ibid., 123.
132. Gibbon 1952, 549.
133. Fuller 1987, 517–518.
134. Sphrantzes 1980, 126.
135. Melville-Jones 1973, 36.
136. Allen 2010, 402.
137. Kinross 1979, 108.
138. Sphrantzes 1980, 128; Melville-Jones 1973, 95, 37.
139. Sphrantzes 1980, 128–129.
140. Melville-Jones 1973, 37.
141. Melville-Jones 1973, 52.
142. Dmytryshyn 1991, 218.
143. Nicolo 1969, 65–66.
144. Allen 2010, 404.
145. Sphrantzes 1980, 130.
146. Melville-Jones 1973, 101.
147. Nicolo 1969, 67; Dmytryshyn 1991, 218; Jones, 123.
148. Ibid., 39.
149. Thomas the Eparch and Diplovatatzes 1976, 235–236 (pp. 3–4 in PDF).

150. Nicolo 1969, 67.
151. Melville-Jones 1973, 39.
152. Melville-Jones 1973, 98–99, 123.
153. Nicolo 1969, 67.
154. Melville-Jones 1973, 123.
155. Sphrantzes 1980, 131.
156. Thomas the Eparch and Diplovatatzes 1976, 235 (3 in PDF).
157. B. Lewis 1987, 146.
158. Melville-Jones 1973, 38, 39, 123–124.
159. Ibid., 39, 112.
160. Sphrantzes 1980, 131.
161. Melville-Jones 1973, 103.
162. Hillenbrand 2007, 175.
163. Melville-Jones 1973, 103–112.
164. Doukas 1975, 234.
165. Gibbon 1952, 552.
166. Melville-Jones 1973, 124.
167. Ibid., 130, 104.
168. Cheikh 2004, 216–217.
169. Norwich 1997, 101.

CHAPTER 8

1. Antrobus 1901, 80.
2. Sehgal 2003, 22.
3. Cardini 2001, 141.
4. Fletcher 2004, 141.
5. Bertrand 1952, 168.
6. Ibid., 167.
7. Grant 1992, 110.
8. Constable 1997, 375.
9. Grant 1992, 81.
10. Allen 2010, 418.
11. Halperin 1987, 123, 26, 93, 7, 120, 77.
12. Bostom 2005, 79.
13. Stark 2012, 210.
14. Ibid., 210.
15. Dmytryshyn 1991, 178.
16. Halperin 1987, 62, 73.
17. Marco Polo 2001, 133–134.
18. Donner 2008, 43.
19. Lamb 1927, 201–203.
20. Daniel 1962, 155.
21. Halperin 1987, 70.
22. Zenkovsky 1974, 214–215.
23. Dmytryshyn 1991, 181.
24. Zenkovsky 1974, 218.
25. Dmytryshyn 1991, 180–181.
26. Zenkovsky 1974, 218.
27. Dmytryshyn 1991, 181.
28. Dmytryshyn 1991, 179.
29. Ibid., 183.
30. Halperin 1987, 71.
31. Dmytryshyn 1991, 185–186.
32. Halperin 1987, 72–73.
33. Troyat 1984, 62.
34. Ibid., 18.
35. Antrobus 1901, 80.
36. Cheikh 2004, 69.
37. Bertrand 1952, 166.
38. Bostom 2005, 619.
39. Madden 2007, 204.
40. Crowley 2014, 245.
41. Crowley 2009, 9.
42. Hillenbrand 2007, 178.
43. Ibid., 179.
44. Cardini 2001, 150.
45. Allen 2010, 413; Madden 2007, 209–210.
46. Lee n.d., 2–3.
47. B. Lewis 1994, 86.
48. Cardini 2001, 150.
49. Allen 2010, 413.
50. Lane-Poole 1890, 201.
51. B. Lewis 1987, 211.
52. Lane-Poole 1890, 122.
53. Crowley 2009, 89.
54. Ibid., 102, 98–99.
55. Curry 1891, 319.
56. Crowley 2009, 124, 130.
57. Ibid., 139.
58. Ibid., 152.
59. Lane-Poole 1890, 155.
60. Crowley 2009, 185.
61. Crowley 2009, 240.
62. Ibid., 275.
63. Ibid., 272.
64. Ibid., 282.
65. Ibid., 286.
66. La Croix 1705, 191–192.
67. Kinross 1979, 341.
68. La Croix 1705, 177.
69. Ibid., 171.
70. Kinross 1979, 341.
71. Ibid., 343.
72. La Croix 1705, 187.
73. Thackeray 2012, 266.
74. Dalairac 1700, 356.
75. Hillenbrand 2007, 181.
76. Thackeray 2012, 266.
77. Palmer 1992, 12.
78. Ferguson 2011, ch. 1 (page unavailable).

79. Pseudo-Methodius 2012, x.
80. Stoye 1964, 238.
81. Ibid., 173.
82. Ibid., 170.
83. Ibid., 242.
84. Ibid., 240.
85. "A True and Exact Relation" n.d.
86. Stoye 1964, 241.
87. "A True and Exact Relation" n.d.
88. Stoye 1964, 239.
89. "A True and Exact Relation" n.d.
90. Fregosi 1998, 345.
91. La Croix 1705, 206.
92. Dalairac 1700, 357.
93. Stoye 1964, 212.
94. Stoye 1964, 213; Fregosi 1998, 346.
95. La Croix 1705, 183–184.
96. Kinross 1979, 346.
97. La Croix 1705, 184.
98. "A True and Exact Relation" n.d.
99. Kinross 1979, 347.
100. Stoye 1964, 263.
101. Dalairac 1700, 364, 359.
102. Thackeray 2012, 268.
103. Dalairac 1700, 360.
104. La Croix 1705, 192.
105. "A True and Exact Relation" n.d.
106. Dalairac 1700, 360.
107. "A True and Exact Relation" n.d.
108. Ibid.
109. Dalairac 1700, 361–361.
110. "A True and Exact Relation" n.d.
111. La Croix 1705, 188.
112. Stoye 1964, 277.
113. La Croix 1705, 189.
114. Holt 1970, 354.
115. B. Lewis 1994, 180.
116. Lane-Poole 1890, 229.
117. R. Davis 2003, 23, 25; see also Khan 2009, 320–351, for more concise information and statistics on Islamic slavery, its institution, theology, history, and Western-imposed abolition.
118. Kizilov 2007, 6.
119. Fisher 1972, 575–594; Bostom 2005, 679–681; Giano n.d., 7.
120. Crowley 2009, 70.
121. Bostom 2005, 200.
122. Foxe 1807, 250–251.
123. Playfair 1972, 12.
124. Herberstein, 65.
125. Kizilov 2007, 13.
126. R. Davis 1972, 40.
127. Playfair 1972, 52.
128. Ibid.
129. Foxe 1807, 251.
130. Kizilov 2007, 15.
131. Playfair 1972, 12.
132. R. Davis 1972, 125.
133. Ibid., 22.
134. Kilmeade and Yaeger 2015, 2.
135. "American Commissioners" n.d.
136. Ibid.
137. "From Thomas Jefferson" 1786.
138. "From George Washington" 1786.
139. Kilmeade and Yaeger 2015, 16.
140. Ibid., 42.
141. Ibid., 87, 14.
142. "United States and the Barbary States" 1860.
143. Kilmeade and Yaeger 2015, 171.
144. Ibid., 176.
145. Ibid., 184.
146. Koran 1806, iii–iv.
147. Lane-Poole 1890, 294.
148. Ibid., 296.
149. Ibid., 297.
150. Ibid., 299.
151. Ibid., 302.
152. Lewis 1994, 17–18.
153. Cardini 2001, 184.
154. Wheatcroft 2005, 238.
155. Akbar 2003, 96.
156. Wheatcroft 2005, 243.
157. Bostom 2005, 665.
158. Akbar 2003, 97.
159. Jamieson 2006, 137.
160. Riley-Smith 2008, 59.

POSTSCRIPT

1. Reuters, "Islamic State Video Calls for Jihad after Brussels Blasts," Yahoo News, March 24, 2016. Accessed April 3, 2018, https://www.yahoo.com/news/islamic-state-video-calls-jihad-brussels-blasts-142945523.html.
2. Belloc 1938, 51.
3. Quote from Bruce Lawrence, in Khan 2009, 4.
4. John Hinderaker, "The American Blood Is Best, and We Will Taste It Soon," Powerline, November 13, 2015, accessed April 2, 2018, http://www.powerlineblog.com/archives/2015/11/the-american

-blood-is-best-and-we-will-taste-it-soon
.php; Duncan Gardham, "'Al-Qaeda'
Terrorists Who Brainwashed Exeter Suicide
Bomber Still on the Run," *Telegraph* (UK),
October 15, 2008, accessed April 2,
2018, http://www.telegraph.co.uk/news
/uknews/law-and-order/3204139/Al-Qaeda
-terrorists-who-brainwashed-Exeter
-suicide-bomber-still-on-the-run.html;
Catalin Cimpanu, "Church Website Defaced
with Ominous Jihadi Message," Softpedia
News, April 25, 2016, accessed April 2,
2018, http://news.softpedia.com/news
/church-website-defaced-with-ominous
-jihadi-message-503385.shtml.

5. Gemma Mullin, "Asian Father of
Four Raped Pub Worker . . . ,'" *Daily Mail,*
December 21, 2014, accessed April 3,
2018, http://www.dailymail.co.uk/news
/article-2882461/Asian-father-four-raped
-pub-worker-three-hours-dragging-street
-saying-white-women-good-it.html; Nick
Gutteridge, "'German Girls Are Just There
For Sex' . . . ," *Express* (UK), January, 19,
2016, accessed April 2, 2018, https://www
.express.co.uk/news/world/635359
/migrant-sex-attacks-Germany-Dortmund
-refugees-Merkel; Daniel Piotrowski, "'All

Australian Women Are Sluts and Deserve
to Be Raped' . . . ," *Daily Mail,* October 5,
2016, accessed April 2, 2018, http://www
.dailymail.co.uk/news/article-3822937/A
-Pakistani-migrant-taxi-driver-declared
-Australian-women-sluts-vile-rant-tribunal
-hears.html.

6. Valentin Wiemer, "Attacken auf
christliche Symbole," The European,
November 9, 2017, accessed April 2, 2018,
http://www.theeuropean.de/valentin-weimer
/11643-anschlaege-auf-gipfelkreuze-und
-kirchen; Darren Hunt, "Christian Statues
Destroyed and Beheaded in Savage
'Religious Revenge' Attack in Germany,"
Express (UK), December 16, 2016, accessed
April 2, 2018, https://www.express.co.uk
/news/world/744379/German-Christian
-statues-destroys-religious-motivated
-attack-revenge-police; Virginia Hales,
"'Not One Day Goes By' Without Christian
Statues Destroyed in Just One Town,"
Breitbart, November 8, 2016, accessed April
2, 2018, http://www.breitbart.com
/london/2016/11/08/christian-statues
-destroyed-town/.

7. Jamieson 2006, 215.

BIBLIOGRAPHY

Abba Anthony. 2014. Coptic Orthodox Patriarchate. Saint Anthony Monastery: California, March, issue no. 3.

Adam, Graeme Mercer, ed. 1906. *Spain and Portugal*. Philadelphia: John D. Morris and Company.

Ahmad, K. J. 1987. *Hundred Great Muslims*. Des Plaines, Ill.: Library of Islam. https:/archive.org/stream/100HundredGreatMuslims/hundred_great _muslims22#page/n447/mode/2up/search/establish+ourselves.

Akbar, M. J. 2003. *The Shade of Swords: Jihad and the Conflict between Islam and Christianity*. London: Routledge.

Akgündüz, Ahmed. n.d. "Why Did the Ottoman Sultans Not Make Hajj (Pilgrimage)?" Accessed October 2017, www.Osmanli.org.tr.

Akram, A. I. 1970. *The Sword of Allah: Khalid bin al-Waleed, His Life and Campaigns*. Karachi-Dacca: National Publishing House LTD.

Allen, S. J., ed. 2010. *The Crusades: A Reader*. Toronto: University of Toronto Press.

"American Commissioners to John Jay, 28 March 1786," *Founders Online*, National Archives, last modified June 29, 2017, http://founders.archives.gov /documents/Jefferson/01-09-02-0315. Original source: Julian P. Boyd, ed. 1954. *The Papers of Thomas Jefferson*, vol. 9, *1 November 1785–22 June 1786*. Princeton: Princeton University Press, 357–359.

Andrea, Alfred, and Andrew Holt, eds. 2015. *Seven Myths of the Crusades*. Indianapolis: Hackett Publishing Company.

Anna Comnena. 1969. *The Alexiad*. Translated by E. R. A. Sewter. London: Penguin Books.

Antrobus, Frederick Ignatius, ed. 1901. *The History of the Popes from the Close of the Middle Ages*. Vol. 3. St. Louis: B. Herder.

Atiya, Aziz Suryal. n.d. "The Coptic Contribution to Christian Civilization." Orthodox eBooks. Accessed online October 2017, http://www.orthodoxebooks .org/sites/default/files/pdfs/The%20Coptic%20Contribution%20to%20 Christian%20Civ%20-%20Aziz%20S%20Atteya.pdf.

———. 1978. *The Crusade of Nicopolis*. New York: AMS Press.

Baha' al-Din ibn Shaddad. 2001. *The Rare and Excellent History of Saladin* (*Al-Nawa dir al-Sultaniyya wa'l Mahasin al-Yusifiyya*). Translated by D. S. Richards. Burlington, Vt.: Ashgate.

Baladhuri, al-. 1968. *The Origins of the Islamic State*. Translated by Philip K. Hitti. New York: AMS Press.

Bar Hebraeus (Gregory Abu'l Faraj). 1932. *Chronography*. Translated by E. A. Wallis Budge. Accessed online, https://archive.org/details/BarHebraeus Chronography.

Barker, John W. 1969. *Manuel II Palaeologus (1391–1425): A Study in Late Byzantine Statesmanship*. New Brunswick: Rutgers University Press.

Baroja, Caro. 2003. *Los Moriscos de Reino de Granada*. Madrid: Alianza.

Bartolomeo de Giano. n.d. "A Letter of the Cruelty of the Turks." Translated by W. L. North. *Patrologia Graeca,* vol. 158. Paris: Imprimerie Catholique. Accessed online, https://apps.carleton.edu/curricular/mars/assets/Bartholomeus _de_Giano.pdf.

Bede. 1990. *Ecclesiastical History of the English People*. Translated by Leo Sherley-Price and D. H. Farmer. London: Penguin Books.

Belloc, Hilaire. 1938. *The Great Heresies*. London: Sheed and Ward.

Benedict XVI (Pope). 2006. "Faith, Reason and the University: Memories and Reflections." Lecture, University of Regensburg, September 12.

Bertrand, Louis. 1952. *The History of Spain*. 2d ed., rev. and continued to the year 1945. London: Eyre & Spottiswoode.

Blankinship, Khalid Yahya. 1994. *The End of the Jihad State*. Albany: State University of New York Press.

Bonner, Michael, ed. 2004. *Arab-Byzantine Relations in Early Islamic Times*. Burlington, Vt.: Ashgate/Variorum.

Bonner, Michael. 2006. *Jihad in Islamic History: Doctrines and Practice*. Princeton: Princeton University Press.

Bostom, Andrew, ed. 2005. *The Legacy of Jihad: Islamic Holy War and the Fate of Non-Muslims*. New York: Prometheus Books.

British Quarterly Review 82 (July–Oct. 1886).

Brockelmann, Carl. 2000. *History of the Islamic Peoples*. Translated by Joel Carmichael and Moshe Perlmann. London: Routledge.

Brooks, E. W. 1899. "The Campaign of 716–718, from Arabic Sources." *Journal of Hellenic Studies* 19: 19–31.

Brotton, Jerry. 2016. *The Sultan and the Queen: The Untold Story of Elizabeth and Islam*. New York: Viking Press.

Brownsworth, Lars. 2009. *Lost to the West*. New York: Three Rivers Press.

Brundage, James A. 1962. *The Crusades: A Documentary Survey*. Milwaukee: Marquette University Press.

Bukay, David. 2013. "Islam's Hatred of the Non-Muslim." *Middle East Quarterly* (summer): 11–20.

Bury, J. B. 1889. *History of the Later Roman Empire*. Vol. 2. New York: Macmillan.

Butler, Alfred. 1992. *The Arab Invasion of Egypt and the Last 30 Years of Roman Dominion*. Brooklyn: A & B Publishers.

Cardini, Franco. 2001. *Europe and Islam*. Translated by Caroline Beamish. Oxford: Blackwell Publishers.

Cheikh, Nadia Maria el-. 2004. *Byzantium Viewed by the Arabs*. Cambridge: Harvard University Press.

Constable, Olivia Remie, ed. 1997. *Medieval Iberia: Reading from Christian, Muslim, and Jewish Sources*. Philadelphia: University of Pennsylvania Press.

Cook, David. 2005. *Understanding Jihad*. Berkeley: University of California Press.

Cowley, Robert, and Geoffrey Parker, eds. 2001. *The Reader's Companion to Military History*. Boston: Houghton Mifflin Company.

Creasy, Edward Shepherd, and John Gilmer Speed. 1900. *Decisive Battles of the World*. New York: Colonial Press.

Crowley, Roger. 2009. *Empires of the Sea*. New York: Random House.

———. 2014. *1453: The Holy War for Constantinople and the Clash of Islam and the West*. New York: Hachette Books.

Curry, E. Hamilton. 1891. *Sea Wolves of the Mediterranean*. Ithaca: Cornell University Library.

Dalairac, François-Paulin, trans. 1700. *Polish Manuscripts*, or *The Secret History of the Reign of John Sobieski, The III of that Name, King of Poland, containing a particular account of the siege of Vienna*. London: Rhodes, Bennet, Bell, Leigh & Midwinter.

Daniel, Norman. 1962. *Islam and the West: The Making of an Image*. Edinburgh: Edinburgh University Press.

Davis, Paul K. 1999. *100 Decisive Battles: From Ancient Times to the Present*. Santa Barbara: ABC-CLIo.

Davis, Robert C. 2003. *Christian Slaves, Muslim Masters: White Slavery in the Mediterranean, the Barbary Coast, and Italy, 1500–1800*. New York: Palgrave Macmillan.

Davis, William Stearns, and Willis M. West, eds. 1913. *Readings in Ancient History: Illustrative Extracts from the Sources*. Vol. 2. Boston: Allyn and Bacon.

Dawson, Christopher. 1955/2005. *Mission to Asia*. Toronto: University of Toronto Press.

Demetracopoulos, John A. "Pope Benedict XVI's Use of the Byzantine Emperor Manuel Palaiologos' Dialogue with a Muslim Muterizes: The Scholarly Background." *Institut für Mittelalterliche Philosophie und Kultur* Archive 14 (2008): 264–304.

Dennis, George T., ed. and trans. 2008. *Three Byzantine Military Treatises*. Washington, DC: Dumbarton Oaks.

Dmytryshyn, Basil, ed. 1991. *Medieval Russia: A Sourcebook, 850–1700*. 3rd ed. Fort Worth: Harcourt Brace Jovanovich College Publishers.

Dominguez, Ortez, et al. 1993. *Historia de los Moriscos; vida y tragedia de una minoría*. No publisher info available.

Donner, Fred McGraw. 1981. *The Early Islamic Conquests*. Princeton: Princeton University Press.

Donner, Fred, ed. 2008. *The Expansion of the Early Islamic State*. Burlington: Ashgate/Variorum.

Doukas. 1975. *Decline and Fall of Byzantium to the Ottoman Turks*. Translated by Harry J. Magoulias. Detroit: Wayne State University Press.

Dunn, Ross E. 2005. *The Adventures of Ibn Battuta: A Muslim Traveler of the 14th Century*. Berkeley: University Press.

Einhard and Notker the Stammerer. 2008. *Two Lives of Charlemagne*. Translated by David Ganz. London: Penguin Books.

Ernoul. n.d. "The Battle of Hattin, 1187." *Medieval Sourcebook* (Fordham University). https://sourcebooks.fordham.edu/source/1187ernoul.asp.

Ferguson, Niall. 2011. *Civilization: The West and the Rest*. New York: Penguin Books.

Fernandez-Morera, Dario. 2016. *The Myth of the Andalusian Paradise*. Wilmington: ISI Books.

Fisher, Alan W. 1972. "Muscovy and the Black Sea Slave Trade." *Canadian-American Slavic Studies* 6 (4): 575–594.

Fletcher, Richard. 2004. *The Cross and the Crescent*. New York: Viking.

Foxe, John. 1807. *An Universal History of Christian Martyrdom*. London: J.G. Barnard, Snow Hill.

Frankopan, Peter. 2013. *The First Crusade: The Call from the East*. London: Vintage Books.

Fregosi, Paul. 1998. *Jihad in the West*. New York: Prometheus Books.

Friendly, Alfred. 1981. *The Dreadful Day: The Battle of Manzikert, 1071*. London: Hutchinson.

"From George Washington to Lafayette, 15 August 1786," *Founders Online,* National Archives. Last modified June 29, 2017, http://founders.archives.gov /documents/Washington/04-04-02-0200. Original source: W. W. Abbot, ed. 1995. *The Papers of George Washington*. Confederation Series, vol. 4, *2 April 1786–31 January 1787.* Charlottesville: University Press of Virginia, 214–216.

"From Thomas Jefferson to Ezra Stiles, 24 December 1786," *Founders Online,* National Archives. Last modified June 29, 2017, http://founders.archives.gov /documents/Jefferson/01-10-02-0483. Original source: Julian P. Boyd, ed. 1954. *The Papers of Thomas Jefferson*. Vol. 10, *22 June–31 December 1786.* Princeton: Princeton University Press, 629.

Fuller, J. F. C. 1987. *Military History of the Western World*. Vol. 1, *From the Earliest Times to the Battle of Lepanto*. New York: Da Capo Press.

Gabrieli, Francesco. 1968. *Muhammad and the Conquests of Islam*. New York: World University Library.

Gabrieli, Francesco, trans. 1993. *Arab Historians of the Crusades*. New York: Barnes & Noble.

Gibbon, Edward. 1952. *The Decline and Fall of the Roman Empire*. Vol. 2. Chicago: University of Chicago.

Glubb, John Bagot. (1963) 1980. *The Great Arab Conquests*. London: Quartet Books Limited. Reprint, Glubb.

Grant, George. 1992. *The Last Crusader: The Untold Story of Christopher Columbus*. Wheaton: Crossway Books.

Griffith, Sidney H. 2010. *The Church in the Shadow of the Mosque: Christians and Muslims in the World of Islam*. Princeton: Princeton University Press.

Guibert of Nogent. 2008. *The Deeds of God through the Franks*. Middlesex: Echo Library.

Guindy, Adel. 2009. *Hikayat al-Ihtilal: wa-Tashih ba'd al-mafahim* [Stories of the Occupation: Correcting Misunderstandings]. Cairo: Middle East Freedom Forum. Excerpts translated by author.

Gullen, M. Fethullah. 2006. *Essentials of the Islamic Faith*. Translated by Ali Unal. New Jersey: Light.

Hakam, Ibn 'Abd al-. 1969. *The History of the Conquest of Spain*. Translated by John Harris Jones. New York: B. Franklin.

———. 2010. *Futūḥ Miṣr wa'l Maghrab wa'l Andalus* [The Conquests of Egypt, North Africa, and Spain]. New York: Cosimo Classics. Excerpts translated by author.

Hakkoum, Karim, and Fr. Dale A. Johnson, trans. 1989. "A Christian/Moslem Debate of the 12th Century." *Medieval Sourcebook* (Fordham University). https://sourcebooks.fordham.edu/halsall/source/christ-muslim-debate.asp.

Halperin, Charles J. 1987. *Russia and the Golden Horde: The Mongol Impact on Medieval Russian History*. Bloomington: Indiana University Press/Midland.

Hanson, Victor Davis. 2002. *Carnage and Culture: Landmark Battles in the Rise of Western Power*. New York: Anchor Books.

Harvey, L. P. 2005. *Muslims in Spain, 1500 to 1614*. Chicago: University of Chicago Press.

Herberstein, Sigismund von. 1852. *Notes Upon Russia*. Vol. 2. London: Hakluyt Society.

Herodotus. 1994. *Histories*. Translated by A. D. Godley. Cambridge: Harvard University Press.

Hill, D. R. 1975. "The Role of the Camel and Horse in the Early Arab Conquests." In *War, Technology and Society in the Middle East*, edited by V. J. Parry and M. E. Yapp. London: Oxford University Press.

Hillenbrand, Carole. 2007. *Turkish Myth and Muslim Symbol: The Battle of Manzikert*. Edinburgh: Edinburgh University Press.

Hitti, Philip K. 1956. *History of the Arabs*. London: Macmillan.

Holt, P. M., et al., eds. 1970. *The Cambridge History of Islam*. Vol. 1A. Cambridge: Cambridge University Press.

Hoyland, Robert G. 1997. *Seeing Islam as Others Saw It: A Survey and Evaluation of Christian, Jewish and Zoroastrian Writings on Early Islam*. Princeton: Darwin Press.

Ibn Ishaq. 1997. *Sirat Rasul Allah* [The Life of Muhammad]. Translated by A. Guillaume. Oxford: Oxford University Press.

Ibn al-Kathir. n.d. "*Fasl fi khabr Malik bin Nuwayra*" [Section on News of Malik bin Nuwayra]. In *al-Bidaya w'al Nihaya* [The Beginning and End], available at www.Library.IslamWeb.net. Accessed October 2017, http://library.islamweb.net/newlibrary/display_book.php?idfrom=714&idto=714&bk_no=59&ID=780. Excerpt translated by author.

Ibn Khaldun. 1958. *The Muqaddimah: An Introduction to History.* Translated by Franz Rosenthal. New York: Bolligen Foundation.

Ibrahim, Raymond. 2007. *The Al Qaeda Reader.* New York: Doubleday.

———. 2010. "How Taqiyya Alters Islam's Rules of War." *Middle East Quarterly* (winter): 3–13.

———. 2013. *Crucified Again: Exposing Islam's New War on Christians.* Washington, DC: Regnery Publishing (in cooperation with the Gatestone Institute).

Irving, Washington. 1970. *Mahomet and His Successors.* Edited by Henry A. Pochmann and E. N. Feltskog. Madison: University of Wisconsin Press.

Jamieson, Alan G. 2006. *Faith and Sword.* London: Reaktion Books.

Jandora, John Walter. 1990. *The March from Medina: A Revisionist Study of the Arab Conquests.* Clifton, NJ: Kingston Press.

Jeffery, Arthur. 1944. "Ghevond's Text of the Correspondence between 'Umar II and Leo II." *Harvard Theological Review,* 37, no.4 (October): 269–332.

Kaegi, Walter E. 1995. *Byzantium and the Early Islamic Conquests.* Cambridge: Cambridge University Press.

Karima, Ahmad Mahmud. 2003. *Al-Jihad fi'l Islam: Dirasa Fiqhiya Muqarina.* Cairo: Al-Azhar University. Excerpts translated by author.

Kedar, Benjamin Z. 2014. *Crusade and Mission: European Approaches Toward the Muslims.* Princeton: Princeton University Press.

Keegan, John. 1994. *A History of Warfare.* New York: Vintage Books.

Kennedy, Hugh. 2007. *The Great Arab Conquests: How the Spread of Islam Changed the World We Live In.* Philadelphia: Da Capo Press.

Khan, M. A. 2009. *Islamic Jihad: A Legacy of Forced Conversion, Imperialism, and Slavery.* New York: iUniverse.

Kilmeade, Brian, and Don Yaeger. 2015. *Thomas Jefferson and the Tripoli Pirates: The Forgotten War That Changed American History.* New York: Sentinel.

Kinross, Lord (Patrick Balfour). 1979. *The Ottoman Centuries.* New York: Morrow Quill.

Kizilov, Mikhail. 2007. "Slave Trade in the Early Modern Crimea from the Perspective of Christian, Muslim, and Jewish Sources." *Journal of Early Modern History,* 11 (1): 1–31.

The Koran. First American edition. 1806. Springfield: Henry Brewer.

La Croix, de. 1705. *The Wars of the Turks with Poland, Muscovy, and Hungary, from the Year 1672, to the Year 1683: Containing a Particular Account of Several Transactions in Those Wars Not Taken Notice of in the History of the Turks. Written in French by the Sieur Le Croy, Secretary to the French Embassy at the Port. Translated into English by Mr. Chawes.* London, Printed by R. Janeway, for R. Basset, at the Mitre in Fleet-Street, and F. Faweet, in the New-Exchange in the Strand.

Lamb, Harold. 1927. *Genghis Khan: The Emperor of All Men*. New York: International Collectors Library, American Headquarters.

Lane-Poole, Stanley. 1890. *The Story of the Barbary Corsairs*. London: T. Fischer Unwin.

Lee, Francis Nigel. n.d. "Luther on Islam and the Papacy." www.Historicism.net: http://www.historicism.net/readingmaterials/loiatp.pdf.

Leo the Deacon. 2005. *The History (of Leo the Deacon)*. Translated by Alice-Mary Talbot and Denis F. Sullivan. Washington DC: Dumbarton Oaks.

Levi, Scott, and Ron Sela, eds. 2010. *Islamic Central Asia: An Anthology of Historical Sources*. Bloomington: Indiana University Press.

Lewis, Bernard, ed. and trans. 1987. *Islam: From the Prophet Muhammad to the Capture of Constantinople. Vol. 1: Politics and War*. New York: Oxford University Press.

———. 1993. *The Arabs in History*. Oxford: Oxford University Press.

———. 1994. *Islam and the West*. New York: Oxford University Press.

———. 2003. *The Middle East: A Brief History of the Last 2,000 Years*. New York: Scribner.

———. 2004. *From Babel to Dragomans: Interpreting the Middle East*. New York: Oxford University Press.

Lewis, Geoffrey, trans. 1988. *The Book of Dede Korkut*. London: Penguin Books.

Lindsay, James E., and Suleiman A. Mourad. 2015. *The Intensification and Reorientation of Sunni Jihad Ideology in the Crusader Period*. Leiden: Brill.

Little, Donald P. 1976. "Coptic Conversion to Islam under the Bahiri Mamluks." *Bulletin of the School of Oriental and African Studies* 39 (3): 552–569.

Madden, Thomas F., ed. 2004. *Crusades: The Illustrated History*. London: Duncan Baird Publishers.

Madden, Thomas F. 2007. *The New Concise History of the Crusades*. New York: Barnes & Noble.

Manuel Palaiologus. 2009. "Dialogues with a Learned Moslem." Dialogue 7, chapters 1–18 (of 37). Translated by Roger Pearse. http://www.tertullian.org/fathers/manuel_paleologus_dialogue7_trans.htm.

Maqqari, Aḥmad ibn Muḥammad. 1964. *The History of the Mohammedan Dynasties in Spain*. Vol. 1. Translated by Sir Gore Ouseley. New York: Johnson Reprint Corp.

Maqrizi, Taqi al-Din al-. 1873. *A Short History of the Copts and Their Church*. Translated by S. C. Malan. London: D. Nutt.

Marco Polo. 2001. *The Travels of Marco Polo*. Translated by William Marsden and Manuel Komroff. New York: Modern Library.

Marozzi, Justin. 2004. *Tamerlane: Sword of Islam, Conqueror of the World*. New York: Da Capo Press.

Matthew of Edessa. 1993. *Armenia and the Crusades, Tenth to Twelfth Centuries: The Chronicle of Matthew of Edessa*. Translated by Ara Edmond Dostourian. Lanham: National Association for Armenian Studies and Research; University Press of America.

Maurice. 1984. *Strategikon: Handbook of Byzantine Military Strategy.* Translated by George T. Dennis. Philadelphia: University of Pennsylvania Press.

Melville-Jones, John R. 1973. *The Siege of Constantinople 1453: Seven Contemporary Accounts.* Amsterdam: Hakkert.

Michael Psellus. 1966. *Fourteen Byzantine Rulers (The Chronographia).* Translated by E. R. A. Sewter. London: Penguin Books.

Moczar, Diane. 2008. *Islam at the Gates: How Christendom Defeated the Ottoman Turks.* Manchester: Sophia Institute Press.

Morgan, David. 1988. *The Mongols.* Oxford: Basil Blackwell.

Muir, William. 1891. *The Caliphate: Its Rise, Decline, and Fall.* London: Religious Tract Society.

——. 1923. *The Life of Mohammad from Original Sources.* Edinburgh: John Grant.

Munqidh, Usama ibn. 2008. *The Book of Contemplation: Islam and the Crusades.* Translated by Paul M. Cobb. London: Penguin Books.

Muqaffa, Sāwīrus ibn al-. 1948. *History of the Patriarchs of the Coptic Church of Alexandria.* Translated by Basil Evets. Paris: Firmin-Didot.

Nicolle, David. 1992. *Romano-Byzantine Armies: 4th–9th Centuries.* Oxford: Osprey Publishing.

——. 1993. *Armies of the Muslim Conquest.* Oxford: Osprey Publishing.

——. 1994. *Yarmuk 636 AD: The Muslim Conquest of Syria.* Oxford: Osprey Publishing.

——. 2013. *Manzikert 1071.* Oxford: Osprey Publishing.

Nicolo Barbaro. 1969. *Diary of the Siege of Constantinople.* Translated by J. R. Jones. New York: Exposition Press.

Norwich, John Julius. 1997. *A Short History of Byzantium.* New York: Vintage Books.

O'Callaghan, Joseph F., trans. 2002. *The Latin Chronicle of the Kings of Castile.* Tempe: Arizona Center for Medieval and Renaissance Studies.

O'Callaghan, Joseph F. 2004. *Reconquest and Crusade in Medieval Spain.* Philadelphia: University of Pennsylvania Press.

Ockley, Simon. 1847. *The History of the Saracens.* London: Henry G. Bohn.

Ostrogorsky, George. 1969. *History of the Byzantine State.* Translated by Joan Hussey. New Brunswick: Rutgers University Press.

Palmer, Alan. 1992. *The Decline and Fall of the Ottoman Empire.* New York: Barnes & Noble.

Patrick, Theodore Hall. 1996. *Traditional Egyptian Christianity: A History of the Coptic Orthodox Church.* Greensboro: Fisher Park Press.

Paul the Deacon. 1907. *History of the Lombards.* Translated by William Dudley Foulke. Philadelphia: University of Pennsylvania Press.

Peters, Edward, ed. 1971. *First Crusade: Chronicle of Fulcher of Chartres and Other Source Materials.* Philadelphia: University of Pennsylvania Press.

Pipes, Daniel. 1981. *Slave Soldiers and Islam.* New Haven: Yale University Press.

Pirenne, Henri. 1939. *Mohammed and Charlemagne*. London: George Allen & Unwin LTD.

———. 1974. *Medieval Cities: Their Origins and the Revival of Trade*. Translated by Frank D. Halsey. Princeton: Princeton University Press.

Playfair, R. Lambert. 1972. *The Scourge of Christendom: Annals of British Relations with Algiers Prior to French Conquest*. New York: Books for Libraries Press.

Pseudo-Methodius. 2012. *Apocalypse & An Alexandrian World Chronicle*. Translated by Benjamin Garstad. Cambridge: Harvard University Press.

Ramelah, Ashraf. 2017. "Copts of Egypt: History of Repression through Today." *Secure Freedom Quarterly* (1st Quarter): 4–8.

Riley-Smith, Jonathan, ed. 1995. *The Oxford Illustrated History of the Crusades*. Oxford: Oxford University Press.

———. 2008. *The Crusades, Christianity, and Islam*. New York: Columbia University Press.

Robinson, James Harvey, ed. 1904. *Readings in European History*. Vol. 1. Boston: Ginn and Co.

Robinson, Nugent. 1887. *A History of the World with All Its Great Sensations*. Vol. 1. New York: P. F. Collier.

Ross, James Bruce, and Mary Martin McLaughlin, eds. 1977. *The Portable Medieval Reader*. New York: Penguin Classics.

Rubenstein, Jay, ed. 2015. *The First Crusade: A Brief History with Documents*. Boston: Bedford/St. Martin's.

Runciman, Steven. 2004. *The Fall of Constantinople, 1453*. Cambridge: Cambridge University Press/Canto.

Santosuosso, Antonio. 2004. *Barbarians, Marauders, and Infidels: The Ways of Medieval Warfare*. New York: MJF Books.

Scott, Emmet. 2012. *Mohammed & Charlemagne Revisited: The History of a Controversy*. Nashville: New English Review Press.

———. 2014. *The Impact of Islam*. Nashville: New English Review Press.

Sehgal, Ikram ul-Majeed. 2003. *Defence Journal* 6.

Sell, Edward. 1914. *Muslim Conquests in North Africa*. Calcutta: Christian Literature Society.

Shatzmiller, Maya, ed. 1993. *Crusaders & Muslims in Twelfth-Century Syria*. Leiden: Brill.

Sidway, Ralph H. 2010. *Facing Islam: What the Ancient Church Has to Say about the Religion of Muhammad*. Louisville: Kalyve of Blessed Seraphim.

Smith, Collin, et al., eds. 2014. *Christians and Moors in Spain*. Vol. 3. Oxford: Oxbow Books.

Sphrantzēs, Geōrgios. 1980. *The Fall of the Byzantine Empire: A Chronicle*. Translated by Marios Philippides. Amherst: University of Massachusetts Press.

Stark, Rodney. 2009. *God's Battalions: The Case for the Crusades*. New York: HarperOne.

———. 2012. *The Triumph of Christianity*. New York: HarperCollins.

Stewart, Devin. 2013. "Dissimulation in Sunni Islam and Morisco *Taqiyya*." *Al-Qantara* (July–December): 439–490.

Stoye, John. 1964. *The Siege of Vienna*. London: Collins.

Stratos, Andreas N. 1972. *Byzantium in the Seventh Century: 634–641*. Translated by Harry T. Hionides. Amsterdam: Adolf M. Hakkert.

Suyūṭī. 1970. *History of the Caliphs*. Amsterdam: Oriental Press.

Tabari. 1964. *Tarikh Al Tabari*. Cairo: Dar Al Ma'ruf.

———. 1993. *Tarikh al-Rusul wa al-Muluk. Vol. X: The Conquest of Arabia*. Translated by Fred M. Donner. Albany: State University of New York Press.

Tabari, Muhammad ibn al-Jarir al-. 1992. *The History of al-Tabari*. Translated by Yohanan Friedmann. New York: State University of New York Press.

Thackeray, Frank W., et al., eds. 2012. *Events that Formed the Modern World*. Vol. 1. Santa Barbara: ABC-CLIO.

Theophanes. 1963. *Chronographia*. Munich: Georg Olms Verlagsbuchhandlung Hildesheim. Excerpts translated by author.

———. 1982. *The Chronicle of Theophanes: Anni Mundi 6095–6305 (A.D. 602–813)*. Translated by Harry Turtledove. Philadelphia: University of Pennsylvania Press.

———. 1997. *The Chronicle of Theophanes Confessor*. Translated by Cyril Mango. Oxford: Clarendon Press.

Thomas Aquinas. 1975. *Summa Contra Gentiles. Book One: God*. Translated by Anton C. Pegis. Notre Dame: University of Notre Dame.

Thomas the Eparch and Joshua Diplovatatzes. 1976. "Account of the Taking of Constantinople." Translated by William L. North, from the Italian version in A. Pertusi, ed., *La Caduta di Costantinopoli: Le Testimonianze dei Contemporanei*. Milan: Mondadori, 234–239. Available at: https://apps.carleton.edu/curricular/mars/assets/Thomas_the_Eparch_and_Joshua_Diplovatatzes_for_MARS_website.pdf.

Thornton, Bruce. 2004. *Plagues of the Mind: The New Epidemic of False Knowledge*. Wilmington: ISI Books.

Tierney, Brian, and Sidney Painter. 1970. *Western Europe in the Middle Ages: 300–1475*. New York: Knopf.

Tolan, John V. 2002. *Saracens: Islam in the Medieval European Imagination*. New York: Columbia University Press.

Treadgold, Warren T. 1997. *A History of the Byzantine State and Society*. Stanford: Stanford University Press.

Treece, Henry. 1994. *The Crusades*. New York: Barnes & Noble.

Troyat, Henri. 1984. *Ivan the Terrible*. Translated by Joan Pinkham. London: Phoenix Press.

"A True and Exact Relation of the Raising of the Siege of Vienna and the Victory obtained over the Ottoman Army, the 12th of September, 1683," pamphlet, "Printed for Samuel Crouch at the Corner of Popes-Head Alley next Cornhill,

1683," in *German History in Documents and Images, vol. 2, from Absolutism to Napoleon, 1648–1815.* Accessed October, 2017, http://germanhistorydocs.ghi-dc.org/sub_document.cfm?document_id=3580.

Tuchman, Barbara W. 1980. *A Distant Mirror: The Calamitous 14th Century.* New York: Random House.

Twain, Mark (Samuel Clemens). 1869. *The Innocents Abroad.* New York: Grosset and Dunlap Publishers.

Tyerman, Christopher. 2006. *God's War: A New History of the Crusades.* Cambridge: Belknap Press of Harvard University Press.

"United States and the Barbary States." 1860. *Atlantic Monthly* 6, no. 38 (December).

Vaporis, Nomikos Michael, ed. 2000. *Witnesses for Christ: Orthodox Christian Neomartyrs of the Ottoman Period 1437–1860.* Crestwood, NY: St. Vladimir's Seminary Press.

Vasiliev, A. A. 1952. *History of the Byzantine Empire: 324–1453.* Madison: University of Wisconsin Press.

Waqidi, Abu 'Abdullah Muhammad Ibn 'Omar al-. 1997. *Futuh al-Sham* [The Conquests/Openings of Syria]. Beirut: Dar al-Kotob al-Ilmiyah. Excerpts translated by author.

Watts, Henry Edward. 1894. *The Christian Recovery of Spain: Being the Story of Spain from the Moorish Conquest to the Fall of Granada (711–1492 A.D.).* New York: G. P. Putnam's Sons.

Wheatcroft, Andrew. 2005. *Infidels: A History of the Conflict between Christendom and Islam.* New York: Random House Trade Paperbacks.

William of Adam. 2012. *How to Defeat the Saracens.* Translated by Giles Constable. Washington, DC: Dumbarton Oaks Medieval Humanities.

Wolf, Kenneth Baxter, trans. 1990. *Conquerors and Chroniclers of Early Medieval Spain.* Liverpool: Liverpool University Press.

Ye'or, Bat. 2010. *The Decline of Eastern Christianity under Islam: From Jihad to Dhimmitude.* Cranbury, NJ: Associated University Presses.

Zenkovsky, Serge A., ed. 1974. *Medieval Russia's Epics, Chronicles, and Tales.* New York: Penguin/Meridian.

INDEX